MW01129245

The "Companion Text" to Law School: Understanding and Surviving Life with a Law Student

By

Andrew J. McClurg

Professor and Herbert Herff Chair of Excellence in Law
Cecil C. Humphreys School of Law
The University of Memphis

WEST®

A Thomson Reuters business

Mat #41060112

© 2012 Thomson Reuters

    610 Opperman Drive
    St. Paul, MN 55123
    1–800–313–9378

Printed in the United States of America

ISBN: 978–0–314–26741–2

To Mona Lisa, my 1L companion

Preface

In a decade-old article in a law school magazine, the wife of a law student pleaded: "We make great sacrifices for our loved ones as they attend law school, sacrifices that are often crucial to their success, and we need support. Please don't ignore us."[1]

If you're in or about to be in a similar position, take heart. You are ignored no longer. This book is for *you*—people in relationships with current or prospective law students. You may be a significant other, parent, friend, sibling, or even child to a law student. Whichever, this book will equip you to ride shotgun on your law student's journey down the twisting road of legal education.

Law school, as you are about to learn, is indeed an adventure for the entire family. Law schools recognize this. Roughly half of them offer special sessions during their orientation programs dedicated to married students or students with families. Law students know it as well, even before starting. Each year I give all my incoming students a questionnaire asking, among other things, "What is your biggest fear about law school?" One of the most common answers is interference with outside relationships.

In 2009, I published a book for incoming law students called *1L of a Ride: A Well–Traveled Professor's Roadmap to Success in the First Year of Law School*. In Amazon.com customer reviews of the book, a relevant thread can be found:

- [A] "must read" to a member of the family who is starting law school in the fall.

- If you truly want your loved ones to understand what you will be going through—make them read this book.

- [F]riends and family members of future lawyers might benefit just as much from McClurg's inside look at the 1L experience.

- I highly recommend this book for ... even parents of students in law school. I know my mom would love to have an idea of what I have gotten myself into so that she can offer her support in a more informed way.

1. Lori Ebinger Sullivan, *The Emotional Roller Coaster of Marriage to a First–Year Law Student*, STUDENT LAW., Apr. 2001, at 27, 31.

I appreciate those comments because they reflect the strong desire of law students to be understood by their loved ones. But while law school prep books such as *1L of a Ride* do illuminate law school in ways from which non-student loved ones could benefit, the bulk of their content is devoted to topics of interest only to law students. Prep books also largely fail to address the emotional and psychological impact of law school on students and on their outside relationships or to otherwise prepare non-students for the on-slaught that is law school. Law student loved ones need their own book, I decided.

Here it is! In the pages that follow, you will learn everything you need to know about legal education, law students, and the overall law school experience—including the potential for it to disrupt outside relationships—to enable you to survive, hopefully even thrive in, your student's pursuit of a Juris Doctor degree.

Throughout, you'll be hearing and learning not only from me, but from real law students and their significant others.[2] I have a lot of experience teaching law students, but I don't know all the answers, so I turned to the source, surveying law students and their significant others with relevant questions. Most of the surveys were conducted at the University of Memphis Cecil C. Humphreys School of Law. With the publisher's help, I also surveyed law students and their partners at Cal Western University School of Law in San Diego and Seattle University School of Law. Additionally, I reached out via Facebook and email to former students at other law schools where I've taught, and also sought input from lawyer friends who weren't my students. In total, I received input from more than 200 current or former law students and their significant others. Their comments are scattered throughout the book, but most heavily concentrated in the later chapters. In some chapters, I let students and their loved ones do most of the talking.

The survey comments offer a direct window into the hearts and minds of real law students and their loved ones who are enduring or recently endured the same experience you and your student are about to share. Many types of students and partners participated in the surveys: 1Ls, 2Ls, and 3Ls, traditional students straight out of college and older couples with kids, full-time and part-time students, same-sex couples, and minority students. You'll find the voices of the students and significant others to be sometimes amusing and sometimes poignant, sometimes uplifting and some-times discouraging, but always interesting and authentic.

2.   This book is for all loved ones of law students, but for practical reasons, I limited my surveys of non-students to significant others.

My principal qualification to write this book—apart from my fascination with the dynamics and anthropology of law students and longstanding interest in researching legal education—is my experience as a law professor who has taught literally thousands of law students of every style, shape, and model at six different law schools from the East Coast (Miami) to the West Coast (San Francisco) and points in between (Boulder, CO, Little Rock, AR, Memphis, TN, and Winston–Salem, NC).

For resume-type credentials, see the About the Author page at the end of the book. Worth mentioning here, I've written and published quite a bit of "legal humor" (which some people think is an oxymoron). That's relevant because, as you'll see, I try to keep readers engaged with a lively voice and doses of amusement. On the other hand, being a "serious" law professor compelled me to back up assertions with research, resulting in the inclusion of quite a few footnotes. Consider them your first introduction to law. The law loves footnotes. If the law could have romantic relations, it would be with a footnote. It wouldn't be pretty, but a lot of things in law aren't. You'll learn something else from studying the footnotes: the law's obsession with precision. All footnotes conform to the citation style called for by the *Bluebook*, the dominant style manual for legal writing. The *Bluebook*'s almost pathological fixation with the tiniest of details (e.g., whether a particular comma in a legal citation should be italicized) serves as a microcosm of the pressure-packed perfectionism demanded from law students.

Before getting started, let me offer—as any good law professor would—some caveats, disclaimers, and other qualifications. First, it is assumed most readers will be using this book before or at the beginning of their student's law school journey, so much of the book focuses on the first year of law school.

To the extent portions of this book can be construed as offering "relationship advice," the nature of such advice is elementary repetitive, comprising basic strategies toward healthy relationships that would occur to any reasonably astute person. The only novel aspect of the advice is that it is applied specifically in the context of law school and law students.

Regarding the student and significant other comments, they're anecdotal in nature and aren't offered to "prove" anything. My surveying strategy was to obtain insightful first-person narrative, not empirically valid statistical evidence. For the most part, the comments coincide with my own opinions and ideas based on experience.

I made minor style-adjustments and punctuation and grammatical corrections in the comments, but did not change their meaning.

Many comments were lengthy and presented two sides of an issue. To make discrete points, I often excised selected portions of a lengthier comment or used one part of a comment in one place and another part in another place. Thus, while I did not change the meaning of the comments, some of the contextual balance from a particular comment may be missing or appear in a different place. When names were used in the comments, I changed them or substituted generic references such as "my husband" or "my wife."

The nation's law students are split roughly 50–50 between men and women. Rather than weigh down the book by saying "he or she," "him or her," and the like ten thousand times, I refer to students in a variety of ways. Often, I alternate randomly between feminine and masculine pronouns. Other times, I use grammatically incorrect plural pronouns, such as "they" or "their" to refer to an individual. Occasionally, I do say "he or she" or "him or her."

At times, it may sound as if I'm trying to elicit too much sympathy for the "poor misunderstood law student." But only by emphasizing the many pressures and demands legal education places on students can one hope to understand law students, and, in doing so, better understand and improve relationships with them. In truth, much of the book should be read from a "poor misunderstood loved one" perspective for having to put up with the crazy world and just plain craziness of law school and law students.

Portions of the book may sound overly negative. You may find a few of the chapters—such as those dealing with law student psychological dysfunction and how law school can alter students' personalities—to be discouraging. My intention is not to bring you down or taint your view of law school. It is a great place to be for all involved. I love being a law professor. It's a privilege to be surrounded day in and day out by so many intelligent and motivated young people. I even liked being a law student, although I found the first year to be rough both emotionally and physically. I also strongly believe in the power and majesty of the law and legal profession and the potential for any law student to make a great life in it.

A few reasons coalesce to explain what might come across as an overemphasis in some places of the dimmer sides of legal education. First and foremost, a primary purpose of this book is to alert loved ones to the pitfalls law school can present both to students and their relationships, a purpose that can only be fulfilled by highlighting the potential problem areas. Second, virtually all of the existing empirical research of law students regarding happiness levels and psychological functioning, much of which is discussed in these pages, has yielded negative results.

Adding to the less-than-blissful picture of legal education is the fact that the most interesting and thoughtful comments I obtained from students and their loved ones address the stresses and difficulties of law school. Positive responses to my survey questions are under-represented in this book largely because they tended to be short and offer less insight. Thus, for example, answers to the question whether law school has caused stress or conflict in a relationship that simply said "No" didn't make the cut for inclusion even though, significantly, several people did give that answer.

It is a well-established phenomenon that people are more likely to report negative aspects of an interaction than positive aspects. Extensive research of customer relations in a business context, for example, shows that consumers are more than twice as likely to tell others about a bad experience with a company as a good one. Here, that effect is multiplied by the fact that law students are notoriously fond of grumbling about law school and also because the many good things about law school have a longer incubation period, making them harder to recognize and appreciate in the moment.

Finally, not everything said in this book—good or bad—will apply to you and your law student. In teaching at law schools in different parts of the country, I've always been struck by the remarkable similarity among law students in their reactions to the trials and tribulations of law school. In part, this is attributable to the substantial uniformity in the content and structures of U.S. legal education across law schools. The essential likeness of law students is what makes generalizations like those in this book possible.

But, of course, no two human beings and no two relationships are truly alike. Also, different groups experience law school differently. Older or part-time evening division students experience law school differently than younger full-time students. Minority students experience law school differently than non-minority students. Top-performing students experience law school differently than lower-performing students. When all is said and done, there are as many different legal education experiences as there are law students and as many types of law students as there are people.

Table of Contents

THE "COMPANION TEXT" TO LAW SCHOOL: UNDERSTANDING AND SURVIVING LIFE WITH A LAW STUDENT

CHAPTER 1
CONGRATULATIONS AND CONDOLENCES

Congratulations and condolences! If you're reading this, you must be in a close relationship with a current or prospective law student, either as a significant other, family member, or friend.

Congratulations are in order for both your student and you. Attending and graduating from law school will grant your student the secret key to enter one of the oldest and noblest of all the professions. People are fond of criticizing lawyers, but lawyers have always been and always will be vital to society. The public tends to think of doctors as the only life-saving professionals, but day in and day out, lawyers represent people in a myriad of contexts in which, in a popular sense, their clients' lives depend on the result.

For every person facing an emergency appendectomy, dozens are being evicted from their homes, domestically abused, fired from jobs, denied benefits, involved in child custody disputes, faced with criminal charges, threatened with deportation, or confronted with other life-consuming issues that only lawyers have the knowledge and power to manage. Even in the absence of crisis, in our heavily regulated society, many individuals and all businesses big and small must depend on lawyers to lead them through the legal morass. Tell your student not to listen to the lawyer-haters. They will be the first ones calling for help when they get in trouble.

Experience has shown time and again that lawyers are the only group with the conviction and courage to consistently stand up and fight for justice when it's unpopular to do so. Lawyers created the liberties we cherish and have fought to protect them for more than two hundred years. Thirty-three of the fifty-five framers of the U.S. Constitution were lawyers. And take a guess as to what percentage of the nation's presidents graduated from law school. The answer is in one of the "Stump Your Student" questions in the last chapter, so I'll keep you in suspense until then, but you will probably be surprised.

Getting admitted to law school is no small feat. Simply by meeting the technical requirements for admission (i.e., an undergraduate degree), your student has already distinguished herself. Only 28 percent of the U.S. adult population holds a bachelor degree.

Your student will tell you that getting into law school is highly competitive. How competitive is it? In truth, it depends on how one looks at it. Roughly two-thirds of applicants were accepted to law school in 2010, up from 56 percent in 2004.[3] A two in three chance of admission might not sound like a staggeringly high barrier to overcome, but Phil Handwerk, a researcher for the Law School Admission Council (the good folks who administer the Law School Admission Test or LSAT), points to several factors that make the two-thirds acceptance figure misleading.

Most students do not get into their law school of choice. More than 25 percent of applicants apply to ten or more schools, precisely because the admissions process is so competitive, substantially increasing their chance of getting admitted *somewhere*. Also, a small number of low-ranked private law schools with liberal admissions policies extend large numbers of offers to fill their classes, as many as nine times the available seats, skewing the acceptance numbers. Handwerk reports that the average acceptance rate across law schools is less than 40 percent. At the University of Memphis, currently a third-tier law school in the *U.S. News & World Report* rankings, we accept only about one of every three or four applicants, depending on the year. In short, the admissions process at most accredited law schools remains highly

---

3. In 2010, the Law School Admission Council (LSAC) reported that 87,900 people applied to law school, of which 60,400 were accepted. *LSAC Volume Summary*, LAW SCH. ADMISSIONS COUNCIL, 1 (2010), http://www.lsac.org/LSACResources/Data/PDFs/LSAC-volume-summary.pdf.

selective. So thumbs up to your student for getting into law school.

More congratulations are due for the enormous intellectual and professional leap your student is about to make. Law school opens horizons to an exhilarating world of new friends, new ideas, and a whole new way of thinking. It will challenge your student like nothing before. Your student will learn more in the first year of law school than in any other single year of life. The knowledge law students acquire makes them more thoughtful, socially aware, and open-minded people. The methodologies of law school teaching, for all their criticism, will transform your student's brain into a high-functioning machine powered by excellent critical reasoning skills that will serve your student well in all facets of life, *except* maybe some aspects of relationships, as we'll see. The professionalism that law school instills makes law students more focused, disciplined, and responsible. So again, congratulations to you and your student. Be proud of them.

But—there's *always* a "but" in law—condolences also are warranted. Life with a law student is no bed of roses, which, as a law student would be careful to explain, is not necessarily a bad thing because rose thorns can cause personal injury, thus likely rendering any such flora-bed a defective product under the risk-utility analysis followed by most courts in products liability cases. The student may go on to explain that since roses are treated with pesticides, using them for bedding purposes could violate the Federal Insecticide, Fungicide and Rodenticide Act (FIFRA).[4] A particularly astute student might even pause to contemplate the potential intellectual property law implications of living a happy "bed of roses" life without giving proper attribution to Christopher Marlowe's sixteenth-century poem, *The Passionate Shepherd to His Love*, where the phrase was first mentioned.

You will quickly learn that the life of a first-year law student—"1Ls," as we call them—shrinks to the size of a pebble and that pebble is solid law. New law students are obsessed with talking about the law and law school to everyone. The fact that the people they are talking to know nothing about these subjects does not deter them in the

---

4. It's fun to say "FIFRA." Go ahead, try it. The law and law school have acronyms and abbreviations for everything, and you're definitely going to be hearing some of them. The Glossary at the back of the book covers some of the more common ones.

slightest. *Anything* can trigger a law-related, analytical response from a law student. Some examples:

"Honey, hold my hand."

"Hand! Good old Judge Learned Hand. Now there was a great judge. Have I told you about the famous opinion he wrote in this case where a barge broke free and ..."

"Would you like tomatoes in your salad?

"You know, some people argue that tomatoes are a fruit, but in 1893, the U.S. Supreme Court, in *Nix v. Hedden*, ruled that tomatoes are actually a vegetable. What happened was that the Tariff Act of 1893 declared a 10 percent duty on all vegetables entering the country, but allowed fruit to enter duty-free ..."

"My parents are coming over Saturday for the garage sale."

"Glad I fixed that broken porch step. On the other hand, as social guests, your parents are mere 'licensees' to whom we owe no legal duty to make the premises safe. But then, that could change if they bought something at the garage sale. They might be considered 'business invitees.' Maybe we should call off the whole thing."

Law students don't just talk about law school. They *become* law school. Law school irrevocably alters law students, often without them even being aware of it. It changes what they think and how they think about it. It changes the way they talk, debate, and argue. It changes their views on the world around them and how they approach problem-solving in all areas of life. It can even alter their personal value systems.

Law school also takes an emotional and physical toll on students, which can be painful for loved ones to witness and can spill over into relationships. As discussed in Chapter 10, several studies show that law students suffer high rates of anxiety, depression, and substance abuse, much higher than the public at large and higher even than medical students, another stressed-out group of professional students. Here's a grim introduction to law student-life offered by one professor:

> Law students get sick more frequently than others: headaches, stomachaches, colds, allergies. They have problems in their relationships with friends or family. They worry more than they work. They are continually agitated or lethargic. They gain or lose weight. They take up or increase their chemical crutches, such as caffeine, nicotine, alcohol, or cocaine. They often become angry and bitter—especially at their teachers, sometimes at their colleagues or at the profession—or they withdraw, dropping out, skipping classes, or simply avoiding getting to know their classmates. When called upon in specific stressful situations to use reserves of courage and confidence, they may be debilitated; and they often have no reserves to call upon.[5]

Even some of the positive aspects of law school can be problematic for unwary loved ones. Law students develop deep friendships with each other, for example, which is great. But law school friendships can often leave family, preexisting friends, and significant others feeling neglected. Because "outsiders" find it hard to relate to the law school experience, law students tend to turn to other students to share their joys and sorrows, people who can better appreciate their accomplishments, empathize with their frustrations and setbacks, and enjoy endless conversations about arcane legal concepts and cases. Be aware of this from the very beginning, when it's easiest to integrate yourself into your student's new law school life. As one spouse of a law student wrote:

> I have a hard time with the separation of "my husband" vs. "the law student." There is a part of him that I will never be able to fully connect with because I really don't get the point of a lot of things. It's like he could be living a double life, but I doubt it with all the work he has to do. I feel like one day he will find nothing in common with me because I do not understand his profession the way his companions and coworkers will.

5. B.A. Glesner, *Fear and Loathing in the Law Schools*, 23 Conn. L. Rev. 627, 631 (1991).

As we'll discuss in detail, most law students and their partners agree law school adds stress and conflict to relationships. As one student put it, "[L]aw school is like a pressure cooker when it comes to relationships. A year of dating in law school is like three years of dating in the real world." Sometimes the impact is quicker and more dramatic. Asked to complete a relationship survey, a 1L wrote: "I would love to complete your survey; however, I am one of those lonely souls who is single. I was dumped the day before classes started as my boyfriend felt I would not have time for him." As Professor Nancy Levit puts it, the first year of law school is itself like a new girlfriend or boyfriend. The highs are higher, the lows are lower, and students feel out of control much of the time.

You may be thinking: "McClurg, surely you're exaggerating all of this stuff for rhetorical effect. And not too shabbily, I might add. But what could possibly make law school so different, so life-altering, so all-encompassing? I went to college and it wasn't anything like that." No, it wasn't. Law school is completely unique from other higher educational disciplines in several crucial respects:

- Only law school uses the terror-generating Socratic method of teaching, in which professors cold-call on students and interrogate them in front of their peers, demanding intelligent answers to questions they've never thought about before.

- Only law school requires students to learn from mysterious texts called "casebooks" that make little to no effort to actually explain the subject matter to readers.

- Only law students are deprived of performance feedback until a single all-or-nothing final exam at the end of the semester, making it impossible for them to know whether they're "getting it" until it's too late.

- Only law school places such extreme importance on grades and class rank, especially first-year grades, in obtaining both internal and external rewards, including jobs, which causes fierce competition and can promote feelings of inadequacy among the 90 percent of students who don't make the golden top 10 percent.

- In terms of workload, only medical school rivals law school among graduate and professional degree programs.

But you don't have to take my word for it. Chapter 14 contains dozens of comments in response to a survey question asking students to explain what they think non-law student loved ones need to know and understand about the ways in which the demands, stresses, and pressures of law school differ from undergraduate or other graduate school programs. Here's a preview of their answers:

- Loved ones need to know that just about the only similarity between undergraduate school and law school is that it is school. Other than that, law school is at an entirely different caliber—requiring so much more than undergrad that it does not even compare. Loved ones need to know that when we say we must get ready for class, it doesn't mean the same thing as that did in undergrad. They need to know that when they ask "When will you be done studying?" there is actually no good answer because we could probably spend every waking hour outside of class studying and still not be done. The only answerable question would be: "When are you going to stop studying tonight?" The stress of law students is greatly more intense than undergrad. While we try not to take it out on our loved ones, it will happen and they should know that we do not mean it.

- I don't care what the most stressful thing you have ever done in your life is. It wasn't as stressful as law school. I don't care if you think you can recall a time when you were under a lot of pressure. It was nothing in comparison to law school. Undergrad is a joke compared to law school. Most people during undergrad b.s.'d every paper, hardly did their reading assignments, and were more concerned with an education in intoxication. In law school, you actually have to read. And you have to do it for every class. And you better understand what you read. And there is no b.s.'ing. Ever.

- There is always stress from day one. Unlike undergrad, it seems like every day there is some type of pressure on you. Whether it is just reading for class, knowing that you are behind on outlining, meeting deadlines for law review or moot court, and trying to find a job. Then, of course, there is always that little thing of knowing that even if I graduate, my life is over if I don't pass THE BAR. Combine all of this with the ordinary challenges of relationships and life in general and it seems that sometimes I am just the little boy holding his finger in the dam.

• Please understand that law school is FAR more intense than undergraduate education. If your loved one made it to law school, she is a good student. She knows how to perform academically in an undergraduate environment. But now she is suddenly in the midst of a very humbling experience. She may even have a crisis of self-confidence, because while good grades always came so easily before, they suddenly have become very difficult to obtain. It is not an easy adjustment for one who always felt so certain of her academic abilities. She'll pull it off in the end, but it might take her a while to adjust. And she may display insane behavior in the meantime.

• If it seems like your law student is "overdoing" the studying, keep in mind that each class requires hours of preparation. Cases are dense and difficult (especially at first), and the student must be prepared to discuss every case with the professor and eighty other students listening in and scrutinizing every word. It is daunting, to say the least. And your student faces two to four classes like this every day. We really, really need to study hard. The best way I can sum it up is to say that when your law student starts out, she feels as though she is learning to swim by being thrown into the middle of the pool. It's not easy! We apologize in advance for our craziness! Know that your loved one must completely reprioritize her time. Please don't take it personally!

As even this sampling of comments reveals, law students are desperate that their loved ones appreciate and understand what they are going through. They want you to cheer their successes and sympathize with their failures, real or perceived. And, of course, you will want to do these things, but you won't be able to without an understanding of law school and legal education, which this book will provide.

For example, suppose your law student comes home and announces excitedly that they received a *B* in Contracts, a required first-year course. Here are some possible responses:

"*B*? But you always got *A*s in college."

That might seem like a reasonable reply. After all, your law student enjoyed academic success their entire life. Unfortunately, so did everyone else in law school, so this is a *wrong* answer. It might require years of psychotherapy to recover from it, maybe even cause a brain aneurism. Don't risk it. Here's another possibility:

"*B*? That's not too bad, right?"

This reply is light years ahead of the first answer, but still needs tweaking. Let's try one more:

"*B*! That's fantastic. I'm so proud of you! Let's celebrate!"

This is the *only correct* answer. As we'll discuss, high grades are hard to come by at most law schools compared to most undergraduate or other graduate programs. A *B* in Contracts may be worth a lung to a law student because law schools and potential employers make grades, particularly first-year grades, so important. One of my former students from more than a decade ago said she is still miffed that her family did not appreciate the significance of her writing the "Top Paper"—the term commonly used in law school to refer to the highest-scoring exam in a particular course—in her Property course, which was taught by one of the hardest professors at the law school. To her family it was: "That's very nice, dear. Congratulations." To her it was: "Are you kidding? I rule the entire freaking world!"

Same thing with failures. Without a crash course in legal education, one can't possibly appreciate the extent to which law school can transform talented, intelligent people into feeling like failures, or how seemingly insignificant events can deeply bruise a law student's ego and confidence. Asked for comments about what they wished their loved ones better understood about law school, one student wrote:

Family cannot fathom the effects of a bad day in class. They don't understand the feeling of crushing defeat associated with those brief thirty seconds during which

Professor So-and-So calls on you and then moves swift-
ly on to a presumably better-prepared student because
your answer wasn't good enough. No matter how many
conversations you have describing these situations and
how upset you are at the time, they seem trivial to
them.

This book is going to make it all make sense. We'll begin
with an overview of U.S. legal education and the briefest of
summaries of the U.S. legal system. Next, we'll talk more
specifically about how law schools function, including: the
courses your student will be taking in the first year, the
twilight world of uncertainty in which law students dwell, the
unique law school teaching methodologies known as the
Socratic and case methods, and that devil's-spawn single-
exam testing format.

Then we'll move on to law students. You'll learn a lot
about them: what they like to talk about, things you should
never say to them, the potential negative impact of law school
on their psyches, their sources of stress, how law school can
change their personalities, what students love about law
school, and what they think loved ones like you need to know
about legal education.

In the home stretch, we'll switch to what my research
assistants came to call "the relationship chapters." These
chapters discuss the effects law school can have on outside
relationships, how law students weigh the pros and cons of
being in a committed relationship while in law school, and
tips for successfully managing a relationship with a law
student. In these chapters, I let law students and their
partners tell most of the story.

We'll wrap things up with a description of the types of
jobs that will be available to your student on graduation,
including the pros and cons of each. The last chapter contains
twenty fun multiple-choice "legal" questions you can use to
stump your law student. Use them to turn the tables when
your student insists on talking to you nonstop about law
school. At the back of the book is an Appendix containing a
sample case and a Glossary that will help you keep track of
some of the new language with which your student (and you
through your student) are about to be inundated.

Strap yourself in and hang on tight. Your student is not
the only one in for a wild ride. Your life is about to change
too.

CHAPTER 2

U.S. LEGAL EDUCATION: THE BIG PICTURE

To give you some context to process what follows, we'll begin with a capsule overview of U.S. legal education (this chapter), followed by a synopsis of the U.S. legal system (next chapter), with a product warning that both chapters are heavy on information.

Basic Background

Law school is a three-year post-graduate professional degree program for full-time students and a four-year program for part-time students. While an increasing number of occupations are attempting to lay claim to professional status, a true "profession" is a distinct breed. Criteria commonly associated with professional status include: (1) the occupation is one that has achieved a particularly high level of status and prestige in society; (2) advanced education and training, usually of an intellectual nature, are required to participate in it; (3) the services its members provide are generally of a non-manual nature; (4) members are expected to serve the community rather than operate solely out of self-interest; (5) members operate under the umbrella of a self-regulating organization, such as the American Bar Association (ABA) for lawyers; and (6) the types of services members provide are essential to the community and cannot be obtained from other sources.[6]

6. *See generally* RICHARD MALMSHEIM- (collecting and commenting on various
ER, "DOCTORS ONLY": THE EVOLVING IMAGE definitions of "profession").
OF THE AMERICAN PHYSICIAN 7–11 (1988)

Law graduates receive a Juris Doctor degree, which raises a question students frequently wonder about: Can a lawyer go by the title "Dr."? Here's your first chance to tell your student something they don't know (keeping in mind that once they start law school, they will think they know everything).

In the late 1960s, as the Juris Doctor degree was being phased in to replace the previous LL.B (Bachelor of Laws), an ABA ethics committee took the position that lawyers should not refer to themselves as "Dr." because it would be "self-laudatory." The ABA later switched positions, but no current ABA or state ethics rules specifically address the issue. The question has come up in a few state bar ethics opinions and the modern position appears to be that a lawyer is not prohibited from using the appellation "Dr." unless it's misleading. (Ethical rules prohibit lawyers from misleading the public.) In 2004, for example, the Texas Bar reversed its previous position that lawyers were prohibited from calling themselves "Dr.," but said it still would be impermissible to use the title in a way that misled the public, giving the example of a medical malpractice attorney using it.[7] So tell your student that, at least in social contexts, they're free to insist that "there's a doctor in the house!"

Legal studies in the United States are much different than in other countries. In most countries, law is studied more like a major in undergraduate universities, rather than as a separate graduate program. The entire academic process to become a lawyer in other countries generally consumes five years, rather than seven as in the United States (i.e., four years of undergraduate school and three years of law school).

Some countries do, however, require formal internships after graduation, which are not required in the United States. Many have argued that U.S. legal education should be changed to require only two years of classroom training, followed by some form of clinical interning similar to what medical students do in their upper-level years. Arguably, the third year of law school is redundant and unnecessary. For

---

7. *See* Kathleen Maher, *Lawyers Are Doctors, Too*, A.B.A. J., Nov. 24, 2006, http://www.abajournal.com/magazine/ article/lawyers_are_doctors_too/ (tracing the history and explaining the modern positions on the question).

the most part, students spend the third year simply taking more of the same types of courses in different subject areas. In the 1970s, a movement existed among law professors and practitioners to abolish the third year. While the initiative lost traction, the argument that the third year adds little as currently structured still carries weight. One survey found that 43 percent of law students believe the third year is "largely superfluous."[8]

As of 2011, the United States had 200 law schools accredited by the ABA, as well as a few dozen unaccredited law schools. Quite a few new law schools, particularly private, for-profit schools, have opened in the past couple of decades. With many recent grads currently unemployed or underemployed, some have predicted that this trend will reverse and that some existing schools will close.

Graduating from an ABA-accredited school allows graduates to take the bar exam and practice in any state, whereas graduating from an unaccredited school generally limits students to taking the bar and practicing in the state where that school is located. As you might imagine, unaccredited law schools are easier to get into and held in lower regard than accredited law schools. Large states have several law schools, while a few states have only one. California has a whopping sixty-five law schools, twenty of them ABA-accredited.

During the application process, you're likely to hear your student talk about the *U.S. News & World Report* rankings of law schools. Each year, the magazine publishes a ranking of all ABA-accredited law schools. These rankings are widely criticized for focusing on a limited number of criteria that ignore the overall quality of education offered by a law school, such as the quality of the teaching and student life, but they have nevertheless become a kind of gold standard for applicants and law schools alike for assessing the quality of a school. Even while criticizing the rankings, schools invest substantial resources jockeying for a better position. A 2010 survey of nearly 1400 people taking the Kaplan LSAT prep course found that a law school's ranking is the factor consid-

8. Mitu Gulati et al., *The Happy Charade: An Empirical Examination of the Third Year of Law School*, 51 J. LEGAL EDUC. 235, 246 (2001). The researchers surveyed 1100 third-year students at eleven schools in 1998–99. Forty-three percent agreed with the statement that "[t]he third year of law school is largely superfluous."

ered most important in deciding where to apply to law school,[9] which I'm confident even the folks at *U.S. News* would agree is short-sighted if not ridiculous.

The good news for applicants is that, due in large part to the uniform ABA standards to which all accredited schools must adhere, legal education is remarkably consistent and of high quality from place to place. In teaching at schools within each of the four tiers of the *U.S. News* rankings, I've always been struck much more by the similarities than the differences among law schools. So if your student is upset because she didn't get into Big Name Law School, tell her not to worry. She is likely to get just as good an education at Small Name Law School.

In some ways it may be even better. Lower-ranked schools may be more student-centered. They usually concentrate on teaching students the fundamentals of being well-rounded, competent lawyers. Law schools considered to be "elite" tend to be larger, thus more impersonal. Limited survey data suggest that graduates of top-ranked law schools are "significantly less satisfied" with their career choice than graduates of lower-ranked schools.[10] And while it is true as a general proposition that graduating from Big Name Law School will bring more and higher-paying initial job opportunities, a 2010 study found that receiving high grades is a better predictor of high salaries than the status of the law school the person attended.[11]

9. *Kaplan Test Prep Survey: Aspiring Law School Students Place Rankings Above All Else*, Bus. Wire (Nov. 16, 2010), http://www.businesswire.com/news/home/20101116005536/en/Kaplan-Test-Prep-Survey-Aspiring-Law-School. The survey asked: "What is most important to you when picking a law school to apply to?" Thirty percent picked a law school's ranking as the most important factor, followed by location (24 percent), academic program (19 percent), and affordability (12 percent). Only 8 percent of the survey participants said that a law school's job placement statistics are the most important factor in deciding where to apply. Answering a separate question, 86 percent said a law school's ranking is "very im-portant" or "somewhat important" in their decision-making process. *Id.*

10. Ronit Dinovitzer & Bryant G. Garth, *Lawyer Satisfaction in the Process of Structuring Legal Careers*, 41 Law & Soc'y Rev. 1, 23 (2007).

11. Debra Cassens Weiss, *Law School Grades More Important to Career than Elite School, Researchers Say*, A.B.A. J., Aug. 3, 2010, http://www.abajournal.com/news/article/law_school_grades_more_important_to_paycheck_than_elite_school_researchers_ (discussing data analysis by law professors Richard Sander and Jane Yakowitz that "indicates that the salary boost for achieving high grades more than makes up for the salary depreciation associated with attending a lower-ranked school").

Law Students

Law school applications go up and down from year to year. Explanations for the variations range from the state of the economy to the popularity of the latest lawyer show on television. In 2010, total law school enrollment was 145,239 students, of which 53 percent were men and 47 percent women.[12] In the same year, 44,004 students graduated with their Juris Doctor degree.[13] In his 1985 song, *One Million Lawyers and Other Disasters*, folkie Tom Paxton rued the day when the nation would have one million lawyers. America now has 1.1 million lawyers.

If you think that sounds like too many, a lot of people would agree, including many lawyers who are finding their practices squeezed by competition, but it's important to note that many people in need of legal help are unable to obtain it. The Legal Services Corporation, the publicly funded non-profit organization that furnishes free legal services to low-income people through local offices nationwide, turns away roughly one million cases each year because of inadequate resources—and that's just counting the people who actually contact one of their offices seeking help.[14] Only one in five low-income people with legal problems actually seek out legal counsel.[15] And because general "legal insurance" is relatively rare in the United States (it's common in some European countries), even middle-income earners often don't have the resources to hire a lawyer when they need one. In some states, as many as 90 percent of divorces involve one party unrepresented by a lawyer and large percentages of people charged with minor crimes face the music without representation.

Law Student Demographics. Here are some other data about U.S. law students:

- In 2010, about 88,000 people applied to law school and 69 percent were admitted. Among those admitted, roughly 82 percent decided to enroll.[16]

12. *Enrollment and Degrees Awarded, 1963–2009 Academic Years*, AM. BAR ASS'N, 1–2 (2010), www.abanet.org/legaled/statistics/charts/stats%20–%201.pdf.

13. *Id.* at 1.

14. LEGAL SERVS. CORP., DOCUMENTING THE JUSTICE GAP IN AMERICA: THE CURRENT UNMET CIVIL LEGAL NEEDS OF LOW-INCOME AMERICANS 8 (2d ed. 2007).

15. *Id.* at 13.

16. *LSAC Volume Summary, supra*, at 1.

- Currently, 23 percent of all law students are minorities, up from only 7 percent in the 1970s.[17]

- The average law school applicant is between twenty-two and twenty-four years old. One in five students is over the age of thirty. Applicants over the average age are less likely to be admitted and less likely to enroll if they are admitted.[18]

- For the last five years, the University of Florida has produced the most law school applicants, with UCLA and the University of Texas–Austin coming in at a close second and third.[19] As a Florida alumnus, what can I say but Go Gators.

- About 40 percent of law school applicants take less than one year off after graduating from college before applying to law school.[20] These are what are known as "traditional students." About 25 percent of this group takes the LSAT at least twice.[21]

- Roughly 9 percent of the nation's first-year law students either voluntarily drop out or are academically dismissed before their second year. In the 2L and 3L years, the attrition rate declines steeply: only 207 third-year students dropped out nationwide in 2009–2010.[22]

The Special Situation of Part–Time Evening–Division Students. For the most part, this book discusses law students generically, but I want to include a special note

17. *First Year J.D. and Total J.D. Minority Enrollment for 1971–2010*, AM. BAR ASS'N, 1 (2010), http://www.americanbar.org/content/dam/aba/migrated/legaled/statistics/charts/stats_8.pdf.

18. Kimberly Dustman & Phil Handwerk, *Analysis of Law School Applicants by Age Group*, LAW SCH. ADMISSIONS COUNCIL, 2 (Oct. 2010), http://www.lsac.org/LSACResources/Data/PDFs/Analysis–Applicants-by-Age–Group.pdf.

19. *Top 240 ABA Applicant Feeder Schools*, LAW SCH. ADMISSIONS COUNCIL, 1 (2010), http://www.lsac.org/LSAC Resources/Data/PDFs/top–240–feeder-schools.pdf.

20. *LSAC Volume Summary, supra*, at 1.

21. *LSAT Repeater Data*, LAW SCH. ADMISSIONS COUNCIL, 1 (2010), http://www.lsac.org/LSACResources/Data/PDFs/RepeaterData.pdf.

22. *Total J.D. Attrition 1981–2010*, AM. BAR ASS'N, 1 (2010), http://www.americanbar.org/content/dam/aba/migrated/legaled/statistics/charts/stats_17.pdf.

about a significant group of law students who are often overlooked. Most of the nation's 145,000 law students attend law school full-time during the day and graduate in three years, but approximately 16 percent of law students attend one of the nation's eighty-four part-time evening-division law school programs. Let's call them "day" (full-time) and "night" (part-time) students for convenience.[23] Night students take the same curriculum from the same professors as day students, but take fewer credit hours per semester. As a result, they require four years to graduate, rather than three.

When most day students have left campus, night students are just arriving, usually after a long day at work in their regular jobs. Their classes typically are held four nights a week, three hours a night. Their reading assignments are just as long and dense and their classes are just as intense. Just about everything is the same as for the day students except the number of courses they take in a semester (usually three for night students, as compared to five for day students).

Many night students get up at the crack of dawn to get their kids ready for school, rush off to full-time jobs and work all day, then hurry to law school, stopping to grab a bite of dinner in between if they have time. It's a grueling schedule and we haven't even mentioned the studying part. Oops, there go the weekends. No other time, literally, is available for night students to do their course work.

Night law students are fascinating people who come from all walks of life: social workers, police officers, doctors, nurses, accountants, homemakers, you name it. The life experiences they bring with them add tremendously to the classroom experience.

Some part-time evening-division students start law school worried they will get a lesser legal education because it's "night school." Not true. As mentioned, they take the same courses from the same professors. Significantly, their actual classroom experiences may prove to be even more vital and

---

23. Not all part-time law students are evening-division students. Some day students attend part-time as well.

exciting than many day classes in large part because, unlike many young traditional students, night students are less afraid to express their opinions and "mix it up" a bit in class discussions.

Night students are older, more mature and settled in life, and more likely to be attending law school for a reason other than that they earned an undergraduate degree in "Things that Happened in England in 1288 A.D." or "The Unpublished Doodles of Henri Matisse" and can't think of anything else to do with it. Because of this, and also because they simply don't have time, night students and their relationships are more immune to some of the common annoyances of being with a law student. They are less likely to be obsessed with law school talk and class rank than day students. They also are less likely to get deeply involved in the law school social scene. They definitely do, however, develop their own camaraderie and enjoy getting together for small gatherings, usually at a pub now and again after class since that is their only available common time slot.

Thus, while being with a night student requires a whole different level of acceptance by loved ones that the person is going to be largely unavailable during law school, it carries upsides as well. My most important heads-up tip for your night student is this: The night students who don't succeed almost always are students who didn't arrive at law school with a plan for how to manage what are essentially three full-time jobs: their regular job, family, and law school. They fall behind and can't catch up. Your night student needs to figure out this plan *before* they get to law school.

Law Professors

Rest assured that your student will be in good hands regardless of which law school he or she attends. The overall caliber of law professors is extremely high. Becoming a law professor is a highly competitive process, with far more qualified applicants than available positions. Because so many well-qualified lawyers want to be law professors, faculty hiring is a buyer's market for law schools. Even lower-ranked schools easily attract top faculty talent.

Nicer Than You'd Think. Prior to starting law school, your student is likely to hear horror stories about law professors. Some famous print and screen accounts of law school portray law professors as sadistic ogres. In modern times, those stories are more urban legend than reality. In asking a group of new students to name their biggest surprise about law school, one of the most common answers related to the professors defying the stereotype of cruel dictators bent on humiliating students. Ease your student's mind by reading these responses to them:

• The biggest surprise has been the attitude of the professors. After reading Turow's *One L*, which was recommended by many friends as an accurate depiction of first-year life, I expected professors to create a clear barrier between themselves and the students. I anticipated a class environment based heavily in fear, with an undertone of student humiliation. I may have just been lucky in my draw of sections, but I have found that the professors actually enjoy what they do (or are great actors). In all classes, there is a relaxed feeling in the dialogue and discussion. This certainly has not taken away from the fear—but for me it has shifted the fear from a fear of public humiliation to a fear of disappointing. In discussions with my classmates, everyone seems to share the same view—that the desire to be prepared and understand the material is not to avoid being humiliated in class, but to live up to the expectations that we place on ourselves and that the professors place on us.

• The surprise would go back to a misguided belief in professors who are emotionally detached from their students. The professors seem to be genuinely concerned about the students understanding the material, raising their own opinions, asking questions, and not getting overwhelmed in the whole process. I think I would find it hard as a professor to remember names in a class of seventy to eighty students; however, I have already noticed that occurring in most of my classes.

• My biggest surprise has been the personality of the professors. While they have all made it very clear that we are to be prepared before class, I never felt as though they were trying to embarrass or belittle us. That being said, the professors are still quite intimidating.

Not every professor at every law school is kind and caring, but in general, law professors are not mean-spirited people out to get students. In fact, law schools are getting "nicer" all the time—too nice, some would argue—as a new generation of professors raised in the esteem-building era takes over for the older, retiring Socratic traditionalists. Tell your student not to worry about mean professors.

Idiosyncratic Ivory Tower Dwellers. Many law professors tend to be idiosyncratic individualists, which is a nice way of saying we can be a bit quirky. Not necessarily quirky in a bad way. Just different. In part, it's because academia overall attracts highly intelligent people who don't fit comfortably into normal corporate or other business environments. Also, once on campus, the nature of the job encourages people to let out what might otherwise remain hidden eccentricities in other settings.

Autonomy, which is largely absent in private practice, is one of the major draws of the job. Law professors can dress as they wish, say what they want to whomever they want, and come and go pretty much as they please. They enjoy more or less complete control over their work lives. Small wonder they let their inner-selves show through more than most other workers. Imagine your law student coming home from class on the very first day. You ask him, "So how was it?" And he tells you that a professor pulled out a machete in class and threatened to kill him. Just another day in legal education, as this significant other reports:

> On my husband's (boyfriend at the time) very first day of law school a couple years ago, his professor, after taking roll, welcomed everyone to law school and said they should all be proud to be there. Then, after a pause, he said he meant everyone except my husband, who should not have been admitted. The teacher said he was disgusted that my husband was there—and that my husband should leave or the teacher would kill him. My husband laughed. The teacher asked why he wasn't afraid. My husband said there was no reason to believe the threat. The teacher pulled out a machete.

Still talking and threatening, he advanced to my husband, crawled up on the table and put the machete to my husband's head.

The significant other reported that her husband laughed as he told the story and said the professor was just trying to make a point (most likely about assault and battery), but added that she would have been freaked out. Me too.

Law Professor Demographics. Here are some general facts about the nation's law professors:

• Most of the nation's 9,500 full-time law professors are white males, although the number of women and minority professors has increased substantially in recent years. In the early 1970s, women and minorities together constituted only 8 percent of all law school faculty members. Today, roughly 34 percent of all law professors are women and 22 percent are minorities (with some overlap between those two groups).[24] Given that most women and minority professors have entered the profession recently, they're more likely to be younger and untenured.

• Professors of Legal Research and Writing, a course you will hear a lot about from your student, are disproportionately women. Due to the fact that these jobs traditionally have not been tenure-track positions (and pay lower salaries as a result), this subset of law faculty jobs is often referred to by law professors as the "pink ghetto." Currently, 71 percent of full-time legal writing instructors are women.[25]

• Forty-seven percent of law professors hold a Juris Doctor or an advanced law degree from just eleven "elite" law schools, with 21 percent coming from Harvard and Yale. (My alma mater, the University of Florida, has generated ninety-two profs for about one percent of the total. Once again, Go Gators.)[26]

---

24. *See* Ass'n of Am. Law Schs., Statistical Report on Law Faculty 2007–2008 4–5 (2008), [hereinafter Statistical Report on Law Faculty], http://aals.org/statistics/report–07–08.pdf.

25. Ass'n of Legal Writing Dirs., Legal Writing Inst., 2010 National Survey Results 55 (2010) [hereinafter 2010 ALWD Survey Results].

26. *See* Statistical Report on Law Faculty, *supra*, at 27–28. As of 2007–08, the following number of professors held Juris Doctor or advanced law degrees from these eleven schools: Columbia University (368), Georgetown University

- Law review membership and other academic honors, such as Order of the Coif (top ten percent of the class), are common credentials for law professors.[27]

- Many law professors hold advanced law degrees (i.e., an LL.M or S.J.D.) in addition to their J.D. degree, and a growing number also have Ph.Ds in other disciplines.

- Disproportionate numbers of professors have held one or more federal judicial clerkships, a prestigious kind of internship working for a judge.

- A majority of law professors had some practical experience in either government or private practice prior to becoming professors, although the preference to hire professors with practical experience is more pronounced in lower-ranked law schools.[28]

- Politically, more law professors probably lean left than right, although no recent data exist to support this assertion. As a general proposition (with many exceptions), law faculties at schools on either coast tend to be more liberal, while law faculties in the heartland tend to be more conservative.

Overview of Law School Curricula

So what goes on during those three (or four for part-time students) years of law school? Subsequent chapters will flesh out the answer in detail, but in general, law school begins with a first-year slate of required courses in core subjects, such as Contracts, Property, and Torts. The purpose of first-year courses is both to teach the rules of law in the particular area (most first-year courses are tested on the state bar exam) and, just as important, to train students in the art of conducting legal analysis.

One of the great misapprehensions about law school is that the primary purpose is to teach students rules of law to

(233), Harvard University (1179), New York University (304), Stanford University (242), University of California–Berkeley (245), University of Chicago (339), University of Michigan (374), University of Pennsylvania (190), University of Virginia (199), and Yale University (805). *Id.*

27. The two most powerful predictors of a law professor's first teaching appointment are the status of the law school from which the professor graduated and the professor's academic achievements while in law school. James R.P. Ogloff et al., *More Than "Learning to Think Like a Lawyer": The Empirical Research on Legal Education*, 34 CREIGHTON L. REV. 73, 130–31 (2000).

28. *Id.* at 131–32.

memorize, but that's only one component of legal education. If I had to put a figure on it, I'd say memorization of rules is about 40 percent of the total package. Particularly in the first year, much of the focus is on training students in legal reasoning. This is accomplished through the notorious "Socratic method" and "case method" of teaching. These methods are so integral to a law student's existence and psyche as to warrant their own treatment in Chapter 6. For now, suffice it to say that they are unlike anything students in other educational fields experience and are a primary cause of angst and confusion in new law students.

Entering students are split into sections, typically two, but it can vary by law school and by course. These sections average seventy to eighty students, which is one of the fundamental defects in legal education. Everyone agrees first-year classes are too large. Seventy to eighty students are simply too many to conduct the kind of one-on-one dialectics envisioned by the Socratic method. As discussed in future pages, large classes and the student-teacher ratios that come with them contribute to making law students feel alienated and isolated. So why don't law schools make classes smaller? The main reason is money. More sections would require more faculty and more classrooms.

Students spend their first year taking the same courses taught by the same professors in the same rooms with the same students. Because most law schools use assigned seating and students tend to choose the same seat for each course, many students literally sit next to the same people day in and day out for the entire first year. Students not only become closely attached to their seatmates, some get attached to their actual seat. As one student wrote:

> Sometimes I feel as attached to my seat as my loved ones. I always get to exams early to sit in my same seat. Even in later semesters, I always try to get that same seat. It has become a comfort zone of normalcy and reliability in the midst of the chaos.

The second and third years of law school are referred to as the "upper-level curriculum." For the most part, the upper-level curriculum is more of the same. Students take mostly the same kinds of courses (i.e., doctrinal courses), except in different subject areas, although some new course types are added, including skills courses, seminars, clinics, and externships. Each of these course types is described below.

Some upper-level courses are, like first-year courses, re-quired courses that all students must take, but most of them are electives, meaning students can choose which courses to take. Thus, if a student wants to specialize in an area such as tax law or intellectual property law, the student can take extra courses in those areas, assuming the law school offers them. The larger the law school, the more elective courses, including specialized boutique courses, it will offer. Some schools offer "certificate programs" in specialized areas. If the student takes a certain number of approved courses, his transcript will reflect that he obtained a specialty certificate in the area, which may give the student an advantage in the job market.

The wholly elective nature of upper-level courses is illuso-ry to some extent because most students wisely "elect" to take courses known to be covered on their state's bar exami-nation. Subjects covered on the bar exam vary by state. Depending on the state, the list of "bar courses" can be either long or short. Even when bar courses aren't required, they fill up with large numbers of students who understand-ably want to maximize their chances of passing the bar exam.

All law school courses, both required and elective, fall into one of four categories:

• **Doctrinal Courses.** The most common type of law school course is referred to as a "doctrinal course." Doctrinal courses focus on teaching the body of legal rules (i.e., "doc-trine") in a particular subject area. They usually are "case-book" courses, in which students learn the law from books that package together assorted judicial opinions (i.e., "cases") in the particular subject.

Doctrinal courses include a large sub-category of courses known as "code courses," in which the primary source of law in the subject is a "code" or book of statutes, rather than cases only. Federal Income Tax, for example, is a code course, with the primary sources of law being the Internal Revenue Code (legislation passed by Congress) and accompanying reg-ulations (adopted by the Internal Revenue Service). Courses in the Uniform Commercial Code, which governs most types of commercial transactions, are another common type of code course. Even in code courses, however, students usually learn the law, at least in part, from reading judicial opinions in casebooks interpreting provisions of the relevant codes.

Most first-year courses are doctrinal courses. Legal Research and Writing, a "skills course," is the exception (see below). The traditional first-year doctrinal courses are Civil Procedure, Contracts, Criminal Law, Property, Torts, and, at about half of law schools, Constitutional Law. Most upper-level courses also are doctrinal courses. Examples include Business Organizations, Corporations, Criminal Procedure, Decedents' Estates, Environmental Law, Evidence, Health Law, Intellectual Property, Sales, and Secured Transactions. The content of doctrinal courses is the primary focus of state bar examinations.

• **Skills Courses.** Skills courses are courses that focus on training students in practical lawyering skills rather than doctrinal law. A longstanding criticism of U.S. legal education is that law schools devote too much attention to teaching doctrine and not enough attention to teaching skills. Recently, in the wake of two influential studies (the *Best Practices in Legal Education* and *Carnegie Foundation* reports), a more pronounced push is being made in law schools to add more skills courses. Examples of skills courses include courses in alternative dispute resolution, appellate advocacy, client counseling, legal document drafting, and trial advocacy.

• **Seminars.** Most law students take at least one seminar, usually in their third year. Seminars are very different from other law school courses. For one thing, they are small, often limited to a maximum of twelve students. Instead of an exam, students are required to write a scholarly paper on a topic of their choice and present it to the class. Often, the seminar paper is used to satisfy a law school's "upper-level writing requirement." ABA accreditation rules mandate that all students engage in at least one substantial upper-level writing experience prior to graduation.

• **Clinics and Externships.** One of the most surprising aspects of law school to outsiders is the lack of training students receive in the actual practice of law. Medical students spend their early years of medical school learning from books, but their later years working in clinical settings with real patients. Law school is not like that. The only avenues for law students to work with real clients and cases are through clinical programs and externships.

Most law schools have one or more "live-client clinics" as they are called, in which students earn credit while working on real cases under the supervision of a professor or staff attorney. Most clinics are devoted to providing legal assistance to persons who lack the financial resources to hire a lawyer. Law school clinics are expensive to operate on a per-student basis, much more expensive than regular classes. Thus, clinical opportunities vary widely by schools. A few law schools have no clinics, while some large, well-funded schools have more than thirty. Most small schools (i.e., 500 or fewer students) have two to four clinics.

Externships involve placing the student with a government agency or court, and sometimes with a private corporation or law firm, for a semester, during which time the student earns credit hours while learning under the supervision of experienced lawyers.

Extra– and Co–Curricular Law School Activities

Throughout law school, students work hard to bolster their resumes to increase their job opportunities. All higher education students try to burnish their credentials, of course, but few do it with the passion of law students. Law students voluntarily take on extra- and co-curricular activities that can consume hundreds of hours. You, like many loved ones of law students, might reasonably ask: "Why in the world are you taking on all this extra voluntary work when you already spend so much time with law school?" In large part, it is because the legal job market is competitive and students want to bolster their experience and career opportunities. The "big four" non-required activities you will hear about are:

• **Law Review.** Every law school publishes a "law review," a student-run, student-edited journal of scholarly legal articles written primarily by law professors, but also by judges, lawyers, and students. Law reviews typically publish four to six issues per year, with each issue containing a few primary articles by outside authors, usually law professors, and a few works written by student members of the law review. Some law review articles become influential in the development of the law, while many others are read only by the authors and a few close relatives.

Being on law review has long been the holy grail of law school success. Law review membership defines its holder as an elite academic performer and opens job opportunities that other students simply won't have. Many law firms and most judges will only hire students who were on the law review.

Traditionally, students with superior grades and class rank (e.g., top 5 percent) were automatically invited to participate in law review. Today, most law reviews select candidates via a "write-on competition" held in the summer after the first year, although some law schools combine a limited number of automatic invitations with a write-on competition, and many schools weigh GPA as a factor in the write-on competition.

Once invited to participate on law review, students are required to write at least one substantial scholarly paper called a "Comment" or a "Note." These titles don't do justice to the work product. Law review Comments and Notes are lengthy and contain hundreds of footnotes. They require exhaustive research, writing, and re-writing. The best student works are selected for publication in the law review. In addition to writing their own Comment or Note (and sometimes one of each), law review students edit and "cite-check" (i.e., verify the accuracy of references to authority and make sure they conform to proper citation style) articles by professors and others that have been accepted for publication by the law review. In their third year, law review members may apply for positions on the law review editorial board, which runs the law review. These editorial positions are considered particularly prestigious. Being editor-in-chief or "EIC" of the law review is the law school equivalent of captaining a starship.

Law review work is long and arduous. The comment below, from a 2L, gives us another example of how family members often misunderstand the nature of law student life:

> At dinner the other night with my family, my dad asks how law review is going, and I tell them about my Note topic and how stressed out I am and how our first Bluebooking[29] assignment took more than ten hours. My mom then casually says, "Oh, I thought law review was kind of like high school yearbook." !??!?

29. "Bluebooking" refers to checking and correcting the citation format in footnotes contained in law review articles. See Chapter 4 for more about the *Bluebook* and citation style.

Each school has a primary law review. Many schools also have "secondary journals" focused on particular subject areas, such as tax law or environmental law. Membership on these journals, while not considered as prestigious as the primary law review, is still a good feather in a student's cap.

• **Moot Court, Mock Trial, and Other Competitions.** Not considered as prestigious as law review, but still an excellent credential and a lot more fun and exciting, is the co-curricular activity known as "moot court." Moot court is basically "mock court" in an appellate setting, as opposed to a trial setting. Most law schools have a moot court program. While they vary considerably in their structures, the programs sometimes begin at ground level with a first-year intramural appellate argument competition, often held in conjunction with the course in Legal Research and Writing. Students who continue in moot court in their upper-level years participate in regional and national moot court competitions, of which there are many, against teams from other law schools. The major competitions attract teams from more than 100 schools.

Participants in a moot court competition, whether internal or external, receive a package of materials containing an abbreviated appellate record of a fictitious case that is pending on appeal before a high court, often the U.S. Supreme Court. Students work in teams of two or three. Each team must research and write a lengthy appellate brief arguing one side of the issues and, at the actual competition, argue the issues against other student teams in front of three-person panels of mock appellate judges. Numerous practice argument rounds are held leading up to a competition. Like law review, moot court requires a tremendous amount of work.

In addition to moot court, law schools often sponsor or participate in other types of skills competitions. (Notice how just about everything in law school is a "competition.") Mock trial competitions are the most common type after moot court. Trial competitions involve student teams competing against each other in a simulated trial. Moot court, remember, involves appellate proceedings. Thus, instead of simply making legal arguments to judges, students in mock trial competitions examine and cross-examine witnesses, make objections, admit documents into evidence, and deliver opening statements and closing arguments to mock juries.

Depending on the school, opportunities also may exist to participate in other types of competitions, such as mock negotiation and client counseling competitions.

• **Student Organizations.** All law schools permit students to form organizations related to particular student interests. The range of these organizations is limited only by law student interest. Surfing through law school websites, one can find student organizations devoted to everything from doing community service projects to enjoying single-malt whiskey. Speaking of surfing, one California law school even has a Surf Club. Most student organizations are devoted to more serious matters, such as political or social causes, specific legal subject areas, or particular religious or cultural groups.

Participating in a student organization enables students to pursue and explore legal issues about which they are passionate, network with like-minded people, and add another line on the resume (although these activities do not carry heavy resume weight, certainly nothing like law review or moot court). Especially if your student feels alienated or isolated, as many law students do, belonging to a student group can provide a real boost to motivation and morale.

Many law schools have student organizations for married students. If you are married to your law student, I encourage you to participate. You'll be able to meet people in the same situation as you. Then, when your student is standing around blathering about the doctrine of *res judicata*[30] to another student, you and the other law school widows and widowers can commiserate about what a drag it is to be married to a law student.

Every law school also has a student government association. These organizations hold elections and function similarly to student government associations at the undergraduate level.

---

30. *Res judicata* is a doctrine that basically says once a legal claim has been decided by a court, it can't be relitigated in the same or another court.

• **Summer Jobs.** While not technically an extra- or co-curricular activity, the topic of summer legal jobs fits well here. Beginning in the second semester, law schools become a feeding frenzy of competition among students seeking summer legal jobs, most of which are at private law firms. These positions, called "summer associate" or "summer clerkship" positions, are considered vital by students for obtaining some real-life legal experience to put on their resumes and getting their feet in the doors of law firms for potential permanent associate jobs after law school. ("Associate" is the name of the position for a beginning lawyer at a private law firm, as distinguished from "partner.") Landing a summer legal job is a large stress factor in a law student's life, as discussed in Chapter 11.

Post–Graduation

After completing 58,000 minutes of classroom instruction in good standing, law students get to graduate.[31] Hooray! A time of joy! A time for celebration! For about fifteen minutes, after which the student has to buckle down and start studying for the bar. To become licensed to practice law in a particular state, a student must take and pass a state bar examination.

Bar examinations are comprised of two primary parts: the Multistate Bar Examination (MBE), also known as "The 200 Hardest Multiple-Choice Questions Ever Written," and a state-specific portion, which may include both essay and multiple-choice questions. Nearly every state administers the MBE (another well-known acronym among law students) as part of its bar exam. The state portion varies by state, both in terms of format and the subjects covered.

More than half of states have recently added the Multistate Performance Test (MPT) as a component of their bar exams. The MPT is designed to test lawyering skills, such as the ability to analyze a legal problem, rather than just knowledge and understanding of substantive law. Forty-six states also require students to take the Multistate Profession-

---

31. No joke. ABA accreditation standard 304(b) specifies that a law student must complete a course of study of no fewer than 58,000 minutes of instruction time with at least 45,000 of those minutes being in the form of attendance at regularly scheduled classes, also known as "butt time" (i.e., the amount of time students must be planted in a classroom).

al Responsibility Exam or MPRE, a two-hour, sixty-question multiple-choice exam, held separately from the regular bar exam, that tests knowledge of the rules of ethics governing lawyers. Bar examinations are given twice a year, in February and July. Most students graduate in May and take the July exam.

As you can imagine, the bar exam is incredibly stressful. It's more than a little daunting to have just finished three of the hardest and most expensive years of one's life only to face the prospect that it might all have been for naught if the student can't pass the bar exam. Most students do, but certainly not all. According to data collected by the National Conference of Bar Examiners, in 2010, nationwide, 68 percent of bar-takers (54,448 out of 79,953) passed the exam.[32] While unsuccessful takers are permitted to retake the exam, one professor estimates there are 150,000 law school graduates in America who have never passed a bar exam.[33]

So don't be surprised when you learn that your penniless, debt-ridden student is shelling out more than two thousand dollars for an intensive bar exam review course to be taken in the weeks immediately following law school. Obvious questions to a non-law student would be: "Why do you have to take an expensive course after law school to prepare for the bar examination? Isn't that what law school is for?" At least those would be obvious questions in a normal world. But law school, as you will learn in these pages, is not a normal world. Far from it.

The culmination of the legal education process occurs when, after passing the bar exam, one is officially sworn in as a member of the bar. As the very last step on the wearying road to earning the title of "attorney,"[34] taking the lawyer's oath is a capstone event.[35] From that moment forward, your

32. 2010 STATISTICS, NAT'L CONFERENCE OF BAR EXAM'RS, 9 (Mar. 2011) http://www.ncbex.org/fileadmin/mediafiles/downloads/Bar_Admissions/2010_Stats.pdf.

33. Jane Yakowitz, *Marooned: An Empirical Investigation of Law School Graduates Who Fail the Bar Exam*, 60 J. LEGAL EDUC. 3, 15 (2010).

34. "Lawyer" and "attorney" are often used interchangeably, but technically, a lawyer is one who is learned in the law and an attorney is one licensed to practice law. Of course, they usually overlap, since most lawyers are attorneys.

35. At least it's supposed to be. My swearing-in was more like a scene from a *Seinfeld* episode. In Florida, one had to be sworn in by a state judge. The federal judge I worked for as a law clerk sent me over to the chambers of a state trial judge friend for swearing-in. When I arrived the judge was about to begin a hearing in chambers, so he ushered me into his bathroom, no bigger than a

student will be licensed to wield the awesome power of the law.

shower stall. Standing nose-to-nose, he said "Raise your right hand and repeat after me," and proceeded to read the oath. But he didn't stop and let me repeat it line by line. He zipped through the entire 344 words. When it came time to repeat it, I couldn't remember past the first sentence, so we were trapped in that bathroom for what seemed like a long time. Not quite the pomp and circumstance I anticipated, but I still felt proud exiting the bathroom as an official attorney. Hopefully, your student's swearing-in will be a bit more decorous.

CHAPTER 3
THE WORLD'S SHORTEST SUMMARY OF THE U.S. LEGAL SYSTEM

You didn't buy this book to learn all about law and the legal system. If you were that into it, you'd go to law school yourself. (Actually, you'd be surprised how many law student relatives end up coming to law school.) But you may feel like you are in law school at times simply from being involved with a law student. Loved ones of law students often complain they feel like outcasts to the exclusive club of law students. Here's part of your ticket to the inside. With your law student talking so much about law, you'll benefit from having at least a passing familiarity with a few fundamentals of our legal system. The Glossary at the back will also come in handy. We're talking real basics here, and even then I'm only going to give you information that will help you understand the law school experience.

Court System

The United States is a "federalist system" in which a federal, or national, court system operates both independently from and interdependently with separate court systems in each of the fifty states. Each system—that is, the federal judicial system and the judicial system of each state—has a set of trial courts, one or more intermediate appellate courts, and a single high court, called the supreme court in the federal system and in most states. Picture a triangle: The trial courts would line the bottom, a much smaller number of intermediate appellate courts would fill a layer in the middle, and a single supreme court would sit at the top.

Most U.S. courts, both federal and state, are courts of "general jurisdiction," meaning they can and do hear all types of cases. A few specialized court systems also exist. For example, in the federal system, there is a separate system of bankruptcy courts and some states have specialty courts in areas such as family law and probate law.

Types of Law

Law is commonly divided into two classifications: "public law" and "private law." The basic distinction is useful, but far from full proof, as several areas of law contain elements of both categories. Simply put, public law is law that regulates the relationships between individual citizens and the government. Criminal law is a good example of public law. Criminal law pits the state (or the federal government) against individuals. Much of constitutional law and administrative law (i.e., law emanating from regulations passed by government agencies) is also public law.

Private law is law that regulates relationships between individuals. Torts, Contracts, and Property—all required first-year courses—are good examples of courses that focus on private law. In tort, contract, and property cases the plaintiff usually is a private citizen or corporation seeking to recover damages or other remedies from other private citizens or corporations.

Most first-year courses focus on private law, with Criminal Law, and Constitutional Law if it's offered in the first year, being the exceptions.

The Common Law System

The United States follows what is called a "common law" legal system. We borrowed it from England. Given our tendency toward U.S. exceptionalism—that is, the belief of Americans that we lead the world in everything—it might come as a surprise that most of the world follows an entirely different legal system than we do. Only a few major countries other than the United States (e.g., Australia, Canada, England, New Zealand) follow a common law legal system. Most countries, including all of Europe and Latin America, adhere to what is known as a "civil law" system.[36]

"Civil law legal systems" need to be distinguished from the way we use the term "civil law" in the United States. In the United States, civil law refers to all non-criminal areas of law. In a civil law legal system, the term describes the entire body of law, both non-criminal and criminal. A better descriptor for a civil law legal system might be a "code law system."

Common law is judge-made law, derived from and developed through case precedent. Case precedent is composed of the judicial opinions that your student will be studying day in and day out. By comparison, in civil law systems, law is derived primarily from codes—i.e., books of neatly organized statutes passed by legislatures. In theory, judges have no power to make law in civil law systems, as they do under common law systems. Their job is to follow the rules set forth in the codes. It doesn't really work that way in real life, as all legal language requires interpreting, whether it's in a code or in a judicial opinion. And any time a court interprets law, it makes law to some extent.

The common law system is one reason why the most accurate answer to most legal questions is "It depends." On what? The facts of the particular case. Case results are driven by facts as much as by law. A change in a single fact can change the result of a case. This built-in indeterminacy of the common law will drive your student crazy at first. Many students come to law school expecting the law to be a neat package of rules to memorize. When they find out that's not the way things work, they get exasperated. "Why the heck don't they just write all the rules down in one place? That way, everyone would know what the law is!"

Someone actually tried to do that once. In the eighteenth century, Frederick the Great implemented the Prussian Code under Prussia's civil law system. The Prussian Code was an attempt to write a complete set of rules intended to foresee and govern the entire range of human conduct. It contained more than 17,000 provisions setting forth specific rules designed to govern specific fact situations. It didn't work. Seventeen thousand provisions were insufficient to cover all

36. In the United States, Louisiana is an aberration. It is the only state that follows a civil law legal system rather than a common law system.

varieties of human conduct. Seventeen million provisions would not be enough.

Although the United States will always be a common law system, one criticism of U.S. legal education is that the "case method" of teaching (see Chapter 6) requires students to focus too much on the common law (i.e., judicial opinions), obscuring the fact that American life is increasingly governed by statutes passed by legislatures and regulations adopted by administrative agencies. As one example, crimes originally were defined by judges as part of the common law, but today all crimes, both state and federal, are defined by statute. Yet in many first-year Criminal Law courses, students still study the judge-made common law elements of crimes.

Appeals

Due to the case method of law school study, law students spend most of their time studying the work product of appellate courts. Appellate courts, both state and federal, usually hear cases in panels that comprise three judges, with the major exception being the U.S. Supreme Court, which has nine justices. To have a right to appeal in the United States, one party to a lawsuit—normally it's the losing party, of course[37]—must be able to point to some specific error that was made in the pretrial or trial proceedings. Examples: the trial court wrongly dismissed the case, the evidence was insufficient to support the jury's verdict, the trial judge gave incorrect instructions on the law to the jury, etc. Simply losing and being unhappy about it is not a sufficient ground for appeal in the United States, which is different from some countries where an automatic right of appeal exists.

Simplistically, appeals work like this: The party pursuing the appeal—called the "appellant"—files a brief identifying an alleged error(s) in the trial or pretrial proceedings below and arguing why, under the facts and law of the case, the error requires a reversal of the trial court. A brief is a written legal argument, explaining the facts, issues, and law in support of the argument. "Brief" is another misnomer because appellate briefs generally run from thirty to forty pages. The other side—called the "appellee"—then files its own brief

---

37. But not always. Sometimes the winning party believes they should have won better or bigger than they did in the trial court and will appeal.

rebutting the appellant's arguments. The court then sets the case for what's called "oral argument." This is where the lawyers get up and argue their case in person in front of the appellate judges. (Law students typically spend a big chunk of their second semester writing an appellate brief and making an oral argument to a mock appellate court—see Chapter 4.) After the oral argument, the judges meet in private and vote on the result. At that time, one of the judges is assigned to write the opinion in the case on behalf of the court.

Judicial Opinions

Reading and analyzing appellate judicial opinions is the grist of U.S. legal education. If you ask your student what she spends most of her time doing, she'll say "Reading cases." What are "cases"? One of my student research assistants said her boyfriend, a police officer, thought this meant she was studying the types of case files he was used to seeing in his job: thick folders of witness statements, etc. That's not what law students do. In law school, a "case" simply means an appellate judicial opinion.

A judicial opinion is a written document in which an appellate court rules on the issues raised in an appeal. A typical opinion begins with a recitation of the relevant facts of the case, including an explanation of the procedural events that landed the case in the appellate court, followed by a discussion of the issue raised on appeal, the law relevant to that issue, and the application of that law to the particular facts of the case. Opinions can be as short as one page or longer than one hundred pages. The Supreme Court's decision in *Buckley v. Valeo*,[38] involving campaign financing, is 274 pages long. I've attached a much shorter sample judicial opinion at the end of the book as an appendix—the infamous Iowa "spring-gun" case, *Katko v. Briney*, which most 1Ls study—so you can see what we're talking about. I wanted to attach *Buckley* as the appendix to confer "tome" status on the book, but the publisher wouldn't let me. Just kidding.

---

38. 424 U.S. 1 (1976) (upholding some parts and rejecting other parts of a federal law limiting campaign financing). As discussed in Chapter 4, your student will spend a lot of time worrying about legal citation style. It gets complicated and is *very* picky about the fine points, but the basics of citing to a case are pretty simple. This citation to the *Buckley* case tells us it was decided in 1976 and can be found in volume 424 of the U.S. Reports (a collection of books reprinting U.S. Supreme Court cases), beginning at page 1.

You may hear your student talking about "majority," "dissenting," and "concurring" opinions. As mentioned, after the appellate argument, one of the judges will be assigned to write the opinion for the court. If all three judges agree, which they usually do, that will be the only opinion of the court. If one judge disagrees with the other two, she may write a "dissenting opinion" (also called a "minority opinion") to the court's "majority opinion." If a judge agrees with the result, but not all the reasoning of the majority, or if the judge wants to add additional reasoning not contained in the majority opinion, she may write a "concurring opinion." At the U.S. Supreme Court, with nine justices, the Court's ruling may include several concurring and/or dissenting opinions, which is a big reason why studying Supreme Court cases is difficult and confusing. Often, a majority of the Supreme Court can't agree on one opinion, so Court-followers of all types, including law students, are left to try to figure out which opinion or parts thereof garnered the most support. These parts are called the "plurality opinion."

One word you are likely to hear from your new student is "holding." The holding of the case is essentially the court's ruling on the legal issue involved. One of the most common questions professors ask in class is "What did the court hold?" or "What was the holding in the case?"

The fact that law students spend almost all their time studying appellate judicial opinions is one of the strangest aspects of U.S. legal education. The vast majority of both criminal and civil cases are resolved without a trial. Approximately 95 percent of criminal cases are dismissed before trial or resolved by a plea bargain. The same is true of civil cases. Roughly 95 percent are dismissed before trial or resolved by a settlement agreement.

That leaves about 5 percent of cases that go to trial. But only about 15 percent of the cases that go to trial are appealed. So now we're down to only about seven out of every one thousand cases that are left for potential study in law school. Thus, the vast majority of your student's legal education will be consumed with studying the end product in very unusual cases: the less than 1 percent of cases that go to trial, get appealed, and result in a full written opinion from an appellate court. And even in those cases, students study only the final result—the appellate opinion—not the years of litigation that preceded the appeal. Weird stuff. Chapter 6 explains the "case method" which is at the root of this odd arrangement.

Trials

It might seem strange that appeals would be discussed before trials—since appeals happen after trials—but as we just learned, law students don't study trials. They study appeals. For the small percentage of cases that actually make it to trial, the right to trial by jury is a fundamental distinguishing feature of the U.S. system from most other legal systems around the world. Even in England, from which we got the jury trial system, the right to trial by jury has been severely restricted. In the United States, the right to a jury trial in both criminal and civil cases is guaranteed by both the federal and state constitutions.

Most criminal cases that make it to trial are jury trials, although a defendant can waive his right to a jury trial and have the case tried by a judge only. In civil cases, the opposite is true. Contrary to the public perception that comes from watching lawyer television shows and movies and reading John Grisham or other courtroom dramas, the majority of civil cases that go to trial in the United States are "bench" trials; that is, trials before a judge only, with no jury. In civil cases, one of the parties must demand a jury or the right will be deemed waived. In the majority of civil cases, the parties opt for a trial before a judge only. The major exception is in tort cases (i.e., personal injury cases), in which the plaintiff almost always demands a jury trial.

One of the most fundamental lessons law students have hammered into them in the early weeks of law school is the different roles of judge and jury in a jury trial. It is commonly said that the judge is the "judge of the law" and the jury is the "judge of the facts." In other words, it's up to the jury to determine "what happened" in a case, including which witnesses are telling the truth. It's up to the judge to determine the proper law to instruct the jury on after all the evidence has been heard.

You may hear the term "fact-finder" tossed around by your law student. The fact-finder is the person or persons who determine the facts of the case (i.e., what happened). If the testimony of witnesses is in conflict, as it usually is, the fact-finder decides which witnesses are credible. In a jury trial, the jury is the fact-finder. In a bench (judge-only) trial, the judge is the fact-finder.

* * *

Obviously, the above summary of the U.S. legal system is truncated and oversimplified to the extreme. A thorough review could, and does, fill hundreds of volumes. But I'm betting you are totally down with my approach. I may already have told you more than you want to know. So let's move on to some specifics about what your law student's new life will be like.

CHAPTER 4
THE FIRST-YEAR CURRICULUM

This chapter describes the first-year courses your law student will be taking, which will help you keep track of their daily lives and conversation. To say that legal education does not change radically would be a sweeping understatement. As the authors of the 2007 *Best Practices in Legal Education* report stated, "[t]ypical classroom instruction at most law schools today would be familiar to any lawyer who attended law school during the past hundred thirty years."[39] Nowhere is this truer than in the first-year curriculum. Your first-year student is likely to take the same courses I took as a 1L more than thirty years ago. While some variations exist among schools, it's a safe bet your student will be enrolled in the following courses during his or her first year:

Civil Procedure

Contracts

Criminal Law

Legal Research and Writing

Property

Torts

All of these except Legal Research and Writing are "doctrinal courses." The focus of each course will be on teaching students the body of basic legal principles that make up the particular subject area, while at the same time training students to understand and engage in legal analysis. Legal

---

39. *See* ROY STUCKEY ET AL., BEST PRACTICES FOR LEGAL EDUCATION: A VISION AND A ROADMAP 98 (2007).

Research and Writing is a "skills course" and a completely different animal—a big, scary beast of an animal. Here are brief descriptions of each first-year course:

Civil Procedure

In the previous chapter, I mentioned the distinction between public and private law. An even simpler division for our purposes is between two basic types of legal cases: civil and criminal. Civil cases encompass every type of legal controversy outside of the criminal courts. Examples are endless, but a sampling includes divorce cases, probate cases, landlord-tenant disputes, breach of contract claims, personal injury claims, and discrimination or other civil rights suits.

All civil lawsuits are controlled by a book of procedural rules cleverly titled "The Rules of Civil Procedure." The Rules of Civil Procedure tell the lawyers and the parties what they must do and may do in the pretrial and trial stages of a lawsuit, as well as how and when to do it. Criminal cases are controlled by a different set of rules, the Rules of Criminal Procedure, but courses in criminal procedure usually are upper-level electives.

Students spend much of their time in Civil Procedure studying this book of rules and cases interpreting them. Although states have their own civil procedure rules for lawsuits in state courts, Civil Procedure courses usually focus on the Federal Rules of Civil Procedure, which apply to actions in federal court. Most states' rules are similar to the federal rules.

A substantial portion of "Civ Pro," as students call it, is devoted to the topic of "personal jurisdiction." A court has the power to hear a lawsuit only if it has jurisdiction over all the parties—i.e., the authority to make binding decisions on them. The basic concept is that each party to a lawsuit must have some connection to the court's geographic jurisdiction for the court to have personal jurisdiction over them. For example, if I take a vacation to China and a Chinese citizen negligently knocks me down in a train station causing a broken arm, I can't come back home and sue him in the United States because the court would not have personal jurisdiction over the Chinese citizen. Similarly, if I take a vacation to Colorado (I'm a citizen of Tennessee) and someone negligently knocks me down at a bus stop causing a broken arm, I can't come home to Tennessee and sue the person, for the same reason. A Tennessee court would not have personal jurisdiction over a Colorado citizen absent additional facts. I'd have to file the suit in Colorado.

It doesn't sound like it from the simple examples I gave, but personal jurisdiction is one of the most complex topics of the first year, and is always heavily tested on the final exam. Your student will likely be fretting a great deal about it. (Tell your student you heard it from a good source: law professors usually test the more difficult material rather than the simpler material.)

In most first-year courses, law students study state court, rather than federal court, cases. Civil Procedure (and Constitutional Law, if it is offered in the first year) is an exception. Personal jurisdiction is studied through a series of famous U.S. Supreme Court cases. Each case modifies the one preceding it, leaving students wondering why they can't just study the most recent one, since it contains the most up-to-date treatment of the law. One answer is that a full understanding of complex legal doctrine sometimes can be achieved only by studying its historical evolution. Another answer is that Civil Procedure professors are in starry-eyed love with personal jurisdiction.

The grand-daddy of these cases is an 1877 artifact called *Pennoyer v. Neff*.[40] Every 1L course has at least one classic case that all law students remember studying and for Civ Pro that case is *Pennoyer*. Quoting Shakespeare's *Macbeth*, one law professor said about *Pennoyer*: "Confusion now hath made its masterpiece."[41] I won't try to explain *Pennoyer v. Neff*. I'm still not sure I understand it. But here are some fun historical facts to spring on your student if he ever starts talking or complaining about *Pennoyer*:

The original plaintiff was a colorful character named J.H. Mitchell. So already you can see how your law student will be confused. Shouldn't the plaintiff be named Pennoyer? These are the kinds of little things that drive law students crazy. Anyway, Mitchell started out as a schoolteacher in Pennsyl-

---

40. 95 U.S. 714 (1877).

41. Wendy Collins Perdue, *Sin, Scandal and Substantive Due Process: Personal Jurisdiction and* Pennoyer Re- *visited*, 62 WASH. L. REV. 479, 479 (1987). Repeating "479" is not a typo. It's a *Bluebook* rule of citation style. I'll spare you the explanation.

vania, where he seduced a fifteen-year-old girl, was forced to marry her, left teaching and took up law, headed west in 1860, established himself as a successful lawyer, got married again without ever bothering to divorce his first wife, sued Neff, got elected as a United States Senator in 1872, became scandalized when the trial judge in *Pennoyer v. Neff* came into possession of love letters Mitchell had sent to his second wife's younger sister with whom he was having a five-year affair, and got re-elected to the Senate four days after the letters were published in the newspaper![42]

None of these facts have anything to do with the case, but they should interest and impress your law student and his friends. Just casually bring them up at the first mention of *Pennoyer v. Neff*. "Oh, you're studying *Pennoyer*? What a coincidence. I was reading about it just the other day and learned some very interesting facts. Did you know that the plaintiff ..." Or you could just shock them during a get-together by suddenly exclaiming *"Pennoyer v. Neff!"* and watch their eyes widen in terror.

Other topics commonly covered in Civ Pro include rules regarding subject matter jurisdiction, pleadings, motions, pre-trial discovery, class actions, summary judgment (a mechanism for judges to dispose of cases without a trial), and the doctrines of res judicata and collateral estoppel (which determine whether a case or claim that has already been heard once can be re-litigated).

Many students would concur that Civil Procedure is the most difficult first-year course. This is attributable in part to the fact that the subject matter is unfamiliar ("Not even covered on TV!" wrote one student) and also because the rules are technical and not intuitive. Moreover, civil procedure rules usually have to be interpreted in the context of lawsuits involving other areas of law (e.g., contract, property, and tort disputes), areas that students are trying to learn at the same time they're trying to learn civil procedure.

Contracts

Contracts focuses on the formation, performance, and breach of oral and written agreements. Much of the course involves the three essential ingredients to the formation of a

---

42. *Id.* at 481–90.

binding contract: offer, acceptance, and consideration. To have a binding contract, one party must make an offer to form a contract, the other party must accept the offer, and each side much give consideration for the contract. "Consideration" is the requirement that each party give something of value to the other as part of the bargain. It's the inducement or reason why people enter into the contract. So, for example, if I hire someone to paint my house, the consideration is, for the house painter, the payment he will receive, and, for me, that I'll get my house painted. Of course, as with everything in law, infinite permutations exist regarding each of these requirements that make them much more complex than they sound.

In addition to offer, acceptance, and consideration, Contracts students learn about the scope of contractual obligations, remedies for breaches of contracts, excuses for performance such as impossibility, and something called the parol evidence rule, which relates to what, if any, extraneous evidence outside a contract can be considered in interpreting the contract. No point trying to explain it here. As a student who finished number one in her class wrote: "I still could not fully explain to you how the rule operates."

As is true of all law school courses, student enjoyment of Contracts varies, with descriptions ranging from "frustratingly boring" and "the driest first-year subject" to "one of my favorite courses."

I mentioned that every law school course, no matter how dry, has its own classic, often amusing, cases or doctrines. In Contracts, one of those gems is the "hairy hand" case, *Hawkins v. McGee*,[43] in which the defendant doctor guaranteed plaintiff, a young man with a burned hand, "a hundred per cent perfect hand" if he would let the doctor perform surgery on him. Instead of a perfect hand, plaintiff ended up with one that grew thick hair on it because of a skin graft from his chest. *Hawkins* never fails to entertain law students. I conducted a scientific poll to determine exactly why. After months of investigation, the only statistically valid answer turned out to be: "There's just something funny about a hairy hand."

43.   146 A. 641 (N.H. 1929).

Criminal Law

Criminal Law is the study of criminal offenses and defenses. Because criminal cases are intensely covered by the media and are a favorite subject of television and cinema, law school outsiders, as well as new students, reasonably assume criminal law will receive a lot of attention in law school. That's not the case. Most students will take only a couple of courses related to criminal law in their three years of law school: the basic required first-year Criminal Law course and an upper-level course called Criminal Procedure that covers the constitutional rights of persons suspected or accused of crime.

In first-year Criminal Law, students spend most of their time studying the "elements" of various crimes. All criminal offenses are composed of elements; that is, the individual parts of a crime that the prosecution must prove beyond a reasonable doubt. If any element is missing, a completed crime has not occurred. A great deal of class time is devoted to understanding the two most fundamental elements of a crime: *actus reus* (the criminal act itself, such as pulling the trigger on a gun) and *mens rea* (the mental state required to be convicted of a particular crime). Regarding the latter, there's a big legal difference between: "I pulled the trigger because I wanted to kill that S.O.B." and "I pulled the trigger because I thought the gun wasn't loaded."

Crimes commonly covered include homicide, theft, and burglary, and what are called "inchoate crimes," such as attempts, conspiracies, or solicitations to complete a crime. If Suzy attempts or conspires to murder Henry, or solicits someone else to do it, that's a crime even if the murder is never carried out. Defenses to crimes also have elements that must be proved. In addition to the elements of crimes and defenses, students study and discuss the societal policies behind criminal punishment and sentencing.

In most first-year doctrinal courses, students study the common law. The common law, remember, is the body of judicial precedent which judges and juries are required to follow when making decisions. But today, most criminal law is written into statutes passed by legislatures, so depending on the professor, your student may be spending most of her time in Criminal Law studying and dissecting statutes, rather than just reading cases. This can be confusing to law students who have been studying judicial opinions until this point. Reading and interpreting statutes is a very different skill from reading and understanding judicial opinions. A whole separate body of rules exists called "rules of statutory construction" that students now have to master.

As you might imagine, Criminal Law cases can be interesting in a "juicy" way. Take *Regina v. Dudley*,[44] a classic case from England. This is the tale of some castaways who, after being stranded on a lifeboat for twenty days with nothing to eat but two cans of turnips and a turtle, cannibalized a seventeen-year-old cabin boy. Four days later they were rescued by a passing ship. Oops! Back in England, the three survivors faced a variety of criminal charges, including "assault with a deadly molar" and "abdominal possession of a fibula." Also, murder. The crewmen defended on the ground of "justification." The defense of justification says you can commit a crime without penalty so long as it is committed in the interest of avoiding a greater harm.

The defendants argued it was better that one cabin boy die than all four of them starving to death, which isn't a bad argument. But oops again. The defendants never consulted the cabin boy for his thoughts on the matter before slitting his throat and feasting on him. The jurors rejected the justification defense and sentenced the defendants to death. However, the English Crown commuted the death sentence to just six months imprisonment, thereby implicitly accepting the justification defense.

Students coming out of Criminal Law often experience polar-opposite reactions to the subject. Some students go into the course thinking they won't like it and come out wanting to practice criminal law. Others complete the course swearing they will never have anything to do with a criminal case.

Legal Research and Writing

While first-year doctrinal courses differ in content, most of them are extremely similar in format. They each will involve similar daily reading assignments of judicial opinions from a casebook, some mix of Socratic Q and A and lecture about those cases in class, and the same single-exam evalua-

44. 14 Q.B.D. 273 (Queen's Bench 1884).

tion method at the end of the semester. But Legal Research and Writing is completely different. You will hear an exaggerated amount of complaining and angst-letting from your 1L about this course, perhaps more than for all of their other courses combined. One of the main reasons is that the workload for Legal Research and Writing strikes students as disproportionately large, yet the credit hours awarded for the course usually are fewer than for other first-year courses.

Legal Research and Writing[45] courses are part of the mandatory first-year curriculum at virtually every law school. They almost always extend through both semesters (as in Legal Research and Writing I and Legal Research and Writing II). Roughly a quarter of law schools require a third legal writing course in the fall semester of the second year. The fundamental goal of the courses is to teach students how to research and analyze legal issues in writing and, in the second semester, orally.

If the purpose of the other first-year courses is, as it is so often said, to teach students to "think like a lawyer," the primary goal of legal writing could be described as teaching students to "write like a lawyer thinks." Legal writing isn't about how to construct sentences. It's about how to clearly and accurately conduct and convey legal analysis in a written form. Because Legal Research and Writing is so different from other first-year courses and consumes so much student energy and attention, we'll delve into it a bit more deeply than the other first-year courses.

Legal Research. Typically, legal writing begins with a research component, which usually includes exercises designed to train students to find and use different types of legal resources in the law library (e.g., case reporters, statute books, legal encyclopedias). Every 1L remembers traipsing around the library on treasure hunts for particular sources. As one student described it:

> I remember thinking to myself how stupid all us little 1Ls must have looked trekking through the library looking for all the old books while doing our physical

---

45. This course travels under a variety of names at different law schools, including Legal Research and Writing, Lawyering, Legal Methods, Legal Skills and Values, and Legal Writing and Analysis.

research assignments and finding our way around. All the 2Ls and 3Ls were in there trying to study while we bumbled about muttering to each other or asking for their assistance. I remember looking forward to the day when I could watch all the neophytes do that as well.

Another student described legal research exercises more bluntly as "scavenger hunts straight from hell."

Most schools still require students to learn how to do book research, even though most modern legal research is done on computers, using subscription-based databases such as Westlaw and LexisNexis. You'll become well aware of these services as both companies inundate students with logo-laden merchandise (pens, coffee mugs, T-shirts, lanyards for ID badges, sticky notes, etc.) as part of their on-campus marketing efforts.

The Law Office Memorandum. Get ready for the term "the memo" to become part of your student's daily lexicon. "The memo" is short for the law office memorandum requirement that forms the foundation of most Legal Research and Writing courses in the first semester. Within a few weeks of starting law school, students begin working on an internal law office memorandum from an associate (the student) to a fictitious partner analyzing the law as applied to a given set of facts. These memos, common in real-life law practice, basically ask the student to explain and analyze particular legal issues in a client's case so the partner can make informed decisions about how to proceed.

It's common to assign two such memoranda in the first semester, often denoted as the "minor memo" and the "major memo." Often, the minor memo will be a "closed universe memo," meaning the professor will provide students with all the necessary research needed to complete the memo (e.g., cases and statutes), while the major memo will be an "open universe memo," meaning the students have to conduct their own research.

Feedback: Be Careful What You Wish For. As discussed in future chapters, a major aspect of law school distress is the lack of feedback during the semester. In most courses, students receive no reports on their progress or lack thereof until their single make-it-or-break-it exam at the end of the semester. Legal Research and Writing is the exception. Students get feedback, often including grades, on their memos and drafts of their memos as they progress through the semester.

You might think this would be a good thing, and it would be except that law school grading is not like undergraduate or other grad school grading. A law professor would describe it as "much more rigorous." A student would say "it's impossible to get an *A*!" Both groups would agree law school grades are much lower than grades in other educational programs. In many graduate programs, *A* averages are the norm. Law students can only dream of such a world.

One can almost hear the self-esteem bubbles bursting when the first wave of legal writing feedback is distributed. As one student put it: "As law students, the majority of us are used to receiving *A*s and when you get that first draft of your first memorandum back with a *C-* on it (and believe me, this happens even to the students who finish at the top of the class), it can be discouraging." She should know. She ranked second in her class.

Negative feedback in legal writing courses can be particularly disheartening because most law students arrive in law school thinking they are good writers. Many of them are, but legal writing is different from the type of prose that, for example, English majors are used to. One top student explained:

> Most of us come into law school feeling confident about
> our writing skills if nothing else, so this course really
> crushes our self-worth where it matters. Legal writing
> is so extremely formulaic. A law student could have
> won a Pulitzer in literature, but that does not matter
> if they cannot master IRAC or CREAC.[46] The writing is
> almost algebraic, which is why I think students really

---

46. IRAC and CREAC are mnemonic devices that serve as frameworks for legal analysis in written documents such as memoranda, briefs, and, for IRAC, law school exams. IRAC stands for Issue, Rule, Analysis, Conclusion. CREAC stands for Conclusion, Rule, Explanation, Analysis, Conclusion.

struggle. Spontaneity and creativity are sacrificed for consistency. We are forced to use the same verbs and phrases over and over. Things we have previously learned to be mortal sins of writing seem to be embraced, and it is hard to just "give in." You basically have to unlearn almost as much as you have to learn to be successful in a legal writing class.

Citation Style. One maddening component of Legal Research and Writing is learning legal citation style. "Citation style" refers to the form and format in which legal authorities (such as cases, law review articles, and books) are referenced or documented. You've seen legal citation style in the footnotes in this book.

The standard legal citation manual is *The Bluebook: A Uniform System of Citation* (19th ed. 2010). The *Bluebook*, weighing in at a hefty 511 pages, tells legal writers what citation information to include (e.g., volume, page number, date), what font to put it in (e.g., big and small caps, italics), when to use abbreviations and what they should look like, where to insert commas and periods, and many other details. It's somewhat similar to the MLA (Modern Language Association) style book you might have used in undergraduate school, except about twenty billion times more detailed and complex.

The *Bluebook* is famously hyper-technical and obsessed with minutia. I laughed when I read a comment from a student advising new students to pay attention to the *Bluebook* because an entire letter grade can be lost on a writing assignment "if you leave off just one comma!" That's right. One comma. The comment brought back memories of a humor column I published in the *American Bar Association Journal* satirizing a *Bluebook* rule that required a comma in a particular place under particular circumstances. An excerpt will give you a taste of what your student will be up against when dealing with the *Bluebook*. The setting for the column was a fictitious meeting of the board of *Bluebook* editors:

Irving: We need that # * % # # & * comma! Rule 15.2 means nothing without The Comma. I'll gladly die for it.

Frieda: *Accord.* [A *Bluebook* reference.]

Dan: *Accord.*

Wendy: Put down the gun, Irving. The *Bluebook* was meant to bring peace.

Irving: Not until I have proof of everyone's commitment to The Comma. I've decided to quit law school and become addicted to amphetamines so I can contemplate The Comma twenty-four hours a day.

Dan: I'm going to have Rule 15.2 tattooed on my thigh, right below the rules for Separately Bound Legislative Histories.

Frieda: I'll cut out my husband's entrails and form them into the shape of one huge comma.

Irving: What about you Wendy?

Wendy: My parents died in a plane crash yesterday. I have to go to the funeral.

Irving: Doesn't The Comma mean anything to you?

Wendy: Alright, I'll send flowers.

Exaggerating obviously, but here's a funny comment showing how the *Bluebook* infiltrates the lives of real law students:

> I was up late putting the finishing touches on my office memo. This primarily consisted of my checking my memo against all the relevant *Bluebook* rules. I started to get really sleepy so I went to bed. I woke up in the middle of the night and looked drowsily at my nightstand to check the time. When I did, I noticed that my *Bluebook* was sitting on top of my Bible on the nightstand. I knew right then that my religion had changed.

It's fun to make fun of the *Bluebook*. Heck, I started my legal humor career doing it. One afternoon in the summer of 1995, frustrated by the strictures of academic writing, I exited a footnote and dashed off *The World's Greatest Law Review Article*, a heavily-footnoted, over-the-top parody of law review footnoting and the *Bluebook*.[47] But all joking aside, as I said back in the Preface, the precision demanded by the *Bluebook* is a tangible and telling symbol of the high bar of perfection that the law and law school set for students.

47. Andrew J. McClurg, *The World's Greatest Law Review Article*, A.B.A. J., Oct. 1995, at 84.

Depending on which school your student attends you might be hearing about a different citation style manual called the *ALWD Manual*, published by the Association of Legal Writing Directors.[48] The *ALWD Manual* has fans who like its simplified approach to legal citation style, but most law schools use the *Bluebook*.[49]

The Second–Semester Appellate Brief and Oral Argument. The second semester of Legal Research and Writing usually focuses on written and oral advocacy. Advocacy is very different from the neutral and objective analysis called for in the first-semester law office memoranda. Advocacy is basically "arguing." Typically, students research and write an appellate brief and make an oral argument to a three-member panel of mock appellate judges. Page limits vary, but briefs usually run thirty or more pages. Composing the appellate brief is excruciatingly time consuming and the subject of much complaining by second-semester students.

As for the oral argument, it's probably both the most exciting but also most frightening event of the first year. It's exciting because the oral argument is often the first law school exercise in which students get to act and feel like "real lawyers." The fright aspect comes from a generalized fear of public speaking accentuated by the fact that appellate oral arguments are public interrogations. They're not monologues. The judges drill students with lots of questions during the argument, sometimes beginning before the student finishes her first sentence. The skills your student develops in oral advocacy may come back to haunt you in your relationship (see Chapter 12).

Property

In Property, students study the principles of law governing the ownership and transfer of personal property (stuff not attached to land) and real property (land or structures attached to land). Your law student's casebooks, for example, are items of personal property. The floor they slam them

---

48. DARBY DICKERSON, ALWD CITATION MANUAL: A PROFESSIONAL SYSTEM OF CITATION (4th ed. 2010).

49. The Association of Legal Writing Directors 2010 survey showed that, of 187 responding schools, 124 use the *Bluebook*, 29 use the *ALWD Citation Manual*, 13 use both, and 12 leave it to the individual professor. 2010 ALWD SURVEY RESULTS, *supra*, at 19.

down on in frustration is part of real property. Most of Property—and most of what students are tested on—focuses on the law of real property.

Unlike the law of most other subjects, which has evolved over time, many of the rules governing property rights were frozen in place centuries ago. Thus, historical context can be more important to understanding Property than in other 1L courses. Your student will likely find herself studying ancient cases from the 1800s, at least early on. As a good rule of thumb, the older the case, the more incomprehensible it will be. Modern judges, and their law clerks, usually are good, clear writers, but judges from back in the day wrote in an archaic, unwieldy style, using a lot of terminology that has long since been abandoned.

In trying to understand conversations about Property with your student, keep in mind this big picture point: a person does not "have" property, but rather has an "interest" in property. That interest can be acquired, lost, given away, or conveyed. The interest can be absolute or conditional. The interest can be partial or whole. Much of the study of property is simply how the law treats various interests in real property.

Well, "simply" is a bad word choice. Property is filled with alien concepts such as adverse possession, easements, restrictive covenants, the fee system, and what are known as future interests. Tackling the latter can be a particularly mind-numbing experience. The law of future interests is a maze-like set of rules regulating the ability of one to convey interests in land to someone in the future, such as by way of a will or trust. Future interests are the ultimate legal rules for control freaks. Essentially, they allow people to say: "Here's what you can and can't do with my property even though I'm long since dead and gone. Ha, ha."

One notorious future interests rule—the Rule Against Perpetuities—is so ridiculously complex that the California Supreme Court once suggested that it's impossible for a lawyer to commit malpractice for misunderstanding and misapplying the rule. In *Lucas v. Hamm*,[50] the attorney made a mistake in interpreting the Rule Against Perpetuities with the result that an intended inheritance in a will was invali-

---

50. 15 Cal.Rptr. 821, 364 P.2d 685 (Cal. 1961).

dated. But the court let the attorney off the hook based on its view that the Rule Against Perpetuities is so confusing that it isn't negligent for attorneys to screw it up.[51] You gotta love that, along with the fact that some of the doctrine's satellite rules—such as the "Bad as to One, Bad as to All" and "Unborn Widow" rules—sound like they could have been classic blues tunes by Muddy Waters or Howlin' Wolf.

For an amusing highlight from Property, I offer the "fertile octogenarian rule." The fertile octogenarian rule is a binding legal presumption that any person—no matter how old—can bear a child. Eighty years old? No problem. Might as well start stocking up on disposable diapers, or just let the baby use some of yours. Ninety? Invite any living friends to a baby shower. One hundred years old and live in a padlocked iron lung? Doesn't matter. The law says it's possible for the person to have children. Strange, but true.

Torts

You might think you have no idea what a "tort" is. Maybe you think it's a dessert, but that's a "torte." In fact, Torts is actually a legal subject that non-lawyers are more familiar with than they realize. Have you ever heard about the McDonald's coffee spill lawsuit?[52] That was a tort case. So are all the lawsuits covered in the media involving prescription drugs, asbestos, tobacco, and other harmful products. Medical malpractice suits are tort cases. So are automobile accident suits. Basically, any time a person or his property is injured through the conduct of another, whether in a train derailment or through cyberspace bullying, the potential for a tort suit arises. Tort law is also part of a controversial national political agenda known as the "tort reform movement" that receives a substantial amount of media play.

A tort is a civil wrong other than a breach of contract (which is also a civil wrong) for which the law allows a plaintiff to seek money damages as compensation for his

51. *Id.* at 690 ("[F]ew, if any, areas of the law have been fraught with more confusion or concealed more traps for the unwary draftsman.... [A]n error of the type relied on by plaintiffs does not show negligence or breach of contract on the part of the defendant.").

52. For an early "date night" with your student, consider renting "Hot Coffee," HBO's 2011 pro-plaintiff documentary version of this case that has been portrayed by many as the poster child for what is wrong with the American tort system.

injuries. Most torts involve physical injuries, but not all. For example, defamation, interferences with business relationships, and the infliction of emotional distress are torts.

Most tort courses begin with a study of the seven basic intentional torts; i.e., claims arising from intentionally, rather than negligently, inflicted injuries. The seven intentional torts are: battery, assault, false imprisonment, intentional infliction of emotional distress, trespass to land, trespass to chattels, and conversion. The latter two involve situations where someone has intentionally taken or damaged another's personal property. Since intentional tort cases involve interesting, accessible fact patterns and are covered early on when students are uncontrollably excited about discussing law school, you are likely to hear about some of these cases. If a five-year-old boy pulls a chair out from under an elderly woman trying to seat herself, can he be successfully sued for committing a battery? These are facts from *Garratt v. Dailey*,[53] a case your student will probably read in the first week of law school and tell you about. The answer is "yes." The boy lost.

Next come the defenses to intentional tort claims, such as consent, self-defense, and necessity. Did you know that you can legally blow up your neighbor's house with dynamite if circumstances of public necessity justify it?[54] Your student will enjoy studying intentional torts because, as mentioned, they are interesting, and also fairly intuitive and comparatively easy to understand.

The bulk of every Torts course is the topic of negligence. Negligence law is essentially the study of legal responsibility for "accidents." People are liable for damages under negligence law when they fail to exercise reasonable care and that failure causes injury. When the words "reasonable" and "unreasonable" start infiltrating your student's daily vocabulary—which they will—blame Torts.

Negligence principles are mostly intuitive but can be difficult to get a grasp on because they are so amorphous. What exactly, for example, constitutes "reasonable care"? And when can we say that a defendant's act is the responsi-

---

53. 279 P.2d 1091 (Wash. 1955).

54. *See* Surocco v. Geary, 3 Cal. 69 (Cal. 1853) (holding that the defendant was legally permitted to blow up the plaintiff's house with dynamite during the great San Francisco fire of 1849 in an attempt to stop the fire from spreading to adjoining property).

ble cause of an injury? If Bloodymess Productions makes and sells a violent video game to Alex, a minor, and Alex subsequently engages in violence against others after playing the game, did Bloodymess fail to act reasonably? Was Bloodymess a cause of the ensuing violence? These are the types of issues students grapple with in trying to solve the puzzles of negligence law.

Torts is where students study one of the most famous and memorable cases in American jurisprudential history: *Palsgraf v. Long Island Railroad Co.*,[55] a wacky, confusing case with opinions from two heavyweight judges, including the great Benjamin Cardozo, about an exploding package of fireworks that supposedly knocked a heavy scale on top of Helen Palsgraf at the Long Island train station in 1924. *Palsgraf* may be the only law school case that every lawyer remembers. If you know a lawyer, test my assertion. Ask if he remembers studying *Palsgraf*. If the lawyer says no, call the state bar to make sure he's not an imposter.

Tort cases, like those in Criminal Law, can make for fascinating reading because of the real-life drama involved when people injure each other, either intentionally or negligently. Sex,[56] drugs,[57] and rock and roll[58]—Torts offers a little bit of everything. *Katko v. Briney*, the sample case included as an appendix, is a tort case.

* * *

So there you have them: six first-year law school courses, sixty bottles of ibuprofen, six hundred panic attacks, and six million conversations (conservatively estimated) about them with your student. Enjoy!

55. 162 N.E. 99 (N.Y. 1928).

56. *See, e.g.*, Doe v. Moe, 827 N.E.2d 240 (Mass. App. Ct. 2005) (suit against ex-girlfriend alleging that negligence during intercourse caused plaintiff to suffer a fractured penis).

57. *See, e.g.*, Hegel v. Langsam, 273 N.E.2d 351 (Ohio Ct. Com. Pl. 1971) (suit by parents of college student against university alleging negligence in not protecting their seventeen-year-old daughter from using drugs).

58. *See, e.g.*, McCollum v. CBS, Inc., 249 Cal.Rptr. 187 (Cal. Ct. App. 1988) (suit against rock singer Ozzy Osbourne on behalf of teenager who committed suicide after listening to Ozzy's song, *Suicide Solution*).

CHAPTER 5
THE LAW STUDENT'S PLIGHT: FEW RIGHT ANSWERS

When I asked a group of law professors to name the single most important piece of advice to give new law students, one spoke up quickly and emphatically: "To embrace and accept uncertainty!" One lesson of the law that new students struggle to come to terms with is that many legal questions simply do not have clear right or wrong answers. Law epitomizes the truism that there are two sides to every story. Many of the cases law students are required to read are purposely chosen by the casebook authors because they raise issues that can be persuasively argued both ways.

The lack of certainty in the law can be disorienting, not to mention frustrating, to new students, most of whom arrive at law school believing that legal principles are black and white only to find themselves stumbling blindly through clouds of gray. Seems like every time a student is convinced he's nailed the "right" answer in a class discussion, the professor will take the wind out of his sails by pointing out flaws in it.

Clarity and certainty simply do not exist in much of law. As discussed in Chapter 12, being immersed in such an ambiguous, multi-angled world can cause law students to change the way they approach not only the law, but life itself, including relationships. In the meantime, your student's inability to pin down the law may cause anxiety or frustration that also can spill over into outside relationships.

Let's look at a few examples to illustrate what I'm talking about. *Lucy v. Zehmer*,[59] a Contracts case, is a good candidate to start things off. You may even hear about *Lucy* from your student, since students are fond of bringing home fact patterns they learn from interesting cases and posing them to their loved ones to get their opinions or just to show off how much they know.

On a Saturday in 1952, Zehmer and his wife were hanging out and drinking alcohol with W.O. Lucy at Ye Olde Virginnie Restaurant in McKenney, Virginia. They got to talking about a farm owned by Zehmer. This led to Zehmer scribbling on the back of a restaurant receipt: "We hereby agree to sell to W.O. Lucy the Ferguson Farm complete for $50,000, title satisfactory to the buyer." Zehmer and his wife both signed it.

Lucy sought to enforce this as a binding contract to sell the farm. Zehmer testified it was a joke, that he "was high as a Georgia pine" when he signed it, and that the whole transaction "was just a bunch of two doggoned drunks bluffing to see who could talk the biggest and say the most." He also claimed he never delivered this "contract" to Lucy, but that Lucy simply picked it up, stashed it in his pocket, and offered him $5 on the spot to "bind the bargain," which Zehmer refused to accept.

What do you think the result should be? Binding contract or simply a non-binding joke? On the one hand, it seems unfair to Zehmer that he should have to sell his farm if we was simply playing a joke while drunk. But what about Lucy? Zehmer wrote out a contract with reasonably certain, if simple, terms. Shouldn't Lucy be able to rely on that? Consider the consequences of ruling for Zehmer: Every time a person entered into a contract they'd have to guess what the other person was secretly thinking or intending, regardless of what the contract said.

The court ruled it was a binding contract and that Lucy was entitled to the farm under the terms written on the restaurant receipt. The court reasoned that the internal mental assent of the parties is not necessary for the formation of a contract. What they say and do outwardly is what counts. If Lucy reasonably believed the agreement was valid,

59. 84 S.E.2d 516 (Va. 1954).

it was enforceable even if Zehmer never intended it to be a binding contract.

We learn two important things from this example. First, that drinking and talking often are a bad mix. Second, that even cases that seem easy on their face can turn out to be anything but easy. Admit it. Your first instinct probably was that Zehmer should have won because he meant it as a joke. Or maybe not, in which case *you* might be the one who belongs in law school.

Here's another example: a criminal law issue from a drug-trafficking case. A federal statute, 18 U.S.C. § 924(c)(1),[60] imposes a mandatory minimum enhanced sentence of five years for one who uses or "carries" a firearm during and in relation to the commission of a drug-trafficking crime. Sounds clear enough. Everyone understands what "carries" means, right? If you have your iPhone in your pocket, purse, or backpack, you're carrying it. If you forget it and leave it at home, you're not. Surely such a simple word and concept could never create a big legal dispute. Guess again.

In *United States v. Foster*[61] the police pulled over the defendant and arrested him for drug-trafficking when they found methamphetamine in his pickup truck. They also arrested him for "carrying" a firearm during the commission of a drug-trafficking crime. But the gun wasn't found on the defendant's person. It was discovered in the bed of his truck under a buttoned-down tarp. Was he "carrying" the gun within the meaning of the statute? It took years to find out the answer.

The trial court ruled he was carrying it. But nine years of appeals and many pages of judicial opinions later, a U.S. Court of Appeals finally held that the defendant was not carrying the gun within the meaning of the statute. His conviction on the firearm charge was reversed. Nine years of appeals over the meaning of *a single word*. If highly esteemed

---

60. Citations to statutes work somewhat similarly to citations to cases, previously explained in another footnote. The first number (18) refers to the volume of the set of particular statute books, the middle part identifies that set of books (in this case, the United States Code), and the last number tells us the particular section of the statute in which the cited provision appears (section 924(c)(1)). Mess with your student's head by memorizing this footnote and explaining statutory citation style to him while he's floundering with his first encounter with it. Talk about fun! He's likely to fall to his knees and worship you in awe.

61. 133 F.3d 704 (9th Cir. 1998).

and credentialed judges can't agree on what the law means, how could one expect a mere law student to figure out the answers?

Even U.S. Supreme Court justices rarely agree on the law with unanimity. Here's a real example. *McConnell v. Federal Election Commission*[62] was a campaign financing law case that made it to the Supreme Court. The basic question was whether the McCain–Feingold Act, a federal statute that imposed restrictions on political contributions, violated the First Amendment free speech rights of potential contributors. A challenging issue no doubt, but certainly not too tough for the mighty U.S. Supreme Court to clear up, right? *Wellll*.

With nine justices voting, the result could have been as simple as 8–1, 7–2, 6–3, or 5–4 in favor of one side or the other. The nine wise ones chose a slightly more complicated path. Here is the Court's actual voting lineup straight out of the case:

STEVENS and O'CONNOR, JJ., delivered the opinion of the Court with respect to BCRA Titles I and II, in which SOUTER, GINSBURG, and BREYER, JJ., joined. REHNQUIST, C. J., delivered the opinion of the Court with respect to BCRA Titles III and IV, in which O'CONNOR, SCALIA, KENNEDY, and SOUTER, JJ., joined, in which STEVENS, GINSBURG, and BREYER, JJ., joined except with respect to BCRA § 305, and in which THOMAS, J., joined with respect to BCRA §§ 304, 305, 307, 316, 319, and 403(b). BREYER, J., delivered the opinion of the Court with respect to BCRA Title V, in which STEVENS, O'CONNOR, SOUTER, and GINSBURG, JJ., joined. SCALIA, J., filed an opinion concurring with respect to BCRA Titles III and IV, dissenting with respect to BCRA Titles I and V, and concurring in the judgment in part and dissenting in part with respect to BCRA Title II. THOMAS, J., filed an opinion concurring with respect to BCRA Titles III and IV, except for BCRA §§ 311 and 318, concurring in the result with respect to BCRA § 318, concurring in the judgment in part and dissenting in part with respect to BCRA Title II, and dissenting with respect to BCRA Titles I, V, and § 311, in which opinion SCALIA, J., joined as to Parts I, II.A,

62. 540 U.S. 93 (2003).

and II.B. KENNEDY, J., filed an opinion concurring in the judgment in part and dissenting in part with respect to BCRA Titles I and II, in which REHNQUIST, C. J., joined, in which SCALIA, J., joined except to the extent the opinion upholds new FECA § 323(e) and BCRA § 202, and in which THOMAS, J., joined with respect to BCRA § 213. REHNQUIST, C. J., filed an opinion dissenting with respect to BCRA Titles I and V, in which SCALIA and KENNEDY, JJ., joined. STEVENS, J., filed an opinion dissenting with respect to BCRA § 305, in which GINSBURG and BREYER, JJ., joined.

Who won? I have no idea. Pretty ugly, but believe it or not, things have gotten even worse. Look at the voting lineup in this recent case:

Kennedy, J., announced the judgment of the Court in which no one agreed except Mrs. Kennedy and even she wasn't too crazy about parts of it. Scalia, J., booed. Roberts, C.J., dissented vigorously from Part A, E, I, O, U and sometimes Y until told there was no such part, so he wrote his own, then unleashed a vitriolic assault against it. Breyer, J., concurred in Part II–A, dissented from Part II–B, was mildly amused by Part II–C, wadded up Part II–D and stuck it under his desk to keep it from rocking, and used Part II–E to make paper airplanes that he and Thomas, J., shot down with rubber bands. Kagan, J., joined in the dissent from Part II–E so she'd have paper for her own planes. Alito, J., dissented, changed his mind and dissented from his dissent. On petition for reconsideration, he dissented from the dissent to his dissent, at which point he lost track of which side he wanted to win and abstained. Sotomayor, J., concurred in part in footnote 6, dissenting from it not being numbered 7. Ginsburg, J., dissented from Sotomayor's partial concurrence on the ground that the issue whether footnote 6 should be renumbered as footnote 7 was not preserved for appeal and was not properly before the Court. Sotomayor then filed a Supplemental Dissent canceling her RSVP to Ginsburg's dinner party on Saturday.

The second one is not real, of course, but the real one is almost as wild and crazy as the parody. Not all cases are as fractured as *McConnell,* but the fact that the highest jurists in the land can disagree so extensively about a point of law is emblematic of the unpredictable world that your student will be living in.

If you ever find your law student pounding his head against the wall moaning, "No, no, no! It's not possible! The law can't be this confusing!," simply pat the part of his head that's not swollen or bleeding and assure him that, "Yes, dear, I'm afraid it can be." Seriously, your student will be working *so* hard to try to understand the law and it really *is* frustrating when the answer to most questions is "It depends." If your student is struggling with Not Enough Right Answers Syndrome, tell them about the examples in this chapter. Say: "It's not you. And, *no-oo,* it's not me. It's the law."

CHAPTER 6
LEARNING TO "THINK LIKE A LAWYER": THE SOCRATIC AND CASE METHODS

Perhaps the most uttered cliché about law school is that the purpose of legal education is to teach students to "think like a lawyer." What does that mean? Do lawyers really think differently from other people? Well, yes. Asking a group of incoming students "What made you decide to come to law school?," one student replied:

> I worked for a public affairs/political consulting firm in Washington, D.C. alongside several non-practicing lawyers. I found that whatever the issue or problem a client was faced with, the people I turned to who were consistently able to develop successful strategies were the lawyers. As they told me, they credit their level of thinking and analysis to their legal education.

Lawyers possess more highly developed critical-thinking skills than other people. This is one of the highlights of law school. Your student will emerge from law school much smarter, or at least sounding and acting much smarter, than when they went in.[63] After a year, their brains will be functioning like a 40G data network compared to the dial-up

---

63. Even doctors, who can't find much they like about lawyers, respect their intelligence. In a survey of physician attitudes toward lawyers, doctors identified "intelligence" as the most positive aspect of working with lawyers. *See* Paul E. Fitzgerald, Jr., *Doctors, Lawyers Evaluate Each Other in New Study: Building Trust, Opening Communication Lines Could Improve Doctor/Lawyer Relationships*, PHYSICIAN EXECUTIVE, Mar.–Apr. 2002, at 20, 21–22.

speed they entered with. How lawyers acquire this mental astuteness is the subject of this chapter.

The process starts on day one. If you attended college, think back to those first days of a new semester. If they were anything like my undergraduate days, the professor would mosey in, sometimes late, introduce himself, chit-chat a bit about the course, maybe hand out a syllabus, then let the class go.

Now let's look at how a first-year law school course might begin. The professor struts in,[64] opens her casebook and notes, picks a student's name randomly from the class roster and BAM:

> *Mr. Smith!* A shoots at B, but misses and hits C, who loses control of her car and crashes into D, driving a school bus full of children—H, I, J, K, L, M, N, O and P—down a winding mountain road. The school bus careens into a gas pump at the exact second lightning hits the pump. In the explosion, a piece of glass, E, hits F, walking his dog, G, nearby. G gets loose and attacks Q, a law student, carrying an armload of casebooks up a staircase. The books fall on R, causing head injuries. R is rushed to the ER by EMTs, gets CPR from an RN and an IV from an MD, but it's too late. He's DOA. Who wins? [Three second pause.] Quick, quick, Mr. Smith! We don't have all day.

Within minutes, perhaps even seconds, of beginning their first law school classes, students are introduced to the Socratic method, law school's "signature pedagogy."[65] Few things define and distinguish legal education as much as the Socratic method and its companion, the case method. The Socratic method involves professors calling on students, typically without prior notice, to recite and analyze appellate judicial opinions and the legal principles raised therein.

You will no doubt hear a lot about the Socratic method from your student, as it ranks high on the long list of law student stressors. Here's how the Socratic and its inseparable companion, the case method, came about.

---

64. Law professors are more likely to strut than mosey.

65. *See* WILLIAM M. SULLIVAN ET AL., EDUCATING LAWYERS: PREPARATION FOR THE PROFESSION OF LAW 23–24 (2007) [herein-after CARNEGIE FOUNDATION REPORT] (report by the Carnegie Foundation for the Advancement of Teaching characterizing the Socratic method in these terms).

Once Upon a Time There Was a Law School Dean Named Christopher Columbus Langdell

The Socratic method is credited to and named after Socrates (470–399 B.C.), a Greek philosopher who engaged in continuous questioning of his students in a quest to discover moral and ethical truths. Along the way, he exposed their fallacies in reasoning, first, by getting the answerer to commit to certain assumptions and then asking questions designed to expose the contradictions or other flaws in those assumptions. A hallmark of his method—one that continues to haunt law students more than two thousand years later— is that Socrates only asked questions. He rarely provided answers.

The origins of the Socratic method in law school teaching are traceable back to the 1870s and the inception of what is known as the "case method." To make any sense of the Socratic method, one must understand the case method. The two methods are inextricably intertwined.

In the old days, law was taught in U.S. law schools principally through a lecture method. Much like in modern undergraduate courses, students would read explanations of the law in textbooks, professors would expand on that law in lectures, and students would be tested principally on their ability for rote memorization. But in the 1870s along came Christopher Columbus Langdell, the man credited with, or blamed for, irrevocably changing the way U.S. law students learn.

Langdell, a professor and later dean at Harvard Law School, believed that true mastery of the law could not be achieved by simply memorizing it. Rather, students had to develop a facility for *applying* legal principles to the varied fact patterns that lead to legal disputes, or what he called "the ever-tangled skein of human affairs."[66] By understanding how law is applied, Langdell believed students would be able to transfer what they learned in one context and apply it to other contexts. To implement his vision, he came up with

---

66. Peggy Cooper Davis & Elizabeth Ehrenfest Steinglass, *A Dialogue About Socratic Teaching*, 23 N.Y.U. Rev. L. & Soc. Change 249, 263 (1997) (quoting Langdell).

the idea to replace explanatory textbooks with "casebooks" filled with appellate judicial opinions. Except for some notes following the cases, casebooks do not explain the law to students. The students have to forage for understanding within the cases themselves.

Under the case method, students do the heavy lifting. Instead of sitting passively listening to lectures, the case method requires students to think critically and discover the law on their own in response to questions posed by the professors. The Socratic dialogue method of teaching developed as an instrument for implementing the case method. Think of it as the steering mechanism that guides the case-method vehicle.

The case and Socratic methods are the major reason why your law student will insist on chaining herself to a desk or law school study carrel and can't spend any time with you. Don't take it personally. Studying for law school classes is very different from studying for classes in other disciplines for two principal reasons.

First, it simply takes a lot more time to read and dissect a judicial opinion than to read explanatory text of the type that appears in most textbooks. The opinions are complex and, especially at the beginning, students have to look up every other word in a legal dictionary. The student usually will have to read an opinion at least twice. Also, professors expect students, especially first-year students, to prepare a written "case brief" for each assigned opinion, which is extremely time-consuming. A case brief is a synopsis of the case that includes the facts, procedural history (i.e., how the case got to the appellate court), issue(s) raised on appeal, holding of the court (i.e., the resolution of the issue), and the reasoning. Law students generally are assigned to read and brief from twenty to thirty opinions each week.

Second, unlike students in other fields, law students are highly incentivized to actually do all this hard work both because they want to succeed and because they do not want to be exposed in front of their professors and peers as unprepared if called on in class to engage in a Socratic dialogue. When students get to class, they need to *know* the cases; simply having read them is not sufficient. If you attended undergraduate school, think back. What percentage of students in your classes would you estimate spent hours preparing for every single class? Fifty percent? Twenty percent? Ten percent? In law school, at least in the first year, that figure is close to 100 percent.

Asked what loved ones should know about law school compared to other higher education programs, a student commented:

> Just understanding the process of law student life is probably the most important thing. What I mean is being assigned cases (not text) to read every night, actually reading them (in undergrad people aren't accustomed to actually doing the reading, from my experience), briefing them for class, being prepared to be called on and discuss the law cogently, and later refining class notes/outlining. Some friends expressed surprise that I would bother to type pages of case briefs each night because the only grade is the final exam. This is because they think law school is like undergrad. The sheer time commitment was something I had trouble getting across.

One of my research assistants, an upper-level student, commented on reading the above:

> This is so true! My husband still teases me about my level of preparation for class. He thinks I am a huge nerd for reviewing my reading assignment before class after I have already read it once the night before. I try to explain to him that law students have to do this to ensure even *minimal* competence during the class discussion.

In Chapter 14, you'll find several additional comments about the sheer intensity of law school class preparation and classes, most of which is generated by the Socratic and case methods.

How It Works

The classic portrayal of the Socratic method in law school came from the 1973 movie, *The Paper Chase*, based on John Jay Osborn's book of the same name.[67] Actor John Housman won an Oscar for his portrayal of the curmudgeonly, imperi-

67. A more light-hearted depiction can be found in 2001's *Legally Blonde*, starring Reese Witherspoon as Harvard law student Elle Woods.

ous Professor Charles Kingsfield, a fictional Contracts professor at Harvard Law School, who torments first-year student James T. Hart, played by Timothy Bottoms. The movie is a classic. Watch it with your student. Although the movie is a bit over the top, it will give you a good idea of why the Socratic method strikes so much fear in the hearts and minds of law students.

In the movie, Kingsfield is a terror, famously instructing his Contracts students, in that great John Housman voice: "You come in here with skulls full of mush and leave thinking like a lawyer." When poor Hart screws up in class, Kingsfield tells him: "Mr. Hart, here is a dime. Take it, call your mother, and tell her there is serious doubt about you ever becoming a lawyer."

Is this a dated portrayal of legal education? Of course it is. You can't make a phone call for a dime anymore. You can't even find a phone booth. In today's wireless law schools, Hart would simply minimize his Facebook screen and zip out an instant message to his mom. Housman's performance was exaggerated for dramatic effect, but it did capture the essentials of how the Socratic method operates. The traditional model incorporates these essential components:

- Cold-calling on a student from a seating chart.

- Asking the student to "state the case," which entails narrating the facts and other aspects about the case, such as the procedural history, issue, holding, and reasoning.

- Testing the student's understanding of the case with more questions, which usually include hypothetical fact patterns that require the student to interpret and apply the legal principle(s) from the case. This is the component of the Socratic method most closely connected with the oft-stated goal to teach students to "think like a lawyer."

- Failing to offer concrete answers to the questions asked based on the assumption that the students, through the dialogue, should be able to figure out the answers on their own.

Depending on the skill and technique of the professor, the whole thing can come off as resembling a bizarre treasure hunt in which neither the professor nor the casebook provides the answers, at least not directly.

Why Do Law Schools Use the Socratic and Case Methods?

The Socratic and case methods have faced resistance since their inception. Criticisms include that the methods are intimidating, humiliating, alienating, bewildering, and inefficient. Yet they remain the dominant teaching methodologies in U.S. law schools, particularly in the first year.[68]

Why? Because law professors genuinely believe that the combination of the Socratic and case methods is the most effective way to train new law students to develop the critical-thinking skills they will need to be effective lawyers. Like most students, I hated the Socratic method back in law school. As a professor, however, I came to appreciate the usefulness of dialectical questioning as a tool for teaching students to discover knowledge on their own. Plus, it's fun scaring the hell out of people.

Seriously, the Socratic and case methods, in the right hands, are excellent tools for developing critical-reasoning skills. That's all "thinking like a lawyer" really means: reasoning well. As Langdell recognized, a person could memorize all the legal rules in the world, but still be a lousy lawyer. Good lawyering is about problem-solving and the Socratic and case methods are intended to force students to learn by doing rather than simply by being told how it is done. As one student said, "When the professor is asking questions and things finally 'click' in my head, I'm much

---

68. After visiting sixteen law schools across the country, the authors of the 2007 Carnegie Foundation Report on legal education concluded that "nearly all the law faculty" with whom they spoke endorsed the case-dialogue method as the best way to train 1Ls in "the craft of legal reasoning." CARNEGIE FOUNDATION REPORT, *supra*, at 66. Professor Steven I. Friedland conducted a survey back in the mid–1990s of law professors to determine how they teach. He sent out approximately 2,000 questionnaires, to which he received 574 completed responses. Ninety-seven percent of the respondents said they use the Socratic method at least some of the time in first-year courses, with 31 percent reporting they use it most of the time, and 41 percent reporting they use it often. Comparatively, only 31 percent of the professors surveyed reported that they use a lecture method "some of the time" in first-year courses, a percentage that soared to 94 percent in upper-level courses. *See* Steven I. Friedland, *How We Teach: A Survey of Teaching Techniques in American Law Schools*, 20 SEATTLE U. L. REV. 1 (1996).

more likely to understand and remember what I learned than if the professor just told me straight out."

The Socratic method has other benefits as well. It helps train students to think on their feet and articulate their reasoning, vital abilities for any lawyer. As mentioned, it provides a strong incentive for students to be prepared, substantially enhancing the quality of the classroom experience for all involved. The Socratic method also can facilitate a more interesting exploration of legal issues than pure lecturing, the principal realistic option in large classes.

Is it a perfect methodology? Far from it. First, the success of the method is heavily dependent on the skill of the professor and the preparation and intellectual levels of the students. Not all professors are adept at using the Socratic method. Some professors simply ask questions to see who is prepared or ask random questions without using the answers as means to an end. As one student wrote: "It annoys me when professors use a Q & A just to see if we prepared a brief, rather than to engage in a genuine Socratic dialogue designed to expose fallacies and reveal truth."

Also, the large size of law school classes renders most students passive bystanders in the process at any given time. A true Socratic dialogue envisions one-on-one instruction or small group tutorial. But even students who aren't directly participating learn from watching and listening to Socratic dialoguing. The *Carnegie Foundation Report* on legal education observed that one way in which the Socratic method enhances student intellectual development is through *modeling*; that is, the students learn by watching and modeling the cognitive skills of the professor displayed during case-dialoguing.[69]

Another common criticism is that the Socratic and case methods are inefficient. You might hear your student com-

---

69. The Carnegie Foundation Report classified law school case-dialoguing as a type of "cognitive apprenticeship" in which student intellectual development occurs through faculty-student interaction. Observing professor-student Socratic exchanges at sixteen law schools, the report's authors observed professors employing four basic apprenticeship teaching methods identified by cognitive theorists: *modeling*, by demonstrating in class the type of cognitive skills the professor seeks to instill in the students; *coaching*, by providing guidance and feedback; *scaffolding*, by providing support for students who haven't yet mastered critical-thinking skills; and *fading*, by encouraging students to go it alone when they've shown themselves prepared to do so. *See* CARNEGIE FOUNDATION REPORT, *supra*, at 60–61.

plain that some classes seem like a "waste of time" because such a large portion of them is devoted to Q and A case-dialoguing and ensuing class discussion. The criticism is valid in one sense. Professors could convey many more rules of law by lecturing, and treatise-like explanatory textbooks would be more efficient than casebooks in delivering information about the law. But this perspective overlooks that conveying information is only one goal of teaching law. Training students to reason well and solve legal problems are the principal aspirations of both the Socratic and case methods.

The Socratic method is also frequently attacked for being too harsh and intimidating. Again, there is truth here, but it was much truer in the old days than today. Very few of today's law professors are Professor Kingsfield-types who try to intimidate or humiliate students. But even when the professor is gentle, it can be scary getting called on and questioned without prior notice in front of a large group of peers.

Be sensitive to your student's fears about the Socratic method. Small classroom incidents that may sound trivial to you take on gigantic proportions to law students. In his quintessential book about the first year of law school, *One L*,[70] Scott Turow described a classroom episode in which a professor expressed irritation at a student for being unprepared. The event was so traumatizing to the class that the students organized a protest and circulated a petition. Turow acknowledged that "the Incident," as it became known, might seem "trifling" to an outsider.[71] But, as he noted, in the closeted world of first-year law school, everything gets wrapped up in "the pressures, and the uncertainty, and the personal humblings."[72]

Your student has a justifiable basis for being confused by and somewhat anxious about the Socratic and case methods. But they really do work. Even the Socratic-haters would be hard-pressed to deny that they really did arrive at law school with "skulls full of mush," in Professor Kingsfield's words,

---

70. SCOTT TUROW, ONE L: THE TURBULENT TRUE STORY OF A FIRST YEAR AT HARVARD LAW SCHOOL (Grand Central Publishing ed. 1997). Turow went on to become a bestselling author of legal thrillers such as *Presumed Innocent*, which was made into a 1990 blockbuster movie starring Harrison Ford.

71. *Id.* at 132.

72. *Id.*

yet exited the Socratic arena as facile thinkers and astute legal problem-solvers. As a 1L described:

> Just the other week I was eating lunch with some of my section friends and reading through a case for class. Without thinking, I said something like, "Don't you all think that we are so much better at reading cases now?" They looked at me like I just stated the most obvious thing in the world. I had just never really thought of it like that. When you stop and think about the evolution of your abilities from the beginning of the year to the end, it is really astonishing.

The difference in the way 1Ls think about legal problems at the beginning and end of the first year is dramatically apparent to professors. Keep an observant eye on your student and see if you can detect these enhancements in their mental facility as they occur.

CHAPTER 7

HOW LAW STUDENTS ARE TESTED: A SINGLE BITE AT A BIG APPLE

As I'm writing this chapter, a group of my 1Ls just finished their first year of law school. Good for them! What a terrific achievement. They finally get to enjoy the freedom they haven't seen in nine months. I wonder what they're doing. Relaxing in the shade with a juicy novel? Shopping? Traveling? Enjoying an afternoon out at the pool? Nope. They're obsessing about grades.

Grades for the Spring semester—the final grades of the year—were released today. Like my students, I frequently take breaks from working to check email, Facebook, etc. When I logged onto Facebook, all I could think was "Bless their hearts." The news feed was a minute-by-minute streaming update from anxious students reporting on which grades for which courses had been posted via the law school's online grade portal. Below are some of their status reports (in bold) and comments:

Grades are being posted now ... ahhhh!!

—How do u know?!!

—B/c my Property grade is there now.

—I got nuthin'.

—I have Property too.

—I'm really glad that once again, [my section] is getting screwed by not having any grades. Blah!

—Contracts!

—Torts II.

—Exquisite torture.

Passing thru 4 [four posted grades]. Almost a 2L.

—What's the 4th?

—Crim law is up

—Gracias! Yay for passing! This is much less brutal than getting grades on the first day of class![73]

—Haha. Agreed.

—My Crim Law grade's not up yet. Strange ...

Cannot stop checking ... now that I have two grades up, I want all of them ... NOW!

Grades, grades, grades, grades ...

—It's all happening so fast.

—Are they finished for the day or am I just growing impatient?

—Correction: more impatient.

—Three are up, right?

—Yes.

—Prop, Cont, and Torts

—You already have grades posted? I am very jealous.

Like I said, bless their hearts. As discussed in Chapter 11, exams are one of the most potent stress factors in a law student's life because law schools and legal employers put so much emphasis on grades, especially early grades. The Association of Higher Education compiled a survey of stress in undergraduate, graduate, law, and medical students and found law school to be unique in attaching so much significance to early grades. "[I]n no other university setting," the report concluded, "do grades have the importance at such an early point in one's education."[74]

---

73. They received their grades from the first semester on the first day of classes for the second semester, one more example of the cruel and unusual punishment law school can inflict on its charges.

74. NEAL WHITMAN ET AL., ASS'N FOR THE STUDY OF HIGHER EDUC., STUDENT STRESS: EFFECTS AND SOLUTIONS, ASHE–ERIC HIGHER EDUCATION RESEARCH REPORT NO. 2 53 (1984).

One student described how the primacy placed on grades can translate into real world consequences for law students in obtaining their first jobs:

> What adds substantially to the pressure is the importance of the grades that a law student receives. Unlike undergraduate or graduate programs, grades matter very much in law school. Indeed, the caliber of job a student receives and their salary depend greatly on their GPA and overall class ranking. The difference between receiving a *B-* average and an *A* average could mean a difference in annual salary to the tune of $100,000 (e.g., $60,000 vs. $160,000). Nowhere else is such weight placed on academic performance.

The student isn't exaggerating. An *A* average, which only a small percentage of students achieve, can literally lead to a student obtaining a $160,000 annual starting salary at a large law firm in a big city. Even in smaller markets, six-figure salaries are common for the top-ranked students.

The Single–Exam Format

As if that isn't enough pressure, in most law school courses, students get only one opportunity to "make the grade," just one three- or four-hour exam at the end of the semester. No quizzes, midterms, or papers. No other evaluation—period.[75] Combine the importance of grades with the fact that students get only one exam per course and you have a recipe for a competition so frenzied and full of stress that it could be the basis for a reality television series—held in an asylum.

Law school is the only educational discipline in which students are evaluated based on a single end-of-the-semester exam. It's not done that way in medical school or business school or veterinary school or in any other field. Particularly because so much rides on GPA and class rank in law school, it seems unsound and unfair to evaluate a student's knowledge and understanding of fourteen intensive weeks of complex material based on a single exam.

---

75. Of course, there are exceptions to all general rules. A small percentage of law professors do augment the final exam with a midterm exam or quizzes. Unfortunately for students, because midterms and quizzes usually count for only a small percentage of the final grade, they often have little impact on the final exam grade.

The authors of the 2007 *Best Practices for Legal Education* report noted that effective student assessment tools must be *valid*, *reliable*, and *fair*, and concluded that law school's single-exam format fails all three of these criteria.[76] Flaws in the single-exam format include the time-crunch factor (the system favors students who can read, think, and write quickly), lack of comprehensive course coverage (one exam can't fairly cover 42–56 class hours of material, which are the number of classroom hours in a three- or four-credit course, respectively), and the absence of feedback to students during the semester (students have no way to gauge their progress until after the final examination, when it's too late).

Part of the explanation for the single-exam format is historical. In the earliest days of American legal education, exams were administered weekly or even daily. The transition to the modern format came as a response to Christopher Langdell's case method back in the 1870s. As we've discussed, the goal of the case method is to train students to analyze and apply, rather than simply memorize, law.

To test these abilities, law professors developed the modern "issue-spotting/problem-solving" essay question, described more fully below. The knowledge and training in legal analysis required to tackle this type of exam can be acquired only over time. New students simply aren't capable of effectively analyzing a legal problem until they've become acclimated to legal analysis. Of course, this doesn't explain why the single-exam format is used throughout all three years of law school.

More modern justifications include a legitimate concern that incorporating other exams, such as midterms, into the semester distracts students from their ongoing course work. It's true. When students have a midterm in one course, their attendance and class preparation suffer in other courses.

A practical explanation for why most law professors don't give exams during the semester, one that professors might be reluctant to concede, is that they simply don't want to take on the job of grading them. This is one more drawback of the large student-faculty ratios in law school classes. Grading law school exams, if done diligently, is a substantial burden. It can take several weeks to properly grade final examinations

---

76. STUCKEY ET AL., *supra*, at 177.

in a large class. A three-hour law school essay exam generates answers ranging from two to five thousand words, or seven to seventeen double-spaced typewritten pages. Multiply those numbers by the seventy to eighty students in the average first-year class section and we're talking about a thick mass of writing for the professor to scrutinize.

Unlike in other educational disciplines, law professors do not rely on teaching assistants or graduate students to grade papers. And contrary to popular perception, most law professors (albeit not all) work hard. They put in long hours preparing for classes, doing administrative work such as serving on law school committees, and, especially, researching and writing. In legal academia, tremendous pressure exists to "publish or perish." I'm not trying to justify the practice, just explain it. The bottom line is that it takes an unusual professor who is willing to take two or three weeks out of the middle of a busy semester and devote them to grading a midterm exam or paper.

The Issue–Spotting/Problem–Solving Essay Question and Other Diabolical Law School Exam Devices

Law school exams, like the exam process itself, are completely unique. They don't resemble any kind of exam students have seen before. In other educational disciplines, a student who has studied hard and consistently can go into an exam feeling reasonably confident in her ability to perform well. That's not true in law school.

Consistent with the goals of legal education discussed in the previous chapter, law school exams do not reward memorization of the law, but the ability to engage in sound, organized analysis of it. While students obviously have to know the law in order to apply it, a student could know all the law in the world and still fare poorly on a law school exam.

Issue–Spotting/Problem–Solving Essay Questions. The classic type of law school exam question is the "issue-spotting/problem-solving question." These notoriously complicated and convoluted questions involve elaborate hypothetical fact patterns in which various actors interact in ways that raise legal issues among them. As the name suggests, students must first spot the issues, then solve them through cogent legal analysis. Some issues might be easy to spot, but some might be very difficult to spot. Depending on the exam, a particularly tricky issue may be identified by only a handful of students in a large class. Obviously, if a student can't spot an issue, she has no possibility of analyzing it. An issue-spotting question may have from three to ten issues, with the norm probably being around a half dozen, but the instructions don't tell students how many issues they are supposed to be looking for.

If the exam isn't crafted well, which they often aren't, even well-prepared students may be left scratching their heads wondering what the professor wants the student to discuss. Despite excelling in law school, I entered every exam with a lurking fear that I was going to read the exam and have no clue what the professor was looking for. Usually the fear was unfounded, but once, in a Corporations course, the exam content was so foreign that I actually went to the professor's office to make sure he handed out the correct exam.

Once students spot an issue, they must give a complete well-reasoned analysis of it by accurately stating the relevant legal rules and applying those rules to the facts of the question. In doing so, the student must address the relative strengths and weaknesses in each argument and offer a conclusion as to how each issue should be resolved.

Meanwhile, in the background, the clock is going tick, tick, tick, like a time-bomb. Most exams are held within strict time limits, three hours being the norm. The professor usually writes the ending time on the board as the last step before the exam begins. Unfortunately, some professors craft exams that can't possibly be adequately completed within that time frame, adding even more pressure.

In short, just about everything involved in this most popular of all law school exam question types seems almost intentionally designed to induce extra pressure: the content, the format, the time frame, everything.

Other Types of Essay Questions. Although the issue-spotting/problem-solving question is the classic model, law professors use other types of essay questions as well. These can include short essay questions focusing on a single issue, instructions to draft a statute or judicial opinion, or what is known as a "policy question." Policy questions don't test students' ability to apply law to facts and solve legal problems. Depending on the question, they don't necessarily even test one's knowledge or understanding of specific principles of law. Rather, they focus on a student's ability to construct a thoughtful argument or analysis regarding a policy issue relevant to the course material.

Some professors intentionally ask policy questions addressing issues never discussed in the course because they want to see how students apply what they learned to new situations. The story might be apocryphal, but I once heard of a law school exam question that asked simply: "What is law?" Most policy questions aren't that broad, but by their nature, grading policy questions is subjective in the extreme.

Multiple–Choice Questions. Many, if not most, professors also use some multiple-choice questions. Good news for students, you would think, and in some ways it is. For one thing, multiple-choice questions facilitate broader coverage of the course material. But law school multiple-choice questions, like everything else in law school, are different from anything students have previously encountered. They require the ability to read, manage, and analyze complex text, and like the law itself, often don't have clear right answers.

Most law school multiple-choice questions are styled after the format used on the Multistate Bar Examination (MBE), given as part of most states' bar exams. One indicator of how hard these questions are is that, depending on the state, students can pass the MBE by getting as few as 125 of the 200 questions correct. That's only 63 percent of the total. Under standard grading scales, a 63 would be a *D*.

MBE-type multiple-choice questions consist of a one- or two-paragraph fact pattern in which events of legal significance transpire among named actors, followed by the "call of the question," followed by four or more answer choices. (The "call of the question" is the part that tells the student what issue to address.) The problem for students is that the answer options often include choices that seem partly right or partly wrong, but not clearly right or wrong. The essence of law school multiple-choice questions is perhaps best captured by an odd piece of advice I remember hearing for the first time many moons ago while taking the bar review course in preparation for the Florida bar exam: "Remember that on the MBE, you're not looking for the right answer. You're looking for the *best wrong answer*." Okay, great.

Here's a sample law school multiple-choice question:

#. Caspid went out for a Sunday drive in his Bentley automobile. He decided to leave the city, crank up the music and just unwind for the afternoon. The farther out into the country he drove, the sparser the population became. Soon he was driving down a deserted winding road through the woods. He opened the sunroof and put in a nice relaxing jazz CD. Caspid was driving carefully around a curve when a 300-pound wild boar ran out in front of his car. He slammed on the brakes, but could not stop in time. He ran into the boar, killing the large animal and damaging the front of his automobile. Caspid got out of his car to survey the situation. He felt bad about killing the animal, but also felt bad about the crumpled front bumper on his Bentley. Shaking his head in disgust, he backed up, turned his car around, and headed back to the city. Ten minutes later, Dort was driving down the same road. He came around the curve and ran into the boar, which was lying in the road. This caused him to lose control of his car and crash into a tree. Dort sustained a head injury. If Dort sues Caspid, the most probable result will be:

(a) Judgment for Dort, because of strict liability for harm caused by animals.

(b) Judgment for Dort, because Caspid created an unreasonable risk that he had a duty to eliminate.

(c) Judgment for Caspid, because Caspid was not negligent in creating the risk.

(d) Judgment for Caspid, because Caspid owed no duty to Dort.

(e) Judgment for Dort based on implied primary assumption of risk.

Not that it matters, but in case you're curious, the correct answer is (b). Normally, under the law, one has no legal duty to aid or protect others. Such inaction is known as nonfeasance; i.e., a mere failure to act. For example, if Caspid overheard two men plotting to rob a convenience store and kill the clerk, he would have no legal duty to do anything to protect the clerk, not even a duty to dial 911. But the law is filled with exceptions and one exception to the "no duty to aid or protect" rule is that if an actor creates an unreasonable risk, even innocently, he has a duty to exercise reasonable care to eliminate the risk. Even though Caspid did nothing wrong in creating the risk (the question says he was driving carefully when the boar ran in front of his car), he had a duty to act reasonably to remove the boar from the road or warn approaching drivers.

* * *

Perhaps the day will arrive in U.S. legal education where students get several attempts to prove their knowledge and ability in a law school course. Perhaps one day humans will travel to another galaxy or learn to make oil from water. In the meantime, be prepared for your student to turn into a basket-case each time those all-or-nothing exams approach.

While exams are hellish for students, they are no picnic for loved ones either. The closer exams get, the more stressed out students become and the more they isolate themselves, either alone or with other students in study groups. They have outlines to finish and practice exams to work through, not to mention keeping up with their ongoing course work. This is definitely not the time to complain about your student not paying enough attention to you. Rather, it is *the* most important time to muster all the patience and support you can. There are tangible things that loved ones can do for their students during this stressful period to ease the burden and strain. One student said of his extremely supportive wife:

> Here are just a few things that my wife did for me to help me get through my first set of exams: (1) Made me flashcards with case names on one side and the legal doctrine on the other; (2) Quizzed me using these flashcards; (3) Walked the dogs (usually my job); (4)

Took care of dinner every night (a task we usually split); (5) Watched TV with headphones on; (6) Made trips to Kinko's to print out and bind my outlines. She was a lifesaver!

He finished number one in his class. Sounds like his wife deserves part of the credit.

But it's not necessary to do all of these things to be a lifesaver during exams. Many students will simply want to be left alone. Just giving your student space and letting them know you are there if they need you will provide an unseen yet deeply felt comfort. If you get lonely, approach your student and imitate Piglet from A.A. Milne's Winnie the Pooh stories: "Piglet sidled up to Pooh from behind. 'Pooh!' he whispered. 'Yes, Piglet?' 'Nothing,' said Piglet, taking Pooh's paw. 'I just wanted to be sure of you.'"[77] Your student may feel the same need, before quickly returning to studying.

77. A. A. MILNE, *The House at Pooh Corner, in* THE WORLD OF POOH 151, 261 (1957).

CHAPTER 8

THINGS LAW STUDENTS LOVE
TO TALK ABOUT

I think the hardest part was the fact that I ate, slept and breathed law school and didn't understand why my family/significant other didn't just LOVE hearing about every minute detail of school/class/studying, etc.

—Former law student

You're going to learn right away that most law students, especially 1Ls, are both consumed by and consume law school. They eat, drink, breathe, and even sleep law school. That's right, *sleep*. Dreaming about law school is common. One student's significant other said about his partner, "I have heard her once or twice going over a case in her sleep." Another told how his law student had a dream in which he, the loved one, was being sued for treating a woman unkindly: "Fortunately, my partner was able to settle things in the dream by informing the woman that the statute of limitations had passed so there was nothing she could do about it." A third said about his wife: "It's all law school 24/7. From the time we wake up, when she's informing me about a dream she had—where she was required to sing a solo as a part of her Contracts Exam—until she's done studying Con Law at midnight."

My favorite dream story came from a student I had several years ago who told me about a grisly nightmare in which I had him tied to a stake while peppering him with questions about the tort of battery. Each time he answered, I shouted, "Wrong!" and lopped off one of his limbs with an ax, saying "Is that a battery? Is that a battery?" Obviously, the dream was farfetched. A law professor never would ask such easy questions.

Students so desperately want to talk about law school they may even resort to trickery to get you to listen:

> During my first few months in law school, I was so excited about everything I was learning that I tried to tell my husband *everything*. Now that the excitement has died down, I've resorted to asking him hypotheticals. I intentionally tailor the questions to make sure that they are somewhat controversial to spark his interest. Then when he takes the opposite side from what I want him to take, I explain all the policy reasons behind the particular legal doctrine. It is really a terrible thing to do but I do find it somewhat entertaining.

Why is it like this? Same thing I've been saying and we'll hear over and over from students throughout the book. Law school is not just school. It's a way of life, an insatiable black hole of focus and effort. Practically speaking, because everything is a completely new experience, there really *is* a lot for your student to talk about: a new language, new way of studying, new teaching methods, new ideas, new classmates and professors, and a whole magnificent legal system to unravel.

The closeted environment of law school also contributes to the preoccupation. Law schools are somewhat like prisons, except the cellmates have names like Ashley and Kevin instead of Trixie and Rocko. As mentioned, law students spend all their time with the same people, especially in the first year. They take the same courses from the same professors in the same rooms with the same classmates. They work on the same assignments. They study together. Most of them form study groups. Functioning in such close-quarters quickly converts classmates into something akin to family. The fact that they are joined so closely in the same mental quagmire makes it difficult for them to separate themselves from it.

Also, because law pervades society, just about anything that happens in daily life can spark a legal commentary from a law student. "Many law school discussions come up naturally," one student explained. "For example, we passed a wreck on the Interstate and suddenly I found myself discussing whether or not bystanders have a legal duty to stop and assist injured people."

Not all law students talk non-stop about law school. Some students make a pointed effort of not talking about it to loved ones, specifically as a way to find respite in their lives. One first-year student said she talks so much about law school with her classmates that she is relieved to get home and talk about other things with her husband, whom she called her "oasis from law school." Others look at the issue reasonably from an "if the shoe were on the other foot" angle, explaining that they don't enjoy hearing their partners going on and on about their jobs, so it's not fair to expect them to listen to continuous law school talk. As one student said, "I refuse to talk about the law with my wife because she's a veterinarian. If I told her about every interesting facet of law, I'd have no excuse to run from stories about Fluffy or Fido."

One study of married law students at a Midwestern urban university suggested that while nearly all students share their law school experiences with their partners initially, this "spousal incorporation" declined for male students as time wore on, but not for female students.[78] One speculated reason was that men are more likely to compartmentalize the law school experience as if it were a nine-to-five job.[79] The study was too small to support any definite conclusions (it involved only twenty-three students, of which eleven were men), but my own unscientific survey sampling lends some support to the idea. I received several comments from male students stating that they preferred to compartmentalize law school and not discuss it with their loved ones.

But students who don't like to talk about law school are atypical. Even if they don't necessarily enjoy talking about law school, many students suffer from a compulsion to do so. One of the goals of this book is to prepare you for this information overload, so here's what you can expect.

---

78. Deanna Boyd McQuillan & Carrie Elizabeth Foote, *Law School and* *Marriage: Making It Work*, 42 MARRIAGE & FAM. REV. 7, 30 (2008).

79. *Id.* at 25.

"These Are a Few of My Favorite Things"[80]

What do law students love to talk about? *Everything* related in any way to law school would be an accurate answer for many students, but we'll narrow that down. The Socratic method and exams, already discussed, are popular topics. Other than those, 1Ls talk primarily about their professors, classmates, classroom episodes, "the law," and their course work. In the second semester, co-curricular activities such as law review or moot court may enter the picture. For upper-level students, finding a permanent job becomes the major preoccupation. A 3L put it tersely: "My discussions now go like this: job, job, job, job, bitching about classmates, job, job, and more job." For many students, law school talk may follow a progression not unlike the one described below by another 3L:

> The answer to the question of what I talk about changes every year. In my first year I spent a lot of time talking about the concepts we learned in class. I think almost every day I shared tidbits from Torts with my spouse. I also spent a lot of time complaining about Legal Research and Writing; i.e., the "memo." Like most students, I stressed about every legal writing assignment and was crushed by most of my grades in the class. My husband endured a lot of "woe is me stories" in my first year. I also subjected him to various reenactments of my getting called on in class so that he could tell me whether I "sounded okay." By my second year, I was still talking about the law, but I was also spending more time talking about my classmates. I would often share stories with my spouse of in-class antics and Socratic method disasters. I think I spent more time on this topic my second year because at that point he had met many of my classmates, so the stories had more relevance to him. I am currently a 3L and I spend most of my time talking about jobs with my husband. That subject seems to consume most 3Ls. I don't share as much with him about what I am learning in class anymore, perhaps because I finally realized that he doesn't really care!

80. RICHARD RODGERS & OSCAR HAMMER-STEIN, MY FAVORITE THINGS (1959).

I'm assuming your student has recently started or is about to start law school, so let's back up to the first year.

Their Professors

Especially at the beginning of law school, students talk a lot about their professors. In part because the 1L universe is so small, the professors become the center of it. Student lives revolve around the professors, in one sense literally since many law school classrooms place professors smack in the middle of horseshoe-shaped seating.

Professors control students' daily existence. They tell them what to read and when to speak. They scrutinize and often correct their comments. And, of course, they are the ones who will grade that single final exam. As one student (not one of mine) put it:

> The class is a world in itself.... All attention in class is directed on the professor on the stage. He is *the authority* in the class. An analogy can be drawn between the professor's relationship to the students and the relationship between a king and his subjects. The king is in control of his kingdom, and the professor's kingdom is his class. The subjects in the class view the professor as an omnipotent authority on the law. What the professor says is the law.[81]

The veneration and awe that some students have for their professors at the beginning of law school is amusing, even embarrassing. At a social gathering during a fall orientation many years ago, I was standing in the restroom at a urinal when a young man next to me exclaimed, "I can't believe it! I'm peeing next to Professor McClurg." I'm pretty sure he was serious.

Law students pay attention to and talk about not only the professors' teaching styles, but their physical appearances, mannerisms, and quirks. You'll hear stories about which professors are nice, demanding, confusing, funny, attractive, etc. Students also enjoy speculating about their professors' personal lives. One student manuscript reader wrote here:

81. James R. Elkins, *Rites de Passage: Law Students "Telling Their Lives,"* 35 J. LEGAL EDUC. 27, 40 (1985). The author had his students compile journals as they progressed through the first semester. The quotation in the text is from one student's journal.

"This is so true. Students love sharing the 'You'll never guess who I saw at [fill in the blank]' gossip about professors." She added, "But some professors generate more intrigue than others. The 'quirky' ones definitely get talked about the most."

One easy way to stay connected to your student's daily existence and also more easily follow their conversations is simply by getting to know the names of their professors. Asked what loved ones should know about law school, one student said:

> My boyfriend commented that the things that were most difficult for him when I talked about school were: (a) keeping up with students' names that I frequently mentioned; and (b) keeping the professors' names straight. He finally just forced himself to memorize which professor went with each subject. He still struggles with student names though. I would become frustrated when I constantly had to repeat who each person was for him, but once he learned the professors' names, I wasn't as frustrated. It was probably because I only had to repeat the students' information. That made my story-telling much easier. So that would be a good tip for a loved one of a student. If they can just remember professors' names, it won't feel like the conversation barrier is as large.

Get a list from your student of their professors and the subjects they teach. Go to the law school's website and click on the "Faculty" link, then click on the links to the individual professors. Every law school website features bios of the professors, almost always with a picture. Not only will you gain familiarity with who your student is talking about, you'll be impressed and comforted that such highly credentialed people are teaching your student.

Find time to sit in on a couple of classes with your student. Most professors allow students to bring visitors to class. Asked for advice they would give to others, one significant other who visited a class with her student said, "I recommend observing a class. It helps to get a little idea of what your law student goes through every day. It also makes all the stories you will hear less boring when you can put faces to the names of the professors and the students." You'll also get a clearer picture of how the Socratic and case methods operate than by simply reading about them. This advice applies to all loved ones. Many of my students bring not only their partners, but parents, siblings, friends, and even children to class and it's always great to meet them.

Their Classmates

As the first year progresses, law professors begin losing their mystique and allure. At the same time, students are getting to know their classmates much better. As a result, classmate-centered talk takes over.

New BFFs.[82] One popular topic will involve your student's new friends. Perhaps the single best thing about law school are the friends students make, friendships that often end up lasting a lifetime.

Law students meld easily and closely, in part because of the psychological bonding effects of group terror. In one famous social psychology experiment, researchers put a group of monkeys in the same cage with a group of lions. Monkeys and lions usually don't socialize because the lions eat the monkeys, which causes hard feelings. Early in the experiment, it appeared events would follow this pattern as the lions began chasing the monkeys and the monkeys began bonking the lions on the heads with coconuts. At this point, the researchers inserted a Contracts professor into the cage who began conducting a Socratic dialogue about the doctrine of promissory estoppel.[83] An amazing transformation occurred. The lions and monkeys immediately locked paws and began singing pub songs. Within a few minutes, the lions were giving the monkeys foot massages and the monkeys were encouraging the lions to get in touch with their inner cubs.

Seriously, people in group fear situations really do interact and bond more cohesively than other groups. In one real study, researchers solicited college students to participate in what they were told was a study of sexual attitudes. They

---

82. For you non-texting, non-Facebooking parents out there, BFF is tech-slang for "best friends forever."

83. Promissory estoppel is a doctrine of contract law holding that if one party changes his position in justifiable reliance on a promise from another party, the former may be able to enforce the promise even though the essential elements of a contract (offer, acceptance, consideration) are missing. The person making the promise is "estopped"—i.e., legally precluded—from claiming there is no valid contract.

divided the students into three groups and put them in rooms containing different objects on a table in the center of the room. In the "fear group's" room, the table contained two electric generators that gave the appearance of shocking devices and some documents stating that the purpose of the study was to compare the subjects' physiological reactions to shock and sexual stimuli. The documents also included a "shock release form." Studying the interactions of the three groups and surveying them afterwards, the researchers concluded that persons placed in a group fear situation were more likely to affiliate and engage in collective coping than other groups.[84] Other "fear affiliation" studies have reached similar results.

Another explanation for the close bonding among law students—well-supported by social psychology "liking" research—is simply that we like people with whom we have things in common. Because law school is such an opaque and mysterious world to outsiders, law students rely on other law students to share their joys and sorrows. No matter how different the backgrounds of law students, they have one big thing in common: law school, and that's enough to form a basis for bonding. Asked what they love most about law school, students replied (see Chapter 13 for more):

- Camaraderie. I have enjoyed the feeling of having a group of people who have gone through the same struggles and hardships as I have. When I complain about the work that a professor gives me or the grade I received in a certain class, there are always people who know exactly where I am coming from and feel my pain.

- What I love about law school is that I am surrounded by people like me and I am lucky enough to call most of them friends. I turn to them for advice or to complain when everyone in my normal life thinks I'm being over-dramatic.

- Law school friends are amazing because they can understand where you're coming from in almost every situation because they're coming from the exact same

---

84. *See* William N. Morris et al., *Collective Coping with Stress: Group Reac-* *tion to Fear, Anxiety, and Ambiguity*, 33 J. Personality & Soc. Psychol. 674 (1976).

place. You're all experiencing it for the first time, and it's wonderful to know other people are overwhelmed or confused or tired; it makes you feel better about feeling that way yourself.

Hear what they're saying, which is that when times get tough, and especially if they feel misunderstood by the non-law students in their lives, law students turn to other law students for support and commiseration. Except for you (because you're reading this book), only other law students "get" a law student's fascination with *Marbury v. Madison*,[85] going gaga over a *B* in Property, or falling into crushing despair after giving a weak answer in class.

It's important to non-student loved ones that they *do* get it so they don't get locked out of the student's new life. One of the best ways to preempt the risk of your law student neglecting your relationship is to become part of your student's law school experience, including getting to know and socializing with his or her new friends. Don't settle for being a law school outsider.

Gossip, Some of It Unflattering. You're also likely to hear negative comments about classmates. In the cloistered, pressurized, highly competitive environment of law school, law students love to gossip about and sometimes verbally pummel certain classmates. Some of this gossip may sound mean-spirited. Asked what they like to talk about to their loved ones, a 2L said: "Rude or inconsiderate classmates are fun to discuss because everyone can relate to having to deal with a schmuck."

If your student participates in the grand tradition of classmate-bashing, it doesn't mean they're a bad or mean person. Gossiping is part of human relationships and is accentuated in closed, stressful environments. Several studies have found that gossip promotes social bonding by generating feelings of closeness and solidarity in relationships. One study specifically found that negative gossip works to build deeper friendships than positive gossip. In an experiment

---

85. 5 U.S. (1 Cranch) 137 (1803) (landmark Supreme Court case establishing the principle of judicial review; i.e., that the Supreme Court gets the last word in reviewing actions of the executive and legislative branches of the government).

involving college students, researchers found that sharing a dislike of a third party with someone promotes friendship and bonding more powerfully than sharing positive information or feelings about the person.[86] Reading a draft of the manuscript, a research assistant wrote here: "I never thought about this, but it's true. I've noticed that making fun of the people around you (out of earshot) to those you are talking to is a way to bond with them and get to know them and laugh together."

On the other hand, don't condone overzealous bad-mouthing of your student's colleagues. It can become a bad habit and contribute to your student's law school-induced transformation into an overly acerbic person. One study of law students suggested that students who rely less on venting as a coping mechanism have more positive attitudes toward their legal education.[87] But expect some catty commentary and understand that, within reasonable limits, it is a natural part of the law school environment.

Relationships and Other Social Drama. Warning: Listening to your student's commentary about classmates may cause an out-of-body experience in which you have flashbacks of not being invited to your junior prom. One perennial favorite category of law student gossip involves relationships and other social dynamics. Comparisons of law school social drama to high school or even middle school are among the most common remarks I hear from students. There's even a Facebook group called "Dear Law School: High School Called, They Want Their Drama Back." At last check, it had more than 7,000 members.

Nowhere is this drama more apparent than in law student relationships. Asked to name their biggest surprise about law school, one student wrote:

> Honestly, my biggest surprise has to do with my fellow classmates. I almost feel like I am back in high school again. There is so much drama between guys and girls

---

86. Jennifer K. Bosson et al., *Interpersonal Chemistry Through Negativity: Bonding by Sharing Negative Attitudes About Others*, 13 PERS. RELATIONSHIPS 135, 147 (2006).

87. Mary E. Pritchard & Daniel N. McIntosh, *What Predicts Adjustment Among Law Students? A Longitudinal Panel Study*, 143 J. SOC. PSYCHOL. 727, 737 (2003).

as well as just between girls. I thought at this age people would be over worrying about who likes who, etc., but that does not seem to be the case. I guess that's what happens when you are with the same seventy people every day all day!

Pack a bunch of bright, attractive people together and some of them are going to get together romantically. No surprise there. Many of these relationships turn out to be deep and long-lasting, often resulting in marriage. But a lot of other law school relationships are short-lived and messy. A 1L, halfway through her first semester, cautioned:

> There are already, regrettably, people getting "reputations" here and I'm sure if I were on the market (and remotely attracted to men who are about a year over the drinking age and thus about seven years younger than me) I'd be one of them. Best advice I can give my fellow law students is: "Date someone who gets it. But don't date anyone in your section. Also, don't get drunk and have a one nighter with a 3L because that will haunt you for the rest of your law school career."

If you're in a committed relationship with your student, you're doing the student a favor just by being with them—it keeps them out of relationship pickles and the accompanying distractions.

Gunners. The Socratic method involves a lot of questions being asked by the professor, including many "What do you think?" questions. Most first-year law school class sections include a small number of students who are more willing to volunteer answers than the other students. And I say to them on behalf of law professors everywhere: Thank you! Someone has to answer those questions. From a professor's perspective, a frequent volunteer beats the heck out of the students who sit silently all year long never engaging in the class. The most interesting and exciting parts of law school classes always involve class discussion.

Unfortunately, frequent participators sometimes get labeled by the law school slur, "Gunner." Probably because classes and the Socratic method are a focal point of their lives, students love to talk about these folks. It's unfortunate because the fear of being labeled a gunner deters many good students with good ideas and answers from participating in class. In general, younger students, who are more sensitive to peer pressure, seem overly concerned about being portrayed as a gunner as compared to older students. That's one thing I love about teaching part-time evening-division students (night students), who are much older as a group. They could care less about what someone thinks of them for participating in class. If they have an idea, they just spit it out.

Tell your student not to worry about being labeled a gunner. True gunners—the ones who engender dislike from their classmates—are rare. I haven't had one in class in years. Real gunners are students who not only volunteer frequently, but do so obnoxiously, with a misplaced air of superiority. Or they routinely offer extremely conservative or extremely liberal viewpoints with a "My position is the only right one" attitude that offends one-half of the class. Students need to understand, but don't, that being a gunner is much more about attitude than frequency of participation. Recently, I had an older full-time student who *loved* to raise his hand, several times in each fifty-minute class. But he did it out of an almost-childlike wonder and excitement for the law, not because he liked to hear himself talk. He was beloved by his classmates and professors alike.

Of course, a lot of students don't participate in class simply because they are afraid, not because they're worried about being called a gunner. One of the best pieces of advice you can give your law student is to participate in class. Tons of research shows active learning is more effective than passive learning. By participating in class discussions, your student will feel better about themselves and their law school experience. Research suggests that students who are highly engaged in law school are happier students.[88] Many professors even raise those all-important final grades based on class participation. Most important, professors appreciate and *get to know* students who participate, which can be a huge practical benefit for your student.

---

88. NANCY LEVIT & DOUGLAS O. LINDER, THE HAPPY LAWYER: MAKING A GOOD LIFE IN THE LAW 132 (2010) (discussing study of life satisfaction among law students and concluding that "highly engaged law students are more likely to become happier lawyers").

"The Competition." As discussed in Chapter 11, the competitive aspect of law school is a big stressor for students. One consequence of the extreme emphasis on grades and class rank is that law students are constantly sizing up their peers. They talk about whether they think other students are smart or not based on their classroom comments and try to predict who will do well and who won't. When grades come out, they talk endlessly about other students' grades and class ranks. Even though grades and class ranks are not publicly posted, law students can't seem to keep their mouths shut about them. If a student reveals her grades to one person, the word will travel at warp speed to other students. Your student won't listen to this advice, but give it to her anyway. Tell her not to share her grades with anyone, except you, of course.

Students who do well and then brag about it are among the least liked students, both by other students and professors. A law professor at another school recently told me about a student who received an *A* on her memo assignment in Legal Research and Writing, then proceeded to carry the memo around, with the *A* clearly showing, on top of her stack of books for three weeks until my professor-friend had a "chat" with her about it. "Her classmates were about to crucify her," the friend reported.

Classroom Episodes

You will definitely hear stories of classroom episodes involving both professors and students. Law students enjoy regaling their loved ones with funny stories about what happened in class. Most of these stories are of the "you had to be there" variety. More accurately, they are "you had to be there *and* be in law school" stories.

One problem is that most law school stories require an in-depth context to understand. Also, due to the intensity of law school classes, humorous episodes or remarks get an exaggerated comedic boost associated with stress release. In other words, the stories are funny in comparison to everything else about law school that is so not-funny. One student explained his experience telling his family about funny things that happen in law school: "I always build up the story, only to finish it thinking, 'Hmm, this is the point where they are supposed to laugh, but I don't think they've laughed yet.' It hasn't stopped me from sharing stories though!"

A lot of law school stories are actually pretty amusing. Many involve professors who embarrass students in class or students or professors who embarrass themselves in class. Here are samples from my legal humor website, law-haha.com, which collects, among other things, funny law school stories sent in by law students and lawyers.

First, we have, in the grand Socratic tradition, a professor poking fun at a student. The nature of the Socratic method— back and forth dialogue between the professor and students— provides abundant opportunities for professors, who are in the driver's seat, to take advantage of the discussion. The only context you need to know for this story is that nearly all law students use computers to take notes in class:

> In my Property class, the professor asked a class-mate, "Do you notice that when you talk all the typing stops?"
>
> "Yes, sir," the student replied.
>
> "Why do you think that is?" asked the professor.
>
> "I guess because I am wrong," the student answered.
>
> The professor quickly responded, "You should have more faith in yourself, Mr. _____. I am *sure* you are wrong."

So we see that even the funny parts of law school can be rooted in self-esteem lowering.

Next is an example of a student embarrassing herself without an assist from the professor. The student misapprehended the rule of defamation law (i.e., libel and slander) that for a defamatory statement to give rise to a valid legal claim, the defendant must have communicated the statement to at least one person other than the plaintiff; as we say in the law, to at least "one third person":

> We were in first-year Torts and discussing slander. The professor stated that one of the elements of slander was that the defamatory statement must be heard by "one third person." A student raised her hand and told the professor she didn't understand. The professor went on to explain how if one third person didn't hear

the statement it wasn't considered published and didn't fulfill the elements. The student, still obviously confused, asked: "But I still don't understand which one-third of the person has to hear it!"

One can almost hear the laughter echoing through the classroom. As for professors embarrassing themselves, law-haha.com has received tales about a bald, white professor who raps in class, a professor who acts like nothing unusual has occurred when a tooth flies out of his mouth and bounces off a table during a lecture, a professor who begins teaching class from the wrong book, a legendary Torts professor who walks smack into the door on the way in and proceeds to teach the entire class with blood streaming down his face, and a famous Property professor who stalks the classroom for an entire hour with toilet paper hanging out the back of his pants.

The Law

For goodness' sake, by the time finals rolled around my husband could define and apply *res ipsa loquitur* better than I could. You know things are bad when your spouse can answer your flashcard[89] questions before you get a chance.

—Former law student

The law itself is another choice topic of law student conversation, especially for 1Ls. That's one reason I gave you those first-year course descriptions in Chapter 4—so you can at least try to follow along.[90] Whatever else can be said about

---

89. Flashcards is the shorthand name for the *Law in a Flash* series of law school study aids, consisting of cards with questions on the front and answers on the back.

90. *Res ispa loquitur*, mentioned by the student, is a doctrine learned in first-year Torts holding that some types of accidents are sufficient proof of negligence by the defendant even when no evidence exists except the happening of the event itself. Translated from Latin, the term means "the thing speaks for itself." Thus, in the seminal 1863 case of *Byrne v. Boadle*, 159 Eng. Rep. 299 (Ex. Ch. 1863), studied by virtually all law students, the plaintiff was walking on a sidewalk when a barrel of flour rolled out of the window of an adjacent flour business and conked him on the head. The plaintiff did not know and could not find out how or why the barrel flew out the window (and, not surprisingly, the defendant, if it knew, wasn't telling). The defendant argued the plaintiff should lose because he couldn't prove a specific negligent act by the defendant. The court created the doctrine of *res ipsa loquitur* and the plaintiff won. As the court said tersely, "A barrel could not roll out of a warehouse without some negligence." In other words, the thing spoke for itself.

the law, most students find it interesting. When students enter law school, the law presents itself as a gargantuan, impenetrable black box, but with each passing day the box becomes a *little bit* more transparent. This part of the learning process is exciting. I still remember as a student the sense of pride and achievement I felt each time another piece of the legal puzzle fell into place.

But, of course, with new law students being crazed and obsessed, a little knowledge can prove to be a dangerous thing to loved ones. The below comments from a 1L explaining what she likes to talk about to her boyfriend had me laughing out loud:

> Recently, my boyfriend and I went to a wedding. It was very liturgical and the priest went on forever about promises. So naturally I started thinking enforceable promises—that is, contracts. I perked up in the ceremony and started listening very intently and my boyfriend was sitting there wondering why I was so interested (like most men, he was probably quaking in his boots that I was expecting to catch the bouquet). Seconds after the ceremony was over, I busted out with, "It's a contract! There was offer, acceptance, and the rings are consideration!" Sometimes I tell him "what I know" but I don't tell him the rule or anything. I guess I do this just to make him realize I really am learning a lot here. Like, for example, we passed a cat that was in the middle of the median on a country highway, fixing to catch a mouse. I told him I could tell him who the cat belongs to, even though it was a stray (law of capture, rules about wild animals on state property). Once I tickled him and he told me to stop, and I kept going and told him "You know, this is a battery. I'm battering you right now." I also told him about the rules of engagement rings if an affianced pair of our friends happened to call it off before the wedding. I wore his robe and told him I was "trespassing on his chattels," and explained that if I took it home with me, it would be a conversion. Torts actually comes up a lot. But, come to think of it, I really don't tell him anything from Civil Procedure.

Poor bloke. I picture him shaking his head thinking, "Why couldn't she have gone for an M.B.A. instead?"

It's common for students to come home brimming with hypothetical fact patterns involving legal issues they covered in class that day and, emulating their professors, asking their loved ones, "What do you think?" "Hypos"—as they are called—are law school's favorite teaching tool. These discussions can be fun and are a good way to get involved in your student's law school experience. You'll be surprised how often your layperson's common sense instinct as to how a case should be resolved will accord with the law.

If you keep an open mind and ears, you'll find that a lot of legal doctrines are interesting because they have practical relevance to everyday life. In Torts, students learn about liability for dog bites and injuries to guests in their homes, automobile insurance policies, consumer rights and manufacturer responsibilities for defective consumer products, worker compensation laws that affect all employees, and, importantly, how to avoid conduct that could result in an injury to someone and get you sued.

In Contracts, students learn about warranties, what constitutes an enforceable contract, when contracts can be voided, and remedies for breaching a contract. You may not realize it, but you enter into binding contracts all the time. For example, every time you click "I Accept" online, you are entering into a binding legal agreement.

In Criminal Law, students learn the elements of crimes and defenses, that ignorance of the law is no excuse, and the procedural knowledge to offer expert play-by-play commentary while watching lawyer television shows.

In Property, students study rules related to home buying and selling, marital property rights, landlord-tenant law, and a doctrine called "adverse possession" that seems to hold universal fascination for students and loved ones alike, even though it is seldom invoked in real life. Overly simplified, adverse possession is a rule that says a person can take lawful title to someone else's land—steal it, basically—simply by occupying it openly and hostilely over a certain period of time. I'm sure your law student can and will give you the details. It will be a good time, I promise.[91]

---

91. One student reported this adverse possession colloquy with his significant other:

I found it amazing that someone can "steal" someone's property just by being a trespasser for a required amount of

In Civil Procedure, students learn about ... um, they learn about ... okay, well, not every class teaches rules with everyday application. Civil Procedure is directly relevant mostly to lawyers. Indirectly, it's highly relevant to any person involved in a civil lawsuit because it will often control the outcome of the case.

Because the cases often involve interesting facts and matters to which laypersons can relate, you might hear more about cases from Torts and Criminal Law than other subjects. As one student said about the latter, "I mostly speak about Crim Law because spilling a little blood is always interesting."

I've had more than one student tell me they actually read Torts cases to their loved ones. One student told me he read a particular case, *Breunig v. American Family Insurance Co.,*[92] to his kids as a bedtime story and said his kids requested it again the next night. No joke. So law school really is for the whole family. In *Breunig*, the plaintiff was injured when the defendant ran her car into his truck. Pretty boring so far, but it gets better. As the court explained:

> The evidence established that [the defendant], while returning home after taking her husband to work, saw a white light on the back of a car ahead of her. She followed this light for three or four blocks. [The defendant] did not remember anything else except landing in a field, lying on the side of the road and people talking. She recalled awaking in the hospital.

> The psychiatrist testified [the defendant] told him she was driving on a road when she believed that God was taking ahold of the steering wheel and was directing her car. She saw the truck coming and stepped on

time. For some reason, my girlfriend was really interested in the subject. Her take on it, though, really surprised me. Our conversation went something like this:

Girlfriend: If you don't want people to steal your land then stop being lazy and go tell them to get off the land.

Me: Well, what if you own a lot of land and it's too much for you to keep tabs on the property lines?

Girlfriend: Too bad, you should have known that someone built something on *your* property and if you didn't find it important enough to kick them off when they did it you didn't deserve the land to begin with.

Me: Sweetheart, have you thought about going to law school?

92.   173 N.W.2d 619 (Wis. 1970).

the gas in order to become air-borne because she knew she could fly because Batman does it.[93] To her surprise she was not air-borne before striking the truck but after the impact she was flying.[94]

Pretty interesting, although I'm still trying to picture how the story-telling incident went down:

Dad: Okay, kids, time for a bedtime story. What will it be tonight? Snow White? The Three Little Pigs? Suzy, it's your pick tonight.

Suzy: Breunig v. American Family Insurance Company!

Kids (chanting in unison): Breunig, Breunig, Breunig!

Dad: Alright then, here we go. Once upon a time there was a woman who thought her car could fly because Batman can fly . . .

Here's a shocker: not all kids find the law fascinating. One wife of a law student wrote: "One time my daughter brought one of her books to my husband for him to read to her while he was studying. He read the book, and then began to read his Property outline to her. She lasted ten seconds."

As an aside, the vignette about the *Breunig* case offers another insight about the nature of legal education that can impact students. Some areas of law, most notably Torts and Criminal Law, are filled with tragedy. In Torts, virtually every case students study involves someone who has been injured or killed. Obviously, there's nothing truly amusing about a psychotic woman experiencing a delusion that causes a car accident, but a long law school tradition exists of professors and students alike having fun with any kind of case involving weird facts. In large part, this is simply a way to get some relief from the tedium—some of the law is pretty boring. But a potential side effect of being immersed in tragic cases day after day while remaining neutral and aloof to the suffering of the real people involved is that students learn to detach themselves from their emotions, an attitude that can bleed over into their non-law school worlds. We'll talk more about this issue of emotional detachment in Chapter 12.

93. Invariably, some astute student will point out that the defendant clearly was acting unreasonably because Batman cannot fly. Superman can fly, but not Batman.

94. 173 N.W.2d at 622.

Their Courses, Especially Legal Research and Writing

Distinct from talking about the law itself and the professors who teach it, your student will be talking to you about their courses and course assignments. You may hear about things like case briefs and course outlines, the difficulty and length of the reading assignments, CALI (Computer Assisted Legal Instruction) exercises, and practice exams.

The course you are likely to hear the most about is Legal Research and Writing, which, as explained in Chapter 4, generates disproportionate complaining from law students. Specifically, you will become well-versed, whether you like it or not, in the intricacies of drafting a law office memorandum (first semester) and writing an appellate brief and presenting an oral argument (second semester).

Even non-law students can appreciate why the latter—getting up in front of a group of judges and arguing their very first case—would be a big deal to a law student. The preoccupation with the first-semester law office memorandum—"the memo"—is more difficult to fathom. A reasonable reaction would be: "How could anyone possibly care so much about one paper in one course? It's insane." Yes! You're getting it now. Law school makes people insane.

I asked students to explain why the law office memorandum is so all-consuming and they responded with several reasons. First, as mentioned previously, the disproportionate workload per credit hour awarded in Legal Research and Writing compared to other courses causes a lot of griping. Also, the legal writing memo is, as one student said, "the first opportunity to create something that is our own." Law school does not offer many outlets for creativity. It's not like the law office memorandum throws the door open for prose stylists or performance artists. Strict rules regulate just about every aspect of the memo, including structure, length, even font size and margin widths. But still, as the student said, it is the first and often the only opportunity students get in the first semester to make something that is their own.

Along the same lines, the memo is a law student's "first turn-in homework," as one student called it. In their other first-year courses, students just read cases, day after day. Diligent students prepare case briefs for each case, but these are not turned in to the professors. They also spend tons of time preparing course outlines, but same thing: these are not turned in.

And last, but certainly not least, the memo not only gets turned in, "It's graded!" Because law students receive no other evaluative feedback during the semester, students become consumed by their memo feedback. So be prepared to be barraged with discussion about the memo even though it is probably among the least interesting law school topics to outsiders. As one spouse put it: "I don't really care when his memo is due or how many pages it has to be!"

Co–Curricular Activities

Late in the first year, your student may start talking about law review and/or moot court, the two major law school co-curricular activities that play such a large role in resume- and credential-building. Both are described in Chapter 2. If your student ends up participating in one or the other or both, those activities will become all-consuming in and of themselves. As one partner decried:

> In terms of my student going "over the top" in their obsession with law school, the moot court phase and the selection of her Note topic for law review both come to mind. With moot court, she rehearsed those arguments so many times I was repeating them myself. And if she changed her topic one more time for that dang law review Note, I was going to pull my hair out.

General Complaining and Whining

In addition to all of the above, you'll hear a lot of general griping about the everyday trials and tribulations of being a law student, of which there are many. They can include: the horrible parking situation; difficulties with the financial aid and career placement offices; classrooms that are too hot or cold; classes that start too early or end too late; the heavy, expensive casebooks and the expensive study aids needed to understand them; sleep deprivation; gaining weight from sitting at a computer all day and night while living on junk food or losing weight from being too stressed out to eat properly; too many stairs to go up and elevators that don't work or take too long; computers that crash and printers that malfunction or run out of paper or ink; having to wait too long for grades to be released ... the list could keep going.

What Loved Ones Find Most and Least Interesting About Law School

I asked loved ones of law students to describe which law- and law school-related topics they find most interesting and which they find least interesting. Their answers were a hodgepodge.

As for most interesting, they listed: "comical mannerisms or quotations from professors," "inside jokes about class-mates," "learning how our legal system works and arguing with him when a part of it seems broken or out of sync," "law school gossip," "weird cases like the woman who went to get her clock fixed and had the crazy clock man come on to her,"[95] "the quirky professors and annoying students," "the HILARIOUS case where the five-year-old boy pulled the chair out from underneath the old lady and she took the kid to court,"[96] "Labor Law and Torts because they have some intersection with my work," "how cutthroat these students are," and "how law school has made watching *Law and Order* with my wife a completely different experience."

The list of the most uninteresting topics included: "Civil Procedure," "her research and writing homework," "stories about professors doing their 'bad cop' weeding out of stu-dents," "listening to her expressions of self-doubt as she prepared for her oral argument," "the repeated complaints about law school's difficulty," "any conversations about the cute boys or professors," "the dry and boring legal doc-trines," and "anything he prefaces with 'You probably won't find this interesting, but....'" And you gotta love this answer: "I'm least interested in hearing about the law when I get into a disagreement with my husband."[97] One partner had a somewhat longer list of uninteresting law school topics:

95. W. Union Tel. Co. v. Hill, 150 So. 709 (Ala. Ct. App. 1933) (woman suing Western Union for assault when employ-ee who was supposed to fix the clock at her place of business reached out across the counter and said, "If you will come back here and let me love and pet you, I will fix your clock").

96. Garratt v. Dailey, 279 P.2d 1091 (Wash. 1955) (famous Torts case in which elderly woman successfully sued five-year-old child for battery for pulling a chair out from under her, resulting in a fractured hip).

97. For more on how law school can cause students to be more argumenta-tive and overly analytical during discus-sions, see Chapter 12.

Least interesting? I don't know if I have the time to write it all down. Torts cases, Civil Procedure, Property, Estates and Trusts ... eyes glazing ... case law, Secured Transactions, statutes, codes, zzzzzzzzzzzzzzzzzzzzzzz ... Business Organizations, Income Tax ... seriously, stop. Just reading some of the pages of my husband's books make my eyes and my brain hurt.

How Loved Ones React to Law School Talk (and How You Should React)

If you find that all the law school-talk makes you feel left out, you will have lots of company. Here's what some significant others had to say about that:

● I get frustrated at times when we are hanging out with a large group of law school students. They do tend to talk mostly about teachers, classmates, and cases that I know nothing about. I have expressed this frustration to my husband.

● I met some of her friends at a law school social event who were nice and it was an honor to meet them. But, of course, they were all talking "law" or about things that happened in class. Not only did I not know what they were talking about, at times they were laughing hysterically and I did not understand what was so funny. All I can say is thank God for the iPhone.

● The only time I have socialized with his law school friends, we met for dinner downtown one Saturday night. Out of the group of seven, I was the only one not in law school. I'd say 70 percent of the conversation revolved around classes, classmates, assignments, and professors. The other 30 percent was about evenly split between them apologizing to me for only talking about law school and them begging me to tell them what was going on in the "world out there."

Some loved ones react to talk about law school by tuning it out. More than one partner to a law student reported incidents of "eyes glazing over" or similar reactions:

Saying that most students "love to talk about the law and law school" would be a gross understatement.... I can't begin to tell you the least interesting thing, mainly due to the fact that I have this innate ability to "tune out" things that I can tell wouldn't interest me. This is usually the case, I realize, when I'm asked, "So what do you think about that?" and I'm unable to recall even the slightest detail of whatever law synopsis I was just told.

Many loved ones get frustrated by the flood of law talk. They don't understand the compulsion and just want it to stop:

As I am sitting there enjoying myself drinking a beer, engulfed in my awesome video games, I hear this noise in the background. It begins to get louder. I realize it is my wife talking about case briefs. I normally don't pay attention. This even goes on during all television shows. Despite the fact that at some point she realizes I am not paying attention, she still goes on. I don't mind talking about law school with you, but not all the time. It shouldn't rule your life. Have a real conversation with me every once and a while!

Other loved ones, however, report that they willingly listen to anything their student has to say. Even if they don't find it to be comprehensible or particularly interesting, they're happy that their student is excited:

• Just because I find some of the things my husband tells me to be uninteresting does not mean I don't want to hear them. I know talking through these topics helps my law student get a functional/working knowledge, which means more to me than my level of interest.

• Least interesting: Nothing really! My student usually only tells me things that excite him, which excites me because there are only a few things on this planet that excite him. Wink! Wink!

• My first response is that I am interested in any topic that excites her, which can change from day to day depending on the class or the actual lessons or cases being learned.

To the extent you can stand it without feeling the need to imitate Edvard Munch's famous painting, The Scream, try to be a good listener to your student. He or she is *excited*, one of the most heart-warming of all emotions to witness in a loved one. Help promote and sustain that excitement. It won't, unfortunately, last forever.

Your student is also highly stressed out. If you aren't there to listen to them, they'll go to their classmates or, worse, repress themselves. Of course, there's nothing wrong with law students turning to other law students to talk about what they have in common. It makes sense. They're all in it together. Let them talk themselves silly, as they often do. Everyone has individual interests that are more easily shared with others with the same passion.

But law school is more than a hobby or interest or even a typical job. As has been said, it's a whole new way of life. As a 2L put it, "Non-law school loved ones should understand that the law student probably feels like law school is a life or death situation, even though they know it is really not." The inability or unwillingness of non-law student loved ones to share in the law school experience is part of what pushes law students closer together and possibly farther away from their non-student relationships.

Being a good listener may even help your student with their academic success. Several students reported that their attentive loved ones helped them not only emotionally, but academically:

• My partner always listens patiently and tries to ask relevant questions even when she's obviously confused. Her patience gave me the opportunity to verbalize my thoughts on the law, which helped me to understand the law better. I think she knew it would benefit me just to talk about it, and I'm thankful she was willing to lend her ear.

• I think that reading cases aloud to a tolerant and curious loved one is the best study tool there is. It forces the student to explain what's going on whenever there's a legal term or a confusing procedural history, and the loved one gets to kind of understand what type of things the student is learning. It's wonderful.

* * *

Here's cause for a sigh of relief: As students progress through law school their conversation about the law and law school usually diminishes. At the beginning, when everything is fresh and exciting to them, students will likely want to talk about, well, *everything*, as I started out saying. As the excitement subsides and the student realizes that most non-law students don't really care about law school, their conversational preoccupation with it decreases. A 1L explained:

> In the beginning of law school I found myself talking about Torts cases all the time because they are the most interesting to people outside of the school. My husband liked to hear about Contracts as well. After a while though the cases wore out their welcome, and now no one wants to hear about school! Now when they ask how it is going, all they really want to hear is "good."

In the meantime, nothing said here should be misconstrued as a free pass to the student to wear down everyone around them with non-stop legal blather. Law students have an obligation to: (1) restrain themselves from nonstop talk about law school; (2) make a determined effort to include you in their law school social circle and insist in those settings that the talk not always revolve around law school; and (3) when they are talking about law school, to explain things on a level that permits an interested listener to understand what the heck they're saying.

CHAPTER 9

EIGHT THINGS TO **NEVER** SAY
TO A LAW STUDENT

Poor, poor pitiful you.[98] You're going to be stuck with this lunatic law student who will be stressing out about everything under the sun and moon and when you try to help by being reassuring, the student might bite your head off. That's just one of the issues addressed in this chapter listing eight things never to say to a law student. Law students can be touchy little creatures. Sometimes you have to walk on pins and needles around them when their stress levels are at their zenith, such as, for example, every single day of the first year. Sometimes you may feel like sticking those same pins and needles in their eyeballs. Read on and learn more about subjects you are better off avoiding:

1. "Don't Worry. You'll Do Fine." Encouragement. Nothing beats it. Hmm, but then why did a law student give the quoted language when asked to list things that loved ones should *never* say to a law student? And why did other students offer these eerily similar answers?

- How hard can it really be?
- You've got this. You have always made good grades.
- You're awesome. You'll kick their butts.

Such statements are, of course, well-meaning. They are intended as "can do" encouragement. And encouragement can help. But these types of sentiments also might frustrate or even irritate your student because the student knows they

98. *See* WARREN ZEVON, POOR, POOR
PITIFUL ME (Asylum 1976).

amount to little more than uninformed platitudes bordering on misrepresentation.

The fact is that many law students do *not* do fine. Depending on how one defines "fine," only 10–20 percent of students end up doing fine. And how hard can it really be? Harder than anything a law student has ever attempted. As for having always made good grades, nearly all law students made good grades in their previous educational experiences. That's why they got into law school. Your student might be awesome, but could still get his butt kicked. Law schools are overflowing with awesome people.

When grades were coming out for a recent semester and all the students were obsessing over them on Facebook, I noticed that someone's grandmother posted a comment, "I'm sure you did great, honey!" With all due respect, there's no way the grandmother could be sure her student did great. What if the student didn't do great? Comments like that just add more pressure on the student. I've even known students to lie about their grades to their families because they didn't want to disappoint them.

Asked to state the most important thing non-law student loved ones should know about law school, a 1L wrote:

> They should know that while it is wonderful for them to be supportive and empathetic, they should never downplay the stress and pressure the law student is going through. Saying things like "Everything is going to be okay" or "You have always gotten through it before" makes it seem like the stresses are not legitimate.

Asked if law school adds stress to relationships, a student shared this story:

> Law school has definitely added stress to my relationship. I have learned that when I have had a bad day and am stressed out about school, I want her to acknowledge what I am going through and be supportive, but the worst thing that she can do is to tell me not to worry and that I am going to do great. While I know she means well, her false sense of confidence drives me crazy. For example, about a month before exams in the spring of my 1L year, I accidentally saved my Contracts outline over my Criminal Law outline

(about fifty pages), which I had not yet backed up onto a USB drive. To put it mildly, I became hysterical and tried frantically for hours to recover the file. The entire time, my loved one was trying to keep me calm and reassure me that everything was going to be alright. She even offered to retype the outline for me. While I knew she meant well and was only trying to help me in my state of panic, I yelled at her, telling her that her retyping my outline was not going to help me and that I was going to fail my exam because there was no way I could redo the outline properly before the exam. As it turned out, I spent ten hours the following day recreating my outline. My loved one stayed very quiet the next day and only stuck her head in my office to see if I needed anything to eat. It all turned out fine and I did very well on the exam, but in that moment of panic, it seemed as though the world was caving in and no one really understood the magnitude of what happened and what it could mean for my grade on that exam.

Instead of saying things like, "Don't worry. You'll do fine," say something like: "I've been reading in this book about how tough law school is. Wow. I honestly had no idea it was that grueling or competitive. Hang in there and do the best you can. That's all you can do." Or do what the above student's partner did on day two of the Disappearing Outline Crisis: offer to help, but otherwise just stay quiet and out of the way.

2. "Remember, It's Only a Test." In the same vein, come exam time, do not make the common mistake of telling your law student that their final exams are "only tests." If you ignore this advice, I highly recommend practicing a defensive ducking maneuver in advance for when the student lobs a casebook in your direction. Again, we have another well-intentioned sentiment—one delivered with the goal of getting the student to keep things in perspective—that can cause an adverse reaction. While you're offering reassurance, your student's amygdala, the almond-shaped portion of the brain that processes emotions, including fear, may be hearing and thinking way more than you're saying:

It's just another test. Keep it in perspective. Don't let the fact that YOUR ENTIRE LIFE depends on passing make you nervous. So what if you FAIL? Feelings of FAILURE AND WORTHLESSNESS can be dealt with by qualified MENTAL HEALTH PROFESSIONALS. They have excellent MEDICATION these days for DE-PRESSION. Don't worry about how you're going to PAY BACK YOUR STUDENT LOANS if you FLUNK OUT OF LAW SCHOOL. Sure, the lender may SUE YOU, but if you don't have a job, you won't have any money, so look at the BRIGHT SIDE. And there are always jobs available in the FOOD SERVICE SEC-TOR. So relax! It's just another test.

A law school exam is not just another test for the reasons already discussed: (1) Under the single-exam format, every-thing rides on that one exam; and (2) Grades and correspond-ing class rank are crucially important in law school, more important than in other educational disciplines.

3. "Maybe You Weren't Meant to Be in Law School." From the other end of the spectrum are loved ones who do just the opposite. Instead of seeking to offer reassur-ances, as unhelpful as they might be, the person accepts the student's panic as justified, making them feel even worse. Here are some samples of what I'm talking about:

Student: I can't do this! I'm going to flunk out.

Other: Not everyone is good at everything. Maybe you weren't meant to be in law school.

Student: You wouldn't believe how dumb I sounded in class today. I gave the stupidest answer ever spoken in a law school classroom!

Other: Maybe no one was paying attention.

Student: My memo is crap! I can't write at all. I'm the world's worst writer.

Other: Maybe the university offers remedial writing classes you could take.

People who give these kinds of responses to problems are just as well-meaning as the people who freely dispense reas-surance. They tend to be analytical people who accept what people tell them at face value and try to reason ways around problems when confronted with them. Thus, their responses are often combined with advice-giving, another no-no for people not well-versed in the situation.

When your student starts freaking out about things and depicting the situation in the most dire light possible, they often are simply catastrophizing and wanting you to reassure them that the world is not really ending. Just listen sympathetically and point out that things most likely are not as bad as they seem. This tip may sound contradictory to what I said above, and admittedly there can be a fine line between giving empty assurances on the one hand and buying into the student's catastrophizing on the other. But there is a difference. For example, reasonable responses to the above samples could include:

Student: I can't do this! I'm going to flunk out.

Other: I really doubt that. From what I've been reading, only a very small percentage of people flunk out of law school, less than 10 percent. I think you're probably just catastrophizing unnecessarily.

Student: You wouldn't believe how dumb I sounded in class today. I gave the stupidest answer ever spoken in a law school classroom!

Other: I'm sure a lot of students feel that way every day. I doubt if it's true.

Student: My memo is crap! I can't write at all. I'm the world's worst writer.

Other: I've read your writing and you're a good writer. It's probably more about learning to write in this new format they're teaching you.[99]

While such answers do constitute a kind of reassurance, they are more restrained and more likely to be accurate statements than unfounded affirmations such as "You'll do fine."

---

99. Of course, sometimes giving blunt advice—such as seeking help from the university writing center—is a good idea. Obviously, it depends on whether the student really has an issue with something and needs help or is just venting and seeking reassurance.

4. "Is That the Best You Could Do?" The most objectionable brand of feedback is anything questioning why the student didn't perform better than he or she did. This is a much worse offense than giving too many assurances or too much advice. Law school victories are few and far between. High grades and other accolades are hard to come by. As has been noted, the fact that a student has received *A*s her entire life is not a reliable predictor of how the student will perform in law school. Many students with chart-topping undergraduate grades become only average law students.

If your student performs well *by law school standards*, don't rain on her parade by suggesting she could or should have done better. Receiving a *B* in a law school course or on a legal writing assignment, for example, is a great achievement. In law school, *B* is the new *A*. Simply giving a good answer in class can make a student's day.

If your student comes home thrilled about an accomplishment—*any* accomplishment (a good grade, a good answer in class, finding a good parking space)—trust that she knows enough about law school to have good reason to be excited and share in her joy and sense of achievement, even if you don't understand what all the fuss is about. Reply to any good news, no matter how insignificant it may seem to you, with: "That's fantastic! I'm so happy for you!"

Law school, as we'll discuss more fully in Chapter 10, crushes self-esteem on its own. You don't want to render an assist.

5. "Do You Really Have to Work on That To-night?" It will be very tempting to pose this or similar questions to your student, especially if the student is your significant other. You are likely to feel neglected by your student, as future chapters will discuss. Don't take it personally. Many loved ones of law students find it unfathomable that their student has to work so hard.

Undergraduate students may have to burn the midnight oil to cram for an exam or meet a paper deadline, but those are only occasional events. For law students, every day and night are like that. They can't put off or skip a night preparing for the next day's classes. Remember, they could get called on and embarrassed in front of a large group of people. The professor may even dock their grade if they are unprepared. Most important, a law student cannot fall behind and have any hope of excelling in law school. The material is too difficult and voluminous to play catch-up.

I still remember my then wife and her family struggling to understand why I couldn't participate in a relaxing Thanksgiving with them during my first year. With that first set of exams closely following Thanksgiving, my main thanks that year, sorry as it may sound, was having four days without classes or other interferences to work on exam prep. Don't be surprised to find your student acting similarly.

Don't harass your student about working too hard. Not only can it cause friction in the relationship, but if the student gives in out of love or guilt, you could be hurting their chances for success. Instead, be proud of them for their commitment and perhaps newfound work ethic. Remember, law school is only temporary. Chapter 11 discusses the workload issue in more depth.

6. "What Kind of Lawyer Do You Want to Be?" This seems like an innocuous and quite logical question. But it can make students antsy because nearly all of them will lack an answer for it, and hearing the question repeated over and over can stress them out because they feel that they *should* have an answer for it. You will figure this out early on, but you could help your student by explaining to family members or friends not to pester the student with this question, which is otherwise likely to arise at every family gathering. In response to a survey question regarding satisfaction with their decision to come to law school, a student wrote he was happy with his career decision, but added: "I just wish that when everyone asked what kind of lawyer I want to be I had an answer. When I answer with 'I don't know,' they look at me like I have been wasting my time. That is really getting annoying."

Some students have a vague idea of the kind of law they want to practice when they apply to law school, but those ideas frequently get shoved aside. Often this occurs simply because students don't really know much about the law or legal profession before they get to law school. Many discover that the field they were interested in isn't so appealing after all, or they develop a passion for a different type of law or law practice they didn't know existed.

Many lawyers' career paths end up being determined purely by fortuitous circumstances, such as where they happen to land a job. My older brother became one of the most prominent bankruptcy attorneys in the country, listed in that field in the *Best Lawyers in America* book. I once asked him how he ended up as a bankruptcy lawyer. He said that when he took his first job at a large law firm, he was assigned an office that just happened to contain the law firm's set of *Collier on Bankruptcy*, a multi-volume treatise that is the bible of bankruptcy law. Other lawyers started coming into his office asking him bankruptcy questions simply because he had the set of *Collier*'s in there. He said he started looking up answers to the questions and the next thing he knew he was a bankruptcy lawyer.

Students feel like they should know what they want to do. They come to me all the time agitated about it. "Professor, is something wrong with me? I have no idea what kind of lawyer I want to be. And people keep asking me and that makes me feel like I'm missing something." I tell them not to worry, that there's no reason they should know the answer because they haven't been exposed to enough yet. Often, they won't figure it out until they graduate and start practicing. I didn't find my ultimate career path until six years after graduation.

7. "Do You Have a Job Yet?" This one applies mostly to upper-level students, although it can also apply to second-semester 1Ls looking for their first summer legal job. Even many top students don't land jobs until close to or after graduation. Many others don't find jobs until after they take and pass the bar exam, several months after graduation. Good legal jobs have been particularly hard to come by in the aftermath of the economic downturn that began in 2008, which battered the legal profession along with every other job sector.

Students are keenly aware that they don't have jobs and that they need one. Asking them whether they have a job just puts them on the spot and embarrasses them. I have to plead guilty to frequently asking this question of 3Ls who I run into in the halls, mainly as a way to make small talk. But I stopped after getting this comment from a research assistant: "I would add to this chapter's list: *'Do you have a job yet?'* EVERYONE asks me this and it is really annoying because, of course, the answer is 'no.' " (I'm happy to report she subsequently found a great job.) Of course, if you're close to a student, you will know whether they have a job, but family members and other friends might not, so it wouldn't hurt to warn them that this can be a touchy subject.

8. "Have You Heard the One About the Lawyer, the Shark, and the Pornographer?" Everywhere lawyers and law students go, people want to tell us lawyer jokes or otherwise bash our profession. True story: I went on a canoeing trip with a group of law professors. You can imagine what a rollicking adventure that was. The woman at the canoe rental place asked what I did and I said, "Law professor." Without hesitating, she said, "I hate lawyers." Without hesitating, I said, "I hate people who rent canoes." She was shocked and appalled I would say something so rude. Although the irony escaped her, I felt good about standing up for my profession. Plus, I really do hate people who rent canoes.

Seriously, the legal profession is the only occupation in the world where people, even complete strangers, feel completely comfortable denigrating your life's avocation to your face. Think about it. Would you make butt-crack jokes to your plumber? Kid your doctor about medical malpractice suits? No, but lawyers get it all the time.

Lawyer jokes are so plentiful that there are even lawyer jokes about lawyer jokes, as in: "How many lawyer jokes are there? Answer: Only three. The balance are documented case histories."[100] Law professor Marc Galanter estimates that 500–1000 lawyer jokes are in circulation.[101]

Unlike the other items listed in this chapter, lawyer jokes may not bother your student. I came up with this one on my own. Your student may laugh at lawyer jokes. He may even tell them. Sometimes students tell me lawyer jokes, or try to before I cut them off, explaining that I don't like lawyer jokes and they shouldn't either. It's not because I don't have a sense of humor. It's because lawyers have a hard enough time getting a fair trial in the court of public opinion.

100. MARC GALANTER, LOWERING THE BAR: LAWYER JOKES AND LEGAL CULTURE 3 (2005).

101. *Id.* at 15. Galanter's interesting book analyzes "humorous" lawyer portrayals in nine categories, including: "corrupters of discourse," "economic predators," "fomenters of strife," "betrayers of trust," "enemies of justice," "allies of the devil," "morally deficient," "objects of scorn," and "candidates for elimination." *Id.* at 16.

An ABA study of public perceptions of lawyers found that "lawyers have a reputation for winning at all costs, and for being driven by profit and self-interest, rather than client interest." They are perceived as "greedy," "manipulative," and "corrupt."[102] In a 2010 Gallup poll of integrity rankings, participants were asked to rate the honesty and ethical standards of twenty-one professions. Only 17 percent of respondents ranked lawyers as having "very high" honesty and ethical standards.[103]

While no empirical evidence exists, it stands to reason that the public's overt disdain for lawyers contributes to lawyers' documented heightened states of psychological distress, depression, and substance abuse. Research shows that people are much happier in their jobs when they feel they are doing something that matters.[104]

Everyone wants to believe they make a positive difference in this world, and lawyers really *do* make a positive difference. The problem is that a lawyer's job often necessarily involves hurting one party while seeking to help another. This is, in fact, my primary theory as to why lawyers are more unpopular and easily susceptible to personal attack than, say, doctors. In their professional capacity, doctors are always trying to help people. They may not always do a perfect job of it or carry it out with the most pleasant of demeanors, but their assignment every day when they get to work is to treat the sick and heal the injured. Lawyers are always trying to help people too, but only *some* of the people involved in a dispute. Their ethical responsibility to zealously champion their client's interests implies a subsidiary duty to defeat, some might say hurt, the opposing party. As one legal commentator put it in comparing lawyers and doctors: "Imagine if it worked like that with doctors. One doctor tries to heal you while the other tries to make you sicker. How popular would doctors be then?"[105]

Certainly, no one wants to travel through life thinking they cause only harm. If everywhere you turned, people

102. *See Public Perceptions of Lawyers: Consumer Research Findings*, SECTION OF LITIG., AM. BAR ASS'N, 7 (Apr. 2002).

103. Jeffrey M. Jones, *Nurses Top Honesty and Ethics List for 11th Year,* GALLUP (Dec. 3, 2010), http://www.gallup.com/poll/145043/nurses-top-honesty-ethics-list-11–year.aspx.

104. LEVIT & LINDER, *supra*, at 83.

105. *Hate Lawyers?*, Albany Lawyer (May 7, 2009), http://albany-lawyer.blogspot.com/2009/05/hate-lawyers.html.

trashed your profession, called you sleazy, and compared you to a shark, you'd probably feel pretty lousy. Law students should be encouraged to honor their new profession, not smear it.

* * *

Like I started the chapter saying, poor you. It's hard to honor some of the advice in this chapter without violating other parts, as shown by this example from a 2L:

> The first law exam I ever took was Contracts and I walked out of the room firmly believing that I had bombed the exam. For two days my wife tried to console me that I hadn't done badly. She did a very good job at first, but then she made me upset when her consolation shifted to telling me that it wasn't a big deal if I did poorly on the exam because "really in the long run, how important is it?"

So the spouse couldn't win either way. At first, she tried to convince him that he really hadn't done poorly on the exam (he hadn't, by the way). When that didn't seem to be getting the job done, she switched gears to accepting that, okay, maybe he really did bomb the exam, but that wouldn't be the end of the world. That didn't work either.

Naturally, you are going to want to support your law student, especially after reading about all the stresses weighing on them. It would be abnormal not to want to comfort them. And giving comfort is a good thing. But in many situations, the best course of action may simply be to be a good listener and let the student vent or even cry.

Once again, my research assistants proved that they are at the top of their classes for good reason: they're smart and astute. Here's what one had to say after reading this chapter:

> Taking this chapter as a whole, it is hard to think of what one could safely say to a law student in the middle of a freak-out, but it is really not fair for anyone to have to walk on eggshells all the time. I think the best thing to do is probably to give a reassuring hug and an offer of help—offer to bring supper to the student a couple nights a week in the library so they don't have to worry about how to eat; try to listen to their problems and offer advice if they ask; see if they need a flashcard buddy or someone to practice their oral argument on; just ask how you can help.

CHAPTER 10

THE DARKER SIDE: ANXIETY, DEPRESSION, SELF-DOUBT, AND SUBSTANCE ABUSE IN LAW STUDENTS

PRODUCT WARNING: You may find this chapter and parts of the next two chapters to be disheartening. A law professor friend who read them wrote, "This is breaking my heart. I had no idea students were struggling like this. I remember we were all so 'chill' back in law school." Knowing her personality, maybe she was "chill." Me, not so much, at least in the first year. She added, "Maybe it's because we didn't have to worry about getting jobs like today's students." She's correct that the tough legal job market, discussed in the next chapter, is aggravating stress in law students. But the studies about law student psychological dysfunction discussed below predate the downturn in the legal job market, by decades in some instances. The studies also accord with my own stress-filled 1L year, which occurred more than thirty years ago. But, hey, we all made it through okay and your student will too. Don't let this or the next chapters cause despair. Learn from them as to what to keep an eye out for in your student, recognizing that all students are different and not everyone suffers psychological distress from law school or experiences it to the same degree.

Just months before I started law school in 1978, a new book came out: Scott Turow's *One L*. It's the classic book about law school. *One L* tells the story of Turow's experience as a first-year law student at Harvard Law School. The book scared the heck out of me at the time. I didn't really remember why until recently rereading it, when I realized that a dominant theme of the book was negative affect. I counted specific references to: fear, anxiety, stress, panic, vulnerability, self-doubt, shame and grief, wounded self-esteem, unhappiness, paranoia, embarrassment, oppression, and insanity. Turow's 1L story turned out to be my 1L story and the story of many law students since.[106]

Many law students, even successful ones, suffer disproportionately from psychological distress. One study found that 60 percent of law students consider quitting.[107] We've talked a little about stress in general terms. This chapter delves more deeply into the toll law school can inflict on the psyches of law students. It's a particularly important chapter for you because these effects can be harmful to your student, you, and your relationship together.

It's important to emphasize, as I did in the "black box" product warning[108] above, that not all law students are overly anxious or depressed. Outwardly at least, most law students seem happy to me, although appearances can be deceiving. But it is true that some students appear to be genuinely unaffected by the aspects of law school that cause other students high anxiety. Some of this can be explained genetically. Extensive happiness research shows that from 40–80 percent of a person's happiness level is determined by genetics.[109]

If your student is an easygoing, happy person by nature and continues that way in law school, be thankful for it. Also be aware, however, that some "no sweat it" law students are laidback simply because they do not care enough about law school or succeeding in it to undertake the same workload with the same motivation as some of their "peace of mind"-challenged classmates. Some of these students suffer from an

---

106. I recounted parts of my own rollercoaster 1L experience in a law review essay. *See* Andrew Jay McClurg, *Neurotic, Paranoid Wimps—Nothing Has Changed*, 78 U.M.K.C. L. Rev. 1049 (2010).

107. Marilyn Heins et al., *Law Students and Medical Students: A Comparison of Perceived Stress*, 33 J. Legal Educ. 511, 520 (1983).

108. "Black box" warnings on prescription drug products are the most potent type of warning required by the federal Food and Drug Administration. They indicate the possibility of a particularly severe side effect or other risk.

109. Levit & Linder, *supra*, at 33 (discussing studies of genetic contributions to happiness levels).

exaggerated sense of their abilities. They rarely perform at a high level.

Conversely, many of the most successful law students are obsessive-compulsive worriers. As James Hetfield of Metallica would sing, "Sad but true."[110] If your student falls into that category, use this information to comfort them. When you find them lying in a fetal position in the corner of the closet, say: "Hey, keep it up. I'm reading a book that says this could actually be a good thing!"

With that introduction, prepare yourself for some disquieting information about law students.

Anxiety and Generalized Psychological Distress

That a competitive, demanding professional degree program like law school would cause students to be anxious is no big surprise. But the situation is worse than that. Studies have found that psychological distress in law students significantly outpaces not only the general population, but other graduate student populations, including medical students.

As early as 1957 a study comparing law students and medical students found that law students scored higher on an anxiety scale, both in the first year and also at graduation.[111] A 1980s study of 232 law students and 262 medical students at the University of Arizona found that law students scored significantly higher than both the general population and the medical students in nearly every category of psychological dysfunction measured, including anxiety, depression, feelings of inadequacy and inferiority, hostility, and obsessive-compulsiveness.[112] A study of lawyers in Arizona and Washington found that 30 percent of male lawyers and 20 percent of female lawyers exceeded the clinical cut-off for measuring generalized anxiety disorder, compared to 4 percent of the general population.[113]

While law school attracts some people already inclined toward anxiety (such as over-achieving obsessive-compulsive

110. James Hetfield & Lars Ulrich, Sad but True (Elektra 1993).

111. Leonard D. Eron & Robert S. Redmount, *The Effect of Legal Education on Attitudes*, 9 J. Legal Educ. 431 (1957).

112. *See* Stephen B. Shanfield & G. Andrew H. Benjamin, *Psychiatric Distress in Law Students*, 35 J. Legal Educ. 65 (1985).

113. Connie J.A. Beck et al., *Lawyer Distress: Alcohol–Related Problems and Other Psychological Concerns Among a Sample of Practicing Lawyers*, 10 J.L. & Health 1, 49–50 (1995).

types), evidence suggests a causal relationship between law school and psychological dysfunction. A later study of University of Arizona law students found that law students begin school with psychopathological symptoms similar to the general population, but that those symptoms become substantially elevated during law school and stay that way after graduation. Researchers administered a battery of psychological tests to groups of law students before, during, and after their legal education. Depending on the particular symptom, 20–40 percent of the students reported significantly elevated symptoms above the normal population after starting law school for anxiety, obsessive-compulsiveness, hostility, interpersonal sensitivity, paranoid ideation, and psychoticism (social alienation and isolation).[114]

A more recent study reached similar conclusions about 1Ls.[115] Researchers administered a battery of tests to entering law students at Florida State University to measure their state of happiness, life satisfaction, physical symptoms, and depression. Their scores were compared to a set of advanced undergraduate students at the University of Missouri who took similar tests. The comparison showed that the law students began law school as a contented, normal group, with higher positive affect and life satisfaction scores than the undergraduates. By the end of the first year, however, the law students showed significant reductions in positive affect, life satisfaction, and overall well-being, and increases in negative affect, depression, and physical symptoms.

Several studies suggest that women law students suffer greater anxiety and depression and are more apt to drop out of law school than men, but other studies have found no significant gender differences. A 2000 study of students at the University of Denver, for example, found that beginning students suffered higher negative affect and depression as they progressed through the first semester, but found no gender differences. The same study found that a month before the end of the first semester, 24 percent of the students agreed or strongly agreed that they considered drop-

114. G. Andrew H. Benjamin et al., *The Role of Legal Education in Producing Psychological Distress Among Law Students and Lawyers*, 1986 AM. B. FOUND. RES. J. 225, 236 (1986).

115. *See* Kennon M. Sheldon & Lawrence S. Krieger, *Does Legal Education* *have Undermining Effects on Law Students? Evaluating Changes in Motivation, Values, and Well–Being*, 22 BEHAV. SCI. & L. 261 (2004) [hereinafter Sheldon & Krieger, *Does Legal Education have Undermining Effects on Law Students?*]

ping out of law school, but again, with no gender differences.[116]

Anxiety, ranging from mild to extreme, affects nearly all law students. The effects can be both psychological and physiological. Anxiety comes in too many forms for us to try to explore here. The American Psychiatric Association breaks anxiety down into several different disorders in the Diagnostic and Statistical Manual of Mental Disorders (usually called DSM–IV),[117] including panic disorders, obsessive-compulsive disorders, phobic disorders, and the catch-all generalized anxiety disorder. As a layperson, be on the lookout for *excessive and prolonged* worrying that appears to be *impairing* your student's ability to function. Short of a professional evaluation, you may be in the best position to identify a problem.

One reason you need to be attuned to symptoms of psychological distress is because your student may not recognize them in herself. Once I had a first-year student rush out of class thinking she was having a heart attack. I ran out after her and found her sitting on a bench clutching her chest. Her face was flushed and she was sweating and trembling. But it wasn't a heart attack. It was a panic attack. She recovered quickly after some gentle conversation and a few deep breaths.

An overly sensitive Nervous Nellie/Ned? No. She went on to be not only an outstanding law student, but a star at moot court, one of the most courageous activities known to legal education. It requires students to routinely stand before panels of judges who grill them with tough questions. Law school anxiety does not prey only on the weak. The point of the story is she had no idea she was under such stress or suffering such anxiety. Not only are people good at hiding their distress from others, we often expertly hide it even from ourselves.

Depression

Law students also suffer disproportionately higher rates of depression than the general population and other professional school students. On depression scales, 17–40 percent of

116. Pritchard & McIntosh, *supra,* at 735.

117. *See* AM. PSYCHIATRIC ASS'N, DIAGNOSTIC AND STATISTICAL MANUAL OF MENTAL DISORDERS (4th ed. 2000) [hereinafter DSM–IV].

law students in the second University of Arizona study mentioned above were found to suffer from depression,[118] much higher rates than exist among the general population. According to a 2010 nationwide survey conducted by the U.S. Centers for Disease Control, 9 percent of the U.S. adult population experiences some depression symptoms, while 3.4 percent meet the definition for clinical depression.[119] A 2000 study of University of Michigan law students found that more than half of law students showed symptoms suggestive of clinical depression by the end of their first year, and that these high levels remained throughout their law school careers.[120]

Comparing the law students' scores on the Center for Epidemiologic Studies Depression Scale to scores for other groups subject to extreme stress yielded somewhat startling results. The 50 percent of law students who scored above the depression cutoff compared to rates of 30–45 percent for unemployed people, 30–45 percent for people testing HIV-positive two weeks after they received notice, 50 percent for people experiencing the death of a spouse or marital separation in the past year, 50–60 percent for persons being treated for substance abuse, and 50–70 percent of homeless people.[121] This isn't to suggest, of course, that being a law student is as bad as or worse than experiencing the listed traumatic events, but law school can strongly push the brain's depression buttons.

As with anxiety, the gloominess pattern continues after graduation. A Johns Hopkins University study found that lawyers ranked fifth in the overall prevalence of depression out of 105 occupations.[122] When the data were adjusted to focus on the association between depression and the particular occupation (by taking into account non-occupational factors contributing to depression), lawyers moved into first place.[123] The study of Arizona and Washington lawyers men-

---

118. Benjamin et al., *supra*, at 247.

119. Ctr. for Disease Control & Prevention, *Current Depression Among Adults—United States, 2006 and 2008*, 59 MORBIDITY & MORTALITY WKLY. REP. 1229, 1231 (2010), http://www.cdc.gov/mmwr/pdf/wk/mm5938.pdf.

120. Alan Reifman et al., *Depression and Affect Among Law Students During Law School: A Longitudinal Study*, 2 J. EMOTIONAL ABUSE 93, 101 (2000).

121. *Id.*

122. *See* William W. Eaton et al., *Occupations and the Prevalence of Major Depressive Disorder*, 32 J. OCCUPATIONAL MED. 1079, 1082 tbl. 1 (1990).

123. *Id.* at 1085 tbl. 3.

tioned above found that 21 percent of male lawyers and 16 percent of female lawyers exceeded the clinical cut-off measure for depression, significantly higher than depression rates found in the general population.[124]

Symptoms of depression to watch out for in your student include:

- Loss of interest or pleasure in activities they normally enjoy
- Social withdrawal
- Reduced (or sometimes increased) appetite
- Decreased energy
- Feelings of worthlessness or guilt
- Persistent irritability or anger
- Feeling "blah"
- Brooding
- Obsessive rumination about minor failings
- Difficulty concentrating
- Memory difficulties
- Insomnia or other changes in sleep patterns
- Loss of interest/desire in sex
- Recurrent thoughts of death or suicidal ideation[125]

As is true of other types of mental distress, many students don't know they're suffering from depression. Even if they are aware of it, many choose to suffer silently. Their classmates don't know. Their professors don't know. You may not even know. If you think your student might be suffering from depression, *talk to him.* I talk to my students in class about depression and, each time, at least a couple of them contact me confidentially to thank me and say that simply having someone acknowledge the issue helped them feel less alone.

Don't dismiss expressions of depression as illogical or irrational, a common tendency in observers of depressed people.[126] The law students who experience the most psycho-

124. Beck et al., *supra*, at 49–50.

125. *See* DSM–IV, *supra*, at 349–52.

126. Phyllis W. Beck & David Burns, *Anxiety and Depression in Law Students: Cognitive Intervention*, 30 J. LE-

GAL EDUC. 270, 275 (1979–1980) ("When a non-depressed observer evaluates the thoughts of a depressed individual, he usually perceives that many of these cognitions are irrational, illogical and unreasonable.").

logical distress are sometimes the highest achievers. People with LSAT scores in the 99th percentile can be complete nervous wrecks. Are their feelings illogical? Yes, but they still feel them. Telling a law student (or anyone else) that they shouldn't be or have no reason to be feeling a certain way is counterproductive. It might only make your student clam up more.

Stay alert to your student's moods. While no substitute for a professional evaluation, a lot of good information exists on the web regarding anxiety, depression, and other psychological disorders. Visit this site run by the American Psychiatric Association for information about each type of condition: http://www.healthyminds.org/.

Most universities have counseling departments where students can obtain free, confidential counseling services. At my university, it's rumored that law students are the most common clients at the university counseling center. It might be true because the center recently began holding counseling sessions directly on the law school campus, which is located several miles from the main campus.

Tell your student there is no shame in experiencing psychological distress or seeking counseling for it. Simply unloading one's pent-up feelings to a neutral listener can be therapeutic. I've seen students who I referred to the university counseling center bounce back looking and feeling better.

Self–Doubt

I'd tell him to improve his ability to bolster her self-esteem because she's going to need it.

—Significant other's advice on how to be in a relationship with a law student

Law school is the undisputed champion of causing talented people, people who have achieved at a high level their entire lives, to almost instantly begin questioning their self-worth. As one student put it, "It seems that law school is *designed* to make the student feel unsure of himself and inadequate." The following comments, all of them quite sad, lend support to the assertion:

- Law school is where smart people go to feel dumb. It is difficult having gone through life being at the top of the academic heap to deal with the stress involved in having to lower one's expectations for performance.

- I feel like I came here being a really good public speaker and writer. I've won awards for both. Somehow, law school has managed to turn that on its head. I'm apparently a bad public speaker and a mediocre writer at best.

- My biggest change in personality is a complete loss of self-confidence and feeling of self-worth.

"Cognitive distortion" is a psychological term used to describe a condition that occurs when a person internalizes neutral or mildly negative external stimuli as signs of severe personal failure.[127] Law school establishes optimal conditions for this to occur. Everything a student does is judged and it never seems good enough. There's no such thing as a perfect answer or work product. Usually, the best affirmation a student can hope for is a "Not bad, *but* ...," with the "but" quickly overtaking and consuming the "not bad." "You write well," my legal writing instructor scribbled on the last page of my first memo in Legal Research and Writing. Hallelujah! My very first law school feedback. "But," he continued, "you made a substantive error of malpractice dimensions." Shucks.

Every word uttered is critically scrutinized. Professors often critique student classroom comments even when they wholeheartedly agree with them. It's the nature of the Socratic beast. Some students shrug it off, but many take it personally and let it diminish their self-image. As Beck and Burns said:

> As part of his internal recurring, cognitive pattern, [the student] globalizes and catastrophizes. He views any evidence of substandard performance as ... cataclysmic to himself, his friends and family. For instance, the student may evaluate his classroom performance as poor. When reciting in class, he fumbles, blanks out or is told by his professor that he is wrong. He views his inadequate performance as conclusive evidence that all his classmates are superior to him (globalizing). He

---

127. *Id.* at 273.

is convinced if he continues in school, he will humiliate himself, his friends and family (catastrophizing). He will be dropped or placed at the bottom of the class.[128]

A big part of the problem is that most law students have never before felt over-matched by their classmates. Their previous educational experiences taught them they were the best. Now comes law school, filled with smart people and administered in a way that puts one's work habits and thinking-skills on public display every day. Here's how one student described law school's bludgeoning of his self-concept:

It's hard to have this image of yourself as a Top Student crumble. I hear that from many other students, and I think that if one doesn't realize that EVERYONE is feeling this, it may seem that everyone else has it all together and you're the only one struggling. Most people who come to law school have probably heard all their lives, from first grade onward, that they are "smarter." In college, scholarships get thrown your way, you win special fellowships or work for your professors on special projects. You have this feeling of being "good" at this school thing and feeling competent. I think the Socratic method (hearing someone give an answer that seems so much more intelligent than whatever you were thinking), and the evaluation method (not having feedback through assignments and midterm tests and what not) can really mess with you. I received an email from a fellow student. She's a student I think people assume "has it all together," and she said, "I feel like I'm hanging on by my fingernails."

It's important for your student to understand that, as the student above noted, most other students are feeling the same way, even the students who appear to have it all together. Despite receiving high grades, law school shook my confidence so deeply that it took until halfway through the first year before I voluntarily raised my hand in class for the first time.

Our Property professor was everyone's favorite, a great teacher with a great sense of humor. One day he asked a

---

128. *Id.* at 274.

simple question. "What is the legal relationship of bank to bank depositor?" Several hands went up. "Bailor-bailee?" "Wrong." "Assignor-assignee?" "Wrong." "Mortgagor-mortgagee?" "Wrong." This kept going until the class had tossed out every possible combination of two words ending with "or" and "ee." All but one. I thought I knew the answer.

This was it. My moment of glory. I took a deep breath and stabbed my hand in the air.

"Mr. McClurg?"

"Lendor-lendee?"

"Wrong!"

Dang. The correct answer turned out to be debtor-creditor. Double "or"-words! Who would have thought? Another law school trick on the mind. O for 1. In *One L*, Scott Turow described a similar experience and crisis of confidence when he gave a wrong answer in Criminal Law. He said it made him feel "horribly embarrassed—worse than that, corrosively ashamed."[129]

Again, make sure your student knows he is not alone in his fears and self-doubt. Read him one of my favorite quotations from motivational educator, Stan Dale:

> It all changed when I realized I'm not the only one on the planet who's scared. Everyone else is, too. I started asking people, "Are you scared, too?" "You bet your sweet life I am." "Aha, so that's the way it is for you, too." We were all in the same boat.

Substance Abuse

Lawyers like to drink. Alcohol flows freely whenever and wherever they gather socially. Several studies have documented alcohol problems in the legal profession. A survey of North Carolina lawyers found that nearly 17 percent reported consuming three to five drinks a day. A study of Washington lawyers concluded from a random sample that 18 percent of practicing lawyers were "problem drinkers." One researcher of alcoholism among lawyers estimated that at least 15 percent of lawyers are alcoholics, compared to 7–8 percent of the general population.[130] Although the data are less exten-

---

129. TUROW, *supra*, at 103.

130. Patrick J. Schiltz, *On Being a Happy, Healthy, and Ethical Member of*

sive, statistics also show that lawyers abuse other substances. Alcohol and other substance abuse reportedly are involved in from 50–75 percent of all disciplinary actions against attorneys.[131] Small wonder that every state bar organization maintains a lawyer assistance program for substance abuse and other mental health problems.

Law students enjoy alcohol as well, no doubt, as is the case with lawyers, in part as an outlet for their stress. In one survey, more than one-third of law student respondents answered affirmatively to the question: "Do you think you drink too much?"[132] And those were the ones who recognized they had an alcohol issue. Many people don't. A George Mason University study found that 11 percent of law students experienced eight or more hangovers during the previous semester, while 36 percent experienced one to three hangovers.[133]

Substance abuse is an issue at all law schools, just as it is at all undergraduate institutions. This is not surprising since most law students are only shortly removed from undergraduate school. But the stress of law school may exacerbate drinking issues. A 1994 report by the Association of American Law Schools Special Committee on Problems of Substance Abuse in Law Schools found that alcohol consumption is a problem at all levels of law school, but that it apparently gets worse as students progress. Specifically, the report found that third-year students reported significantly higher alcohol usage than first-year students.[134]

Research shows that 75 percent of a heavy drinker's social network consists of "drinking buddies," compared to only 30 percent for normal alcohol users.[135] That's exactly what many law school friends become: drinking buddies. Law students turn to each other for mutual support and frequently cele-

an Unhappy, Unhealthy, and Unethical Profession, 52 VAND. L. REV. 871, 876–77 (1999) (collecting and reporting on these studies).

131. Betty Reddy & Ruth Woodruff, Helping the Alcoholic Colleague, PROF. LAW., May 1992, at 1, 4.

132. Heins et al., supra, at 521.

133. See Gerald W. Boston, Chemical Dependency in Legal Education: Problems and Strategies, 76 MICH. B.J. 298, 299 (1997) (discussing this study).

134. Ass'n of Am. Law Schs., Report of the AALS Special Committee on Problems of Substance Abuse in Law Schools, 44 J. LEGAL EDUC. 35, 42–43 (1994).

135. Ronald B. Cox, Jr., Alcohol Abuse and Relationships: Implications for Relationship and Marriage Education, NAT'L HEALTHY MARRIAGE RES. CTR., 3–4, http://www.healthymarriageinfo.org/docs/alcoholabuseandrelationships.pdf (citing study).

brate or drown their sorrows together—one more reason to not let your law student spouse or significant other abandon you to hang out exclusively with his or her law student buddies.

Excessive alcohol or other substance abuse is problematic for law students on several fronts, but it also can have a damaging impact on relationships. Numerous studies show a link between alcohol use and marital dissatisfaction and divorce.[136] In fact, alcohol and drug use rank third, just behind infidelity and incompatibility, as a cause of divorce.[137] On the other hand, there is good news for married couples in studies showing that marriage can have a "protective effect" on alcohol abuse,[138] in part because couples spend more time together and less time with peers (i.e., the drinking buddies).

* * *

Pretty grim chapter, but law school isn't all gloom and doom. The research just tends to make it look that way. No one has ever seriously studied the positive aspects of law school, of which there are many. In Chapter 13 students explain things they love about law school. In the meantime, a few points bear noting. First, the studies showing higher rates of psychological dysfunction in law students do not predict an outcome for any individual student. Your student may end up being completely "chill," to quote my law professor friend at the beginning of the chapter.

Also, take comfort in the fact that law school inflicts its most visceral impact on students in the first year. The old saying about law school is that "in the first year they scare you to death, in the second year they work you to death, and in the third year they bore you to death." There is definitely truth in this cliché. While the studies discussed in this chapter show that law student psychological dysfunction continues into the third year and even past graduation, the most intense whirly rides of anxiety and emotion occur in the first year, especially the first semester, when there is so much uncertainty.

After that, things settle down and life falls into a more or less normal pattern. Stressors undergo reordering in terms of priority. Panic over the Socratic method and exams is re-

136. *Id.* at 2 (citing study).   **138.** *Id.* at 4.
137. *Id.* at 3 (citing study).

placed by external worries about finding a job and paying back student loans. Indeed, the biggest problem with 3Ls from a teacher's perspective is that they become disengaged from law school. In the 2009 Law Student Survey of Student Engagement, to which more than 26,000 students at eighty-two law schools responded, one-quarter of 3Ls reported that they frequently come to class without completing their reading assignments, a relaxed approach that is far different from first-year students.[139]

My first year was marked by heavy stress. But by the third year, I was loving law school so much I didn't want to leave. Loved it so much, in fact, that I decided to come back and stay forever. As you're counting the days until your student becomes a 3L, let's consider more closely some explanations for the law school freak out.

139. LAW SCH. SURVEY OF STUDENT ENGAGEMENT, STUDENT ENGAGEMENT IN LAW SCHOOL: ENHANCING STUDENT LEARNING, 2009 ANNUAL SURVEY RESULTS 8 (2009) [hereinafter 2009 LAW SCHOOL SURVEY OF STUDENT ENGAGEMENT].

CHAPTER 11
A DOZEN LAW STUDENT STRESSORS

What exactly is it about law school that has students singing "It's just my nineteenth nervous breakdown"[140] on the nineteenth day of class? This chapter discusses twelve top law student stressors, not in rank order. Several of the items listed below have already made an appearance, although not specifically in the context of being a stress factor. Several of them are intertwined. Keep this list in mind when you're tempted to lose patience with your student.

1. Uncertainty

At the very beginning of law school, the cloud of uncertainty that envelopes students is the over-riding stressor. Several times, I've polled incoming law students with this question:

As you begin your 1L quest, what is your dominant feeling?

- Confidence
- Excitement
- Fear or anxiety
- Lack of confidence
- Pride
- Stress
- Uncertainty

---

140. *See* MICK JAGGER & KEITH RICH-ARDS, 19TH NERVOUS BREAKDOWN (Decca 1965) (Rolling Stones song with the re-frain line, "It's just your nineteenth nervous breakdown.").

"Uncertainty" is the most common answer, usually receiving as many votes as the other choices combined. Because law school is so completely different from anything students have encountered, uncertainty lurks at every turn. Researchers have long studied uncertainty as a contributor to stress. In psychological terms, uncertainty is defined as "the anticipation of a poorly defined threat."[141] Studies show that exposure to unknown potential dangers can actually be more psychologically threatening than exposure to known dangers. As two researchers put it, we tend to prefer the devil we know over the devil we don't know.[142]

Makes sense. Think of all the times in your life you dreaded something only to find it never transpired or, if it did, it wasn't nearly as bad as what you imagined. Law school is like that in many ways. The Socratic method is a good example. Many students are literally terrified of the Socratic method until they see it in action and realize that, while it can be stressful, it's not a torture device.

The stress of uncertainty subsumes many of the more specific stress factors below. Much uncertainty is generated from the uncertain nature of law itself, covered in Chapter 5. Simply figuring out the physical lay of the land and the mechanics of functioning in a new environment can cause an unsettling feeling, with questions arising over everything from "Where can I park?" to "How do I register for a TWEN site?"[143] The most oppressive uncertainty involves the performance aspects of law school: "When will I get called on?" "Am I going to embarrass myself when I do?" "Is everyone here a genius except me?" "Am I going to flunk out?"

Fortunately, the total-immersion nature of law school means that uncertainty about most aspects of law school begins diminishing quite quickly. Within just the first couple of weeks, students are visibly more relaxed. They know their way around the building. They're more comfortable in class as they start to figure out how the Socratic and case methods

141. Jacob B. Hirsh & Michael Inzlicht, *The Devil You Know: Neuroticism Predicts Neural Response to Uncertainty*, 19 PSYCHOL. SCI. 962, 962 (2008).

142. *Id.* at 966. People with neurotic tendencies experience even greater anxiety from uncertainty. *Id.*

143. TWEN stands for The West Education Network, run by Thomson West, the publisher of this book. Nearly all professors set up online TWEN sites on which they post assignments, syllabi, and other course materials.

function. They begin making friends. The professors become known quantities. Unfortunately, as discussed below, the biggest uncertainty of all—whether they can succeed and at what level—remains a mystery until the first semester is over, and the disquietude from this big question mark is always weighing on students.

2. The Socratic Method

We covered the Socratic method extensively in Chapter 6. In short, we learned that, not surprisingly, getting called on without warning in front of a large group of peers and interrogated with tough questions can be intimidating. I once surveyed a group of new students, asking the question: "What are your biggest stressors or causes of anxiety after two weeks of law school?" The first three answers I read were:

- Waiting to be called on creates a lot of stress for me. It's like you're sitting in every class knowing that it could be your name that comes up at any time and you're not completely confident in what you will say. It's like waiting on the other shoe to drop!

- I have noticed in class that when questions are left open for students to answer, I find myself going blank in my head because I am fearful that the professor will revert to the seating chart and go directly to the clueless Mr. _____. However, when the question is directed at a specific student (not me), the pressure is off and I seem to be able to come up with the right answer. I think it is a confidence issue.

- My biggest stressor is that I will be called on in class and will not have the slightest clue of the answer, or make a really off-the-wall statement. That hasn't changed because I haven't been called on just yet. Please don't call on me now that I've told you that.

Even when wielded by nice professors, the Socratic method can leave students feeling vulnerable and exposed. Everyone wants to look good in front of their peers and professors, but under the Socratic method, even well-prepared students can come across as clueless. No amount of preparation will be sufficient to answer some of the questions law professors ask. As one student described:

Law school professors essentially require students to know every aspect of every subject at every moment of every class. The ever-present anxiety of being called on to answer a question to which you do not know the answer, combined with the incredibly competitive nature of law school, creates a stressful classroom environment. While class can certainly be enlightening, thought provoking, and even enjoyable, every law student feels a little nervous when they hear the professor say: "Would you please tell us the facts of today's case, Mr. _____?"

Some students live in fear of being called on throughout law school, but for most students, after witnessing the Socratic method and especially after being called on once or twice and successfully negotiating the Socratic terrain, anxiety over the method lessens.

3. Fear of Failure/Not Meeting Personal Expectations

Every year I give my incoming students a questionnaire that asks them to name their biggest fear about law school. Failure is the most common answer. If failure is defined to mean failing to achieve and maintain the minimum GPA necessary to remain a student in good standing (generally a 2.0)—i.e., getting kicked out of law school—the picture isn't as bleak as most students imagine. Because admissions standards at most ABA-approved law schools are high, the attrition rate is low, below 10 percent at most schools.

A common variation of the failure fear is the fear of not living up to one's own expectations. This concern is much more well-grounded than the fear of being academically dismissed. As we've discussed, law schools are full of high achievers. Instead of competing against students like their undergraduate roommate who sat in the dorm room all night smoking a bong and listening to Radiohead, your student is competing against motivated, talented people with solid track records of academic accomplishment. Okay, some of them may still be smoking bongs and listening to Radiohead, but only after they've read and briefed all their cases for the next day.

Many smart people who are fine law students and who will become excellent lawyers do not get the grades they want and expect. If your student comes to law school expecting As, he or she will likely be disappointed. Except at some elite law schools where inflated grades are the norm, high grades are much harder to come by in law school than in undergraduate school or other graduate programs, even for good students. Generally, only about 10–15 percent of the students in a first-year law school class receive any form of A grade (i.e., A+, A, or A-), which translates to roughly seven to twelve A grades in an average-size first-year section of seventy to eighty students.[144]

Most students, even if they deny it, arrive at law school hoping they can be one of the top students in the class. Professor Lawrence Krieger, who researches law student well-being, asked his first-year class how many of them wanted to be in the top 10 percent of the class. Ninety-percent of the students raised their hands. As Krieger noted, herein lays a major hindrance to law student well-being. If the "want" to be on top is perceived as a "need," most everyone in the class is going to end up perceiving themselves as a failure.[145]

Get ready for your student to sustain a powerful blow to self-esteem when those first exam grades are released, and stand by ready to lend comfort and support. Your student may feel completely demoralized, in part because they don't see the connection between all their hard work and the grades they received and also because of their growing awareness of the differences in opportunities for those who receive high grades and everyone else.

The impact of receiving lower-than-hoped-for grades may be especially devastating to the current generation of students. Born to Woodstock-generation parents, many of today's students arrive at law school having been showered in self-esteem building since birth. The self-esteem movement has been carried over to schools and other institutions. One

144. Some law schools have raised their grading curves recently in an attempt to help their students better compete in the job market. In 2010, Loyola Law School Los Angeles raised eyebrows when it retroactively increased all students' grades going back several years by adding a third of a point (.333) to every grade issued. See Catherine Rampell, *In Law Schools, Grades Go Up, Just Like That*, N.Y. Times, June 21, 2010, http://www.nytimes.com/2010/06/22/business/22law.html?emc=eta.

145. Lawrence S. Krieger, *What We're Not Telling Law Students—And Lawyers—That They Really Need to Know: Some Thoughts–In–Action Toward Revitalizing the Profession from Its Roots*, 13 J.L. & Health 1, 11 (1998–1999).

study found that twice as many high school seniors had *A* averages in 2006 as in 1976.[146] Some researchers have found undesirable side effects from this constant affirmation, including an unwarranted belief that success is guaranteed in every endeavor in life regardless of one's actual abilities.[147]

Law school, which combines lower grading scales with excessive importance attached to grades, may be exactly the wrong place for such students. Give credit to the student quoted below, who saw value in law school's more honest evaluation of student performance:

> Although the soul-crippling uncertainty of the first semester is just awful, when law school does provide feedback, you know it is sincere. Our first graded assignment was in Legal Research and Writing. The assignment was to state the "Question Presented" for the law office memo. I received the lowest grade possible above a zero, as well as some mysterious comment along the lines of "Are you sure?" *What?! The assignment was just one sentence! I can't even write a sentence?* I continued from there to reach all the typical milestones: the first really stupid thing I said in class; the first disappointing exam grade; the first time a moot court judge caught me without an answer. Most of us were programmed to expect praise and reassurance for everything we did growing up, even if we couldn't actually draw, dance, catch a ball, or do any kind of math past long division. Now when I receive positive feedback, I know I actually deserve it. Law school does not always make us feel great about ourselves, but it helps us recognize our strengths while forcing us to address our weaknesses.

If those first grades bring your student down, remind them why they went to law school in the first place. No one goes to law school just to get three more years of good grades. They go there to get a law degree. All law school graduates get the same diploma, the same entry pass to the profession. It would be a misrepresentation to say grades are unimpor-

146. *See* John Keilman, *A Downside to High Teen Self-Esteem?*, CHI. TRIB., July 4, 2010, http://articles.chicago tribune.com/2010–07–04/news/ct-met-teen-self-esteem-20100704_1_self-esteem-jean-twenge-praised (mentioning this study and discussing generally the "toxic effects" of the self-esteem movement on American youths).

147. *See id.*

tant. They open up early entryways to both internal and external law school advantages, including initial job opportunities. But in the long run, lawyers are judged not by the grades they received in law school, but by their hard work, professionalism, ingenuity, integrity, and ability to get the job done. No client goes into a lawyer's office and asks what his class rank was in law school, just as patients don't ask doctors what grades they received in medical school.

Also, one semester of grades is not determinative of a student's long-term grade fate. This is important to emphasize to your student because too many students give up after their first disappointing set of grades. They accept they are not going to perform at a high academic level and adjust their effort downward accordingly. Tell your student that law school is a marathon, not a sprint. It's *way* too early to give up after just one semester. For people who continue working hard, grades generally go up. For people who start working less, grades generally go down. Urge your student to stay in the race and not slacken the pace.

Students not only worry about failing to meet their own expectations. They want to meet yours too. Many students have told me they felt they let their families down by not getting good grades. Stockpile some encouragement in reserve for the end of the semester so you can give your student a boost when grades come out.

4. Fear of Not Understanding the Material

Another major stressor, especially at the very beginning of law school, is fear of not understanding the material. This anxiety is more preliminary and specific than a generalized fear of failure. Students worry that they will arrive in this new academic world and find that the legal rules they're supposed to be learning are unintelligible ciphers and, worse, that they will be the only one without a decoding manual. This fear is reflected in answers to my "greatest fear" question such as: "That I would be the only person to not understand the reading" and "That everyone will 'get it' and I won't."

I'm happy to report that this fear is also overblown. Coming into law school, the law naturally seems inaccessible and unfathomable because it's a complete unknown. Some of the first cases read in law school are old and written in an archaic style, confirming students' worst fears about not being able to grasp the law. Below is an excerpt from a famous Torts case decided in 1616 by the King's Bench in England that beginning students often are assigned in the first week of law school. The case, *Weaver v. Ward*,[148] is the earliest known judicial decision expressly recognizing that a defendant might not be liable for damages for a purely accidental injury occurring without any fault on his part. But it's doubtful many students ever figure that out from the opinion itself, which reads like this:

> And upon demurrer by the plaintiff, judgment was given for him; for though it were agreed, that if men tilt or turney in the presence of the King, or if two masters of defence playing their prizes kill one another, that this shall be no felony; or if a lunatick kill a man, or the like, because felony must be done animo felonico; yet in trespass, which tends only to give damages according to hurt or loss, it is not so; and therefore if a lunatick hurt a man, he shall be answerable in trespass; and therefore no man shall be excused of a trespass (for this is in the nature of an excuse, and not of a justification, prout ei bene licuit), except it may be judged utterly without his fault.

Er, could you run that by us again? Why couldn't those old English judges speak ... well, English? Modern opinions aren't nearly as bad. Once students get past the moldy-oldies still included in casebooks because of their historical significance, the reading gets easier because most modern judges write lucidly in plain English. If your student begins freaking out over cases like this, show him the sample judicial opinion (*Katko v. Briney*) included as an appendix at the back of the book. It might be fun to read it with him and then ask him questions about it.

As with so many other life challenges that seem overwhelming when we first encounter them, learning the law becomes less intimidating with each passing day as students begin figuring out basic legal terms and procedures. One of my favorite parts of teaching 1Ls is watching the satisfaction, even joy, as the light bulbs go on, as the students start to

---

148. 80 Eng. Rep. 284 (K.B. 1616).

realize, "Hey, I really can understand this stuff. I really can learn the law!"

Don't get me wrong. A lot of the material is difficult and not all students grasp the law equally well. Law school may be the only educational discipline where students feel compelled to buy "study aids"—extra books that explain the law in clear terms—to help them understand what they're supposed to be learning from their assigned casebooks. But most students who put in the necessary effort will understand most legal principles. Reassure your student that she has been carefully prescreened by the law school admissions committee, which has determined she possesses the ability to understand law.

5. Competitive Atmosphere

Even if they don't admit it (perhaps even to themselves) most law students are quite competitive. Often they are that way by nature, but even if they aren't, law school forces them to be competitive by making nearly all of the available prizes and accolades—grades, law review, research assistant positions, scholarships, first jobs—into a competition. My current institution, the University of Memphis law school, is a relatively small law school with about 400 students. Sitting at a recent commencement ceremony at which 127 students graduated, I counted the number of honors and awards (which included the top exam-grade awards for each course) listed in the program: 398! Most of them were distributed among a relatively small group of students.

Asked at the end of their first year to name one thing they wished they had known when they started law school, two students said:

- I think that competition is the white elephant in the room in terms of discussion of the law school experience. Everyone is in a marathon race against the other. Everyone is aware of this—some simply care more than others.... There are people who will go out of their way not to help you lest they give up some tiny thread of comparative advantage.

- To believe people when they warn how competitive law school is. Looking back, college was like running a 5K race for a cause where everyone wanted you to succeed. People are there along the way giving you water and cheering you on. Even the slowest runner is praised for participation. Law school feels more like roller derby. While racing to the finish line, your competition is beating on you, intentionally tripping you up and pulling your hair out all in an effort to pass you by.

Boy, that doesn't sound good at all. But wait. Compare the two comments above with these two:

- I love that everyone is so supportive. The horror stories that I have heard so far have proven to be completely false. After class the first time I got called on in Civ Pro and had the spotlight on me, numerous people came up to me and told me how well I did. Later that afternoon at the lockers someone who I hadn't even noticed before said, "Congrats for doing so well today." I don't think that I will ever forget how good other people made me feel when I didn't even think I did well to begin with. Along with the support of my classmates, it seems that the 2Ls and 3Ls go out of their way to make sure we "get it."

- I love the camaraderie among the students at law school. You really feel like you are all "in this together." One of the things I miss most from the first year is having class together with all the same people in my section. While law school can be competitive, one thing I have loved is feeling like so many of us really are rooting for each other. When we graduate, I know I will have a whole cheering section out there.

Are these folks talking about the same place? The true state of competitive affairs probably lies somewhere between the two extremes. In general, my experience as a professor has been that ruthlessness is uncommon and that, overall, law students are quite supportive of one another. I frequently observe students going out of their way to help their classmates, sometimes to extraordinary lengths. But there is no denying that competition permeates law schools. Even among friends, with everyone vying for the same limited laurels, an inherent tension exists between being supportive and being competitive. A first-year student explained it well:

Some days my classmates are comrades, sharing in a tough experience together. Other days they are my worst enemies, silently laughing at how much better prepared they are, how much more easily they understand the material, and how I'll never be able to achieve my goals because I can't compete evenly against them. In short, even the good things in law school can be twisted by the "bad things."

The competitive environment will add to your student's stress level because competition, by its nature, implies "winners" and "losers." I asked students what they love about law school and one wrote:

Law school is littered with competitions and awards. Almost every activity that a law student undertakes is incentivized with some sort of award or certificate, and I could not imagine law school without them. I am a person who has always been driven by competition and will thrive in an environment where everything is accompanied by a ranking or an award. At the commencement of the 1L year, most entering students are probably aware that every student will be ranked at the end of each semester based almost entirely on their exam performance. However, most are probably unaware that there are also awards for, to name a few, best memo, best appellate brief, highest grade in each class, best oral advocate, best moot court team, best *Bluebook* editing, and best case comment for the law review write-on competition. To an outside observer this all may seem ridiculous and superfluous. However, law school would feel less like an experience and more like just school if these competitions and awards were eliminated, and that is something I would hate to envision.

So this student *loves* the competition. But that's no big surprise because he wins all the time. He's ranked at the top of his class and has earned several of the accolades he mentioned. Would he love the competitive part as much if he was "losing" instead of "winning"? I suspect not. Well, heck, let's stop and ask him.... Okay, I just emailed him and asked. He wrote back:

I can definitely understand how the competitive nature of law school could become a source of stress and anxiety for those students whose performance does not meet their expectations. A successful student will relish the competitiveness of law school because of the benefits that inherently come with a high rank or GPA. However, a student who puts in the required effort on a daily basis throughout the course of a grueling semester but nonetheless finishes in the middle of the pack could easily start to perceive his or her rank as a constant reminder of unmet expectations.

To the extent competitiveness is an issue, it gets worse after the first semester, largely because of that first set of grades. In the first semester, everyone is in the same boat, struggling to stay afloat. The shared experience creates a communal bond. But once those first grades are released, there may be a feeling—both among some high achievers and some lower-than-hoped-for achievers—of "Hey, you're in *that* boat and I'm in *this* boat." Reading this section, a research assistant commented:

> This is definitely true. One thing that surprised me in law school was its clique-ish nature. Very early on groups of people became friends and always hung around each other. This became even more pronounced in the second semester after grades came out. It seemed that students in each clique generally received similar grades, thus reinforcing their companionship— seemed like everyone was in their own boats now.

Tell your student to compete only with himself; that is, to be the best law student he can be. In the end, that's all he has control over. If he works hard and earnestly, he will earn people's respect—both professors and other students—regardless of his grades.

6.   The Workload

The workload in law school is the biggest and most well-founded stressor of them all. Law school is relentless. Every day brings new cases, new rules, new complexities. Each set of rules builds on the ones before it. If a student gets lost or falls behind at step three, steps four, five, and six won't make sense either. Loved ones have a hard time understanding the enormity of the workload, which can be frustrating to students:

- The biggest thing that I think my girlfriend doesn't understand is that, unlike in undergrad, every class and assignment is important. Also, I don't need to read just for my classes, but to learn things I'll need to know after graduation. No matter how much I tell these things to her, I don't think it ever really hits home. I'm pretty sure she still thinks I'm ignoring her, but as I've tried to tell her: "I've had more homework in the first six weeks of law school than I had in the last two years of undergrad combined." Then she usually just tells me to quit whining.

• The work of a law student is never truly done. It has been extremely hard for everyone in my family to understand how in the world this stuff could monopolize me so much. It takes a lot of effort on their part to trust what I am telling them, like: "This is the hardest thing I've ever done in my life." I could study 'til the cows come home and still not understand *everything*.

• The workload is the number one thing for loved ones to understand. It is very true that the work never ends. There is always something you could be doing. Every waking moment you spend on something non-law related is a moment you could be spending studying the law. Last semester my wife had scheduled, to my dismay, an appointment the very day before the Criminal Law exam to look at an apartment we were thinking of renting. Luckily it didn't take long, but I kept quipping to her that I could feel my grade dropping with each passing moment. The people who succeed at law school are going to be the workaholics.

Students obsessing about getting called on in class or not understanding the material are worrying about the wrong things. The vast majority of the people who do not succeed in law school or who succeed at levels below their potential do so because *they weren't prepared to handle the overwhelming workload*. They get behind early ... and never catch up. Nothing, I repeat, nothing will cause your student more stress and portend of failure to meet expectations than falling behind.

Understanding the nature of the workload is crucial for a couple of reasons. First and foremost, you need to give your law student the time and space necessary to succeed. This doesn't mean giving the student permission to completely abandon you and the pre-law school life you enjoyed, but the reality of a law student's life is that they need most nights and most weekend days to prepare for class, prepare their course outlines, and work on their Legal Research and Writing assignments. Also, being cognizant of the workload will make it easier for you to not take it personally when your student seems to neglect or ignore you.

7. Lack of Feedback

"People need feedback, not a God-awful sense of impending doom!" a law student told researchers studying psychological distress in legal education.[149] The lack of feedback, attributable to the single-exam format covered in Chapter 7, is one of the great deficiencies of legal education. In a survey in which law students were asked to rank the importance of twenty-four suggested changes to legal education, "more feedback on academic process" finished second only to smaller classes.[150]

One researcher of law students has opined that "learned helplessness" contributes to stress in law students because of their inability to control their environment. Learned helplessness as a theory originally emerged from a study of lab animals exposed to electric shock. The animals were divided into three groups: animals that could turn off the shock, animals that could not turn off the shock, and animals not exposed to any shock. Subsequently, when all the animals were put in a box from which they could escape, the second group—the group that could not avoid the shock—showed little effort or motivation to escape. Their behavior was explained by the fact that they had learned to be helpless during the shock-phase of the experiment; that is, they learned that they could not control their situation "and that nothing they did mattered in terms of protecting themselves."[151] The researcher's study of law students involved administering a "helplessness scale" test to them. Several aspects of law school ranked high on the scale she used, including the Socratic method, but lack of feedback scored the highest.[152]

149. Reifman et al., *supra*, at 95.
150. Whitman et al., *supra*, at 56–57 (discussing this survey).
151. Suzanne C. Segerstrom, *Perceptions of Stress and Control in the First*

Semester of Law School, 32 WILLAMETTE L. REV. 593, 597–98 (1996).

152. *Id.* at 601–02.

It's doubtful that any other life endeavor, educational or occupational, requires one to give so much for so long without receiving any feedback, positive or negative, by which they can gauge their performance. Before that first set of grades is issued, nearly every student thinks they have a shot at doing well, *but* they also think they have a shot at flunking out. Small wonder law students live in such a maelstrom.

Think about what a bizarre situation law school is in terms of this feedback issue. Imagine accepting a new job. It's a challenging, difficult job. You work harder at it than at anything you've ever tried. You want desperately to be a success. Days pass, then weeks. You stay alert for any clue as to how you're doing, but none is forthcoming. You have no idea whether you are doing the job completely right or completely wrong. You finally get up the nerve to ask your boss: "Could you please tell me how I'm doing so far? I'm working really hard to succeed and it would help me a lot to know whether I'm doing things correctly or should be doing them differently." The boss says, "Sorry, I can't tell you that. We'll let you know something in three months."

At the end of the three months, you are told you can go online and see how you have been performing; that is, to get your "grade" (law school grades are posted online). You eagerly log on to find a statement that says: "Most of what you have done for the last three months was wrong." That is essentially how law school evaluation can work. Of course, results vary. A student might also happily discover, "Most of what you have done for the last three months was right." The point is that a student's academic performance remains a big mystery until grades are posted several weeks after the semester is over.

8.   Exams

"At one-thirty, wild now with drugs and frustration, I rolled out and began to flail at the mattress: I was *trying* to destroy myself, I shouted; I was *insuring* failure."[153] Drug rehab gone bad? Nah. Just another 1L freaking out the night before his first exam; in this case, Scott Turow, writing in his book, *One L.* Given what has been said, I'm sure you expected that exams would earn a spot on the top law student

---

153.   Turow, *supra*, at 167.

stressors list. Exams as a stress factor are closely related to the fear of failure discussed above. But fear of failure is an abstraction. Exams, and the grades that come with them, are all too real. One student described his first exams as follows:

> Law school exams were unlike anything I had ever experienced. I knew they would be hard, but after experiencing a few of them, I felt as though the professors were backhanding us across the face with their knowledge, demonstrating how little we puny students knew. One student I remember commented that our first-semester Contracts exam "Made the LSAT seem like patty-cake." Even the people who got As on that exam felt like they got Ds or Fs before grades were released.

You know the word "loom"? It means "to appear, take shape, or come in sight indistinctly as through a mist, esp. in a large, portentous or threatening form."[154] That's exactly what law school exams do. From the first day, they LOOM. Indistinct at first, but emerging through the mist and taking clearer shape day by day as students move through the semester. The stress is accentuated by the lack of feedback discussed above. Each day that passes, exams take on additional oppressive weight, such that a student who weighs 150 pounds at the beginning of the semester will be dragging 5,150 pounds around in those final days—1,000 additional pounds of heavy-duty stress per exam.

When "Time's up!" is declared after the very first exam,[155] it's a huge relief and the weight on the student is reduced by 1,000 pounds ... *until* the student walks out the door of the exam room and adds 200 pounds back on by engaging in an exam autopsy. Professors always tell students: "Don't talk about the exam when it's finished. There's nothing you can do about it. Just move on." But students never listen, and neither did we when we were students.

I still recall walking out of my first-year Criminal Law exam, feeling good, until I ran into a classmate who started talking about a big conspiracy issue that I had missed. I stood there feeling like I had just wasted the three hardest months

154. WEBSTER'S NEW WORLD DICTIONARY 797 (3d College ed. 1988).

155. That is literally how it works. Many students write feverishly until the last second, when the professor declares "Time's up! No more writing."

of my life, convinced I had flunked out of law school. This fear haunted me for the remainder of the exam period. As it turned out, I got my first *A* in law school on that exam. Once again, neurotic obsessiveness—a hallmark trait of law students—shows its limitations as a lifestyle.

What happened to me happens to most law students. One of my research assistants read the above and wrote:

> I walked out of my first ever law school exam (Contracts) utterly convinced that I had just failed. My next exam was three days later. The day after my first exam I did not study at all because I figured "What's the point? I just failed my first exam." Thankfully, I pulled myself together.

He pulled it together alright. He received an *A* on that Contracts exam. Another research assistant told a similar tale:

> My first (but not last—slow learner!) taste of the crushing emotional devastation caused by the inevitable after-test chat was after my Contracts exam. We were all talking it up, asking each other how we answered this or that question, and someone asked me, "So was it a firm offer or an option contract? I wrote about both." We'd had an essay question on the sale of a racehorse with multiple issues, a major one being whether the seller had made a firm offer or whether it was an option contract, and I completely missed the distinction, writing instead about something else entirely. I literally spent the whole next day in bed under the covers thinking about *my* options, since it was obvious law school was not working out.

She got an *A* too. The moral of these stories is not that students always get *A*s on exams they think they botched, but that students have no accurate idea how they fared on a law school exam until the grades are released. Comfort your student with these stories when they come home after an exam convinced they just flunked out of law school. Even better, do your student a gigantic favor by convincing him to leave the law school and drive straight home after each exam, not stopping to talk to anyone about the exam. One student urged an even more forceful approach:

I suggest the loved one do *anything* they can to prevent after-test chat. Be waiting outside the room, make dinner reservations, call the student every five minutes when the exam is about to end. *Anything.* If they don't, they'll eventually deal with the consequences.

Once the exams are over, nothing can be done to change them. Worrying, wishing, hoping—it's all wasted effort. Tell your student to look to tomorrow, not yesterday.

Despite the post-mortem second-guessing described above, overall, with each passing exam, the weight does get lighter and lighter, until walking out of that last exam, a student feels so light he might float away. But then the waiting kicks in, and as rocker Tom Petty sang, "The wa-aa-iting is the hardest part."[156] Okay, that's not true. Studying for and taking the exams is the hardest part, but the waiting is still tough. It takes weeks for exam grades to come out. Sometimes students have to start their second semester without having yet received their first-semester grades.

It may appear that your law student is literally going insane around exam time. As with wild animals, psychiatric patients, and angst-filled teenagers, it's often best to keep a safe distance from law students during exams, except maybe to slip them a tray of food through the bars of their cage (i.e., their study room or corner). No amount of comforting is going to relieve the student at this time. It may even backfire, as covered in Chapter 9.

9.   High Student–Teacher Ratios

In most graduate programs, classes are small, often with no more than a dozen students. In law schools, as mentioned, the average size of first-year sections is seventy to eighty students, although many upper-level courses are smaller. These large classes inhibit the development of positive relationships between students and faculty which may contribute to feelings of alienation, isolation, loneliness, and hostility in law students.

In their research of psychological distress in law students, Benjamin and colleagues speculated that high student-teacher ratios may be one of the causes.[157] More than one-third of

---

156. TOM PETTY, THE WAITING (Backstreet/MCA 1981).

157. Benjamin et al., *supra*, at 249 (stating that the distant relationships

law students in a survey reported that they "felt substantial or severe stress because they were unable to establish rapport with faculty."[158] A study of undergraduate students found that positive student-faculty contact is one of the most important components of avoiding "student burnout," which the researchers defined as emotional exhaustion combined with feelings of low personal accomplishment.[159]

Fortunately, there's a partial cure for this ill and, even better, it is one of the few important aspects of law school that lies within your student's complete control. Law professors have received a bad rap over the years for being distant and aloof from students, and certainly some of this reputation is deserved. But many law professors are kind people who really do care about students. Your student will be surprised how much friendlier most professors are one-on-one than when lording over their classroom kingdoms. The professors don't enjoy the high student-teacher ratios any more than the students. Many of them would like to get to know students better, but it's practically impossible to do so with such large classes, *unless* the student does something to help.

This requires effort on the part of the student. Encourage your student to: drop by their professors' offices and introduce themselves at the beginning of the year; sit in the front, not the back, of classrooms; raise their hands to participate in class; hang around after class, when several students usually stay behind to further discuss the day's material with the professor; and show up during the professors' office hours with their questions.

Students have a strong self-interest in getting to know at least some of their professors. Listen to this student's advice:

> Loved ones need to encourage their student to talk to at least one professor a few times throughout their first semester. It is hard, especially for shy students, but making small talk is a lot easier than having to ask one of your professors—out of the blue—for a recommendation or reference letter when summer job and

between law students and faculty attributable to high student-faculty ratios is "related significantly" to student dissatisfaction).

158. Whitman et al., *supra*, at 58 (discussing this survey).

159. Yoram Neumann et al., *Determinants and Consequences of Students' Burnout in Universities*, 61 J. HIGHER EDUC. 20, 28 (1990).

scholarship applications start becoming due. These usually require a reference from at least one professor. Recommendations are part of law school life, and it's hard to ask for one if you know the professor only has a vague idea of which one of the faces in the crowd you are.

And it's just as hard for the professor to *make* a recommendation for such students. The student quoted has it right. Recommendations from professors can be important to students. When professors make recommendations, we're putting our reputations on the line. We can only recommend what we know. Simply being a living, breathing entity who did not throw things in class will not qualify a student for a recommendation.

But just as important as recommendations and other tangible benefits of knowing the professors, having a professor on one's side can make a student feel more connected and less isolated. It's a good feeling simply to have a professor call you by name and say hello when passing in the hallway. Urge your student to get to know their professors.

10.   Debt–Load

Debt load is a major concern and source of stress for law students—and it should be. The average amount a law student borrows to attend a public law school is $66,045[160] and rising, because most states are cutting support for higher education, meaning law school budgets have to be balanced on the backs of students. To attend a private law school, students borrow on average $100,003.[161] A 2011 *U.S. News & World Report* survey showed that the average law student debt by school ranged from a high of $145,621 for graduates of the California Western School of Law in San Diego to a low of $18,603 for Southern University Law Center in Baton Rouge.[162] The 2009 Law School Survey of Student Engagement to which more than 26,000 students responded revealed that 29 percent of students anticipate graduating with more than $120,000 in loan debt, up from 18 percent in 2006.[163]

160. *Average Amount Borrowed for Law School 2001–2009*, AM. BAR ASS'N, 1 (2009), http://www.americanbar. org/content/dam/aba/migrated/legaled/ statistics/charts/stats_20.pdf.

161. *Id.*

162. *Best Law Schools: Whose Graduates Have the Most Debt?*, U.S. NEWS &

WORLD REP., http://grad-schools.usnews. rankingsandreviews.com/best-graduate-schools/top-law-schools/grad_debt.

163. 2009 LAW SCHOOL SURVEY OF STUDENT ENGAGEMENT, *supra*, at 14.

All of the law student stressors described in this chapter will affect you at least indirectly, but your student's debt-load could do so very directly if he or she is your child, spouse, or other intimate partner. Given the importance of financial issues in relationships with law students, we'll talk much more about student debt and other money matters in Chapters 15 and 17.

11. Worries About Finding a Good Job

Closely tied to concerns about debt-load is the worry about finding a decent job. Traditionally, employment opportunities for law graduates have been excellent. Between 1970 and 1987, the "golden era" for lawyers, the legal sector tripled in size.[164] Even in recent years, schools have routinely reported employment rates exceeding 90 percent within nine months of graduation. Many schools continue to report high employment rates, although law graduates have begun raising legitimate questions about the accuracy of these figures.[165]

But there is no question that the economic downturn that started in 2008 inflicted a heavy blow on the legal job market, from which it has not recovered as of this writing. Media reports about shrinking job opportunities for law graduates are ubiquitous. While some believe this is merely a cyclical result of the recession, others are concerned that the curtailment in legal employment is part of a permanent paradigm shift in the profession. Technology advances, globalization, competition among lawyers, and demands by business clients for lower costs have all been given as bases for predicting a permanent slowing down of the legal job market.[166] For the 2008–18 decade, the Bureau of Labor projects that lawyer

164. Amir Efrati, *Hard Case: Job Market Wanes for U.S. Lawyers*, WALL ST. J., Sept. 24, 2007, http://online.wsj.com/public/article/SB119040786780835602.html.

165. In 2009 two Vanderbilt law students started an organization—Law School Transparency—calling on law schools to be more open and complete in disclosing employment figures. Law School Transparency, http://www.lawschooltransparency.com/. Theirs and

similar voices were heard. Beginning in 2011, new ABA rules require law schools to submit much more complete data about the status, type, and locations of jobs regarding their graduates.

166. William D. Henderson & Rachel M. Zahorsky, *Law Job Stagnation May Have Started Before the Recession—And It May Be a Sign of Lasting Change*, A.B.A. J., July 1, 2011, http://www.abajournal.com/magazine/article/paradigm_shift/?utm_source=maestro & utm_me-

employment will grow 13 percent (or 1.3 percent per year), about the same rate as the average for all occupations.[167]

In terms of lawyer salaries, most people turn to the National Association for Law Placement or NALP for current information. The NALP collects salary data nationwide each year through surveys. You know things aren't looking particularly rosy when the NALP's press release about 2010 salaries begins:

> The median starting salary for new law school graduates from the Class of 2010 fell 13% and the mean salary fell 10% according to new research released today from NALP. The research also reveals that aggregate starting private practice salaries fell an astonishing 20% for this class.[168]

The national median salary for 2010 graduates was $63,000 and the national mean was $84,111.[169] For the most part, the dramatic salary drop for 2010 did not occur because individual legal employers were paying less, but because fewer jobs were available at large firms, which are the highest paying legal jobs. In 2010, more law grads turned to smaller firms or non-law firm legal jobs.[170] Significantly, the NALP report noted that few salaries were actually at the median or mean figures; rather, salaries at the bottom and top ends skewed the middle.[171] In other words, many law grads are accepting jobs at figures below the national medians and means, often in the $40–50,000 range.

Don't be overly alarmed by these figures, although they certainly are something for you and your graduate to think about, particularly in terms of trying to keep student loan debt down. It's been a crazy job market in recent years with wild swings in almost all employment sectors. By the time you read this, the market hopefully will have improved.

dium=email & utm_campaign=weekly_email.

167. *Occupational Outlook Handbook, 2009–11 Edition*, Bureau of Labor Statistics, 4 (June 2011), http://www.bls.gov/oco/ocos053.htm.

168. *Class of 2010 Graduates Saddled with Falling Average Starting Salaries as Private Practice Jobs Erode,* NALP (July 7, 2011), http://www.nalp.org/uploads/PressReleases/Classof2010StartingSalaryFindingsPressRelease.pdf [hereinafter *NALP Falling Salaries Report*].

169. *Id.*

170. *Id.*

171. *Id.*

Take heart that people, business entities, and governments will always need lawyers and that over time most lawyers earn good salaries. The national median salary at law firms in 2010 was $104,000.[172] One up-note to keep in mind is that while many starting lawyer salaries may not be much better, and may be even worse, than some jobs not requiring three grueling years of expensive professional school, there is much greater opportunity for income growth over time in the legal field than in most other fields. Most established lawyers live comfortable lives, but it may take several years to get to that position of security. Chapter 18 discusses the types of legal jobs available to recent law graduates, including some additional salary information.

A law student's job worries begin early, in the second semester, as most students feel tremendous pressure to land a summer clerkship (also called "summer associate") position at a law firm. In many cases, this pressure arises from pressing financial needs, but it also stems from an expectation that getting summer legal jobs is something 1Ls absolutely must do to secure a permanent job in the future. That is not necessarily the case, however. It's true that many firms hire associates from the ranks of former summer clerks who performed well, but it's far from an absolute rule. I tell my students not to overly worry about summer clerkships in the summer between their 1L and 2L years. For one thing, many law firms will not hire students after only one year in law school because they don't yet know enough to be useful.

The long and short of it is: try to reassure your student that the job situation will take care of itself if the student takes care of business in law school. The future can't be predicted or controlled, so there's no point worrying about it. Tell your student to keep her eye on the ball.

12. Trouble in Outside Relationships

Last but not least on our law student stressor list is trouble in outside relationships. That's right. I'm talking about you. Well, you and your law student. Law school and relationships do not always blend easily. This issue, which is

172. *Id.*

one of the main topics of the book, is thoroughly examined in Chapters 15–17, so we'll wait until then to talk about it.

* * *

Phew, two less-than-uplifting chapters in a row. Only one more to go before the skies get brighter. In the meantime, to assuage your concerns about law student welfare, here's an inspiring comment from a 2L:

> I feel very blessed to be a law student. In a world of countries where people live on less than a dollar a day, of people who battle terminal illnesses, of natural disasters that can wipe out everything in an instant, how can I for one second complain about law school? It is hard and challenges me in ways I never imagined, but that is a good thing! Opportunities to enrich the mind are too often taken for granted in my opinion. What a blessing to be able to be a law student!

Ahh, the beauty of perspective.

CHAPTER 12

How Law School Can Change Students' Personalities

I've always loved scary movies. When I was a kid, the movie that scared me the most was the original 1956 version of *Invasion of the Body Snatchers*. What a classic.[173] The movie starred Kevin McCarthy as a small-town doctor whose patients start showing up with reports that their loved ones have been replaced by imposters. They look the same and, McCarthy finds on questioning them, have the same memories, but they're somehow different. In a thrilling climax, it turns out that all the imposters were, in fact, law students! Not really. The doppelgangers were created from seed pods from outer space.

But they could have been law students. Law school is not only a life-changing experience—it's a self-changing experience. Students arrive at law school as one person and leave as a different person.

Is it possible that law school could have "such a pervasive socializing influence" on students? One set of law student researchers posed that very question and answered it affirmatively.[174] They pointed to research showing "that professional schools are highly invasive institutions which exert intense control by purposely influencing beliefs, values, and personality characteristics of students."[175] They concluded that no graduate program is as invasive as law school and that, given

173. The movie left a legacy of critical acclaim, including being selected in 1993 for preservation by the National Film Registry of the Library of Congress as a film that is "culturally, historically, or aesthetically significant."

174. Benjamin et al., *supra*, at 251.

175. *Id.* at 251–52.

159

the structure and nature of legal education, it shouldn't be surprising that students turn themselves into the kinds of people law school demands they become.[176]

Individual law students, of course, vary in the ways and degree to which law school alters them, but every student is transformed to some extent by the law school experience. That much can be counted on.

Many of the changes are for the better. Above all else, law school is a period of tremendous intellectual growth. In the first year alone, students learn a mountain of interesting material relevant not only to their careers but to making them more aware and thoughtful people. Law students become better readers and thinkers. They develop effective time management habits. They learn the importance of paying attention to detail. They become more focused and responsible in all areas of life. The analytical skills they develop convert students into astute problem solvers. Know someone with a problem that needs to be strategically worked out in the best way possible under the circumstances? Send them to a law student or lawyer.

Law students also develop into articulate speakers. The other day a friend was lamenting the fact that she worked with an extremely talented young man who she worried was going to be held back by his inability to communicate confidently or articulately, particularly in public settings. She urged him to sign up for Toastmasters International, the non-profit organization dedicated to improving public speaking skills. I said, "Send him to law school. It's like a three-year Toastmasters program." It's true. Even the shyest people emerge from law school as confident public speakers.

In short, law students enter as "newbs," as upper-level students call the 1Ls, and emerge as "professionals." Like caterpillars turning into butterflies, they spread their wings over a period of three years and fly away on graduation day to take over the world. You will enjoy an insider's view of this amazing transformation. One husband summed up the blossoming he saw in his student by saying, "I sense in her an energy fed by the euphoric feeling of learning something significant." The excitement and enthusiasm generated by law school is a wonderful thing to behold.

---

176. *Id.* at 252.

But again with the caveats: Some of the changes that occur in law student personalities are less than ideal. Or better put, some of the changes are ideal for being a lawyer, but may be less than ideal for people who have to be around a law student or lawyer. That's the subject of this chapter. It explores the following personality changes that may occur in law students and crossover to their external lives: becoming overly legalistic, analytical, argumentative, cynical and skeptical, and more detached from their intrinsic values and emotions. Note that I said "may" occur, not necessarily "will" occur. Everyone is different.

Many of the student comments in this chapter came in response to two bonus questions I inserted in my Torts exams over the past couple of years. One question asked students to name to their "biggest change in personality" after, depending on the exam, one semester or one year of law school. Another question asked:

After one year of law school, the following is a "negative" personality change I detect in myself (realizing that some "negative" qualities also have a positive side):

(a) I am more argumentative.

(b) I am overly analytical in my non-law school life.

(c) I am more cynical about the legal system and/or about human nature.

(d) I feel more detached from the values I held when I entered law school.

(e) None of the above. I cannot detect any negative influences of law school on my personality.

The instructions told students to circle as many answers as applied to them. I followed the question with lined space and asked students to provide a short explanation of their answers. By the numbers (emphasizing that this was simply another anecdotal exercise involving a potentially biased question, not statistically valid research), out of a total of seventy-four students who answered the question, thirty-one (42 percent) said they were more argumentative, thirty-eight (51 percent) said they were overly analytical, twenty-six (35 percent) said they were more cynical, twelve (16 percent) said they felt more detached from their values, and thirteen (18 percent) reported no negative changes.

With the Good Comes Some Bad

I've always been a strong believer that most personality traits short of lying, cheating, and serial-killing have both a positive and a negative side. For example, one person might criticize someone for being "anal" or obsessive-compulsive, while others will praise the same person for being well-organized and paying attention to detail. A person can be attacked for being aggressive or complimented for being confident, or denounced as wishy-washy while lauded for not being rash.

It is easy to find support for this "two sides to every coin" view in the personality changes that can occur in law students. Take, as an example, an increased willingness to be confrontational. While some might see that as a negative trait, a significant other saw it as a plus in her law student:

> My partner has become more assertive and confrontational (as opposed to being passive-aggressive). Although my partner was never really a "pushover," he now frequently stands up for himself, me, and others unable to stand up for themselves.

Here's an example from the other side of the coin. Law school makes students more confident interacting in the world around them. That's a good thing. But too much confidence can resemble arrogance, not such a good thing, as this significant other noted about her law student-husband:

> Law school has made my partner develop an inflated sense of self-importance that I can confidently say was never previously apparent. My partner has always enjoyed debates, but since law school, he has acquired a sense of arrogance that can quickly change a civilized discussion into a relationship-ending argument.

So, realizing that with the good comes some bad and vice versa, let's look at some personality and world-view changes you may see occurring in your student, some of which may affect you.

Law Students May View and Approach Life Legalistically

One day my partner was really mad at me for studying instead of watching football or going out to dinner, so she did something ridiculous. I stopped her and said: "I don't know any other way to say this, but you are being *malicious*" [a frequently used legal word]. This made her even more mad because she HATES law talk.

—Law student commenting on whether law school added stress/conflict to his relationship

Law students quickly begin taking what they learn in law school and applying it to their personal lives. Commencing within weeks of starting law school and gradually developing into a permanent condition, law students come to view the universe through a legal lens. This alteration manifests itself in several ways, some amusing and some potentially annoying.

Risk Is Everywhere. Law school teaches students that anything that can go wrong, will go wrong. This is because in every case students study, things went wrong. That's why they ended up as cases. Torts cases are particularly likely to confirm the validity of Murphy's Law to students. Who would ever think, for example, that if a worker cleaned a vending machine with gasoline in a room with a space heater, a rat would run out of the machine, cross the room and take refuge under the heater, catch fire because its fur was permeated with gasoline fumes, then, in flames, run back to where the gas was located, causing an explosion?[177] Only a law student. Who would think a radio station contest to locate a mobile DJ would cause two teenagers searching for the DJ to recklessly crash into and kill someone, making the radio station liable for the death?[178] Only a law student. Who could conceive that if a contractor negligently installed a water heater, a fire would start and a passerby would be injured when a resident

---

177. United Novelty Co. v. Daniels, 42 So.2d 395, 396 (Miss. 1949) (holding that the fact that "the unique circumstance" causing the explosion "was the escape of a rat from the machine, and its disappointing attempt to seek sanctuary beneath the heater whereat it overexposed itself and its impregnated coat, and returned in haste and flames to its original hideout" did not negate the liability of the worker's employer).

178. Weirum v. RKO Gen., Inc., 539 P.2d 36, 36 (Cal. 1975) (holding "[i]t was foreseeable that the [defendant's] youthful listeners, finding the [DJ] had eluded them at one location, would race to arrive first at the next site and in

of the burning dwelling leaped out the window and landed on him?[179] Only a law student.

It's no surprise that law students quickly become attuned to risk and the legal consequences of it. To a normal person, a hole in the sidewalk is something to step around. To a law student, it is a potential tort; i.e., a dangerous premises condition that could lead to personal injuries and a lawsuit.

When my daughter—nicknamed Tortgirl—was about six years old, I taught her to play a game called "Spot the Tort." It worked like this: We'd be in a public place and I'd say "Tortgirl, spot the tort!" and then time her as she sought to identify the nearest dangerous condition on the premises. Sounds sick, right? But it provided loads of family fun. Before you know it, your law student will be spotting potential torts everywhere.

When I asked students to name their biggest change in personality after one year of law school, their answers included:

- I'm always on the lookout for torts!

- That I constantly am noticing potential tort claims around me and avoiding them.

- In every situation, I find myself assessing if it is a tort or if someone could claim something here.

Being careful is good, but some law students and lawyers may go overboard in seeing risk in every situation, suffering from what psychologists call the "availability heuristic." The availability heuristic is a mental shortcut people use to assess the likelihood of harm when they lack adequate information about the actual probability of the harm. They assess probability based on whether they can think of an example of the harm happening.[180] That can be a problem for law students because their days are filled with examples of things going wrong in every conceivable situation.

Over-awareness of risk can affect the daily functioning of law students and lawyers. Constant risk-immersion, for ex-

---

their haste disregard the demands of highway safety").

179. Williams v. Foster, 666 N.E.2d 678, 682 (Ill. App. Ct. 1996) (holding that the passerby, who tried to render assistance to the family, could pursue a claim against the manufacturer and in-

staller of the water heater under what is known as the "rescue doctrine").

180. *See* CASS R. SUNSTEIN, RISK AND REASON: SAFETY, LAW, AND THE ENVIRONMENT x (2002) (explaining the availability heuristic and other mental phenomena that cause people to over-estimate risk).

ample, affected my parenting in raising my daughter. I became the classic over-protective parent. The full extent of this tendency hit me like a ton of bricks (which is another risk to watch out for) one morning as my then five-year-old daughter and I were leaving our third-floor townhouse. Descending the stairs, I cautioned her to hold on to the railing and be careful not to fall. Seemed like a reasonable warning from a parent, but I guess I must have said it too many times because she responded: "I know, Daddy. Because if I don't, I'll fall and *cra-aa-ack* my head open on the sidewalk and there will be blood *everywhere* and you'll have to rush me to the hospital and I'll *die!*" I'm not making this up. I just shook my head and said, "Well, um, it might not be that bad. Just hold on to the railing!"

A former student read this and concurred. Heck, she even blamed me for it:

> The Torts II products liability discussions ruined me. I am a complete nut with my daughter at the playground. My husband gets irritated, but I always say things like, "We don't know if this ground cover is thick enough to prevent a fatal head injury." So, thanks for all the playground hypos, Professor!

But it really wasn't my fault. Torts teaches everyone that the world is a dangerous place. There's a very good chance your student's newfound risk awareness and ability to "spot the tort" will rub off on you:

> My boyfriend, an engineering student, and I were watching HGTV at his mother's. On the show, they cut out a portion of an outside wall separating a patio from a staircase and installed industrial cables across the gap where the wall had been. I said, "Why did they put those there? They're ugly." My boyfriend looks at me like I'm stupid and says, "Don't you know?" "No," I said. "Annie, it would be *tortious* if they didn't. Someone would just walk right through and break their neck." That's how much law school changes your life, Prof. Your boyfriend starts playing "Spot the Tort."

What I love most about this story is that the boyfriend didn't just say, "It would be *dangerous*." He actually said *"tortious*." Beautiful.

Every Action Has Legal Ramifications. Related to the above, law students also become keenly aware of the legal ramifications of their own conduct, as shown by these answers to the "biggest change in personality" question:

• Determining my "legal obligations" in just about every facet of everyday life. I suppose it is good practice, but it can be very distracting.

• I am by far a much more careful person than I was over the summer before law school. I no longer "jump" into things. I spend a lot more time considering the risks and possible liability of my actions.

• That I think about the legal ramifications of most of my actions before I ever attempt them.

This too has both positive and negative ramifications. Acting in ways that avoid creating legal liability is smart, but being overly worried about the legal consequences of every action is neither healthy nor warranted. As with risk generally, law students and lawyers tend to over-estimate the risk of being sued.

You might find your student issuing legal cautions to you and other loved ones about your conduct as part of this development. It may sound like lecturing at times, or worse, chastising. Your student will be doing it to help, but that might not prevent it from being annoying.

"I Know My Rights!" While worrying about their legal responsibilities, law students also become well aware of their legal rights. Everyone has been in situations where they were mistreated—whether by a merchant, service provider, employer, creditor, landlord, police officer, or someone else—and wondered whether they had any legal rights. Knowledge is power and one of the largest personal benefits of being a lawyer is simply having the knowledge to navigate one's own everyday legal affairs, such as in consumer disputes. This knowledge will benefit you and other close loved ones of your student. It will be like having a doctor in the family, only a doctor of law rather than medicine.

But with everything law-related, new law students sometimes get carried away with asserting their rights. After starting law school I became determined that "the man" was never again going to take advantage of me. I still recall a hot summer afternoon sitting in the office of an apartment building in Gainesville, Florida, where I was a 1L at the University of Florida law school, reading a lease agreement in contemplation of renting an apartment. I immediately began encountering lease provisions that offended my newfound keen sense of landlord-tenant justice.

"Excuse me," I said to the apartment complex manager. "This provision is clearly unconscionable."[181] I remember her looking at me as if thinking, "Ahh, another new law student."

"So," I said, "can I cross it out?"

"Yeah, right," she laughed.

Your student may behave similarly at first, but will get over it.

Law Students May Become Overly Analytical

> I analyze everything legally now. My friend told me he hit a deer the other day. My first question was "Was the deer in the road after you hit it?" "Yes." "Did you leave it there?" "Yes." "You had a duty to move it. You created an unreasonable risk." Last year I would have said, "Oh dang, that sucks. Did it mess up your car very much?"

> —Student describing biggest change in personality after one year of law school

Closely entwined with approaching life legalistically, law school's focus on instilling and enhancing critical thinking skills in students can cause students to approach not just law school but all of life more analytically, too much so in many cases. Quite a few students recognized this change in themselves:

- I'm sometimes unable to sufficiently enjoy what a person is saying because I have to analyze the entirety of the situation. I analyze even compliments because I have to determine if they are genuine or just situation-

---

181. "Unconscionable" is a favorite word that students learn in law school. Unconscionability is a legal doctrine that allows courts to refuse to enforce contractual provisions that are unduly oppressive and one-sided. Many students adopt the word as part of their everyday speech and use it in an overly broad, non-legal sense: as in, "No way. He did that? That is completely unconscionable."

al. Although I think it's good to have an analytical mind, I worry that it's going to affect my ability to truly enjoy and develop my relationships.

• I have noticed I analyze everything about everything now. My fiancé always asks if we can just watch a show or drive down the street without me analyzing every fact about what is going on.

• I often find myself thinking that people's reasoning is faulty and many times I have let them know this. Typically, this situation arises in conversations with my wife and sometimes, if not most times, I come off as a jerk.

• I have started to "fact find" when I get explanations from family and friends or when just talking to them in general. I start asking myself the reasoning behind their statements or closely listening to the facts they tell me about a situation to see if I can catch them fabricating or exaggerating a story.

• I find myself dissecting what people say or write in an email to preposterous levels, searching for inconsistencies or different interpretations.

One way being overly analytical will manifest itself will be in a newfound penchant in your student for conducting cost-benefit analyses before making decisions. Much of law involves weighing the benefits of particular actions to society and individuals against the costs. In Torts, all law students study a case called *United States v. Carroll Towing Co.*,[182] in which a famous judge with a great name—Learned Hand—set forth an algebraic economic cost-benefit formula for determining whether conduct that caused injury was *reasonable* or *unreasonable*. If reasonable, the defendant is off the hook. If unreasonable, the defendant is liable and pays damages.

The formula, which you'll probably hear about, is $B < P \times L$. B stands for the burden of avoiding a risk of harm, P is the probability that the risk will actually cause harm, and L stands for the severity of the harm if it occurs. The formula states that if the burden of avoiding the harm is less than the probability of the harm multiplied by the severity of the harm, the conduct is unreasonable. Conversely, if the burden

---

182. 159 F.2d 169 (2d Cir. 1947).

of avoiding the risk outweighs the probability times the severity of harm, the conduct is reasonable.

Here's an example of how it could work in real life: Suppose Dalvin falls over the edge of a crevice into a canyon in a remote area of a large national park and is injured. He sues the U.S. government alleging that it was negligent to not build a fence around the canyon to keep people from falling into it. We'll assume the fence would cost $1 million, decrease the aesthetics of the park, and cause some damage to the environment. Together, these would constitute the burden of avoiding the risk—the B factor in the equation. Under those facts, Judge Hand's formula most likely would lead to the conclusion the government acted reasonably because the burden of building the fence would be greater than the small probability that someone would fall into the remote canyon. On the other hand, if Dalvin showed the canyon drop-off ran adjacent to a well-traveled hiking path, the probability of harm—the P part of the equation—would go way up and his case would be substantially strengthened. Also relevant is the likely severity of the harm, the L factor in Judge Hand's formula. It would make a difference whether the drop-off led to a hundred-foot plunge to certain death or a three-foot fall more likely to cause a sprained or broken leg.

Judge Hand and his formula make a lasting impact on law students, as reflected in answers to my question that asked students to name their biggest change in personality after one year:

- I apply the Hand formula in every situation. I don't do this by choice. It is an automatic response, much like breathing or blinking.

- I think more critically now about my responsibilities in life. It is not that I was careless before, but rather that I was lacking Judge Hand, who is always looking over my shoulder now!

- An infuriating (to the uninitiated, at least) tendency to apply Judge Hand's formula to just about every area of my life.

Consciously or unconsciously, law students and lawyers learn to apply Judge Hand's cost-benefit analysis to guide much of their everyday decision-making. Not only with regard to risks of harm, but to everything. Weighing the costs and benefits of actions prior to acting is a rational approach to decision-making, but being *overly* analytical is not always the best course toward leading a full, spontaneous life. Not all of life's decisions should be grounded exclusively in economic cost-benefit weighing, which excludes the intangible values of feelings and intuition.

Suppose you and your law student are looking to buy a house. You come across a house you both absolutely love. The law student begins conducting a thorough cost-benefit analysis that includes balancing the cost of the of house, resale potential, square footage, floor plan, curb appeal, needed repairs, local school system, taxes, etc. Those are all worthy considerations, of course, but they ignore what may be the most relevant factor in the decision-making process: *that you love the house*!

Law Students May Become Argumentative

Law students are literally taught to argue. Court cases are set for "argument." Not discussion, consideration, or presentation, but *argument*. In the U.S. Supreme Court, the proceedings in every case begin with the Chief Justice saying: "We will hear argument today in [case number followed by case name]."

Your student's intensive training in how to argue will begin on the first day of classes. The Socratic method forces students to argue and defend, not simply recite, their positions. Professors often require students to defend their positions even when the professor agrees with the student. Class discussions are filled with dialogues tracking this model:

Professor: Ms. Smith, what do you think about this rule?

Student: I don't like it.

Professor: Why?

Student: Because it's not fair to plaintiffs.

Professor: That's not a legal analysis. *Why* is it not fair?

Student: Because ... [gives explanation].

Professor: What if we changed the facts to *a*, *b*, *c*? Would the rule be fair to plaintiffs under those facts?

Student: It would be much fairer than in this case.

Professor: Why?

Student: Because ... [gives explanation].

Professor: But what about the defendant. Is the rule fair to defendants?

Student: Yes, I would say so.

Professor: Then is your position wrong?

Student: I don't think so.

Professor: Why?

Why, why, why? Class after class, day after day, week after week, for three full years.

In between getting interrogated in class, your student also will be practicing for and delivering their oral argument in the second semester of Legal Research and Writing, as well as learning to argue to judges and juries in courses in trial advocacy. For students who participate in moot court, arguing becomes the focus of their lives. Here's one barometer for measuring the relative importance that U.S. legal education places on resolving disputes peaceably as opposed to through an adversarial process: only one national law student competition exists in negotiation skills, but dozens of competitions exist for argumentation skills.

Nearly three decades ago, a legal scholar observed "that the singular purpose of most law school curricula was to prepare students for adversarial conflict rather than for the gentler arts of reconciliation and negotiation."[183] Another law professor called "the adversarial ethic" one of the implicit values of legal education.[184] Yet another commentator stated: "Anyone who has had a spouse, sibling, friend, or child go through law school needs no convincing ... that a legal education instills greater disputatiousness.... More than anything else, law school teaches the ability to dispute virtually anything."[185] Small wonder that law students become inculcated with an instinct to argue and challenge and defend every position.

---

183. Benjamin et al., *supra*, at 251 (referring to an observation by Derek C. Bok in an earlier article).

184. Glesner, *supra*, at 640.

185. WALT BACHMAN, LAW V. LIFE: WHAT LAWYERS ARE AFRAID TO SAY ABOUT THE LEGAL PROFESSION 54–55 (1995).

Argumentation skills are among the most valued tools of a lawyer's trade, but do not rank highly on the list of traits considered helpful by psychotherapists to successful relationships. To a law student, the simplest assertion is an invitation to a challenging response. If a mate complains, "You don't give me enough attention," a law student might reply:

> First, we must define the word "attention." Attention comes in different degrees and forms and can reasonably mean different things to different people. Let's assume *A* asks *B* for more attention. In response, *B* dumps a flower vase of water onto *A*'s head. Would *B* be giving *A* attention? In one sense, clearly yes, and yet the act probably would not fall within the scope of the requester's original intent. And what about "give"? Does one really give attention? "Give" suggests a conveyance and since attention is not personal or real property, it can't be conveyed. To discuss this intelligently, we first need to clarify the operative terms.

At this point, the non-law student may simply give up and leave the room or perhaps pick up on *B*'s idea and pour water on the law student as the rebuttal argument.

Several students and their partners described how the student's escalating propensity for argument infiltrated their relationships.

From Law Students:

- After my first year of law school, I was arguing with my wife in the car. I was pretty aggressive in my arguing and she got rather upset. She said, "Is this what they teach you in law school?"

- Much to the annoyance of my wife and family, I always present the other side of issues we are talking about, whether the subject is politics, sports, or whatever. I do this even if I don't agree with the side I'm arguing. They all say all I want to do is argue.

- I will argue with members of my family about anything. If they use an incorrect term, or write something on Facebook that is wrong, I will correct them. I don't like to—no, I *won't*—let an argument go. If I lose the argument on the facts, I will argue about the terms they used when making their arguments. This is a sad development.

From Significant Others:

• We were at a small outdoor gathering with friends. I was enjoying myself and I thought my partner was too—until she pulled me aside to say that law school had finally penetrated the core of her brain. She hadn't been able to stop analyzing all the anecdotes being tossed around for reasoning defects so she could prove them wrong or "play devil's advocate." She couldn't just listen to fun stories anymore—they were *all* cases and arguments to her!

• A negative change, in my opinion, is being extremely argumentative. Argumentative in a way that he is disagreeing with me AND thinking he's always right, better, smarter, and more clever than I could ever hope to be with my pea-brain. It tends to get really annoying after a while.

• He is always being a devil's advocate. It's really annoying and it makes everyone at home mad. I can tell he is using that IRAC method even in his arguments at home.

Even more frustrating, law students learn to be *very good* at arguing, making it impossible to win a debate with them. Law students can argue weak and strong positions equally well; in fact, their weakest positions may actually require the most argument. As one significant other to a law student remarked: "It is stressful and scary that my wife knows the law now and can use it in arguments." A student said his partner complained he didn't argue fairly and "that I was trying to turn everything around, and that I was talking 'like a lawyer.'" Asked what they think loved ones of law students need to know about law school, a 2L said:

Law school reshapes the way that law students view the world as they learn the language of the law and learn to "think like a lawyer." This change can cause conflict in the home as the law student becomes more critical in every discussion that takes place. Suddenly, the loved one may find himself met with a strategic multi-point argument regarding everything from the dishes to world politics.

Always remember that, as annoying as it can be, law students do not intend to offend when they "argue" in legal-mindset mode. To a non-law student, "arguing" may mean "fighting." The constant questioning, nitpicking, and asserting may feel like a personal attack. To a law student, "arguing" is synonymous with "discussing." When loved ones get upset by all the arguing and debating, students may not understand what the problem is. After all, it's what they do or listen to all day long.

An exchange from a *Journal of Legal Education* article about role conflict in law student marriages provides an example:

> Wife: *X* has a tendency to verbally attack me more, not in a sense of being nasty, but to press me with questions.... He will get me into an argumentative mood so that he can see my response. I think of it as verbal battering ... *which he didn't do before. He just started doing this in the last year.* Have you noticed that?
>
> Husband: No.
>
> Wife: Oh, I have![186]

Law students may be sincerely clueless, as this husband apparently was, about both the fact that they have become more argumentative and, just as important, the effect this can have on people who don't live in a world where being a good arguer wins awards. If your student seems overly argumentative, make him or her aware of the issue when it crops up. Explain that it feels personal even though the student may not intend it that way.

So what's the upside of being argumentative? Being willing and able to assert and defend one's position is not only vital to being a good lawyer, it can serve people well in their outside lives. Three students (all women, interestingly) conceded that law school had made them more argumentative, but said they considered this to be a positive development:

> • Now, I definitely want to make my point known. Before law school, if I heard something that didn't sound right or my boyfriend said something I didn't agree with, I would just let it go. Now I'm much more vocal, but I see this as a positive.

186. Errol G. Rohr et al., *Role Conflict in Marriages of Law and Medical* *School Students*, 35 J. LEGAL EDUC. 56, 62 (1985).

- My husband has made it a point to tell me how much more argumentative I am! I do feel like this is positive though, because I stand up for myself more now, by a long shot, than I did before.

- I am much more analytical and argumentative. I do not think these are totally negative. I am now able to stand my ground in arguments.

Law Students May Become More Cynical or Skeptical

Some law students become increasingly cynical or at least skeptical about the law and legal system and the human condition as they move through law school. "The process of learning to 'think like a lawyer,' " wrote one commentator "is fundamentally the development of a critical skepticism about any proposition, no matter how seemingly straightforward."[187] Skepticism is not the same as cynicism,[188] but a study of Yale law, medical, and nursing students found that the law students scored highest on a "cynicism scale."[189]

My students recognized their own creeping cynicism in answering my "biggest change in personality" question:

- The biggest change I have noticed in myself is an increase in knowledge directly proportional to an increase in cynicism.

- I question everything now. I was never gullible, but I liked to think that people had good motives. Now, I think that most decisions in life are reduced to money.

- I no longer assume anything commonly said is true.

Specifically, student attitudes may become more negative about both the legal system and human nature as they progress through law school. One might think that the sheltered, ivory tower world of law school—as compared to the hard-scrabble of real life—would be the ideal place to nurture

187. BACHMAN, *supra*, at 54.

188. The two words are related, but not synonymous. Skepticism is more about doubting or questioning, while cynicism has more to do with not believing at all or holding negative beliefs.

189. Eron & Redmount, *supra*, at 433. The scale was based on questions that asked participants to state their level of agreement with statements such as: "Most people make friends because friends are likely to be useful to them"; "I think most people would lie to get ahead"; and "If you don't look out for yourself, nobody else will."

and kindle students' faith in the legal system. But it doesn't always work out that way. Many people who come to law school are idealists. They arrive thinking the law is about liberty and justice for all. They experience a disillusioning awakening when they discover that the neutral application of legal rules can lead to unfair results. In the words of one student, "I used to have a blind faith in the accuracy of our legal system, but after having seen the inner workings, I find myself more doubtful than anything." (Importantly, several students said law school had the opposite effect on them, making them more confident in the legal system. Some of their comments are included at the end of this section.)

A real case provides an unusually stark example of the injustice that can result from the objective application of legal rules: *In re Estate of Pavlinko*.[190] Vasil Pavlinko and his wife, Hellen, were immigrants who spoke little English. They went to a lawyer to have separate wills drawn up. Both wills left their estates to the same person: Elias Martin, the brother of Hellen Pavlinko. Unfortunately, when it came time to sign the wills, the wills got mixed up and Vasil and Hellen each signed the other's will instead of their own.

After the couple died, Elias Martin—the sole heir under *both* wills—offered Vasil's will for probate. Although conceding that the result was "unfortunate," the Pennsylvania Supreme Court rejected Martin's petition because Vasil had mistakenly signed Hellen's will. Judge Michael Musmanno, one of the most artful judicial opinion-writers in American legal history, wrote a blistering dissenting opinion attacking the injustice that can result from blind adherence to the law:

> Everyone in this case admits that a mistake was made: an honest, innocent, unambiguous, simple mistake, the innocent, drowsy mistake of a man who sleeps all day and, on awakening, accepts the sunset for the dawn.... I know that the law is founded on precedent and in many ways we are bound by the dead hand of the past. But even with obeisance to precedent, I still do not believe that the medicine of the law is incapable of curing the simple ailment here.... We have said more times than there are tombstones in the cemetery where the Pavlinkos lie buried, that the primary rule to be followed in the interpretation of a will is to

190.   148 A.2d 528 (Pa. 1959).

ascertain the intention of the testator. Can anyone go to the graves of the Pavlinkos and say that we do not know what they meant? They said in English and Carpathian that they wanted their property to go to Elias Martin.

Still, Elias lost. Charles Dickens wrote that the law is an arse, and it certainly can be. In most cases fairness does enter the equation, even if not stated expressly in the court's opinion. In defense of *Pavlinko*, a fundamental purpose of having legal rules is to instill some certainty in the law and prevent judges from simply doing whatever they personally believe is fair in a case. Nevertheless, the emphasis on objective analysis over personal feelings and emotions, especially when it leads to unfair results, can cause students to question the system.

Students also come to realize that laypersons' negative perception that lawyers are always looking for "loopholes" is in one sense accurate. Law students are taught to represent their clients "zealously."[191] Developing a winning legal argument or strategy—even if it depends on a legal technicality— is considered to be part of good lawyering. As a student commented:

> I have realized there are exceptions to everything, which makes me feel like the people who win lawsuits are the people who can most creatively craft their argument. It doesn't seem like it comes down to justice.

With regard to cynicism concerning human nature, lawsuits often show off the worst sides of people, causing some students to be less trusting:

- I've definitely become more cynical about human nature (something I thought impossible). I've slowly begun assuming everyone is out for their own personal gains and will get there no matter who they have to go through.

- Unfortunately or fortunately, I am not as trusting of human nature now. I automatically think someone has an angle.

---

191. MODEL RULES OF PROF'L CONDUCT, pmbl. para. 2 (2006) ("As advocate, a lawyer zealously asserts the client's position under the rules of the adversary system."). The Model Rules of Professional Conduct are the ethical rules to which lawyers are bound.

- Every aspect of my life is filled with looking for fault, lies, and inconsistencies.

One source of this skepticism is that legal disputes invariably involve opposing parties giving different versions of the same events. Students see this frequently in the cases they read. Here's a 100 percent real fake example in the form of two conflicting witness statements describing the same automobile accident:

Describe How Accident Happened

Driver 1. I was minding my own business driving practically in slow motion with my eyes glued to the road when my neighbor's death machine suddenly warped out of his driveway aimed straight at me.

Driver 2. With my head turned completely around looking for cars, I was backing out my driveway at approximately one-third of a mile per hour when my neighbor decided recklessly and without warning to launch an assault on the world land speed record.

Describe Damage to Vehicles

Driver 1. My irreplaceable, vintage automobile is a total loss. Amazingly, despite the explosive force of the accident, my neighbor's car has only a tiny dent in one fender.

Driver 2. After I pried myself loose from the twisted wreckage of my vehicle, I immediately inspected my neighbor's rusted-out pile of junk. Miraculously, the heap suffered only a minor, hardly noticeable scratch.

Describe Any Injury to Persons

Driver 1. My spine is practically snapped in two and I cannot move at all. I am having to dictate this witness statement to my chiropractor. Fortunately, my neighbor was not hurt at all, except for a very slight bump on one arm.

Driver 2. It's hard to write with my shattered elbow in this cast. I'll submit an addendum if I ever get out of the hospital, which right now, is in question. Meanwhile, my neighbor was not hurt at all. He passed the time waiting for the police to arrive doing sit ups.

Other Comments

Driver 1. After reviewing the tragic circumstances of this horrible crash, I'm sure you will agree the other driver is guilty as sin and does not deserve the great American privilege and responsibility of holding a driver's license. If he doesn't admit the accident was 100 percent his fault, it's only because he's a pathological liar.

Driver 2. After you carefully investigate this terrible collision, I am confident you will come to the conclusion that I am as free from fault as a newborn baby. If the other driver doesn't confess all responsibility, it's only because lying and bad driving are part of his devil-worshiping religion.

Satire, of course, but the basic thrust is true. Even when people aren't overtly lying, they often perceive events differently. Law students and lawyers become programmed to be skeptical of any one person's version of an event or situation.

But there is an upside to being skeptical, if perhaps not cynical. Law students and lawyers are much less likely to make snap judgments about situations without first hearing all sides. One student said: "I analyze things differently now. When my friends tell me stories, I legally analyze both sides instead of seeing just the drama." Another commented similarly: "Law school has helped me hone in on the essential points of any given situation and to look at both sides of any given issue. My non-law school acquaintances often have a hard time seeing the other side of anything." Avoiding rushes to judgment without knowing all the facts and being open to hearing and considering the different sides of issues should not be underrated as a positive trait.

Finally, as noted, several students said that law school had made them *less* cynical about the legal system. One said he had learned that most of the time, the legal system reaches reasonable results, which is quite true. Usually, the system is able to sort the truth-tellers from the prevaricators and arrive at fair results. Another commented that law school increased his faith in the law by exposing the falsity and distortion in some of the reporting about the legal system, specifically mentioning the grossly misunderstood "Mc-Donald's coffee spill case" that most people have heard about. A third student said: "If anything, I am less cynical about the legal system after a year in law school. The fact that there are intelligent courts struggling to determine the reasonable bounds in which society should live gives me hope."

Law School May Cause Students to Change Their Values

Another way law school can change students is by altering their value systems, not always for the better. On the questionnaire I give to incoming students, I ask why they came to law school. A substantial percentage of students give sincere answers about wanting to help people, often targeting specific groups such as children, the elderly, or the disabled. Very few law students, however, end up pursuing those original goals once they become lawyers. What happens to them? Research by Kennon Sheldon and Lawrence Krieger suggests a plausible explanation.[192]

Sheldon and Krieger conducted a study of law students at two law schools to test a number of hypotheses about declines in law student well-being. They grounded their research in self-determination theory. Self-determination theorists study the connection between human motivations and optimal well-being. In short, self-determination theory, supported by thirty years of empirical research, hypothesizes that people are happier when they are motivated by autonomous (not externally coerced) goals and also when they seek to fulfill intrinsic values rather than extrinsic values.

As applied to law students, Sheldon and Krieger hypothesized that law students experience a decline in their autonomous motivations over the first year of law school and an increase in externally controlled motivations, and that this change is accompanied by a decline in intrinsic values and an increased focus on external values. They further hypothesized that these changes in motivations and values lead to lower levels of happiness and life satisfaction. Their study results supported their hypotheses.

Here's a somewhat oversimplified plain-language example to illustrate their points: Sarah arrives at law school with the goal of becoming a lawyer who will aid people with mental

192. *See generally* Sheldon & Krieger, *Does Legal Education have Under-* *mining Effects on Law Students?, supra.*

disabilities. Her autonomous motivations on arrival are to enjoy the learning process for its own sake and to graduate from law school so that she can pursue that career goal. Her primary intrinsic law school-related value is to serve her community and, more specifically, the people with mental disabilities who live there.

Sheldon and Krieger's hypotheses predict that the coercive environment of law school, with its emphasis on external rewards such as achieving high grades and landing prestigious jobs, will cause Sarah's motivations and values to change. Her autonomous motivation to simply enjoy the learning process and graduate will decline, while the external motivation to achieve out of fear or to please or compete with others will increase. Her intrinsic value to serve her community will decrease, while her emphasis on extrinsic values, such as enhancing her image and obtaining a lucrative job, will increase. Significantly, the more successful Sarah is in law school, the larger the shift in values that will occur.

Ultimately, these changes could lead to Sarah experiencing a lower level of well-being. As Krieger explained:

> Scientific research for the past 15 years has consistently shown that a primary focus on external rewards and results, including affluence, fame, and power, is unfulfilling. These values are seductive—they create a nice picture of life but they are actually correlated with relative unhappiness. Instead, people who have a more "intrinsic," personal/interpersonal focus—on personal growth, close relationships, helping others, or improving their community—turn out to be significantly happier and more satisfied with their lives.[193]

The bottom line: Sarah arrives at law school happy to be there to learn and with a goal of serving her community. She comes out having sublimated her internal motivations and values in favor of externally imposed motivations and extrinsic values such as landing a prestigious, high-paying job. The possible result is that Sarah ends up as an unfulfilled and dissatisfied lawyer. Look at the spooky similarities to hypothetical Sarah's predicament in this student comment:

---

193. LAWRENCE S. KRIEGER, THE HIDDEN SOURCES OF LAW SCHOOL STRESS: AVOID-ING THE MISTAKES THAT CREATE UNHAPPY AND UNPROFESSIONAL LAWYERS 4 (2005).

I came into law school as a crusader. I morphed into a
competitor. Being surrounded by the obsession on status, grades, and being "the best" really took away
from my real long-term goals of promoting justice and
finding a good quality of life.

It can happen to the best of them. As one student who
came to law school with strong social activism values but who
suffered the mixed blessing-curse of doing well academically
wrote after reading the above:

This is a particularly painful thing to face as all my
friends are suiting up for on-campus interviews with
the prestigious law firms, although they came in wanting to do public interest or some other type of fulfilling
work. I'm told all the time that there's no harm in just
doing an interview, that it's always good practice or
something, but there is. Once you do the interview,
you might get the job, and once you get the job locked
in at this stage, it's hard to say no later—especially
because so many law students are so prone to wanting
to please everyone. There's nothing wrong with working in a large firm if that's what you came here for.
But SO MANY people don't, and when real money
comes into play, things change. I had one of my best
friends here tell me that "good grades are wasted" on
me and that it's a shame I don't want to "make
money." That's not true. I do want to make money,
but I also want control and freedom. I am not exactly
sure what the answers are, but any supportive family
member or significant other of a successful law student
who wants to work in public interest law is going to
have to make a lot of difficult choices.

Remind your student to hang on to the person they were
when they entered law school. Encourage them to stay connected to their heart and follow it in plotting their career.
"Follow your heart" is the most essential piece of advice I
give to my students.

Contrary to what people believe, money is only tangential-
ly related to happiness. In their book, *The Happy Lawyer*,
Professors Nancy Levit and Douglas Linder delved into tons
of research about what makes people happy.[194] The most

194. *See* LEVIT & LINDER, *supra.*

overrated factor, it turns out, is money. Asked to name the one thing that would make them happier, most people say "more money."[195] A significant happiness difference does exist between people with high incomes and people with very low incomes. People with incomes above $90,000 are twice as likely to report that they are "very happy" compared to people with incomes below $20,000.[196] But almost no difference in happiness is reported between the highest income earners and middle-income earners. In other words, once a person achieves a salary that allows a comfortable living—Levit and Linder put the number at $75,000 a year—additional money does little to add happiness.[197] Most lawyers will, at least over time, earn salaries sufficient to live comfortable lives. As previously noted, the median income for lawyers in the United States is more than $100,000.

Of course, sometimes loved ones—yes, this could include you—play a role in their student's decision to pursue riches over leading a rich life. Some significant others pressure their students to "go for the money." A former student of mine at another law school called me recently. In an anguished voice, he said he was absolutely miserable in his job at a big law firm and wanted advice. I asked him what kind of legal job would make him happy. "Anything except what I'm doing!" I asked him to be more specific and he said, "I've always wanted to work helping children. That's what I wanted to do when I went to law school. I just saw that there's an opening in the guardian ad litem program here.[198] I was thinking about applying for it." "Do it!" I told him. "I can't," he said. "My wife would kill me. It only pays $35,000 a year."

Wanting your student to be financially successful is completely understandable. After all, loved ones suffer through those lean years of law school right along with the student, and the student's loan debt is going to weigh down the entire family. Everyone wants to live at a comfortable level. But significant others do not appreciate the major qualify-of-life

---

195. *Id.* at 38–39 (citing studies).

196. *Id.* at 10 (quoting study).

197. *Id.* at 10–11. In the book, Levit and Linder put the figure at $70,000, but they later revised it upward to $75,000.

198. Although the details vary by state, guardians ad litem are appointed by the court to represent and advocate for the interests of minors in cases where no one else might be looking out for the child's best interests, such as in child custody divorce disputes or cases where a child has been abused or neglected.

sacrifices that may be required to achieve a high income as a lawyer. Chapter 18, which addresses the different job options available to new law graduates, discusses some of the trade-offs. You will be happier if your student is happy! There are few assertions in this book in which I have more confidence. "Follow your heart!"—post it on your student's refrigerator.

Law School May Cause Students to Become More Emotionally Detached

> I find (and my girlfriend does as well) that I'm a lot more critical and detached in that I see everyday incidents as "cases" rather than actual people. My girlfriend says law school has made me a "butthead" because I'm not as nice as I used to be.
>
> —1L describing his biggest change in personality after one semester

Finally, law school may cause students to become more emotionally detached or hardened. As one commentator said, "[A] certain lack of emotionality and 'hardness' is often advanced as a professional ideal."[199] Thinking from the heart, regrettably, is not regarded as a pathway to either academic or financial success as a lawyer. The lack of contexts in which feelings and emotions are relevant in law school can be demoralizing and alienating, all the more so for students who came to law school with a sincere desire to help people. As one student said, "I'm definitely becoming more detached, mostly because of analyzing everything as a hypothetical rather than something affecting someone's real life."

Pity the poor lawyer who dares to believe or suggest that personal feelings are relevant to the resolution of a case. In *United States v. Johnson*, the defendant was convicted of possession with intent to distribute cocaine. The defendant was arrested during a traffic stop after a drug-sniffing dog alerted police to the presence of drugs. The defendant appeal-ed his conviction, arguing that the dog-sniff inspection was an illegal search under the Fourth Amendment to the U.S. Constitution. Unfortunately for the defendant, after his con-

---

199. James B. Taylor, *Law School Stress and the "Déformation Professionelle,"* 27 J. Legal Educ. 251, 265 (1975).

viction and before his appeal was heard, the U.S. Supreme Court ruled that police do not need a driver's consent to subject a vehicle to an inspection by a drug-sniffing dog. During the oral argument on appeal, the defendant's lawyer expressed personal distress about the leeway that the Supreme Court's decision gives police to make pretextual traffic stops with the secret goal of using the stop to elevate the confrontation to a search and arrest for drugs or other crimes. One of the judges on the three-judge panel hammered the lawyer for articulating his concern:

> **Lawyer:** I'm here because I feel very strongly about this. I mean, my words are probably not being heard by very many people. But I feel it necessary that some people need to listen.
>
> **Judge 1:** Any way to distinguish [the Supreme Court case]? I mean, I understand you object to the premise.
>
> **Lawyer:** I hope you can find one.
>
> **Judge 2:** Well, what you want us to do is overrule the Supreme Court.
>
> **Lawyer:** I want you to find a way to help me to distinguish this, Judge. I'm very disturbed.
>
> **Judge 2:** You can be disturbed on your own time. Why are you intruding on mine? I can't reverse the Supreme Court.
>
> **Lawyer:** Because I want you to be disturbed too.
>
> **Judge 2:** Well, if I am disturbed it's by arguments that have nothing to do with reality.[200]

This is a message law students receive from day one: *Your personal feelings are not important* in developing and advancing legal arguments.

Don't get me wrong. Law professors don't expressly teach students that feelings and emotions aren't important. Kindness, empathy, passion, integrity—no law professor, judge, or lawyer worth their salt would deny that all truly great lawyers display these qualities. They are vital to several aspects of lawyering, such as client counseling, appealing to juries, and knowing when to do the right thing. But subjec-

---

200. Oral Argument, United States v. Johnson, 123 F. App'x 240 (7th Cir. 2005), http://www.ca7.uscourts.gov/ fdocs/docs.fwx?caseno=04–2732 & submit=showdkt & yr=04 & num=2732.

tive feelings and emotions do not figure into the equation of sound "legal analysis." Under the American adversary legal system, cases are supposed to be decided by neutral decision-makers (judges or juries) based on law applied to facts.

Related to disengaging feelings from legal analysis, law students and lawyers learn they must separate their feelings about clients and their causes in order to do their jobs. Within the adversary system, the lawyer's role is to present the client's side zealously, even when the cause is unjust. Lawyers don't have the luxury of selecting only clients with noble causes that they believe in. Very few paying clients arrive at law offices with haloes above their heads.

As a young lawyer, my managing partner assigned me to represent a real estate developer in several cases. In every case, from any reasonable objective viewpoint, the client's position was unjust. One morning I was taking the deposition[201] of a young woman, a former tenant at one of the client's properties, who was suing the developer. I still remember her name and what she looked like. Halfway through the deposition, with the court reporter transcribing everything word for word, the woman stopped and said, "How can you represent these people?" "Excuse me?" I said. "You seem like a nice person. How do you represent these scumbags? How do you sleep at night?"

The event left a deep impression because the truth hurt. To say I did not like the client would be an understatement. If I were a judge or jury, I would have ruled against him in every case. But I still had to represent him the best I could. I couldn't go into court and say, "Your honor, I've determined based on fairness that my client should lose this case." If I had spent my nights as a practicing lawyer considering whether I advanced the cause of justice each day, I really wouldn't have been able to sleep. Few lawyers would. I had to detach myself from my feelings about both clients and cases to be a competent lawyer.

The adversary system, like all complex adjudication systems, has many flaws, but most law students and lawyers believe strongly in it. The major alternative is the system used in most European and Latin American countries, where matters are left to appointed civil servant judges, bureaucrats

---

201. A deposition is where lawyers are able to ask questions of litigants and other witnesses under oath before a court reporter prior to trial.

essentially, to both investigate and decide cases. Nevertheless, being trained to not inject one's personal feelings into cases can't help but affect students, whether they realize it or not.

What I described works in reverse as well. Many clients are the opposite of the client I described. They are sympathetic and in dire straits. Many are suffering not only financially, but physically. They tug at the lawyer's heartstrings. But lawyers can't get emotional about them either. They would quickly burn out. Imagine if a doctor became emotionally involved in every patient's suffering. No lawyer has the emotional capacity to take on every client's troubles as their own.

The upside of developing a facility for separating personal emotions from work is that it is the only way most people can function effectively as lawyers. Critical is being able to compartmentalize that side of lawyering and not allow it to spill over into other parts of life. But that is easier said than done.

Learning About Personality Type

Much of how law school impacts people depends, obviously, on the particular student. It is important for your student, and also you, to recognize that students have different learning styles that are tied to their personality types. I strongly recommend that both your student and you complete and learn about the Myers–Briggs Type Indicator (MBTI), an instrument for measuring personality preferences based on Swiss psychologist Carl Jung's research into psychological types. The real test is available online for a fee. Copycat tests can be found for free, but I recommend the real thing.

The MBTI is designed to help people understand certain core personality preferences that affect the way they gather information, make decisions, organize their lives, and interact with people and the world around them. If the name sounds familiar, it could be that you've already taken the MBTI in a different educational or career context. Extensively validated, the MBTI is the world's most widely administered personality measuring instrument for mentally "normal" (if there is such a thing) people. Millions of people take the MBTI each year.

Your student can learn a lot about their law school learning style from taking and reading up on the MBTI. There's even a book on the MBTI just for law students: *Juris Types*, written by Martha and Don Peters.[202] The Peters are MBTI gurus who have spent decades researching the MBTI and its application to law students. *Juris Types* is filled with practical information about the learning strengths and weaknesses for each of the sixteen MBTI personality types in tackling the core challenges of law school: studying, classroom participation, and exam-writing.

The MBTI can also help your student figure out why they struggle with certain aspects of law school and what kinds of legal jobs will best fit their personality. Here's an example: The MBTI measures personality preferences on four spectrums: Introversion–Extroversion, Sensing–Intuitive, Thinking–Feeling, and Judging–Perceiving. The Thinking–Feeling scale measures how people evaluate information and make decisions. "Thinkers" prefer making decisions based on objective, impersonal weighing of data, whereas "Feelers" prefer subjective, value-based decision-making.[203]

As you can imagine given what's been said, Thinkers are more likely to feel comfortable with law school's emphasis on neutral, objective analytical thinking, while Feelers may find it discomforting. Feelers care more about the actual people involved in the cases.

Just recently a 1L came to see me. He had done well in his first semester, but was laboring under doubt as to whether he wants to be a lawyer or pursue something closer to his heart. To his credit, he had taken the MBTI and studied up on it, concluding that his Feeling side didn't seem to be a good fit with being a lawyer. That's not necessarily true. Feelers have valuable skills, such as people skills, that Thinkers may lack that can be very advantageous to lawyers. The point isn't whether it's better to be a Thinker or a Feeler, but that, by understanding these aspects of self, students will better understand why law school impacts them the way it does, and also their strengths and weaknesses as a law student and for different types of law practice.

---

202. Martha M. Peters & Don Peters, Juris Types: Learning Law through Self-Understanding (2007).

203. *Id.* at 17.

I also recommend that *you* take the MBTI to understand more about yourself, your student, and your relationship with your student. I've learned more about myself and my relationships of all types from the MBTI than from any other single source.

* * *

"They're turning me into someone else. . . . They're making me different."[204] No, this isn't a line from *Invasion of the Body Snatchers*. A classmate of *One L* author Scott Turow told him that during their 1L year. Whether students realize it or not, law school does make them different. Because the transformational process is gradual, law students may not detect the changes.

Armed with the information in this chapter, you may be in a better position than your student to spot these influences taking root. If and when you do, point them out to your student. Going back to the home-buying example, if your student gets too hung up in doing a Judge Learned Hand cost-benefit analysis, stop her and say: "Honey, I love Judge Hand as much as you do. He's awesome. I'm even thinking we should name our first child after him. But he's not going to be living here. We are! We both love the house. We can afford it. We can fix what's wrong with it. Let's go for it!"

204. TUROW, *supra*, at 72.

CHAPTER 13

"WHAT I LIKE ABOUT YOU":[205]
STUDENTS EXPLAIN THE GOOD
PARTS OF LAW SCHOOL

The one thing I can honestly say I love about law school is the feeling that came over me at some unspecified point during my first year—the feeling that I had found my niche in society and that I was following the path I was meant to follow.

—2L

My students call me "Tortman" as a nickname, but by this point you might be convinced a more accurate nickname would be Debbie Downer, Nattering Nabob of Negativity, Death of the Party, Professor Pessimism, or something similar. Admittedly, the last few chapters leaned toward the drearier sides of law school. Here, we switch gears and talk more about the positives.

Unfortunately, existing research, and we've seen there's quite a bit of it, concentrates on the detrimental impact of legal education on students. No one has specifically studied the good things about law school or the positive effects it can have on students. One strong encouraging note can be found in the 2009 Law Student Survey of Student Engagement (LSSSE), to which more than 26,000 students responded. The results showed that 83 percent of law students evaluated their "entire educational experience" as good or excellent,

205. WALLY PALMAR, MIKE SKILL, RICH COLE & JIMMY MARINOS, WHAT I LIKE ABOUT YOU (Nemperor Records 1980) (better known collectively as the Romantics).

190

while only 16 percent rated it as fair or poor.[206] Thus, despite some shortcomings, legal education is a satisfying experience for most students.

With no time to wait for academic researchers to begin examining the positive aspects of law school, I turned to law students for their opinions. No one knows better than students what there is to love and hate about law school. I sent emails and posted Facebook messages to former and current students stating that a body of research shows negative effects of law school on students, but added that there *must* be something good about law school. Why else would everyone be there? Then I specifically asked: "What do you love about law school?"

This chapter is made up of the answers to that question. While most of the responses are from students at one law school, based on my experiences both as a law student and a professor at several law schools, I'm confident that the comments capture many of the essentials of what law students everywhere enjoy about legal education. Hopefully, you'll find this chapter comforting and affirming.

Virtually all of the students who responded to this unscientific survey found something good to say about law school.[207] But not everyone. One former student wrote: "Alcohol. And that's all." An upper-level student wrote: "What do I love about law school? Delayed the real world for another three years." A 1L wrote, "There is nothing I love about law school yet, but I guess I don't hate it either!"

Obviously, the best thing about law school—and the reason students are there—is the payoff at the end: becoming a lawyer. So let's get that one out of the way. As a 2L commented:

> The most obvious, utilitarian reason to like law school is that it offers a career track—not a very romantic notion, but it's true. We, especially all the liberal arts majors, really appreciate the security of knowing that at the end of the tunnel, we will have marketable job skills. Not only that, but these skills will also afford us

206. LAW SCH. SURVEY OF STUDENT ENGAGEMENT, STUDENT ENGAGEMENT IN LAW SCHOOL: ENHANCING STUDENT LEARNING, STUDENT RESPONSES, STUDENT SATISFACTION 5 (2009), http://lssse.iub.edu/pdf/2009 sturesp_studentsatisfaction.pdf.

207. Not everyone responded to the survey question, so it's possible that some students truly couldn't think of anything they love about law school.

the independence and flexibility to do all different kinds of work. I came to law school so that I: (1) could help lots of people; and (2) would never have to have another boss. Whenever I concentrate on these ambitions, I feel totally satisfied with what I'm doing with my life, and that's definitely something to love about law school.

I'm not sure the student will be fortunate enough to never have another boss, unless she opens her own law firm straight out of law school (which about 5 percent of graduates do), but we'll take as a given in this chapter that the overriding best thing about law school is the end game, the pot of gold at the end of the rainbow.

The student comments are divided into categories, although several of the categories and comments overlap. Law school is a holistic experience and it's difficult to neatly compartmentalize the reasons students enjoy or don't enjoy it. As one example, several students commented that they love the intellectual stimulation of law school, while several others said they love the freedom of thought in law school and the new awareness it instills, both of which serve to make law school intellectually stimulating.

To avoid undue repetition, I limited the number of comments in any particular category to five, but this limitation can be misleading because it skews which items were listed most frequently. For example, *many* students listed "friends" as the thing they love most about law school, while a much smaller number listed "the Socratic method," yet both of these categories contain five comments. So keep that in mind as you read.

Friends/Camaraderie

The deep and lasting friendships one makes in law school are perhaps the highlight of the entire law school experience and the students' answers to my "What do you love about law school?" question bear out that assertion. Friendships were the clear number one answer.

I'm still friends with the very first person I met in law school—Mac McCarty—who happened to be seated next to me during orientation because they put us in alphabetical order. Within weeks, we were best buddies, forming a study group and eventually even rooming together. Mac and I enjoyed many memorable nights providing acoustic guitar sing-along entertainment at law school parties. In the basement of the law library, we laid claim to some choice study carrels in a corner that we called our "law office." We taped a dollar bill to the wall that said, "Our first dollar." I still have a photocopy of it. Yes indeed. Those were the days. Several of the survey respondents specifically mentioned "camaraderie." It is the perfect word to describe the atmosphere of law student bonding. Every law student will find their own "Mac" in their first-year class.

Here are some of the many other comments I received touting the friendships one makes in law school:

- Camaraderie. Law school is not unlike boot camp. While the work is tough and the time required is stressful, it is an experience shared with classmates. This encourages us as students to pull together (against a common foe!) and create intimate friendships that, hopefully, will last a lifetime.

- I love the supportive community I've found in law school. Law school gets bashed for being cutthroat, but my classmates are so supportive. People share outlines, cheer each other's successes, and can understand better than my non-law school loved ones the stress our program imposes and offer invaluable empathy and emotional support (yes, I know I used "support" three times).

- I enjoy the camaraderie among my classmates. I've formed meaningful bonds that are different from any friendships I've ever had. My classmates are accomplished and intelligent people, with interesting backgrounds, talents, and expertise—and we've all been thrown together into the same new life. Law school feels a little like a middle-school summer camp at the beginning: it is a regimented, unfamiliar, and emotional experience with strangers. But they are the only ones on earth who can empathize with you. Because of this atmosphere, friendships grow strong rapidly, and I made wonderful law school friends who have become an important presence in my life, along with their parents, wives, pets, boyfriends, best friends, and babies.

• When I read your email my initial response was to say that there was nothing good about law school, absolutely nothing. However, as I thought about it more, I realized that there was one positive aspect of law school: camaraderie. I have never served in the military and have no siblings and never before have had an educational experience so challenging, so this is the first time that I have ever experienced such a feeling of brotherhood among my peers.

• I enjoy the feeling of being part of a community of my peers. I waited three years after undergraduate to attend law school. In that time, I worked several different jobs, but most of my co-employees were much older and besides work, we had nothing in common. Law school is a community atmosphere, and it does not matter what your age or background is—you will make friends. Everyone in law school is in the same boat. We are all working our tails off to eventually earn a J.D. Being surrounded by a large group of people who are all working toward the same goal is very motivating, and helps to ease the stress.

Sense of Accomplishment, Pride, and Empowerment

Justly so, law students feel a strong sense of accomplishment and pride in their pursuit of a J.D. degree. Law school is tough, as we've seen. The material is difficult and the process rigorous. Successfully navigating law school's rites of passage such as the Socratic method, mastering the law, and earning the privilege of being a lawyer all bring a strong feeling of personal achievement and satisfaction. Knowing that, in the end, completing law school bestows on one the power to help others makes it all even sweeter.

• What I love most about law school is the sense of accomplishment I feel after overcoming the major law school obstacles (the first time being cold-called on, finishing the closed memos, exams, etc.). For those of us who are right out of undergrad and aren't accomplished professionals from previous careers, getting through the ups and downs of law school are things to be proud of! Learning something new every day gives me feelings of accomplishment and pride. Knowing that someday I'll be able to use what I've learned to help someone else gives me a feeling of accomplishment far greater than anything else I've ever experienced.

• I loved the sense of accomplishment that came with understanding how to read and analyze the law and being able to use that to effect change and make a difference in people's lives.

• Law school empowered me unlike anything before (well, at least after I graduated and passed the bar exam).

• Simply making it into law school is a worthy achievement that brings with it a degree of prestige. I am the first person in my family to enter the legal arena and I feel a sense of pride and accomplishment when I discuss my time as a law student with my peers and family members.

Intellectual Stimulation and Challenge

A large percentage of students arrive at law school having never been truly challenged in their previous educational experiences. They've always been the brightest bulbs in their classes and school has always been easy for them. All of a sudden they get to law school and find themselves intellectually awakened and challenged, and, as tough as it is, many of them love it. Students who took a break after undergraduate school and worked in less-than-stimulating full-time jobs appreciate their new surge of brain activity even more.

• I love the fact that everyone is genuinely interested and engaged in the work we're being faced with. I don't remember any class in undergrad in which a professor ended a class, and I, along with several other classmates, immediately turned to each other to continue discussing the material. And for that matter, I don't ever remember topics from my other schoolwork incessantly finding their way into my non-school related conversations, as law does.

• What do I love about law school? I love using my brain instead of breaking my back every day. I was in the restaurant business (and a few others mixed in there) for twenty years. While I loved it, you can't wait tables forever. It's also nice not being surrounded by people who champion mediocrity. I doubt I'll ever again hear, "No one's paying you to think."

• Immediately following college graduation, I got married and started a job at a bank. Although I wanted to attend law school, I worked while my wife completed her graduate studies. Similar to many other recent college graduates, I left school with a sense of empowerment and ambition. I soon found out that banking left my desire/need to be intellectually stimulated entirely unfulfilled. I felt as if I was a drone who was wasting away (even though it was only for three years) because I no longer needed to think deeply about anything. I felt intellectually lazy. As a result, law school represented an escape from monotony. I didn't want to feel as if I was settling for a job that didn't push me to the limits. I wanted a challenge, and I have surely found it. So for me, law school is about the pursuit of knowledge and earning a sense of achievement and a feeling of accomplishment—and being happy knowing that I never settled for the first job I got or took the easy and comfortable path to settling down.

• I love the challenge of law school, the fact that I have to think again instead of going through the monotonous motions of mostly mindless work. I love the fact that I am nervous about what's next, the unpredictability of what lies ahead. (I also hate that at times too.)

• The best part about law school so far is that I am able to sit down, clear my head, and think clearly about topics that matter. I love sitting with a book in the library, considering difficult scenarios, working out problems, and enjoying the process of learning. Being able to focus in solitude and quietness nourishes my mind. After too long just drifting through the motions, I felt like my brain was atrophying, and it was unsettling. Law is a refreshing way of contemplating the Socratic "examined life."

Intellectual Freedom

One of the most exciting aspects of law school is that it is a place in which different ideas and points of view are welcomed and encouraged. U.S. Supreme Court Justice Lewis Powell's famous statement in a defamation case that "[t]here is no such thing as a false idea"[208] epitomizes the law school learning environment. Legal education exposes students to competing viewpoints—from professors, fellow students, and reading assignments—on many of the most important issues of our time, while also providing a setting in which to thoughtfully explore them. This is a luxury not available to practicing lawyers, who are under time and billing pressures to simply "get the job done," as lamented by a former student in the first comment below.

- I loved the sheer limitlessness of the discussions. You're surrounded by people who are both smart and intellectually curious as well as by a myriad of legal topics. There's room and time for expanded discussion of hypotheticals and the philosophies behind the law both inside and outside of class. Practicing law is great, but I only practice in two areas and due to time restraints I have to stick on topic and see law as a practical means to an end/resolution as opposed to something philosophical.

- The thing I love most about the experience of law school is that it's still "school." I have time and am encouraged to think about life and ponder the big questions. In the workforce, most people just do their job, then go home and relax. In school, I have to think about the world and what's going on in it. That's what I really enjoy.

- I love that I can find people who share similar political and religious beliefs with me and have some fine discussions with them, but also have good talks with people whose views are totally opposite of mine.

- In everyday life it is often difficult to find people with whom one can discuss one's opinions. Many say that the art of real conversation is dead. Law school

208.   Gertz v. Robert Welch, Inc., 418 U.S. 323, 339 (1974).

has restored my faith in that art. In the course of daily preparation, every student reads the same cases, the same treatises, etc., then we all have the opportunity to dissect the theories, reasoning, and thoughts behind everything. It's like one big book club! Through that conversation, we expose one another to new viewpoints. The learning process is one big dynamic and engaging conversation.

- If I had to say what I love about law school right now it would be the fact that having a different point of view is not discouraged. Undergraduate school was a little bit rigid. I had several experiences where a different approach to a problem was unwelcomed and was told once that it didn't matter if it was a good idea because it wasn't the accepted approach. In law school a different approach to the issue is welcomed, the more points of view the better.

Increased Awareness/Deeper Understanding of the World

Related to the above, law school causes students to pay more attention to the world around them and promotes deeper understanding of important issues that affect all people. Because so many relevant issues in modern times—e.g., free speech, immigration, healthcare, globalization, gun control and gun rights, discrimination, environmental and consumer protection, the limits of presidential and congressional power—are rooted in the law, being a law student works to convert students into well-rounded, better-informed citizens.

- What I love about law school is that it encourages you to seek a deeper understanding of issues that affect our daily lives, not just as future members of the bar, but as U.S. citizens. Students often talk, even out of class, about real issues that affect real people: taxes, fundamental rights, new legislation, etc. While I am a firm believer that everyone benefits from mindless magazine-reading or TV-watching every now and then, it's nice to be able to sit and have a real conversation about something other than who is dating who or which contestant was eliminated from last night's reality show.

- Before I started law school, I was oblivious to how much I didn't understand about everyday life. Now, when I read a story in a newspaper, or watch a scene on a TV show, or hear an anecdote from a friend, I can better understand the whole situation because of law school. Law school has enabled me to better understand the world around me. Of course, this extra knowledge can turn a naïve 1L into a certified "know-it-all." My first month into law school, I was convincing my dad that he had adversely possessed a strip of land behind his house. He advised me to get my law degree first, and then tell him more about his property.

- In this age of talk radio, blogs, and Twitter, people are becoming increasingly opinionated, especially regarding social and political issues. I love that law school provides a structured and civil platform for highly educated and informed students to express and defend their viewpoints.

- What do I love about law school? I love how it builds you into a much more conscious and aware citizen.

Increased Knowledge/Intellectual Transformation

Einstein said intellectual growth should start at birth and end only at death, but the truth is that too many people stagnate in between. Law school not only jump-starts intellectual growth, but propels it to a level that would never otherwise be attainable. I've told you and always tell new students that they will learn more in the first year of law school than in any other year of their lives. It sounds like hyperbole, but it's true. The combination of the sheer amount of material absorbed and the way students are taught to think about it results in a comprehensive intellectual transformation, as the first student quoted below zeroed in on.

- I loved law school. If I could go back to law school and pay my mortgage and loans, I would. Perhaps that was a good thing—as a student, you're on the cusp of adult responsibility, but not yet having to shoulder the burden of a twelve-hour-a-day job. But what I found most amazing of all was how I saw my own mind changing during my first year. I was prepared to learn new things when I entered law school. I was, however, completely unprepared for the mental metamorphosis that resulted, dramatically changing not just what I thought, but how I thought. That, for me, was extremely fulfilling.

• The huge learning curve that most law students experience is exciting and generally beyond compare. It took me three hours to decipher my first case, but by the end of my first semester I could quickly identify the holding, procedural history, and rule of law for my briefs. While the learning curve in subsequent semesters might not be so steep, it's still pretty impressive. The summer after my second year I worked for a legal organization where lawyers expected me to research and write about complex areas of the law. It was exhilarating to be able to synthesize the information from my classes into actual practice. I was actually a little surprised that I could do it!

• While there is a lot of mental anguish induced by the law school environment, the overall rewards are often overlooked. First, we are learning about things in which we are likely interested—things that brought most of us to law school in the first place. I consider these "welcome challenges." I may not always come away from those challenges with an $A+$, but I can safely say that I have already learned SO much law. You can view grades as setbacks and let rankings be discouraging, but there is another option. You can step back and realize that we are lucky to be sitting among the brightest of students while being taught by amazing professors. Only a small fraction of the population can say that.

• I love learning and it's amazing how much we're learning every day. My dad is a lawyer, and before I started he told me that the process would stretch my brain and require me to think in a way I'd never experienced. He was right! I feel like my mind is being forced to rearrange itself to accommodate the massive amounts of information that we're required to learn.

• I love how I have learned so much in such a short amount of time. You would think that my brain would be on overload right now, but it's not. I enjoy learning new topics each day, weird I know, but now every time I read a case for one of my classes, I look forward to finding out the issue and get excited when I figure out the reason for assigning that particular case.

Socratic Method

Given what has been said about the Socratic method, you might think this heading got included in the wrong chapter by mistake. Could anyone other than a masochist find something to love about a teaching methodology that is regularly accused of being terrifying, hostile, humiliating, and alienating? Yes! Several students listed the Socratic method as *the* thing they love most about law school. Their answers surprised even me, a staunch believer in the value of Socratic teaching. Appreciation of the method usually doesn't arrive until one is looking back on it *after* law school. Give these students credit for recognizing that, while the Socratic method can be intimidating, it can also be exhilarating, and it certainly makes for a much more vital and interesting classroom learning experience than standard lecturing.

• I love the Socratic method. In undergrad, it was too easy to daydream or lose attention during a lecture, and not have to worry about it. There was no penalty for daydreaming in class. But the Socratic method keeps me focused in class and, thus, learning more. The Socratic method does make for some late nights reading the material on occasion, but it's so worth it. It's definitely not the big bad monster it's rumored to be, as long as you're prepared for class.

• I love how different the classes in law school are as opposed to undergrad. I love the non-lecture format of classes because they are so much more interesting. Though I was scared of the Socratic method, I find it to be a much better way to learn and makes class much more interesting.

• I enjoy the advanced dialogue that often occurs when using the superior teaching mechanism of the Socratic method. I enjoy going in depth with the material and learning all the ins and outs of the law, rather than just skimming the surface of each topic.

● It's ridiculously gratifying when the professor poses a question and I'm able to recall the answer or use the information I've learned to come up with the correct answer. (Even if I'm not called on or don't volunteer my answer, it's still a mini-victory for the day and I love it!)

● Law school is better than undergrad because you participate in class. You must pay attention in class, and you must do your homework. In undergrad sometimes you don't get much from the actual class, and can learn everything you need to know from your books (super-boring). In law school you learn what you need to know from your teachers, in class. This makes the classes much easier to sit through. They fly by.

The Law Is Interesting

For all its imperfections, the law is interesting. No two cases are alike even in the same subject area. One advantage of the case method is that students see how legal rules affect real people, something that could not be accomplished from reading law in textbook-like treatises. Whenever a student comes to me and talks about quitting law school, my first question is, "Do you enjoy 'the law' itself?" If the student answers "yes," which most do, I try to help them find ways around the other issues that are causing them to rethink their decision to come to law school. It was my love for the law that kept me hanging in there during my stressful first year. Like the students below, I found reading and deciphering cases to be fascinating.

● This may sound rather nerdy, but I really do enjoy reading the casebooks. The cases strikingly reveal the human side of the law—it affects the lives of real people and everyday problems, in addition to providing a broader foundation for our society. It's interesting to study and debate those problems, solutions to the problems, and the ramifications of those solutions. I find the law to be a thing of beauty. The common law is flexible enough both to adapt to the times and to respect the wisdom of past generations. It's individualistic in allowing for human variance, yet it also respects the greater community, past and present.

• One reason I love law school is because most of the material is fascinating. Coming into law school, I assumed a lot of the cases would be dry and boring. For the most part, I have been pleasantly surprised. When the rules meet the facts, the cases come to life.

• What I like most about law school so far is that it is interesting. Yes, it is a lot of work, and yes it takes more time (twelve hours a day) than I thought it would, but the subject material is not boring (except for Civ Pro). If this were twelve hours of math a day I would rather rub a cheese grater on my forehead.

• I love that law school makes me WANT to learn. I actually have a DESIRE to wake up at 6 a.m. so that I can arrive at school by 8 even if my first class of the day does not begin until 11. I do not mind staying until 5 or 6 o'clock even when I am done with my last class of the day at 2. I have never before "wanted" to read, but I actually enjoy reading assignments now. Although law school is difficult (and will only become harder), I have a joy and passion in my heart each and every day I wake up knowing this is what God intended for me to do with my life.

The Material Is Relevant

One reason the law is interesting is because it is relevant, both to everyday life in a society weighed down by law and to the student's career goals. In undergraduate school, students are required to take many courses that have no perceived connection to their lives or interests. We've all sat through classes thinking, "What is the point of learning this stuff? I'm never going to use it for anything!"

From a superficial perspective, one could say the same thing about some law school courses. A student who doesn't plan to practice bankruptcy law or tax law might think courses in those areas are not relevant, maybe even a waste of time. But few students know in law school what areas they will end up practicing in. Moreover, "the law" is a monolithic integrated whole. Legal issues often bleed over from one subject area to another. For example, a personal injury client who comes to a lawyer seeking help recovering damages from the person who injured her might also be on the verge of filing for bankruptcy because of her medical bills. Meanwhile, the Internal Revenue Code has specific provisions as to which types of damages for personal injury are or are not taxable. Thus, to function as a competent lawyer, students need to learn at least the basics about a variety of subject areas outside their specific areas of interest. But beyond that practical consideration, any area of law, no matter how boring the subject may seem on the surface, becomes fascinating once one starts delving into its many intricacies, contradictions, and exceptions.

- During my pre-law school life as a high school math teacher, a common refrain among my students was, "When will I ever use this when I get out of school?" On the really bad days it was honestly hard to come up with a reasonable answer to this question. Going back to my days as a college student, many undergraduate courses, especially general education courses, produced this same question in me regarding a course's relevance and applicability. Thankfully, for the large majority of law school classes, such a query will never leave the lips of students. I love that I am faced daily with problems in class that practitioners encounter in real life on a regular basis. I consistently perceive the real world relevance of the material I am studying and, thus, I do not get the feeling that I am wasting my time or merely satisfying a credit requirement.

- I love how the class material of law school has the potential to be directly relevant to my career (unlike undergrad where I had to take biology and math, yuck).

- I love the fact that, for the first time in my academic career, I feel like I'm actually learning practical information. I'm not just "working to make good grades" so that I can "get a degree" and just move on to the next level. Everything that I'm learning at this point is material that I will use for the rest of my life.

- After students have become acquainted with the law school teaching style (a little daunting), the basic tenets of the law (a little difficult to grasp), and the workload (very intense), many begin to develop specific areas of interest. This, in turn, provides students with a sense of focus about their future and the goals that they want to achieve. I knew generally what I wanted to do when I came to law school, but learning about my area of interest has allowed me to flesh out my career goals and pursue them more intently. I think a lot of students share this sense of enthusiasm and passion about discovering and developing their legal interests.

Rigor and Structure

Law school converts students, most of whom are young and some of whom may have been borderline slackers in undergraduate school, into "professionals." The demanding amount, difficulty, and precision of the material combined with the expectations placed by professors on students to be prepared, punctual, and act professionally all work to instill discipline and focus in students.

Even though they often complain about it, most students appreciate the demanding level of professionalism in legal education. I had a former student who left law school to pursue a Ph.D in another area. He had a hard time adjusting to what he saw as unprofessionalism and laxness among the professors in his new program because he compared everything to law school. He reported that his professors often didn't prepare for class, dressed slovenly, missed scheduled appointments, didn't reply to email from students, and arrived late for class or sometimes didn't show up at all. He said many of the assignments were "blow-offs" and found he could b.s. his way through major papers the night before they were due. Grading occurred haphazardly or not at all. It didn't matter, apparently, because he said just about everyone in every class got an A. You'd think that last part would appease him, but he found he missed the high level of excellence that is the norm in legal education.

We've seen law school's rigor reflected throughout the book. Here are a few comments specifically addressing the disciplined nature of legal education:

● I love that law students are held directly accountable for their work and effort. While this may seem like common sense, my other educational experiences have not always reinforced the principle of accountability. It has often been my experience in school that the "slacker" or procrastinators could simply cram or get the Cliff Notes version of the course material and still perform adequately or even well when it came time for exams. These experiences included my time as an undergraduate and graduate student. However, these methods are simply not an option in law school. I love that law school embodies the old adage, "You reap what you sow." As someone who always puts in the daily effort, I am grateful that hard-working law students are able to see the fruits of their labor in their research, writing, exams, and grades. This realization provides a sense of accomplishment and instills in me a belief that it was all worth it.

• Because there's only one thing to do in law school— law school stuff—my life has been simplified significantly. Before school, I was always working a couple of jobs and volunteering a lot, which meant my schedule was never predictable. I couldn't really focus on anything. This was all right for a while, but I got tired of the chaos, and I definitely wasted a lot of my time. Now my days are structured, sometimes planned to the hour, and each semester presents a satisfying story arc like a TV miniseries (except that it always ends in exams). Free time means so much more than it did before. When class is canceled it's like getting an extra birthday. This isn't because school is so terrible that it makes everything else seem more fun, but when you spend most of your time immersed in one worthwhile pursuit, a little relaxation can be so rewarding.

• Every day has a purpose. I'm a goal-oriented person, both in life and in school. So law school is a perfect fit. I have a list of what needs to be accomplished each day, and it gives me something to work toward. Granted, there are days when I wish for a bit less "purpose," but it's still nice to see progress being made. Finding my purpose for each day makes me feel like I'm one step closer to larger goals like passing finals and becoming a well-educated and knowledgeable attorney.

Caliber of Students and Faculty

One reason law school and law school relationships are so special is because, usually for the first time in their lives, students are surrounded by people—both classmates and professors—of extremely high caliber, intellectually and in terms of their professionalism and dedication. Every law school building in America contains literally hundreds of people worthy of respect and admiration.

- I love what a privilege it is to be surrounded by people passionate about law, and the caliber of the students and professors I get to interact with on a daily basis.

- The students and professors are smart, hard-working people. Intellectual discussions abound in the classrooms, the lounges, and the hallways. I enjoy this environment; it pushes me to work harder and engage more. I think a lot of students derive a sense of accomplishment from every success they have in school partially because it is such an intellectual setting. Answering a question correctly in class, winning a moot court round, or getting a good grade is especially rewarding when your peers are among the brightest around.

- I love the professors. It is often said that the higher you move up in education, the less the "teachers" care about you. Law school has proven this false. The faculty is accessible and almost always willing to answer questions. They support our philanthropic endeavors: for example, at our school, numerous faculty members supported our Race Judicata 5K to benefit legal services for low-income people and donated to our Alternative Spring Break in Miami to assist immigrants after the terrible earthquake in Haiti. They serve as advisors to our student-written publications, and they genuinely care about the quality of the work our students produce.

- The professors are all so outstanding at what they do. Seeing their mastery really inspires me to work hard.

Flexible Schedule

This next item hadn't occurred to me, but I guess that's only because I now take it for granted, having been fortunate to live on an academic schedule for most of my career. But it makes perfect sense. Like full-time students of higher education everywhere, full-time law students enjoy flexibility in their daily lives unavailable to most working adults. Law students work hard, as you've heard over and over, but except for fifteen or so hours of class each week and a few mandatory meetings of various types, they can do it on their own clock. Students who have taken a break between undergraduate school and law school to work in full-time jobs appreciate this aspect of law school even more. (It should be noted that part-time evening-division law students—most of whom work all day before coming to law school at night— cannot relate to this concept of a flexible schedule.)

- I love my schedule. As I approach the "real world," it is a bittersweet feeling. While I will hopefully be making money, I will be losing a lot of free time; i.e., "no class-Fridays." You can't get much better than that. And the nerd in me secretly likes the homework.

- The schedule is amazing. Having had my first 8–5 job this summer, I realized how much I enjoy the student lifestyle. You set your own study schedule around class-time. That sounds simple, but it is such a luxury. We have the rest of our lives to work 8–5 (or more). Law school is a full-time job, but a lot of the scheduling can be set according to individual preferences.

- What I love most about law school is the flexibility. Other than my class schedule, I am free to plan my day and study times at my discretion and choose when I get up in the morning and return home in the evening. For me, this is a significant change from a highly structured office environment where work hours are strictly enforced and employees generally remain in their offices through lunch. Last week I went to the grocery store at 2 p.m. and felt like Christmas had come early! Along with flexibility is personal responsibility. I enjoy knowing that it is my responsibility to complete my work on my own time. I feel a great sense of accomplishment at the end of the day when my assignments are finished.

* * *

So you can see that there really are a lot of positive aspects to law school. And, other than the flexibility of the schedule, they are all deep, important components of living a rewarding, fulfilling academic life. Unfortunately, the positives tend to be obscured not only by the empirical research we've discussed, but by the fact that law students love to partake in the time-honored tradition of complaining about law school. It becomes almost like a hobby to them. In truth, most students probably have something of a love-hate relationship with law school, as the following significant other to a law student noted:

> The funniest thing I've heard about law school is how tough it is as well as how much he loves it. How can you complain about something so much, yet actually really love it? After telling stories about how students are kicked out of class or embarrassed for being five minutes late or how he's already spent fifty hours this week on out-of-class work, he proceeds to talk about how great it is. I just don't understand this.

Many of the best parts of law school, including most of the items listed in this chapter, are more subtle and gradual than the parts that make for daily gripe-sessions. You're much more likely to hear your student come home and groan, "My Contracts professor assigned forty pages for tomorrow," than to burst through the door beaming, "Wow, my world view really got expanded today!" Having read this chapter, use it to help your student see the bright spots in the murkiness of law school. As an exercise, after law school has been in session for a month or so, sit your student down and go through the positives identified in this chapter to see if she recognizes and appreciates them. It should be interesting.

CHAPTER 14

WHAT LAW STUDENTS THINK YOU NEED TO KNOW ABOUT LEGAL EDUCATION

Something I wish my family understood is that no matter how much they think they understand about everything I'm doing/going through, *they do not understand*!

—2L

A primary goal of this book is to help non-law student loved ones like you understand the law school experience, to understand, as the student above put it, what your law student is "doing/going through."

In my surveys, I explicitly asked students to explain what they think loved ones need to know about the ways in which the demands, stresses, and pressures of law school differ from undergraduate school and other educational programs. Their responses are grouped into categories. As in the previous chapter, many of the comments are interdependent and could be placed in multiple categories. For example, law school is "all-consuming" in part because of the "workload" and "intensity" of it, all separate categories below.

I let students do all the talking in this chapter. You've already heard from me on most of the points raised below. Anything I added here would be repetitive. Back in an early footnote, I explained a famous doctrine of tort law called *res ipsa loquitur*, which translated from Latin means "the thing speaks for itself." That's true of the comments in this chapter. They say it all and need no explanation.

Listen carefully! This is what your student will be wishing you knew and appreciated about his or her law school experience.

Law School Is an All–Consuming "Way of Life"

• Law school is completely different than anything I have ever experienced. The demands are constant, the stress only builds throughout the semester, and the pressure to succeed is daunting to say the least. I have always believed that if my family and loved ones could understand the rigors of daily law school life, then they would truly see that it isn't a lack of caring that prevents a student from calling home or visiting, it's simply not always a viable option. Because time is so valuable and scarce, law students must actually plan for phone calls and visits home just like they plan for Contracts or Torts!

• Law school is all-consuming. Reading for class is never optional, and just skimming the material without taking notes or critically thinking about it is not sufficient preparation. This is because the material covered is not simply a list of rules or facts or things to remember; law students are trying to comprehend a system of shifting principles and policies through the complex reasoning of a judicial opinion. Moreover, there are a finite number of good grades due to the curve—not everyone will be satisfied, and with good grades comes even more pressure.

• Once other assignments and activities—moot court, legal writing courses, law review—are piled on top of normal class preparation, literally every minute of the day *could* be spent on law school. This is impossible, of course, but even when your student is enjoying a movie or a nice supper, law school is probably on his or her mind at least in some way.

• Non-law school loved ones need to understand that law school is a totally unique educational experience unlike any other undergraduate or graduate level program, and success in any other program does not necessarily mean that the student will succeed in law school. They should understand that it is an enormous time commitment that must take priority if one is to succeed. The loved one should understand that there is tremendous pressure that comes with an entire grade riding on one final exam. Work cannot be delayed or done later. A law student cannot get behind.

• The entire semester revolves around one exam at the very end which is the only grade a student gets. If we get behind, it just makes it that much harder. I emphasized to my family throughout the summer before starting that once classes started I would be spending a majority of my time each day either at school or studying/doing homework. I think non-law school loved ones need to realize just how much that involves. It's more than adequately preparing for classes the next day. It requires so much extra work to understand and retain very complex material. Law school becomes our lives for the fourteen weeks of a semester. There's no choice but to treat law school that way.

Law School and Law Students Are Intense

• Law students are intense about grades, awards, jobs, internships, and just about anything else that demonstrates success in law school. I went to an elite private high school and a top liberal arts college and I have never seen more competitive students in my life than at law school. The intensely competitive environment is relatively unique to law school so it's hard to explain to my husband what it is like to be around law students all day. Usually the best I can do is say: "This place is driving me crazy."

• In undergrad I never felt the type of academic pressure that I feel at law school. Loved ones of law students should know that most of the students and the professors are very intense and this intensity permeates the law school atmosphere. The professors are intense about class preparation and participation. In undergrad, I always did my homework and participated in class, but the in-class atmosphere was more laid back because the professors did not use the Socratic method. In law school, you need to be prepared not only to volunteer your thoughts in class, but also to respond to unanticipated, difficult questions from the professor. This requires a specific type of class preparation that most people who have not gone through law school would consider excessive.

• They need to know that it is very time consuming and that law school is an extremely pressure-packed endeavor. Not only do students have to complete complex reading assignments in our casebooks, we also must read supplemental study aids, make extensive outlines, write lengthy legal papers, and prepare for exams months in advance. I have seriously done more work this semester of law school than I did my entire undergrad career.

• Law students are typically smarter, or more capable, than the average undergrad student. I've found from conversations with peers, and my own personal experiences, that undergrad really wasn't a challenge. Most of us didn't have to do the required reading and could write papers in one night. My first day of law school completely and permanently changed my work habits. I've done every ounce of reading and every required assignment, and studied seriously for the first time in my life. The time commitment and brain commitment are HUGE compared to anything else. So loved ones may try to compare the work we do in law school to what they've done, but it's on an entirely different level. Recognizing the difference is the first step to appreciating it.

• Most things in law school are "fall off the cliff" types of things, meaning that you have just one shot to get things right. This applies to everything from the single-exam model favored by the vast majority of professors to the daily class work and the stress involved in not understanding something or knowing the right answer. Needing to get everything right in one shot is a phenomenon not usually experienced elsewhere in life.

Law School Classes and Class Preparation Are a Different World

• Even in my almost twenty-year long professional career prior to starting law school, I rarely had to prepare as much as I do just for a single class in law school. The only exception was when I had to prepare to speak at a seminar or conference. But I only did that typically once a year—not two or three times every day! So, patience and understanding is the key to supporting your loved one and trying to understand what they're going through, because it takes a lot of work to really be prepared. Even as hard as I work, I rarely feel fully prepared, which of course leads to STRESS!

• Going to class is like taking a test every day. You have to be prepared enough and know the material well enough to be able to answer questions when called on. One quick read of the material will be insufficient for two reasons. First, a quick read is hard to accomplish due to the complexity of the material. Second, a quick read will not solidify the information well enough to remember the details in class. It takes a lot of time!

• As a law student who is also a graduate student, I would say that the pressures of law school differ greatly from either undergraduate or graduate school. One big difference and stressor in law school is that the student is required to perform at their peak ability at all times. Being put in the hot seat during class requires not only that the student has read the material before class, but also that they understand it well enough to discuss it in great detail while being extensively scrutinized by the professor in front of the entire class. If in the course of this questioning the student shows himself to be less than fully prepared, his final grade in the course could be reduced. This type of intense classroom interaction simply does not occur in graduate courses.

• Everyone had classes in undergrad where you could simply not raise your hand and expect not to be bothered. In law school, however, there simply are no blow-off classes. Every single day presents a minefield of opportunities to be exposed as either a good student or a bad one. There is an immense pressure to be prepared to give the right answer on the spot if called upon in class. I worry less about what the teacher will think if I am unprepared and more about what the other students will think about me.

The Single–Exam Format Is Stressful and Intimidating

• The exam preparation period is probably the most difficult tribulation the law student has ever been through. Remember, each class involves a lot of preparation work and the exam counts for 100 percent of the grade. In the second semester, I was literally sitting in a room for almost sixteen hours a day every day for about two weeks reading and studying. That's enough to drive you crazy. The exams themselves (mind you, they occur in the midst of these grueling studying marathons) are an emotional and mental sledgehammer. Despite a whole semester's work trying your best to learn the law, and those final few grueling weeks studying every hour of waking life, the exams are such that they leave you feeling as if you know nothing and that all your efforts have been in vain. This is particularly true the first semester.

• In undergrad, the most I studied for any single exam was probably five hours, and that was for Invertebrate Paleontology, a pretty tough upper-division class outside of my major. In law school, if I knew I only had five hours to study for an entire exam, I wouldn't even bother to show up. Studying for exams is such an extreme process it almost defies explanation. It is an intense period—beginning months before the actual test—of condensing tons of hours worth of reading, thinking, and listening into digestible bits of information that can be instantly recalled in order to properly identify and competently analyze a number of complex issues. First-year students in particular struggle with even figuring out what it is they are supposed to learn. Many, for example, waste hours memorizing the facts of all the cases we read, only to find them to be of little use.

• Loved ones should know that law school exams test an enormous amount of information. I usually start my preparation four to six weeks before exams, depending on how many exams I have. Every semester, my husband makes fun of me for this. He never fails to tell me stories about how when he was as an undergrad at an "elite" university he studied the night before every exam and still did fine. I have tried to articulate to him the amount of information I need to comprehend and often memorize for each exam. I even try describing it to him using quantitative measurements, as in "I have X number of pages of outlines to memorize" or "I have X number of cases to grasp." It's impossible to convey this to someone who has never been through it. I'm not sure he will ever fully understand how much work it is.

• Your whole future is hanging on one exam. At least that is what you think. It is practically impossible to say anything during this period to make someone feel better about the exam. It is better to just be supportive than lie and tell your loved one everything is going to be all right. Because it won't be until we get our grades back and find out we haven't failed.

• There is only one grade. Exams are extremely stressful and anything outside of school that can be put on hold should be. During this time, I don't want my husband talking about changing jobs or how little Johnny got in trouble at school. Don't complain about laundry, cleaning, or cooking. Don't ask about Christmas plans/presents/where we are supposed to be when, etc. I'll have to figure all that out after exams are over!

Grades and Class Rank Are Crucial

• Loved ones should know that getting good grades in law school, being accepted to prestigious groups (such as law review or moot court), and landing good summer jobs are not just about over-achieving, but have a major impact on the student's future and ability to do what he or she wants to do with their law degree. The legal world is obsessed with grades, class rank, and accolades (all lawyers *were* once law students) and the correlation between those markers of success and landing a good job are stronger in the legal profession than in any other profession. The legal community's often myopic—in my opinion—focus on law school-specific achievements continues to bewilder me.

• Just doing all the assigned work won't get you even to the middle of your class. Those at the bottom of the class have a harder time getting the right internships and eventually getting a permanent job. They aren't always allowed to participate in the extracurricular or co-curricular activities or take the classes they want. They lose any scholarship they're on, and they have more worries about failing the bar exam. Good 1L grades are very important to the initial stages of future careers, and they are very, very hard to get.

• Class rank and GPA dictate what types of law school activities (such as law review) and careers are available for a student much more so than the things over which students have more control, such as leadership positions or volunteer work. At first, you are just competing for grades. But soon, it feels like you are competing for your entire future.

• Grades and class ranking are so important early on at law school. I wish they weren't, but they are. Especially in a weak economy, ranking toward the top of the class is a necessary competitive edge. As an undergraduate, I worried in a general sense about my GPA, but rarely lost sleep over it. My first graduate experience, ten years ago, was pass-fail. We worried about things like "connecting" with the faculty for guidance and reference purposes later on, but never agonized over grades.

• Many law students are, by nature, "overachievers," so it is easy for a loved one to write off their student's long hours as simply a symptom of the student's personality type. It took my husband until the fall of my second year when I started to interview for summer jobs to understand the importance of good grades and law review. When he saw how few people landed jobs, or at least good jobs, he started to understand that my commitment to academic excellence wasn't just a manifestation of my own perfectionism, but rather an essential means to an end—getting a good job that makes me happy.

Law School Makes People Competitive

• It is an incredibly competitive atmosphere where failure and mediocrity are not options. Everyone in the program is used to being successful. So you have 500 overachievers competing with one another: a recipe for disaster.

• The most important thing for loved ones to know is that law school is about competition. It is no longer sufficient, as it might have been in undergrad, for a student to simply be prepared, she must be more prepared than all the other students. In undergraduate school, all of the students in a course could be rewarded with As if they did the work. This was reassuring because the requirements for success were fixed and clearly delineated. In law school, on the other hand, students are graded against each other on the curve. Unless she is naturally more gifted, this means that the student must work harder, more efficiently, and longer than all the other students to earn one of the few As available in a course. When all of the students are neurotic perfectionists accustomed to getting top grades, this environment creates the perfect storm for academic brinksmanship. This level of pressure is difficult for non-law students to understand.

• Loved ones should know that competition in law school can resemble some of the silly competition found in junior or senior high school. Cliques are quickly formed. Some students will only invite "elite" students to join their study groups. Some students will tell others wrong information about an exam, assignment, or case. Finding like-minded, trustworthy fellow students can be difficult.

• There is no escaping the competitive environment of law school! I am not a very competitive person (although my wife will probably disagree) and even I get caught up in it. Your rank among your peers has a significant impact on what opportunities are available to you. If you do well and have a high enough class rank, you have opportunities to participate on law review, be a research assistant for a professor, and interview with the big law firms. There ends up being a relatively small group of people competing for these same opportunities, so there's always gossip amongst the group about who is doing what.

• Never before have rankings and competition been so important than in law school. Medical school is not even like this. My fiancé is in his first-year of medical school, and they are not graded against each other. They help each other out, and the school itself has ample resources and will bend over backwards to en-sure that no one fails. It is more an atmosphere of companionship. While you do make friends in law school, everyone has to look out for his or her self. Sometimes this pressure is not anticipated by incoming law students. For me, I had no idea that it was going to hit me like a ton of bricks after my first set of exams. Then comes law review, moot court tryouts, job interviews, etc. That adds to the atmosphere of compe-tition, and it can be very hard. A lot of students, like me, are probably very humbled by the process. I was thankful that my fiancé gave me my space when neces-sary, bought me flowers during exam week, and our relationship did not suffer as a result.

The Workload Is Enormous

• Law school can be very depressing. From the out-side, my life may seem easy. I get home every day by 3 or 4 p.m., don't have class until 9 a.m., and my weekends are theoretically "free." The worst thing that my partner will do is tell me "Wait till you get out of school and have a real job." My reply is always, "Okay, then switch places and see how long you last!" I think what most people who have "real jobs" don't realize is that much of the work and stress that comes from law school doesn't happen in an office or at a desk during normal working hours. Most of it happens during study time when my partner is either asleep or watching television.

• The most obvious thing is the time commitment. Just between classes and the assigned reading, the expected time requirement per week is anywhere from fifty to seventy-five hours (if one actually does all the reading). This is to say nothing of prepping for finals or getting papers done. Throw in a part-time job, externship, internship or clinic and the potential time commitment is ridiculous.

• Law school provides a unique kind of pressure because on the first day you create a To–Do list that never ends. The rate at which you cross things off is only a fraction of the rate of things being added. It is not that each thing on its own would be so difficult. It's the combination of everything. It's hard to explain to a loved one without sounding like you're whining all the time.

• Perhaps because I'm older and had been out in the real world for a decade, I was arrogant about my ability to perform in law school. I remember reading the early assignments and putting my books away, telling my wife it was easy. I was blown away by how prepared my fellow students were. They were reading the cases multiple times and briefing them—truly "analyzing" them. I didn't think I would need to work that hard to be ready. I remember feeling dejected after classes that first year, even though I hadn't been called on because I was painfully aware of how relatively underprepared I had been. During the first year, my wife would ask me how much time I would need for studying on every upcoming weekend—how much time I would have to be away from her and our daughter. I would leave to study for four hours and return home feeling that, because it takes so long to get through the dense material, I had accomplished so little. I felt so guilty about not being more grateful that she had given me the time, but it never seemed enough. It's hard to explain to a non-student that you're not done working yet, that you'll never be done!

• Law school is a job, and undergrad is not. In undergrad there is still plenty of time for a life outside of school, whereas with law school you must schedule your "old life" around school. When I first started law school and figured out what it would entail, I posted on my Facebook page, "Goodbye old life, see you in three years!" Several months in now, I still feel the same way. It is hard on loved ones as well as the student because you don't have time to talk on the phone or go out like you used to. Holidays entail reading, and any trips out of town are stressful because it takes the whole next week to catch up.

As a hobby, I sing and play in a Memphis classic rock band called The Vynals. Editing this chapter brought to mind the chorus of a song we regularly perform, a 1965 blues-rock hit by a British Invasion band called The Animals: "I'm just a soul whose intentions are good. Oh Lord, please don't let me be misunderstood."[209] Even through the sterile printed words of the student comments, one can feel the almost desperate desire of law students to be understood by their loved ones.

Trust that law students' intentions really *are* good. They don't want to neglect you. They don't want to act like the "crazy" or "selfish" or "whining" people some of them admit to being. They are struggling themselves and need your support. But it won't always be easy to give it. As I'm sure you've figured out by now, being in a close relationship with a law student can be a challenge. Time to tackle that issue head-on.

209. BENNIE BENJAMIN, GLORIA CALDWELL & SOL MARCUS, DON'T LET ME BE MISUNDERSTOOD (MGM Records 1965: Animals U.S. version). The song was originally written in 1964 for jazz singer Nina Simone. *Rolling Stone* magazine ranked The Animals' version at #315 on its list of "The 500 Greatest Songs of All Time."

CHAPTER 15

LAW SCHOOL AS A "PROXIMATE CAUSE" OF STRESS AND CONFLICT IN RELATIONSHIPS

Sorry, couldn't resist slipping in a legal term. It's part of the sickness.[210] We've touched all along on how law school can affect outside relationships. This chapter examines directly the potential sources of stress and conflict that law school presents to relationships with law students, saving tips for managing the issues for Chapter 17. Much of what is said below applies to any close relationship between a law student and non-student, including relationships with parents, children, best friends, and others, but the primary focus is on intimate partner relationships, married or unmarried. Partners are, after all, the ones who apart from the student bear the brunt of the law school experience.

Conventional wisdom has it that law school is deadly for relationships, or at least very hard on them. That's why approximately one half of the nation's law schools offer special sessions during orientation for married students or students with families. It is commonly said that law students suffer higher divorce rates than the rest of the population, although no reliable data exist to support the assertion. The anecdotes below show that law school *can* be a "relationship

---

210. Speaking of sickness, the referenced term—"proximate cause"—is universally regarded as the first-year Torts doctrine most likely to make your student ill. To use a popular law professor saying, getting a handle on proximate cause is like trying to nail a jellyfish to a wall, which, by the way, would be a mean thing to do and could violate animal cruelty laws, albeit only after twelve years of litigation to determine whether a jellyfish is an animal.

killer" for some people, although no doubt in connection with other causes:

- My boyfriend of two years broke up with me his first two weeks at [law school]. . . . Law school definitely kills relationships with undergrad significant others, that's for sure.

- I was in a three-year relationship and it took less than one semester for her to dump me because she never got to see me.

- It ended mine. We were living together and I moved out in November of my 1L year. On the plus side, things got so bad in October and November that I would go and bury myself in work so I didn't have to deal with her. I think that helped with finals.

Even if law school doesn't kill relationships, there's no question it can add stress and conflict to them. You've read enough by this point to guess the main reasons why:

- The immense workload often does not leave students with enough quality time to spend with significant others.

- The intensity (e.g., the Socratic method, single-exam format, competitive atmosphere) and volume and complexity of the material covered can cause students to be preoccupied—to the degree of a diagnosable obsession in some cases—with law school even when they are physically present with their partners.

- Even when students are present and able to stave off thinking about law school, law school can leave them mentally and physically taxed to the point where they don't have the energy to contribute adequately to the relationship.

- The foreign language and esoteric substance of law combined with the close and cliquish nature of law students can leave non-students feeling excluded and sometimes jealous.

- The intellectual advancement and enlarged world view of the student may create a fear that the law student is "outgrowing" the partner.

- The stress of law school on students can spill over into outside relationships, causing friction.

- The time demands of law school may cause students to not uphold their side of the partnership in terms of everyday activities such as housecleaning, errand-running, meal-providing, and childcare.

- The high cost of legal education combined with the fact that the student is not generating income can cause money issues (e.g., too much debt accruing, lower standard of living, resentment from the sole breadwinner).

- Law school inculcates students to be more argumentative, analytical, and adversarial with the result that even well-meaning students may approach relationship issues in off-putting ways.

This chapter addresses each of these potential sources of discord except the last one, which was covered in Chapter 12. Throughout, law students and their partners weigh in with comments. Before tackling the individual sources of potential conflict, we'll look at the big picture and also cover some good news for loved ones of law students who happen to be in school themselves. But first this important qualifier:

Law School Doesn't Cause Problems in All Relationships

Nearly all of the comments in this chapter came in response to a survey question about whether law school had added stress/conflict to an intimate, committed relationship. Most of the respondents—law students and loved ones alike—reported that law school had caused at least some stress or conflict in their relationship. But it's important to start out by noting that several respondents said law school had *not* negatively affected their relationships. Many of these comforting answers, however, were short, offering little insight, so they aren't reprinted below. Examples include "Not particularly" and "Not really." Several other answers took the form of "No, but ...," with a qualifier attached to the "but" (*unbuttoxia l'attachement* as it is called in the law[211]) that amounted to a concession that law school actually had caused some stress or conflict. But a few students who said

211. Kidding. Just want to make sure you're still paying attention to footnotes. If you're going to keep up with your law student, you *absolutely must* embrace footnotes and academic geekiness in general.

law school had not caused any stress/conflict in their relation-ships offered well-reasoned explanations, as in these com-ments:

- It has not added any stress to our relationship. I think that we are at an advantage because we are both several years (or more than several) removed from our college days, and we are used to long hours and stress. I have also made a concerted effort to treat my school days as work days. That means that I use my time in such a way that I do not have a lot of late-night studying. We still have our time together.

- My husband has been a champ about the adjust-ment. I think he understands what I am going through because over the years his career has at times required intense (and all-consuming) months of training. I think that experience helps him understand that I am not pushing him away when I spend time studying. He doesn't take it personally when I can't spend time with him. He understands that this situation is inconven-ient, but only temporary. He's on board. It would be much more difficult for me if he was not!

- Our relationship had never really been tested until we moved eight hours away from home to continue our educations here. We had been together for two years before we moved. I enrolled in law school and she in nursing school. We were the only familiar thing either of us had here. We depended on one another for support and helped one another cope with the foreign and demanding environment. Through this process, we have discovered that we make a great team. Together we can accomplish anything.

While comments like the above were in the minority, keep in mind while reading this chapter that law school does not automatically have a negative impact on every relationship. To the contrary, as the last comment noted, as with many of the struggles and challenges partners face in life, law school can bring people even closer together.

The Big Picture: Get Ready for This

Prepare to make adjustments in your relationship with your student. Reorienting is necessary in relationships with any type of graduate student. Researchers of graduate student relationships emphasize that graduate education is a "family task," one that "entails a realignment of family priorities of time, energy, commitment, and financial resources."[212] As made clear from the comments in the previous chapter, law students would argue that the demands and pressures of law school exceed by a wide margin those in most other graduate programs. Thus, reorienting a relationship with a law student may be both more necessary and difficult to accomplish.

To facilitate the necessary adjustments, everyone involved needs to be aware at the very beginning that some shifts, whatever they turn out to be for the individual relationship, inevitably will occur. Not all of the adjustments will be bad, but it's safe to say that you will not sorely miss many of them when they go away in three or four years.

Here are three wide-angle perspectives from three significant others of law students on the challenges law school can present to intimate partner relationships:

• When my husband started law school, we had a seven-month-old baby at home. I had gone back to work and was not prepared for what we would encounter during that first year. We had gone to the law school family orientation session. We had both been working full-time for years, at demanding and time-consuming jobs. We had even worked different shifts. I thought we would be fine. I did not factor in the amount of time it would take for Thomas to get used to going back to school. I never imagined how much reading he would do or how his class schedule would affect our home life. I also did not realize what I would need to do to make it all work. We never fought or had major conflicts, but now we stay stressed and exhausted all the time. On Saturdays, I would need to buy groceries or make a Target run. I would need to drop off the dry cleaning or run other errands. I would feel so guilty asking Thomas to watch our daughter that I would end up taking her with me. The errands would take twice as long and I would come home frustrated

212. Joshua M. Gold, *Profiling Marital Satisfaction Among Graduate Students: An Analysis of the Perceptions of* Masters and Doctoral–Students, 28 CONTEMP. FAM. THERAPY 485, 485–86 (2006) (citing to other studies).

and tired. In the end, I learned that I would have to run errands during our daughter's nap time or even after we put her to bed at night. I can now tell you where to find all the 24-hour stores in our neighborhood.

• Living with an OCD-perfectionist is hard enough as it is, but when that perfectionist starts law school, it becomes a completely different kind of hell. I would love to say that the start of this journey did not cause any stress between us, but when you are involved with a law student, you come second to their workload. Honestly, you are pushed to the bottom of the list. We had discussed at length what we thought the course load would be like, but we were way off. I knew that the workload was going to be heavy, and I knew that a lot of the responsibilities around the house would fall on me, and I was okay with that. What I wasn't prepared for was when we went somewhere *together*. I would be the one driving with the radio off, sitting in complete silence while she sat with a highlighter and book-briefed cases. Or I would wake at 3:00 a.m. to find her still studying. The laptop became her best friend, got more time with her than I did, and went everywhere we went unless it was to the grocery store.

• The added stress has added conflict. When we were both undergraduates, we spent the weekends partying and didn't do an ounce of homework. Spending a day in the library was unimaginable. I'm still in undergraduate school and can still get away with last minute homework and night-before-exam cramming. Unfortunately, this is no longer the case with him. It's a big change. He is being overwhelmed and this has added stress to both of us, including the occasional fight over how much time I get from him. Now, when we fight I typically always lose. He pulls arguments and words out of his ass that I have never heard of. It is very annoying. He is the same person he was before law school, just way busier and slightly more cynical. I've seen sides of him I never saw when we were younger, like his newfound wonderful time-management skills, which he frequently uses to criticize me for being late.

In just these three comments, we see embodied a number of the themes listed at the beginning of the chapter, including the time demands and intensity of law school, the spillover effect of law school stress, and the changing nature of law students. We also see a unifying, unyielding truth. No matter how healthy and strong the relationship, being with a law student is in all cases going to require, in the words of David Bowie, *"Ch-ch-ch-ch-changes."*[213] No relationship is immune.

Symmetrical vs. Asymmetrical Relationships

You probably don't know if you're in a "symmetrical" versus "asymmetrical" relationship with your student, but if you're in the former group, congratulations. What follows will come as welcome information. As used by family relationship researchers, symmetrical relationships are relationships in which both partners are in graduate school; asymmetrical relationships are those where only one partner is in graduate school. According to the research, this difference can be important.

Several studies have found that students in symmetrical relationships have better quality marriages than those in asymmetrical relationships. In one study, graduate student couples in symmetrical relationships scored higher on marital satisfaction tests.[214] Another study found that relationships in which both spouses were enrolled as college students "ranked significantly higher in quality of marriage than couples in which only one spouse was enrolled."[215] Another researcher found that graduate students in symmetrical relationships are more stable and satisfied with the relationships, while those in asymmetrical relationships "tend to be more volatile, conflictual, and dissatisfied."[216]

What accounts for the difference? Graduate students in symmetrical relationships are more likely to share the same goals, interests, and lifestyles, all of which make them more

213. DAVID BOWIE, CHANGES (RCA Records 1971).

214. Rebecca Groves Brannock et al., *The Impact of Doctoral Study on Marital Satisfaction*, 3 J. COLLEGE COUNSELING 123, 127 (2000).

215. Gerald R. Bergen & M. Betsy Bergen, *Quality of Marriage of Universi-*

ty Students in Relation to Sources of Financial Support and Demographic Characteristics, 27 FAM. COORDINATOR 245, 248 (1978).

216. Michele Scheinkman, *Graduate Student Marriages: An Organizational/Interactional View*, 27 FAM. PROCESS 351, 355 (1988).

compatible.[217] Importantly, in light of what we've been discussing throughout the book, they *understand* each other better. They understand the academic pressures of exams and deadlines, erratic schedules, late-night studying, and other hallmarks of being a graduate student. Both partners are excited about what they are doing and working toward. They are more likely to be on equal footing, both intellectually and financially. It's much easier being dirt-poor when you're struggling together toward similar objectives.

Not so with many asymmetrical relationships. While the graduate student is soaring through an adventure filled with intellectual stimulation and dreams of better days, all the while operating under an aberrant schedule that knows no time-clock, the non-student may be grinding away at a nine-to-five job—often an unfulfilling one—to support both of them. Whereas grad students need to spend much of their nights and weekends with noses in books or eyes locked on computer screens, non-students are interested in leading what one researcher euphemistically called a more "diversified life."[218] Understandably, they want to get out and do things: go to movies, restaurants or clubs, work out together, hang out with friends, or travel. When the non-student says "Let's PAR–TAY!" they don't want to hear back, "Sorry, have to STU–DAY!" Asymmetrical relationships also may be marked by discomfiting feelings of inequality that can be manifested at several levels: in finances, educational attainment, and household responsibilities.[219]

Feelings of resentment can arise on both sides of asymmetrical relationships. The non-student may feel resentful that the student is never available, always too tired to have fun, not performing as many household responsibilities, and adding debt, rather than revenue, to the family budget. The student, meanwhile, may feel resentful that the non-law student does not understand what the student is going through or share in their excitement. The student wants their partner to be supportive and may expect them to pick up the slack in household responsibilities. They also may resent that the non-student partner has more leisure time or that they continually demand time and attention that the student can't presently give.

---

217. *See id.*
218. *Id.* at 354.

219. *Id.* at 357–59.

Several of these aspects of asymmetrical relationships are reflected below in the comments of both law students and their significant others. While unscientific, the comments appear to support the hypothesis that law students and their partners in symmetrical relationships may have a somewhat easier road to travel than their asymmetrical colleagues.

From Law Students:

• Overall, law school has not caused a strain on our relationship. My fiancé is in medical school, and he studies harder than anyone I have ever met. So, we mutually benefit from staying out of each other's hair. When he has an exam week, I will try to have dinner for him or be extra nice, and he offers me the same courtesy. I admittedly get moody around November when law school exams are looming. I feel very vulnerable and I take a lot of my stresses out on him, but I can usually admit when I am doing it. He knows from where the animosity is coming and knows not to take it personally.

• Law school has definitely taken time away from hanging out with my boyfriend, but he is in pharmacy school and going through the same things that I am. We knew the stresses that school would cause and decided before starting that we would not let this get in the way of our relationship and no matter how hard things got to never get mad at each over the stresses and demands of school. There have been times when I would enjoy spending unlimited time with my boy-friend like I used to but we both know we have other priorities that come first right now. It is much easier being able to go through this with someone who is going through something similar and understands, at least to an extent, the stress you have going on in your life.

• Law school did cause some stress and conflict, but this went away after my wife went back to school during my second year. While this created more of a tension on the budget, she has complained less about my time spent doing school and talking too much about school. She is doing something new and exciting, which we both can talk about as well.

From Significant Others:

• I am thankful every day that I am also in a challenging/high demand program of study (nursing school). If I were not in school or in a less challenging field, I believe more stress would be added. It is helpful that we are both extremely busy. This may seem sort of backwards, but because I am also very busy and without much idle time, I understand the high demands placed on my law student. The only extremely high stress time for us is finals, and as time goes on, this stress has been easily relieved by talking out our feelings.

• Law school hasn't added any stress or conflict at all to our relationship. I'm also in professional school and my girlfriend and I study together and we both know what the other is going through and the stresses of school. We don't put any other added stress on each other when we need to study. The one negative is that we don't get to spend quite as much time together as we would like, but it will all be worth it in the end.

• Since we are both in some type of graduate school, we both understand how easy it is to be consumed by the stress of a workload, deadline, or social interaction. But this hasn't added conflict to the relationship, since we both seem to be careful to balance our stressful ranting with listening and our snippy moods with understanding.

Sources of Relationship Conflict Related to Law School

If you're a graduate student, or plan to be, the above section should give you some comfort. But most people aren't in graduate school, and even if you are, it doesn't mean your student's law school experience will be a day at the beach for you. For one thing, while the research suggests that being on the same page with your law student academically can ease your relationship path in some ways, dual-graduate student status may exacerbate other relationship issues, particularly financial ones. Picturing a household occupied by two non-earning, loan-gobbling graduate students can be a terrifying thought! So let's look at some of the major sources of potential conflict in relationships with law students.

Neglect

No one in a relationship wants to feel like they rank anywhere except in first place in the hearts, minds, and souls of their loved ones. Unfortunately, the combination of the time demands, obsessive preoccupation with, and exhaustion caused by law school often leave significant others feeling neglected.

Neglect Due to Time Demands. "[A] compulsive, progressive ... disorder characterized by self-imposed demands, compulsive overworking, inability to regulate work habits, and an overindulgence in work to the exclusion of intimate relationships and major life activities."[220] That's how one psychologist described "workaholics" and how many significant others to law students would describe their partners. Law school has a way of bringing out the inner-workaholic in everyone.

The time demands of law school can be a major source of discontent and disruption in relationships. A national study showed that spouses of workaholics reported greater dissatisfaction with both their relationships and their partners.[221] What Scheinkman said in her work about graduate student marriages fits law student relationships:

> Time is a major problem for most couples. For example, it is quite common for couples to complain about how opposite their schedules have become. While the working spouse goes to bed early so that he or she can go to work the next morning, the graduate student, driven by inspiration or deadlines, works late into the night. While the working partner sees the evenings and weekends as a time to unwind and relax, the student sees these uninterrupted blocks of time as opportunities to go to the library and have a spell of concentrated work. Over time, the graduate student's studies become like a lover to whom the student is totally devoted.[222]

220. Bryan E. Robinson et al., *Work Stress and Marriage: A Theoretical Model Examining the Relationship Between Workaholism and Marital Cohesion,* 8 INT'L J. STRESS MGMT. 165, 165 (2001) (referencing definition from co-author Robinson).

221. *Id.* at 167 (discussing study).

222. Scheinkman, *supra*, at 359–60.

I love that last sentence in light of this comment received from a 1L: "My husband has asked me on numerous occasions if I am having an affair with someone, namely Cecil C. Humphreys." The full name of the University of Memphis law school is the "Cecil C. Humphreys School of Law." Here's what some other law students said about how the time demands of law school impacted their relationships:

- Lack of time spent together is the biggest problem; especially when I am at home but I'm not really "there" because I am doing homework. There are times, such as studying for finals, that my wife hates my computer because I spend more time with it than with her. This was especially true in my 2L year when I worked twenty hours a week on top of being a full-time student. When the end of the semesters rolled around and I had to study for tests and finish writing papers, I'd spend pretty much all day either working or doing homework. There were times she'd try to draw me away, and though I wanted to, I just had so much to do, the breaks would be short—to eat dinner or talk for a bit. I know this bothered her.

- Because my wife is the breadwinner and I am the student, I think we both felt going in that I would have more time, both practically and emotionally, to be available to help with our then infant daughter. She has regularly told our friends that she dreads my return to school after vacations, because I "disappear." Ironically, I have always felt like I could have invested so much more in law school and have held back because of my commitments at home.

- Law school has caused conflict, big time. I completed the first two years of law school working full-time and attending the part-time program. The stress was mainly coming from my complete lack of free time and inability to pay any attention to my husband. I've switched to the full-time program and work significantly less at the present time and this seems to have helped quite a bit.

- One of the hardest times is during exams, especially because each year, my fall exams fall either on or the day after my birthday. My partner did not seem to understand how I could stay closed up during Thanksgiving break, reading and studying and skip out on my birthday! Not even long enough to go to dinner! Another source of conflict or stress happens on Sunday afternoons. I would say, okay, time to hit the books, but my partner would want to go see a movie or go shopping or do something else fun.

• I was in a long-distance relationship that did not survive beyond the winter break. We made it through the first semester, but my significant other was often hurt by the lack of time to talk on the phone, which was our only means of interacting. We only saw each other twice during the fall semester. We talked on the phone briefly each day and at night—but there never seemed to be enough time to truly nurture the relationship. The emotional and mental tug I felt from the relationship began to be too much. Though it's been kind of a sad holiday break, I had to end the relationship before the second semester began. I'm not sure how great an effect law school had on the demise of this relationship—it may have ended anyway—but it is likely that the time and effort I put into my studies, and the anticipated emotional and mental energy needed for the second semester played a role in my decision to break things off.

Neglect Due to Preoccupation With Law School. A common complaint from people who are close to law students is that even when law students are physically present they are mentally absent, preoccupied by law school. An anecdote from a law student recorded by researchers studying the effect of law school on marital relationships offers an amusing snapshot of the problem. The student was describing her thought process on occasions when her husband attempted to be amorous:

There are times on a Saturday or something, he'll try to be all romantic. He'll come to my office, I'm studying, he'll put his arms around me and he'll be like would you come with me? Let's go to bed. And I have had days where, honestly and this is like kinda sick, ... I'm just like wondering how fast we can do this because I have reading to do.... I'm like, "oh my god ok, we gotta make this quick because I have this and this to do." My husband is trying to be romantic and I'm thinking about torts."[223]

Here are some observations about the preoccupation issue from other students and their partners:

From Law Students:

• My boyfriend complained that I spent too much time away from him and was not attentive when I was with him. He said that my mind wasn't present when we were together, and he felt ignored and marginalized by my attitude.

• Law school stresses have caused me to be less attentive. While we're having dinner around the table, I am thinking about the memo that's due in three days.

From Significant Others:

• I miss my husband sometimes, even though he's home. He has to spend so much time reading and working on the computer. It would almost be easier if he were away at a job or something, not sitting there, with his mind someplace else.

• The relationship stress happened before we got married when we weren't living together. After working all day, I wouldn't want to shower, go to him while he studied/ate, then go home an hour later and go to bed. It was as if it wasn't even worth getting ready for. It felt like he really didn't care about the relationship as much as I did. Sometimes I would leave him alone and not speak to him for days, weeks even. I was mad and wanted him to suffer, but I guess it probably didn't hinder him at all, probably helped actually. My frustration mostly came out of "I've worked all day. I don't want to sit here and watch you study and eat."

Neglect Due to Exhaustion/Lack of Energy. Another cause of neglect by law students is that they simply get worn out physically and mentally from the burdens of law school, leaving them with insufficient energy to give to the relationship, as law students explain:

• Law school was a big adjustment in my marriage. Although my husband is extremely supportive, he

223. McQuillan & Foote, *supra*, at 17.

would get frustrated with me and school at times. Usually it would happen when I continued to break our "date night" because I wanted to sit at home and watch TV or sleep when I had free time. Law school is very draining because of all of the attention to detail and stress that I was under to properly prepare for class. So when I had free time, I did not want to do anything except to be alone and not think about anything.

• Oftentimes when I get home I'm tired from a day of waking up early and stretching my brain to the breaking point. After my reading for the night is done, I usually just want to watch a mindless television show or stare at the wall for a few minutes. My wife, on the other hand, loves going outside and doing involved activities. Occasionally she gets frustrated because I'm boring and don't have the drive to do anything fun. I'm not boring! I'm just burned out!

• My husband has complained a little that my attention is lacking, that I never have energy to do the social activities that he wants to do, and that he's concerned that I like to spend more time with my law school friends than with him. These conversations usually arise when we're planning our weekends, or when we're trying to plan "date night." My husband works from home, so when I come home on a Friday night and want to stay in and watch a movie, he wants to go out for dinner or drinks. This often serves as a point of conflict for us.

But don't let these comments get you down. Maybe you're one of those optimistic souls who always looks at the bright side of things, someone who, like the husband below, can put a positive spin on being abandoned by their law student:

Law school hasn't really caused any stress or conflict. It's actually been a lot better for me because now she stays up all night studying, which means the bed is all mine. Then it gets even better when I wake up because she'll still be studying, meaning sometimes I get lucky and my breakfast will already be ready for me before I head out to work.

Jealousy

Subsumed within feelings of neglect can be feelings of jealousy arising from the fact that the student spends so much time absorbed in law school and with their new law school friends. This jealousy can assume the form of "priority jealousy," where a partner feels they've been supplanted in the hierarchy of importance in the other's life and/or "exclusivity jealousy," where a partner worries that the other is acting in ways that violate the exclusive compact of a romantic relationship.[224]

Priority jealousy can arise from both the student's fixation on law school itself and the close bonding that occurs among law students. Partners may resent that they are being made to take a backseat to law school and the student's new circle of friends. As one student wrote: "Jealousy is a problem. Spending so much time with students and books, and talking about them to loved ones, may lead the loved one to think you care more for law than for them, and that your highest priority is not your relationship but law school and law buddies."

Exclusivity jealousy, also called "romantic jealousy," arises from a concern that the student is engaging in behavior that threatens the exclusivity of an intimate relationship. It doesn't have to involve any kind of physical contact, although that may be part of the underlying worry. It includes any behavior that violates the jealous partner's understanding of his or her exclusive relationship rights, for lack of a better term, such as sharing personal information or going to lunch with someone of the opposite sex.[225]

As an example, just recently a student came to me asking for advice on how a handle a situation where his serious girlfriend was extremely jealous that he had begun studying with a female classmate. The girlfriend insisted he stop studying with her and he didn't know what he should do. He insisted the study arrangement was innocent and that he loved his girlfriend. Of course, I didn't try to tell him what to do, but I did point out that sometimes we have to do things

---

224. Padmal De Silva, *Jealousy in Couple Relationships: Nature, Assessment and Therapy*, 35 Behav. Res. Thera- py 973, 975 (1997) (describing these two types of jealousy).

225. *Id.*

that are important to our partners even if they seem unreasonable to us. I also noted that if he insisted on continuing the study relationship, there was a big difference between studying together in the afternoon in the law library as opposed to at night in a bar (some students really do study in bars) and to use his common sense to draw those kinds of distinctions.

In response to my surveys, some students and their partners agreed that jealousy was a problem for them. One student wrote: "Yesterday, one of my study partners called me and my husband asked me why we (my study partner and I) didn't just 'do it already.'" Overall, however, most significant others denied feeling any jealousy of the student's new law school friends. Hopefully, it's because they are all in healthy, secure relationships. But it also could be that the significant others don't understand enough about what goes on at law school social events or how closely law students bond together. Another possibility is that because jealousy is considered an unattractive quality, they suppressed or underreported its existence.

I received two interesting conflicting gender-based comments about jealousy. A female student said "the only instances where I have seen jealousy occur is with male students attending law school and their significant others becoming jealous of the women they are meeting in school." But a male student said exactly the opposite: "My gut opinion is that, as a general rule, female students have jealous boyfriends whereas male students generally do not appear to have jealous girlfriends." Who's right? My guess is both are half-right.

Some significant others expressed low regard for law students in general, which possibly has a root in jealousy, although it may simply be their honest take on law students. One husband said he was "annoyed by [law students'] immature ignorance and can't really stand to be around them for long periods of time." A wife said she's not jealous of her law student's new friends, but rather pities their lack of development and awareness and obsession with law school.

One point that stood out clearly from the student comments was that jealousy is much less of an issue for students who incorporate their partners into their new law school social lives. I received several comments similar to this one: "My boyfriend only expressed jealous feelings toward the beginning of the program when I was hanging out with new friends without him. Once he met my new friends and began attending law school social events with me, most of the jealous feelings seemed to drop off." This observation is in harmony with my advice from the beginning: Get involved in your student's law school experience early.

As everyone knows, jealousy can be a destructive force in a relationship. It can be harmful not only to the jealous person, but to the partner at whom the jealousy is directed.[226] Research supports the common sense proposition that jealousy is related to relationship satisfaction.[227]

Concern That the Law Student Is "Outgrowing" the Other

An oft-spoken fear is that graduate and professional students may "outgrow" their partners, intellectually and otherwise. If true, it may help explain why symmetrical graduate student relationships can work better than asymmetrical ones. Graduate students in symmetrical relationships are growing together. Both partners are expanding their internal and external worlds in ways that feel stimulating and adventurous. But in asymmetrical relationships, it may be that only the student is growing while the other is stagnating, often while slogging away at an unfulfilling job to support the household. Relationship researchers label the unenviable position of such non-student partners as "role captivity."

The intellectual growth of a law student is stunning in its arc. As we saw in Chapter 13, among the things students love most about law school are the intellectual stimulation, rapid knowledge acquisition, and the opening of new vistas onto the world around them. Meanwhile, they're surrounded by unusually smart and accomplished classmates at every step. These developments may be threatening to significant others. One husband of a law student wrote: "I feel insecure that I'm not as smart as her new circle of friends. I have made comments about how I feel but we have not really talked about it."

---

226. *Id.* at 973 (stating that "[o]ften, it appears that the main sufferer is the partner about whom the jealousy is focused—the target, or the victim").

227. *See generally* Mariana Gatzeva & Anthony Paik, *Emotional and Physi-* *cal Satisfaction in Noncohabiting, Cohabiting, and Marital Relationships: The Importance of Jealous Conflict*, 48 J. SEX RES. 29 (2011) (discussing the impact of jealousy on marital relationships).

Here's a piece of advice I would give my daughter (or son, if I had one) if she married a law student—meaning, it's the most honest and sincere advice I can muster: Never put your personal development on hold for the sake of your law student. Many significant others do it, largely for financial reasons, and a lot of times everything works out fine for everyone involved. But a lot of times it doesn't. Some law students abandon the partners who supported them up to or through law school. Occasionally, these events even result in divorce court proceedings by the abandoned partner to recoup his or her investment in the lawyer's career.[228] Talk about turning the legal tables.

But more important than self-protection, continuing to pursue your own passions will make you a more interesting person, which in turn will enhance your self-esteem, make you more attractive to your partner, and help maintain balance in the relationship. Law school will require some sacrifices on your part, but that should *not* include sacrificing yourself.

Spillover Stress

Researchers have long studied the "spillover effect," sometimes called the "stress contagion," of work demands and pressures on non-work relationships. As the name suggests, spillover theory posits that negative aspects of work, including stress, are often brought home by the worker and can affect the worker's family.[229] No big surprise there. While some are better at compartmentalizing than others, it's difficult to separate major portions of our lives and store them in neatly segregated boxes.

---

228. *See, e.g., In re* Marriage of Graham, 135 Cal.Rptr.2d 685 (Cal. Ct. App. 2003) (wife demanding that her ex-husband reimburse her for funding his legal education); Robinson v. Irwin, 546 So.2d 683 (Miss. 1989) (ex-wife of lawyer winning additional alimony for having financially supported him while he was in law school); Scott v. Scott, 645 S.W.2d 193 (Mo. Ct. App. 1982) (wife winning additional spousal support because she put her ex-husband through law school while they were married); Chamberlain v. Chamberlain, 383 S.E.2d 100 (W. Va. 1989) (husband appealing divorce order on the ground that it failed to reimburse him for contributing to ex-wife's legal education).

229. *See* Niall Bolger et al., *The Contagion of Stress Across Multiple Roles*, 51 J. MARRIAGE & FAM. 175 (1989) (discussing stress contagion); Jeffry H. Larson et al., *The Impact of Job Insecurity on Marital and Family Relationships*, 43 FAM. REL. 138 (1994) (discussing spillover theory).

The spillover effect of stress from law school to home life came through loud and clear in my surveys, as in these comments from law students:

- Like, right now I'm at about a seven on the stress scale. I overreact to small stimuli, like the other day my boyfriend made a maneuver in a game we played that virtually clinched that I would lose, and I started crying and told him we never played with that rule before, which is unlike me. I'm usually a good sport.

- Fights have stemmed from everything from "Are there any pretty girls in your class?" to "Is your memo more important than this relationship?" I'm, of course, not always innocent either. One time I remember losing it was one night after a long week of classes when I had a light homework load and fell asleep on the couch watching TV. About fifteen minutes later my girlfriend came in and woke me up because she was bored and wanted to go do something. I wasn't happy about being woken up so I started yelling. We fought for about an hour, but we eventually resolved the fight and I made up for yelling by taking her out to eat.

- When I began law school, it put a lot of stress on my relationship. We would fight a lot about how I wasn't home, wasn't paying attention to my home life, etc. Every time I would come home, I was expected to switch to "home mode," but I can't always do that. Finally, after a series of bitter arguments, we came to an agreement that I need a little "me time" to decompress when I get home.

- I must admit there is some added stress in our relationship due to law school. In fact, this morning, my husband informed me of making plans to go out of town this weekend without mentioning anything to me. I have a great deal of work due next week, so I let my temper get the best of me. Sometimes, he just does not understand the workload, but how can I expect him to understand it?

- In general, I am on a very short fuse now, so a comment or suggestion that I would otherwise consider with a grain of salt can set me off or piss me off. There have been two instances where my emotional intelligence decreased to that of a shrieking three-year-old and a normal conversation with my boyfriend turned into an outlandish fight. I transformed from a normal person into a scary, scary beast.

Household Responsibilities

One of the most dramatic changes in role expectations, and one of the biggest sources of conflict in relationships with a law student, concerns the fair division of household responsibilities, including housekeeping, errands, and childcare. In my surveys, this issue was raised exclusively by women law students. In her groundbreaking book, *The Second Shift*, first published in 1989, Arlie Hochschild documented the inequalities in the distribution of household responsibilities between working men and women. The book's title refers to the fact that many women in dual-career couples come home from a long day at work only to begin their second job: taking care of the household and family.

With regard to higher education students, studies show that women students traditionally have experienced greater role conflict in this regard than men. Instead of adjusting or shifting their existing roles when they become students, many women attempt to simply add their new role as "student" on top of their others (e.g., as worker, parent, spouse) and attempt to perform them all at the same high level; i.e., the "supermom."[230]

Academics who study this gender divide are in conflict as to how much the situation has improved for women in recent decades, with one expert calling it a "highly politicized" issue in the academic literature. There seems to be general agreement that, concurrent with the advancement of women in the workplace, both in numbers and earning power, men have picked up some of the slack around the house over the past decades, as measured by hours spent on housework and

---

230. Patricia A.H. Dyk, *Graduate Student Management of Family and Academic Roles*, 36 FAM. REL. 329, 329 (1987) (discussing studies). Another type of role conflict that can occur is when women out-earn their male partners. Some research shows divorce is more likely to occur in such situations. While no research exists pertaining to law students, theoretically, this type of conflict could affect some law school relationships. One professor who taught a course for married law students commented, "[I]f it's the woman on top, it may cause [the male] to be resentful and jealous—and the marriage starts to deteriorate." Sal Manna, *First Comes Love. Then Comes Marriage. Then Comes Law School. The Tricky Part is Managing All Three.*, STUDENT LAW., Oct. 1986, at 38 (quoting Dr. Clarence Hibbs).

childcare. Meanwhile, the number of hours women spend each week on housework, although not necessarily on childcare, appears to have declined.

Overall, research shows that both men and women are simply doing less housework than in the past. Our houses our dirtier, we order more take-out meals, and, seriously, who irons anymore?[231] But while there is disagreement as to the extent to which the gender gap in household labor has shrunk, most researchers accept that women still do more household and childcare work than men, although obviously many individual exceptions exist.

No research exists specific to law students, but my limited surveys anecdotally suggest that women law students in particular may struggle with issues regarding the fair division of household responsibilities. No male students raised the issue, but several women did:

● Yes, law school has caused conflict. I feel like I need more help around the house and with general household matters. Prior to school I took care of everything, worked full time, and cooked dinner every night. Now, I still feel pressure to take care of the house, but I don't have the time or energy. I definitely am stressed and I am trying to remember that I chose to do this.

● He mentioned that the house is a big mess and I haven't cooked in months. This made me feel really guilty. Then I got over it and went back to studying. Seriously, my priorities have shifted dramatically. Things that I used to take care of for my family have fallen to my spouse now. Fortunately, he has been willing to shoulder the increased burden, but I know it hasn't been fun. I tell him everyday how much I appreciate him.

● Stress has primarily come up for us in terms of household expectations. I feel like my husband should just *know* how stressed I am or what a hard day I had. But he *doesn't*. We have had all kinds of spats when I get home from twelve hours of studying and the dogs

231. *See* Suzanne M. Bianchi et al., *Is Anyone Doing the Housework? Trends in the Gender Division of Household Labor*, 79 Soc. Forces 191, 218 (2000) (setting forth data showing trends in household labor division by sex, including figures showing that the total amount of time spent on household labor has decreased, and explaining how this "undone" labor has been replaced).

need a walk or the dishes need to be washed, and I expect him to just take care of it all. Communication has become key. It's not fair for him to think that I will have the energy to do household chores at the end of the day, but it's not fair for me to expect that he will just take care of it all himself, despite his full-time job.

• We always fight around exam time, which really lasts like a month, about housework. The house gets messy, things don't get done and he gets agitated. I try to make it up to him by thoroughly cleaning the house from top to bottom the day after my last exam.

Without empirical research, one can't speculate about the extent of any gender inequality in the division of household labor in law student relationships. If division of labor is an issue, regardless of gender, the obvious solution is that each party must bear his or her fair share. Of course, agreeing on the definition of "fair share" can be a sticking point. Chapter 17 suggests that partners think this issue through thoroughly and come up with an agreement in advance. In the meantime, you can hope that your partner—male or female—is like the prince of a partner described below:

I know I am an incredibly lucky woman because my husband makes me a lunch every day, cleans the house, washes the clothes, does the dishes, makes dinner, takes care of the dog, EVERYTHING, and usually all before I get home in the evening. Although he does not understand the cases, rules, and theories, he does understand that I need support, comfort, and encouragement. He provides that all day, every day! He allows me to vent, even if he does not understand everything I am talking about. He deals with my being moody or tired for a majority of the time we are together during the week. He NEVER makes me feel guilty for staying at school for 8–12 hours a day, as opposed to coming home and being "Susie Homemaker."

The "Who Has It Worse?" Syndrome

Related to the above is what I call the "Who Has It Worse?" Syndrome, a common situation in which both the law student and his or her breadwinning partner think the other has the easier life. The following comment from a law student provides an example:

> Law school has exacerbated the "who is doing more" tension in my relationship with my significant other. Both parties in a marriage sacrifice for the relationship and this sacrifice is even more pronounced when you have a young child (which we do). Law school added another layer to this dynamic. It's hard to empathize with your spouse's stress and workload when you feel like yours is worse. For example, my husband does not always appreciate that law school is a full-time job. He knows that it is a ton of work, but does not always understand that the work is extremely demanding and often leaves me more exhausted than any job could. By the same token, I don't think I always appreciate that he works a full-time job, on which our family depends, because he gets to watch TV at night and take naps on the weekends while I am studying. We both think the other one has it better.

Law students are often lost in and overwhelmed by their study carrel-sized law school world. Sometimes they can't see beyond it and may appear selfish when it appears they are giving everything they have to law school rather than to their loved ones. Particularly in the first year, students are so wrapped up in the workload and suffocated by the pressures that they can't imagine anything being worse. Meanwhile, non-law students who spend their days "workin' for a living" may have little empathy for someone whose major life responsibility is simply attending "school." These opposing perceptions may cause both parties to end up stuck in competing thought processes like the following (which I made up):

> **Non-law student during the day:** "Great. She's out sipping on a Carmel Macchiato with her 'study group' while I have to work on these stupid reports all afternoon!"

> **Law student during the evening:** "Nice. He's on the couch with a beer playing video games while I have to work on this stupid memo all night!"

One real, and exasperated, law student explained her life this way:

I'm not just playing with my friends all day!!! Sometimes I feel like my husband thinks because it's
"school" and not "work" that it's all fun and games
up here. This is the most academically challenging
program I have ever been exposed to, and it's intense.
I feel like I've been totally immersed into this culture
and have had to learn a whole new language, as if I
had moved to Portugal. It's stressful and intimidating
when you feel like the other people get it and you
don't.

As with most difficult issues in relationships, both sides
have valid positions. To some extent, law school is a better,
easier life than a full-time job, mainly because law students
have flexible schedules and more free time during the day
than most full-time workers. Recall that in Chapter 13 several students listed their flexible schedules as the single thing
they love most about law school. On the other hand, unlike
most employees, a law student's work day usually doesn't end
at 5 or 6 p.m. For many, the hardest parts of the day—
reading and briefing cases, outlining, working on their memos—are just starting. For most students, this carries over to
weekends and even holidays. And while many jobs are stressful and exhausting, many aren't. They may be boring and
unfulfilling, but they aren't necessarily stressful or exhausting. Law students, as we've been discussing, experience abundant doses of both stress and exhaustion.

Financial Issues

In a survey by the American Psychological Association, 73
percent of respondents named money as the number one
stress factor in their lives, putting the issue above other
common causes of stress such as work, health, and children.[232]
In relationships, studies show that money is the most common issue about which couples fight.[233]

Particularly relevant to law students and their significant
others, several studies have found that debt brought into a

---

232. Bradley T. Kontz et al., *The
Treatment of Disordered Money Behav-
iors: Results of an Open Clinical Trial*, 5
PSYCHOL. SERVICES 295, 295 (2008) (mentioning study).

233. *See, e.g.*, Linda M. Skogrand et
al., *The Effects of Debt on Newlyweds
and Implications for Education*, 43 J.
EXTENSION (June 2005), http://www.joe.
org/joe/2005june/rb7.php   (mentioning
study).

marriage can be a thorn in the union, and that worries about debt are linked to negative emotional outcomes, such as depression, for young couples.[234] One study of married college students found that couples with minor debt have much higher quality of marriage scores than couples who depend heavily on student loans for income.[235] On the flipside, not being in debt is a factor associated with strong marriages.[236]

If Captain Kirk were reading this, particularly if he were about to be a 1L at the Starfleet Academy School of Law, he would immediately say, "Scotty, we have a problem." Apart from prior savings or gifts or other support from loved ones, most law students have no significant source of money to turn to other than loans. Students with strong entering credentials may receive scholarships, ranging from partial to full tuition. Some scholarship money may also be available for students who succeed at a high level while in law school. Successful students may be hired as research assistants by professors, although the hourly rates are not high, usually running from ten to fifteen dollars per hour. Most law students seek jobs at law firms in the summers, not always successfully. High-achieving students, especially those from brand-name schools, can rake in some good money if they land a summer clerkship with a large firm, but these jobs are available to only a small percentage of students. Small firms pay much less. Many of my students are spending their summers working for free just to get some experience and have something to put on their resumes. As 2Ls and 3Ls, students at urban law schools often work part-time at law firms during the school year.[237] These potential revenue sources can help, but when all is said and done, the bottom line is that you should not count on your full-time student producing any meaningful income for three years.

In my surveys, financial issues were one of the most commented-on areas among both law students and their significant others.

---

234. *Id.* (discussing studies).

235. Bergen & Bergen, *supra*, at 250.

236. Skogrand et al., *supra*.

237. ABA law school accreditation Standard 304 restricts outside work for full-time students to twenty hours per week. Because of financial pressures or pressures put on them by their employers, some students violate the rule and working more, which presents real risks to maintaining their GPA.

Concerns Arising From Student Loan Debt. As mentioned earlier, loan debt for law students averages $66,000 for public schools and $100,000 for private schools, figures likely to grow due to continuing tuition increases. The non-law student may, understandably so, get agitated or at least antsy about the amount of money the student is borrowing, since debt-load, even if it's in the student's name, will bring down the standard of living for both partners for many years to come.[238] Friction may be more likely where the significant other is the sole breadwinner, and especially if the worker is postponing his or her own educational or other advancement for the benefit of the student.

A few comments help drive home that this is an issue to be aware of and address up front with your law student:

• Law school is expensive. I really don't want his debt. I get mad because he is in law school and he jokes around saying things like, "I want to be an importer-exporter." Well, that is just great because you are in law school wasting away money and causing us financial strain.

• My husband always complains about the size of my law school debt. He says, "We could have had a mansion by now."

• My husband gets concerned with the amount of loans we are taking out. When I talk about going into public service law, I can tell he gets really nervous about our financial situation because we have borrowed money for me to pay for school.

Your student needs to plan on severely tightening his or her budget belt to minimize future indebtedness—for everyone's sake. If you're a couple, both of you need to do so. Chapter 17, the tip-giving chapter, addresses this important issue in substantially more detail.

---

238. This relationship concern is not limited to partners. As a parent, I'm always apprehensive about the prospect of my daughter taking out large student loans. Not only will the debt crimp her lifestyle for many years, but, directly or indirectly, parents usually end up stuck with part of the tab.

Reduced Standard of Living. One of the most common sources of financial stress in relationships with law students arises from couples having to adjust from being dual-wage earners to a partnership with only one wage earner and an expensive sidekick. Inevitably, when this occurs, the couple's standard of living decreases:

- The only stress in my family life that I have associated with law school is related to paying bills and adjusting to a different quality of life. Having worked for six years prior to attending law school, it has not been easy for our family to change our lifestyle with regard to our change in income. Prior to law school my wife and I both had jobs and were living on two incomes. Now that I am in law school, we are living on one income and paying for my tuition as well. This has been a pretty difficult transition for our family and I think that it has resulted in the most stress not only on me but particularly on my wife because she is the sole provider for our family, which has been a heavy load for her to bear at times.

- The biggest complaint and hardest thing for us was to go from two incomes to one income. It has just taken time to adjust to having to budget, not go on weekend trips all the time, and to realize that this is a three-year commitment that will pay off throughout the rest of our lives because I'll be doing a job that interests me and soon we will again have two incomes! Also, I think that budgeting and knowing where our money is going and realizing what we spend on life (all things that have happened since starting law school) is a good thing for any couple to do.

- When she went to school our household income was cut in half and with tuition, etc., our expenses increased. With a child and two mortgages in the picture, watching your savings account shrink while home values and other investments drop over the course of time is a scary thing. My wife still has expensive taste when it comes to coffee drinks, etc. Finding the right balance between being super-stingy and irresponsible when it comes to the weekly budget has been a learning experience. There have been times when I have wanted to walk away or take a sabbatical from my work but knew I couldn't or shouldn't with a child and a wife in school and dwindling savings. These times have put more unnecessary pressure on her to be successful and finish.

The financial impact of law school can present somewhat of a Catch–22 for relationships with law students. The reduced standard of living imposed by law school may add stress, but so will taking on additional loan debt to raise or maintain one's standard of living. Given that the former is much more limited in time than the latter—three years of law school versus ten or twenty years of debt repayment—I strongly recommend opting in favor of the temporary reduced standard of living over incurring more debt. Again, more on this in Chapter 17.

Guilt on the Law Student's Part. Being a financial drain isn't lost on students. While non-student partners may feel concerned or even resentful about rising debt or a reduced standard of living, students may suffer guilt from the same facts:

> I think the other biggest stress comes from the fact that being in law school means that I can't work, so I don't feel like I am financially contributing. I do actually have a 10-hour a week job, but that's almost nothing, so I feel like a bum sometimes. My wife has never held that over my head or anything, but I just feel bad about not helping more to support us.

* * *

As it probably occurred to you in reading this chapter, several of the sources of conflict discussed herein exist in intimate relationships of all types, not just relationships with law students. As examples, jobs and even hobbies can suck too much time and energy from a relationship, stress from any outside source can spill over into relationships, and money issues rank high on all lists of relationship torpedoes. Conflict in relationships of any type (intimate partners, parents and children, co-workers, friends) is inevitable to some extent, and not all conflict is bad. On the other hand, everyone has an interest in minimizing conflict in their closest relationships. Chapter 17 offers some suggestions from law students and their partners on how to navigate relationships with a law student. But before we go there, let's look at how law students perceive the benefits versus the costs of being in a committed relationship while in law school.

CHAPTER 16
LAW STUDENTS WEIGH THE PROS AND CONS OF BEING IN A COMMITTED RELATIONSHIP

Though your lads [and lassies] are far away

They dream of home.

There's a silver lining

Through the dark cloud shining.[239]

While your lad or lassie is toiling away in the law library, they dream of home. They dream of you. If you're in an intimate relationship with your student, *you* are their silver lining. At least that's what research and student survey comments suggest. They both support the proposition that being in a committed relationship can be an appreciable advantage for a law student.

A sizeable body of research shows that being married is linked to better physical and mental health.[240] Studies show that the emotional support and satisfaction that marriage provides can help form a buffer against daily life stressors.[241] Other research shows that marriage encourages healthier lifestyles, in part by deterring partners from engaging in risky behavior such as excessive consumption of alcohol and outside sexual activities.[242]

239. Lean Guilbert Ford, *Keep the Home Fires Burning, in* BARTLETT'S FAMILIAR QUOTATIONS 617:12 (Justin Kaplan, gen. ed., 16th ed. 1992).

240. Scott R. Braithwaite et al., *Romantic Relationships and the Physical and Mental Health of College Students,* 17 PERS. RELATIONSHIPS 1, 1 (2010).

241. *Id.* at 2.

242. *Id.*

Not married? No problem. One study found that unmarried college students in committed relationships enjoy these same benefits. The study, of more than 1600 college students at a large Southeastern university, found that college students in committed relationships experienced fewer mental health problems and were less likely to engage in risky behavior than students not in committed relationships.[243] This "behavioral regulation" hypothesis is believed to be particularly applicable to males.

With regard to law students, a nationwide study of law students designed to identify predictors of law student life satisfaction found that married or cohabitating law students "reported significantly greater life satisfaction than single students." The study involved thousands of law students at fifty ABA-accredited schools.[244]

A study of students at the University of Denver law school reached similar results.[245] Researchers administered questionnaires to students at the beginning and end of their first year in an attempt to measure various factors, including relationship factors, related to law student stress, adjustment, and happiness. The study found students who reported being in happy romantic relationships at the beginning of law school showed higher positive affect and fewer health problems at the end of the first year.[246] To the contrary, students who lacked an intimate partner when starting law school showed greater negative emotions at the end of the first year and also were more likely to consider or plan on dropping out.[247]

My survey results corresponded with the research findings. I asked law students in committed relationships: "Do you think being in a committed intimate relationship has made your law school experience easier or harder than if you were not in such a relationship? Please explain." A clear majority of the respondents said being in a relationship made law school easier, in many cases much easier. "EASIER, EASIER, EASIER!!!" is how one student put it. Many of their answers give credence to the "support hypothesis" regarding the protective, buffering effects of being in a close relationship. Other comments—such as those by students who said

243. *Id.* at 3, 7–8.

244. Nisha C. Gottfredson et al., *Identifying Predictors of Law Student Life Satisfaction*, 58 J. Legal Educ. 520, 526 (2008).

245. *See* Pritchard & McIntosh, *supra.*

246. *Id.* at 741.

247. *Id.*

being in a relationship keeps them from hanging out in bars and looking for love in all the wrong places—may support the "behavioral regulation hypothesis."

Of course, nothing is ever all sweetness and light. A number of students saw both pros and cons to being in a relationship while in law school, while some stated flatly that being in a relationship made their law school life harder. Here's what people in all three groups had to say:

Easier

Emotional Support

• If it wasn't for my wife, I wouldn't be here in the first place. She is a constant source of encouragement and listens to me vent when I need to. If it wasn't for her, I'm not sure I would make it through.

• Three-fourths of the way through each semester I always realize that I should have been doing x or y or $x + 1$ and have a pretty intense panic attack (hyperventilating, crying, the whole sha-bang ... it's pretty dramatic). My significant other is really great at making me feel better, just by holding me and reminding me that most of the pressure comes from my drive to do well and that allowing it to take hold is really just self-sabotage. From my end, it makes me appreciate him more because he always puts things in perspective for me (from his end, I predict, he thinks I'm just crazy).

• I love having someone to go home to. If I did not have my fiancé, I think that those times where I feel sorry for myself and wonder what the heck I was thinking when I decided to go to law school would be so much tougher on me. I love the fact that I can go to him to decompress and get encouragement.

• Having the stability of Karla's vested interest in my success as a person (and as a student) has become a definitive coping strategy for what I hope will become a successful law school experience. If I weren't in a relationship I would only have those other super-stressed out law students to turn to, and as great as my law school friends are, *because* they are in law school they can't be that objective caring voice of reason, support, and concern for which I turn to Karla.

• Definitely easier. I attribute my sanity to my partner. I seriously doubted my ability to survive law school. She never did, and made a point to tell me so. She would let me vent when I needed to and also reminded me that my fate was in my own hands. It's easy for law students to feel overwhelmed. A good partner can be the best asset a student can have.

Household/Daily Life Support

• I have support and someone to come home to and have a glass of wine with. I can choose to talk about law school or I can totally put it out of my mind when I need to. He also understands and helps with housework and that makes life a lot easier! The nights I just can NOT cook, he will have dinner ready.

• Having a partner there to help you every step of the way definitely makes things easier (if they are willing to help). Robby prints out my case briefs and files them away for me in my binders when I don't want to, which is all the time. And if my backpack is heavy, which it is every day, he carries it for me. In our relationship I'm the worrier, and he is the fixer, so whenever I am stressed about getting all the schoolwork done he listens to my problem and tries to help however he can, which is usually just by being nice and comforting, but that's still very helpful.

• Much easier because my partner is so supportive. He takes care of all the little things around the house I don't have time for. He is there to listen when I need to vent. He's my cheerleader. I am so grateful for all his support.

Adds Balance and Stability to Life

• Definitely easier. Our marriage has helped me keep law school from overwhelming the rest of my life. Many students think that law school must be their only life for three years. But it doesn't have to be that way. Being married while attending law school has provided a daily reminder that, while law school is important, the people I love will always be more important.

• I think it has made it easier because now, after working out some kinks, I have a great support system. My boyfriend will listen to my law school problems, but he doesn't try to insinuate himself into my law school experience. It's a good balance, and he helps me to take time away from law school, which is very important to maintaining my sanity.

• Having a wife who is a non-law student has helped me retain a much needed perspective on the experience and to remember that there is so much more in life more important than learning the law.

• I sometimes wonder the same thing. I often think about what it would be like if I had never met Brannon and was single in law school. First, I believe I may have driven myself crazy without him. It has been a great balance to live and love someone who is completely removed from everything that I do at school. I am a bit of a perfectionist. If I was on my own, I think no one would ever see me. I would never come out of my house.

• Definitely easier. Having someone to come home to who doesn't want to talk about adverse possession or how they did on the latest practice exam is wonderful. It's not that I don't like school; it's just really nice to be able to spend time with someone who has absolutely no association with law school and wants to talk about the other things that are important, the stuff that brought us together before law school was in the picture.

Fewer Distractions

• I think being in a serious relationship has made my law school experience much easier than if I were not in the relationship. I see my peers going out and getting into relationship "tangles" and I am so glad that is not one of my worries. I go home to my fiancé at night and I am with him on the weekends so I do not feel the need to go out to bars with some of my classmates.

Don't get me wrong, I think socializing is very important in law school but not to the point where it can affect the real reason why we are here.

• I would not trade places with one of these single kids for anything. I have seen my single law school friends fall in love, fall out of love, struggle with someone they dated before starting to date someone else. It's so nice to already have that out of the way. My classes confuse me enough. I couldn't handle being confused in a new relationship.

• I think that my relationship with Stephanie has made my school experience much easier. Most of the single male students in the class spend quite a bit of time in the bars looking for women, on both the weekdays and the weekends. Because I have absolutely no use for this activity, and I am being encouraged by Stephanie to do well, I don't have any trouble staying focused on school.

Provides Extra Motivation to Work Hard and Be Responsible

• Being in a relationship certainly gives me a greater resolve to do well because I have this other person who is depending on me to be successful at this someday. She also works to keep us afloat financially and helps with the workload around the apartment too. I don't know how I could possibly have managed to get through this without her.

• Even as a 3L, I still believe that success in law school is, in some part, a function of non-class interaction. Because of my wife's commitments at work and our shared obligations at home with our daughter, my ability to participate in extracurricular activities, attend nighttime social events, or contribute to study groups has been limited. I'm not sure my wife would object if I expressed an interest in doing those things, but her support of this endeavor makes it hard for me to, in good faith, commit a great deal of time to "elective" activities.

• Being in a serious intimate relationship and having a family has made my law school experience easier.

Having my family waiting for me at home forces me to focus my energy while at school. I know that if I waste time playing on the internet between classes, I might not have time to read my son a bedtime story. If I skip classes, I may not have absences available to accommodate staying at home with a sick child. Also, I know how much my husband and my son have sacrificed to give me the opportunity to go to law school and pursue this path. This has made me more serious about school and more focused than ever before.

Easier in Some Ways, But Harder in Others

Quite a few survey respondents commented that being in a relationship makes law school easier in some ways, but more difficult in other ways—primarily in that the time and energy required to be in a committed relationship takes away time and energy that could otherwise be devoted to succeeding in law school. Here's a sampling of answers from folks in this category:

- It's been a combination of both. I feel like I could get more accomplished academically if I didn't have to also make sure I don't neglect my relationship with my girlfriend. Sometimes I think it would be easier to make friends, because I'd be more inclined to attend all the social activities, but I can't because my girlfriend is at home and I feel bad that I'm leaving her by herself. At the same time, it's also been very helpful to have her to talk and complain to whenever I've had a long day at class. She's also been there to help put school into perspective for me. I feel like if my only friends were law students, I'd spend so much time at school that I'd eventually lose my mind.

- This is an extremely difficult question, and something that I have considered a great deal since I started law school. Although I have often thought that being single would be easier, because I wouldn't have to worry about anyone else's schedule or who needs the car when, I really believe that my husband has made me better at law school. Despite our challenges, he keeps me balanced, reminds me that there are things that, at the end of the day, are just more important than law school, holds me accountable to working hard, and supports me every single day I feel like giving up. No matter how hard things get at school, I can always come home, curl up on the couch with Alan and our dogs, and know that I have a fantastic support system. I wouldn't give that up for anything.

• In all honesty it depends on the day or week. There are instances that making time for a relationship truly cuts into time that I feel like I should be outlining, studying, or researching. Yet, these times do not outweigh the comfort and stability of a healthy, serious intimate relationship. There are undoubtedly times in law school that you will be depressed, angry, and frustrated. At these times it feels like no one knows what you are going through, and law school is a living hell. Someone who loves you can pull you out of these situations because they are outside of all the law school insanity. My fiancée has an uncanny ability to let me know that life and death are not riding on my Civ Pro final. When times are good, the first person I want to tell is my fiancée. She may not have any idea what I am talking about, but still is happy that I am happy, and that is good enough.

• Overall, being in a serious relationship while in law school has made the experience easier. I would be lying if I said it did not add stress in some ways. Being in a relationship demands that I find time to spend with my loved one and be aware of the stress that my schooling places on her. When I started school, it was an adjustment for both of us, and we had to struggle through some issues, such as finding time for each other, taking care of household responsibilities, and finding time to spend with our family and friends, until we found a system that worked for us. It is not a perfect system, and it has to be adjusted the closer I get to exams, but we always try to find a workable solution. With my focus on preparing for class, working on my law review note, fulfilling my research assistant responsibilities, going on job interviews, preparing outlines, and studying for exams, it is hard to find the time to focus on my personal wellbeing. My loved one is there to keep me grounded. She is always there for me to vent frustration to or run ideas by. If I am feeling overwhelmed, I can cry on her shoulder. She is there every day to remind me that the world is bigger than law school and that I am more than just a law student. She encourages me to find the time to take care of myself—to relax and decompress so that I do not get burned out. So, while being in a relationship does require me to juggle more responsibility, the mental support and emotional stability that it provides has made my law school experience easier.

• It has made the experience much easier in some respects. I am glad I am a bit older than many law students and do not have to deal with the incidents of being in my early twenties and single while in school. My wife has been a source of support and comfort. Conversely, the birth of our daughter in my 1L year made being a 1L harder. I sacrificed some academic performance for the sake of spending time with my wife and trying to help make the new experience of parenthood better. I could have kept my same schedule that spring semester, but I would not have been able to take an active and supporting role at home, which I genuinely wanted. Although grades suffered, my life has been enriched.

Harder, Primarily Because of Conflicting Demands

Some students said being in a relationship made law school harder for them. For the most part, their comments echoed the "con"-side sentiments above: that being in a committed relationship takes too much time and focus away from law school.

• Harder! I have a strong commitment to my relationship. It takes time even when I don't feel that I have time to give it. If I weren't in a relationship, I would work until I felt like stopping, not until I had another thing to do around my house. It is a constant juggle to balance school and my relationship with my husband.

• Being in a relationship made law school a nightmare for me. The constant drama and fighting have affected my concentration and self-confidence. I have more physical problems now than when I did before coming to law school. The person I was involved with did not go to college or grad school, so he had no concept of what kind of work law school involves. I am sorry that I decided to continue in this relationship during year one.

• Harder. If I was single I'd probably be out getting into trouble more, but those relationships carry no responsibility. Now I consciously have to make efforts to spend time with her. I'm not saying the sacrifice isn't worth it, I'm just saying it is difficult. But who knows, I could say the same thing if I were on the other side.

• Harder. In trying to balance my home life with my law school life, I often have to compromise. That may mean not going to a networking event, or skipping afternoon tutoring sessions. It makes it harder on a social level, because my socializing is mostly with my significant other. And it makes it harder on an educational level because I often forego the supplemental sessions (tutoring sessions, etc.) to spend time with him.

• There are only twenty-four hours in a day to give to your commitments. If you can't balance all of them, something will suffer. For me, at times, grades suffered because I was unwilling to lose my wife. So perhaps that made it harder to achieve in school.

* * *

What can be taken away from the comments in this chapter? First and foremost that even though law school does add strain to many relationships, both research and law student opinions support the conclusion that, overall, your student is better off for having you as their traveling companion down the long law school road. Remind your student of this when they act cranky.

But we also see strong support for the old adage that the "law is a jealous mistress," penned by former U.S. Supreme Court Justice Joseph Story in the nineteenth century. Story wrote that the law "is a jealous mistress, and requires a long and constant courtship. It is not to be won by trifling favors, but by lavish homage.''[248] The comments in this chapter show many students are truly torn between their loyalty and dedication to their loved ones and their belief that they must at all times bestow "lavish homage" on the law and law school to succeed at a high level. It's a classic case of being trapped between a rock and a hard place, between Scylla and Charybdis, between the horns of a dilemma ... well, you get the idea. As one student lamented:

> The law student cannot win: if you concentrate on school, you are missing out on life. If you concentrate on life, you are hurting your chances of being successful in school. Every now and then, it feels like I've found the right balance, but it never stays that way for long.

But you and your student can take heart. Finding and maintaining balance *is* possible. The next chapter offers some tips on how to do it. In the meantime, hopefully this chapter has assisted in accomplishing one of the most frequently uttered wishes I heard from law students in writing this book: convincing loved ones *not to take it personally* if the student has to temporarily neglect them because of law school. It's not a choice students want to make. To the contrary, it causes them anguish, as seen in the comments.

---

248. Joseph Story, *The Value and Importance of Legal Studies*, in BART- LETT'S FAMILIAR QUOTATIONS 392:16 (Justin Kaplan, gen. ed., 16th ed. 1992).

CHAPTER 17

TIPS FOR MAINTAINING SUCCESSFUL RELATIONSHIPS WITH LAW STUDENTS

Here it is. The chapter you've been waiting for, the one that explains it all. The pages that hand over the secret keys to not only surviving but thriving with a law student, which, as we've seen, is no easy task for people not trained in Special Ops. Dang, if only I could give them to you!

Some background: A funny moment happened in a conference call with several editors and marketing specialists from West—the publisher of this book.[249] To appreciate the story, you need to know a little about West. Started 140 years ago by a traveling book salesman named John B. West, West developed into one of the largest and most prominent publishers of legal materials in the world. West is the publisher of a long list of venerable casebooks and treatises written by some of the greatest minds in American legal history, including many of the books your student will be assigned to read. In 1887, West created the National Reporter System, which collects and publishes the judicial opinions of every U.S. appellate court—those same opinions your student will be reading. In 1975, West launched Westlaw, one of two competing computer legal research giants,[250] which your student will talk about a lot. You'll also hear frequent references to

---

249. West was acquired by the Thomson Corporation in 1996 to form "Thomson West," which was subsequently acquired by Reuters, but many of us in legal education still call it simply "West."

250. The other is LexisNexis.

"TWEN" online course sites, also established and operated by West.[251]

It was against this backdrop of august history in legal publishing that the aforementioned conference call occurred. During the call—with me in my office at the University of Memphis and the West folks at their headquarters in Minnesota—I spoke animatedly about how I envisioned the book developing. At one point I mentioned that a portion of the book would offer advice to law students and their loved ones about how to manage their relationships.

Someone at the other end said, "You're not planning on giving 'relationship advice' are you?" The implication of the question and obvious answer both sunk in quickly. "Oh, no, of course not." Even from 900 miles away, I sensed approval and relief. Someone said: "West giving relationship advice. Can you imagine?" And everyone, including me, laughed heartily.

West isn't in the self-help book business and I'm not a psychologist, although it has seemed like it at times over my years as a law professor. Let's face it. Your ultimate likelihood of success in a maintaining a good relationship with a law student—whether as a partner, parent or other close loved one—won't depend on this or any other book, but on whether you possess the foundation and tools for a healthy relationship to begin with.

So, no, unfortunately, this chapter does not contain the mystery answers to living a "bed of roses" life with a law student. But what it does offer is also valuable: insider insights from people who have walked a mile in law school-relationship shoes. My surveys asked both law students and their partners: "What is the one piece of advice you would give to other law students and their loved ones for how to successfully manage a relationship with a law student?"

Most of the content below emanated from their answers. Much of the relationship wisdom offered by the students and their partners flows from and is tied to the sources of conflict discussed in Chapter 15. The tips aren't startling revelations. They are things that would occur to any thoughtful person with emotional intelligence—although maybe not soon

---

251. TWEN stands for The West Education Network. See the Glossary for more details.

enough to save the day. Hopefully, hearing the tips from folks who experienced the same issues you will be facing will drive the points closer to home and heart. The fact that so many of the answers from both the students and their partners echoed the same themes suggests there really is such a thing as generic law student relationship advice—er, rather, *tips*.

The chapter is divided into three categories: Tips for Loved Ones, Tips for Law Students, and Tips for Both of You. Some of the tips apply only to partners, such as insisting on participating in law school social events with your student. You parents out there have enough to worry about without ending up in your student's Facebook party pics. But much of the advice is universal to all close relationships with a law student.

Tips for Loved Ones

After all you've read, you might be thinking the number one tip would be "Run for your life!" Nah, things aren't that bad, although one student did advise: "Educate yourself before law school begins. If you cannot handle what you find out, then end the relationship before law school begins—not five weeks before finals." That makes sense. In *1L of a Ride*, I advised new students that if they are in a turbulent relationship they know deep down inside is going to end at some point to go ahead and end it before law school. "No reason," I said, "to jeopardize your success by wasting emotional energy on a relationship you know is already on life support."[252]

Here, we'll think more positively. The fact that you're invested enough in your student to read this book means you've already made the "Most Likely to Succeed in a Relationship with a Law Student" list. Congratulations on that, by the way.

Be Patient

Have you ever seen the television game show *Family Feud*, where contestants have to fill in the blanks of survey questions answered by the studio audience? I used to watch it

---

252. ANDREW J. MCCLURG, 1L OF A RIDE: A WELL-TRAVELED PROFESSOR'S ROAD-   MAP TO SUCCESS IN THE FIRST YEAR OF LAW SCHOOL 8 (2009).

back in the day when the lovably creepy Richard Dawson hosted it, always insisting on kissing and hugging the female contestants. The show has been reincarnated with several hosts since then. In reading the survey answers to my advice-giving question, Dawson's signature tagline came to mind: "Number one answer? Survey says ..." The clear number-one answer from both students and their partners as to the best piece of advice they would give to others in their situation was "patience."

Being with a law student will test your patience on a regular basis. Here are some examples. I cut the original list of eight thousand items down to eight:

• Patience listening to endless dissertations about arcane cases decided by judges who have been dead for 200 years;

• Patience as your student gazes into a computer monitor late at night when they should be gazing at you;

• Patience with endless boring stories about a seemingly endless list of classmates and professors;

• Patience with not only being told that your ideas are bad and your thinking wrong, but with having to endure four multi-pronged, fully reasoned explanations as to why this is so;

• Patience sitting on the couch struggling to be attentive as your student subjects you to the 980th practice run of their oral argument in Legal Research and Writing;

• Patience when hearing that your student is really psyched about the upcoming holiday because they will "finally be able to get some real work done";

• Patience as your student neurotically refreshes the law school's grade posting webpage every five minutes for five weeks beginning five minutes after the end of exams;

• Patience consoling your student when they fail to meet their own high expectations for the first time ... then second time ...

Below are just a few of the "patience" answers from both law students and their partners. There were many others.

From Law Students:

• Patience. That is really it. There are going to be times when a loved one is just going to have to let the law student do his or her thing. This is selfish, but at certain points in the semester, especially finals, it is much easier to just accept that the loved one won't see the law student as much for a few weeks than constantly try and fight to win time.

• Be patient and understanding. He/she WANTS to spend time with you, but they NEED to spend time with their books and notes.

• My biggest piece of advice is just to exercise an inordinate amount of patience. Law school is going to be one of the most stressful experiences of their life, and unless their significant other has been in a similar situation, they just won't really understand what the student is going through. So I would suggest to students that they need to be patient when their significant other doesn't understand why they don't spend as much time focusing on the relationship, and I would suggest to the non-law students to be patient while the 1L suffers through the first semester trying to find a healthy balance.

From Significant Others:

• You have to be extremely patient with their schedule or problems will occur. The time constraints are already hard enough on the law student and any added pressure that you put on them to spend more time with you will not be beneficial to the student and possibly the relationship. I have an interesting situation where I am as busy as she is, if not more busy at times, and even I have to remain patient when I don't get to see her as much. I would like to see her all the time, but I realize that is not going to happen.

• Be patient! Any ideas the soon-to-be law student has about law school will quickly be changed and their world will be turned upside down. It is necessary as a significant other to realize and expect this and be ready and willing to listen, console, and comfort your law student.

- Try to be patient and understanding. They don't want to be buried in books 24/7 any more than you want them to be. It's just part of the game.

While most of the comments address the need for the non-student to be patient, as one student astutely pointed out, patience must travel both ways in the relationship. Loved ones need to be patient with their students, but law students also need to be patient with loved ones. Be honest with your student about your frustrations. Tell them: "Hey, I'm trying hard to understand what you're going through. I'm even reading a book about it! But this is a hard adjustment for me too and I need you to understand me just like you want me to understand you."

Prepare for What to Expect, Including That Life Is Going to Change

Check this one off. You now know what to expect. Heck, you've learned enough to start giving advice to other loved ones of law students, although I'd prefer you just tell them to buy the book. I've already talked about the fact that law school will require adjustments in your relationship and daily lives. Here, students and their partners reinforce the importance of being prepared in advance—*ab initio* (from the beginning) as we say in law.

From Law Students:

- Students need to be candid with their loved ones about the time commitments of law school. Tell your loved ones that for the next three years, you will be physically and emotionally unavailable at times and that this is not a reflection on them. Restate this position often, but be patient with them. It's hard for them too.

- Make sure you know how things are going to work ahead of time! How you are going to communicate about difficult things, how your significant other will be involved (or not involved) in law school, how time will be spent, how to tell your significant other when you need time to be left alone to study or just be grouchy, etc.

- Clear the decks completely. Rid yourself of all other commitments. Forget about Thanksgiving. Schedule a nice vacation over the semester break so you have something to look forward to. If the spouse is needy, the spouse definitely needs to find something else to occupy their time.

From Significant Others:

• It is harder than you would think. I had friends who are law students, so I thought I knew what to expect. But it is completely different when your boyfriend/girlfriend is in school. I did not think I would have any trouble adjusting to William being in school, but it has been much harder than I realized. I've finally come to terms with the fact that school is the number one priority and everything else falls in line behind that.

• Make a plan you can both agree on regarding how you will handle the next three years and then be willing to be flexible. And spend time before school starts to get things in order: set up direct withdrawal for your bills, fix up the house, etc. Once school starts, anything extra will have to wait until Christmas break or worse yet, summer vacation, or even worse still, graduation.

• Don't expect your partner to be like they were in undergraduate school. Instead of spending time perfecting his beer-pong shot, he now spends his time perfecting an "open memo" on something I find utterly incomprehensible.

Do It Together: Get Involved in Your Law Student's Experience

You have a choice: separate yourself from your law student's experience or get involved. I recommend getting on board early. Here's *your* first law school exam. Below are two comments related to the level of law school involvement by a non-student spouse, one comment from a student about her uninvolved partner and one comment from a very involved partner. Read them. Which loved one seems to be enjoying the law school experience more?

(A) My loved one states that I talk too much about law school. He is not willing to understand the time constraints, nor will he ever. He stated he could care less about who was in my class—I only mentioned them to him to share what was going on in my world.

(B) I've met most of her classmates several times now and luckily, we enjoy each other's company—we're even Facebook friends. I first met them at some social events and *yes*, everything they talk about is somehow tethered to law school! But thanks to the daily updates from my student, I know what they're talking about—the cases involved, how the professor feels about it, even how the SCOTUS judges feel about it—so I don't feel left out. Actually, they probably think I'm a weirdo for knowing so much. I get the feeling their significant others do not get into it as much as I do. But I don't see why. Because I get involved at home in listening to my student, I don't feel left out or excluded at get-togethers.

The correct answer is **B**. Pretty awesome that she even used the "SCOTUS" acronym in referring to the Supreme Court of the United States. And doesn't she sound genuinely happy about the whole thing? You don't have to strive to reach her level of involvement. Not everyone has that kind of time, for one thing. But you do not want to go in the opposite direction and erect a barrier between you and your student by purposely excluding yourself from your student's new life.

Here are five easy-to-follow steps for connecting to your student's law school experience (partly a refresher since some have been mentioned previously):

- Get to know the names of your student's professors and closest friends so you can keep up with conversations about them.

- Make a point of meeting and getting to know your student's new friends in social situations. If your student resists that effort for any reason, take him/her to task for it.

- Visit one or more classes with your student, both to get a feel for what law students do every day and also as a convenient way to meet their professors and pals.

- Show interest in your student's new adventure and law school-talk. This is a big deal to them. Treat it that way.

• To the extent you have the time and your student wants your help, lend an assist to your student's studying efforts such as by listening to them practice their first-year oral argument or reading flashcards with them during exam prep. An add-on benefit of this approach is you will be able to spend more time with your student.

Listen to Your Student

It might not always be fun. It might even be painful at times. But simply *listening* to your student will be helpful on two fronts. First, since most students are, at least in the first year, going to want to talk law and law school non-stop, it will be a way to spend extra time with them and stay more connected. Don't understand what the heck your student is talking about at times? No problem. Follow the advice in the comments below and just nod periodically.

More important, your student is going to need a reliable friend to lean on at times to express her worries and frustrations. Be that person! As we talked about in Chapter 9, there may not be a clear "right" thing to say to a law student in times of distress, but just lending a sympathetic ear can be a real comfort. Here's some advice from significant others on the importance of being a good listener:

• Be prepared to listen, even if you do not care about wills or intellectual property or whatever. Even if you just nod and shake your head it is worth the effort.

• I think engaging with your law student—asking questions about what they've learned, and listening intently while they discuss their curriculum—is a productive way to stay connected.

• Sometimes you're not going to know the right thing to say, but just listening will help your law student more than anything.

• Listening is important even if you could care less about the law information. Law is becoming part of their life, so you'd better get used to it anyway.

• Sometimes you are going to understand their problems and other times you will not have a clue about what they are talking about. Just nod your head and be supportive.

Be Supportive and Lend a Hand

In any challenging situation, people want and need the support of loved ones. Law students need both your emotional support and, if you live together, also some physical support with household duties. Now, of course, one would expect law students to say that, but, interestingly, most of the "be supportive" survey replies I received came from significant others. Given the earlier discussion of the traditional gender-based inequality in the distribution of household labor, it's worth observing that the comments below all came from husbands or boyfriends. Way to suck it up, guys!

• My best advice is plain and simple, but it is also sometimes the most difficult to do. It is this: Be understanding and supportive. Understanding doesn't mean comprehending the law and law school, it means understanding what your student is going through, understanding how difficult it is, and how, sometimes, it seems that there is no end in sight. Understanding the stress that your student is under and how that affects them. Being able to support them, not just monetarily, but on a deeper level. I'm not talking about your run-of-the-mill Dillard's bra-type support. I'm talking Victoria's Secret Push-Up bra support. Tell them that they're doing a great job (even if you have no idea what exactly they're working on). Let them know that it's okay if you don't spend much time with them for a day or two while they finish a large assignment. Support their decision to pig-out on ice cream and after a pint, still tell them that they're beautiful. Be loving, caring, and devoted, even when it seems as though they're more devoted to their studies than you.

• You must understand that this is something they want to do and you took a vow to love and support them through better or worse. Law school is part of the "worse." I tell myself everyday that she is tired and does not want to do anything and that in the end all of this will be worth it. Her happiness is what matters and my job is to help her get there no matter what. Even if it means going to Wal-Mart a half-hour away at midnight for printer ink so she can finish printing her cases.

- Be supportive, communicate, and just hang in there! It's not an easy road to say the least. I have had to take on a completely different role in the family in an effort to give my wife the best opportunity at success. I cook, clean, do laundry, and am the primary care-giver for our child. This is all stuff that the law student was in charge of in the past (and will be when she's done with school).[253] For now, I know that law school is stressful enough as it is, so I'm here to support her in any way she needs.

Stay Busy/Pursue Your Own Interests

Many of the significant others who stated that law school had not negatively affected their relationship said it was because they too were busy pursuing their own educational or work careers to feel neglected. Quite a few of them were graduate students in "symmetrical relationships" with law students (see Chapter 15 for a discussion of the benefits of symmetrical relationships). Partners who are extra-busy outside the home simply don't have time to feel abandoned. My advice-giving question generated several responses along the lines of "Take advantage of the time he or she is devoting to studies and pursue your own interests!" and "Get a hobby to occupy your time!" You might recall my advice not to put your own development on hold for the sake of your law student. A tagalong benefit of that is that you'll be much less likely to feel abandoned if you stay busy doing something productive on your own.

Remember, This Too Shall Pass

As a kid, whenever I fretted about a tribulation of life, my mom, in a tone befitting the wisdom of the ages, trotted out the proverb, "This too shall pass." She said it so often I thought she made it up. Of course, being a kid, my response was always "Whatever! I want it to pass now!" As I matured and faced more formidable challenges in life than, say, braces, I took the words more to heart. I also learned they

---

253. Hmm, I wonder if he cleared this part with his partner.

aren't always true. Not every unpleasant thing in life does pass, unfortunately. But law school does.

Students and partners alike advised that one effective way to endure the law school experience is to remember that it is only temporary. There *is* an end to those lonely weekends of solitude, the gasping sound coming from your student's bank account, and those commonly uttered late-night murmurings such as "Augggh! Memo! Memo! Augggh!" Here's some advice on this point from both students and partners:

- As with all things in life, the best things come only after a period of difficulty. This includes going through law school. While it may not seem fun (indeed, it may seem like torture), in the end it will be worth it for both of you.

- Keep a good attitude and have faith that three years pass by quickly. Remember that time spent on studying or school activities (law review, mock trial, moot court, etc.) is an investment your student is making to better your future as well as his/hers.

- Patience, understanding, and faith that law school is a finite period, just one small chunk out of a long life!

- Law school is only a temporary thing. Three years sounds like a lot looking forward, but it's not that much looking back.

- This too shall pass.

Thanks for reading the book, Mom! Kidding. That last comment came from a student.

Not only is law school temporary, importantly, as mentioned, it gets better for both students and their others after the initial adjustment period. A student explained:

Know that it gets better. Your law student will get better at managing time and resources as time goes by. Just try to give them time to adjust to what they're going through, and they'll start to seem like their normal selves at some point in the first year.

Law school does end, *but* ... ahh, here we go again. I hate to throw ice water on this good vibe, but it would be a major omission if I failed to mention that L.A.L.S. (Life After Law School) is hard duty for most graduates. Several of the comments I received from significant others suggest they may be laboring under a misapprehension that once law school is over, they and their newly minted lawyer will be lounging at country clubs knocking back Margaritas and otherwise enjoying the high life. Unfortunately, most lawyers—even those who lounge at country clubs knocking back Margaritas—work long hours in what can be stressful jobs. Chapter 10 mentioned some studies about the levels of anxiety and depression suffered by lawyers. The *Wall Street Journal Law Blog* has written so much about disaffected lawyers that "[u]nhappiness in the law has ... become a distinct subgenre of LB [Law Blog] coverage."[254]

In a national job satisfaction survey, 43 percent of lawyers described themselves as "very happy."[255] You could look at that from a cup-half-empty perspective and feel discouraged, but you could also see it from a cup-half-full view and reasonably believe the odds are in your student's (and thus your) favor. In a country with more than one million lawyers, the 43 percent "very happy" response rate means there are at least 430,000 jubilant attorneys bopping around out there. No reason your student can't be one of them. Being happy as a lawyer is all about finding the right job fit for the particular person.

In that regard, I again strongly endorse the Myers–Briggs Type Indicator (MBTI) as a tool for your student to learn more about himself and, hence, the types of legal jobs and areas of law best suited to his personality preferences. I also recommend as a good gift for summer reading after your student's first year a book I've cited a few times: *The Happy Lawyer: Making a Good Life in the Law*, by Professors Nancy Levit and Douglas Linder. Don't worry about L.A.L.S. now. Everything will work out fine if your student follows his heart in making ultimate career choices.

Meanwhile, like the rest of life, law school will zip by faster than either of you will believe possible. Not necessarily in any particular moment. At times, it will seem intermina-

254. Dan Slater, *What Holds Unhappy Lawyers Back from Leaving?*, WALL St. J.L. BLOG (June 23, 2008), http://blogs.wsj.com/law/2008/06/23/what-holds-unhappy-lawyers-back-from-leaving/.

255. Tom W. Smith, *Job Satisfaction in the United States*, NAT'L OPINION RE-SEARCH CTR., UNIV. OF CHI. 3 (2007), http://www.news.uchicago.edu/releases/07/pdf/070417.jobs.pdf. The survey polled more than 27,500 randomly selected people. *Id.* at 4.

ble. Just today, as I'm writing this, three students came to my office to ask questions about an impending Torts II exam. They looked exhausted and downtrodden, understandable given that they were at the end of the punishing first year and had already taken three exams—Contracts, Civil Procedure, and Property—in the past week. Trying to raise their spirits, I said cheerily, "You're almost done! Only three more days and you'll be finished with the first year!"

Doesn't that sound like sunshine-y news given everything you've read? You'd think they'd jump for joy at the reminder. Well, it didn't unfold *exactly* like that. They all just glared at me until one said, "Professor, we still have our Torts and Criminal Law exams. One day during exams seems like at least a week. So really, it's like we have three more weeks." And you thought *I* was a downer. But trust me, law school really will pass quickly.

Tips for Law Students

While this book was written for you, the following relationship tips directed at students could, if followed, make your life measurably better. Share them with your student.

Manage Time Efficiently

My earlier book, *1L of a Ride*, includes a chapter called *The Top Five Habits of Successful Law Students: A C.R.E.D.O.* The C.R.E.D.O. stands for Consistent, Rigorous, Efficient, Diligent, and Organized. The single best thing your student could do for you and your relationship—not to mention her own law school success—would be to get a firm grip on living an "E"-life; that is, learn to be extremely efficient in managing the scarce hours in each day. Here's some specific advice on that point from *1L of a Ride*:

> **Don't waste time during the day.** Given that time is such a precious commodity, it's unfortunate that many students waste so much of it during the school day. First-year law students frequently complain that class schedules are not designed efficiently in that too many lengthy gaps exist between classes. They don't realize schedules are set up this way intentionally, as a way to encourage (perhaps "compel"

would be a better word) students to stay on campus during the day, rather than just attend their classes and flee the building. As a result, you're likely to have several free hours available each weekday. Use them productively rather than fritter them away.

Study habits and preferences vary by personality. Me, I hated studying late into the night. I realized this at the very beginning of law school. When I studied late at night, I'd end up dreaming about law and working in my sleep all night. I awoke feeling tired and un-rested. After a few weeks of law school, I began developing an awareness of how many hours I wasted during the day. My friends and I began each morning playing ping pong in the student lounge. We'd shoot the breeze between classes, even when there were lengthy gaps between the end of one class and the start of another. At lunch, we'd hang out and talk some more. I don't recall the specifics, but I have no doubt that, in the grand tradition of all 1Ls, many of our lengthy discussions were wasted gossip and gripe sessions about courses, professors, and classmates. One day it occurred to me that if I became more efficient during the day, I'd have more free time at night.

So I changed course. I began using every spare minute of the day productively. Within a couple of weeks, I had refined my system to the point where, by the time I left to go home (i.e., when many of my classmates were just getting ready to begin their studying), I usually had every assignment for the next day read and briefed. I missed spending more time with my friends at school, but the payoff came each night. I found myself with plenty of time to work on my legal research and writing projects and still have time to just hang out and relax. Those long nights of working out legal problems in my sleep ended. I had found a time-management plan that fit me perfectly.[256]

Imagine! Your student free in the evenings to hang out and chill with you. Doesn't that sound fantastic compared to all the comments in this book about students working all night, some of them not even going to bed with their partners?

---

256. McClurg, *supra*, at 156–57.

My approach doesn't work for everyone or in all situations. Obviously, it won't work for part-time evening-division students, who work all day and attend school at night. Also, some people are "night people" who are more productive when the sun goes down. Nor does the strategy apply to weekends, when students may need blocks of unfettered time to work on outlining or other law school projects. And it goes without saying that exam periods will call for elongated days. But the basic point is sound: *Each hour your student wastes during the day is one more hour that must be put in at night.* I liked coming upon this answer to my advice-giving question:

> My advice for future students is something I learned from reading *1L of a Ride*. I learned to use my breaks wisely. Instead of shooting the bull in the hallway between classes or going home between classes, I stay and do all of my work at school. First, this helps because at the school there are ample resources for any type of legal research imaginable and it is relatively quiet and free of distractions. Second, it allows me to generally be done working and researching by around 5 or 6 p.m. every day. If you treat law school as a full time job—working eight to five or nine to six, then keeping up with your relationship isn't very difficult.

1L of a Ride offers a lot of other specific advice to students on how to be efficient and organized, keep stress levels in check, and maintain well-being. Not surprisingly, since I wrote it, I recommend it to your student. The crucial point here is that students can, in effect, create extra time in their lives that can be spent with you, without jeopardizing their law school success, simply by being efficient and organized.

Don't Talk About Law School All the Time

While I've recommended you make a good faith effort to listen to your student's law-talk, students need to make a good faith effort not to drown their loved ones in it. One student framed his advice to other students succinctly: "Shut the hell up about law school and go out and hang out together, often!"

When your student does talk about law school, caution them that you could be a better listener if they slowed down and defined what they are talking about as they go along.

Several loved ones complained that they can't follow law school conversation even when they want to because they don't understand the terminology. As one partner said:

> I find any topic involving law school interesting if it is discussed in a manner courteous to those who are not in law school and who are unfamiliar with law school lingo. Law school students love to talk about law school even around those who do not understand words and concepts usually only used in law school. To make law school interesting to non-students, you have to actually consider those not in law school. This is the step most commonly skipped.

Seek Balance

"Balancing," your student will learn, is one of the fundamental concepts of law. Courts do it every day. In tort cases, courts balance the costs of accident avoidance (e.g., investing in a safer design for a product) against the number and severity of the injuries that could be prevented. In constitutional law cases, courts balance competing social interests and individual versus community rights. In property cases, courts balance land owner rights to use their land as they see fit with the rights of their neighbors. Balancing is necessitated by the recognition that in complex situations there are few interests that warrant being exalted over all other relevant competing interests.

Law students need to do some serious balancing in their own lives. How does one find equilibrium between the competing demands of law school and outside life, including relationships? Several students advised other students to refrain from pressing their thumbs down too firmly on the law school side of the scale:

- Retain balance. It's better to lose a little face in class because you didn't finish all the reading or to get a slightly lower grade than to damage a long-term relationship or neglect someone you love.

- Remember how much you are missing out on and try to weigh that against the amount of studying you want to do. Is it really worth it to miss out on a family dinner just to get a grade a few points higher? Try to draw the line somewhere you can keep your sanity.

- Remember that law school is not the most important thing. If you have to choose between your marriage and an exam grade, choose your marriage. I strongly believe that no success in law school, law, or your career can make up for failure at home.

Good advice in one sense. If one truly had to make a choice between law school and family, or between just about anything else in life and family, family should win out. But I disagree with the suggestions that it's better for your student to leave assignments unfinished or otherwise put their academic success at risk than, for example, miss a dinner with family. As we've covered, your student's grades are going to be very important in determining a variety of internal and external law school rewards.

The best balancing decisions are those that accommodate competing interests without sacrificing either. It *can* be done, in large part by developing efficient time-management skills as discussed above. A student can finish her reading assignments *and* have dinner with family if she's efficient. Maybe not every night, but on a regular basis.[257] The following student's advice fits better within my conception of striking a good balance:

> Maintain a balance. Your life can't be all about school or all about your marriage. I look at law school as a job. I get to school between 7 and 7:30 a.m. and I get home between 5 and 8 p.m. I do school work at school and I keep it separate from my home life. Home should be a place where one can relax and take time to do non-law school things. When you're home, your spouse knows that the time you spend with each other is yours and devoted to maintaining and developing your relationship. Bringing school home can cause stress, tension, resentment, and anxiety.

I'm not sure complete separation of law school and home-life is achievable or even desirable, but his basic point is correct that law school does not have to interfere egregiously with outside life if your student manages his time efficiently.

---

257. Admittedly, the nation's roughly 23,000 part-time evening-division students will have a much harder time achieving a good balance between family and academics. Candidly, it may be impossible. For night students and their families, remembering that "this too shall pass" may provide the best sustenance.

Don't Constantly Whine and Complain

At times your student will need a shoulder to lean on and even cry on. But there's a difference between sharing one's feelings and engaging in nonstop barrages of negative energy. At some point, negativity can become a self-perpetuating habit. If your student seems to be getting "stuck" in law school tirades, as opposed to occasional venting, try to gently interrupt the cycle with something like, "Stop! Tell me one *good* thing that happened at school today." Do it in a positive, fun way. Don't scold. Try to get your student to see when they are caught in a loop of whining or complaining.

If you're feeling less kind at the particular moment, you could just remind your student that if they spent less time complaining, they'd have more time to do all the work they're complaining about. But try the soft approach first.

Help Out With Household Responsibilities

While law students may need a break from some share of their household responsibilities, especially during exam periods or the days before a legal writing assignment is due, no one should expect or be given a free ride in a relationship. It's not fair to the other person and will, as we've discussed, predictably cause conflict. If you reside with your student, map out a reasonable division of household responsibilities *in advance* that the student can perform without substantially impinging on his or her study schedule, recognizing that everyone will have to be flexible in implementing the plan and making adjustments as events unfold.

If you have the resources, band-aids are available. One of my research assistants said she and her husband hired a housekeeper and that it made a world of difference in their hectic lives trying to juggle jobs, law school, and a young child. Take-out meals, dry cleaners, single-cup coffee makers—more great time-saving stuff. But only take advantage of them if your student can afford to do so *without using student loan money*. Otherwise, just let the house be a little messier, eat more ramen noodles, and wear wrinkled clothes.

Show Appreciation

Law students can be a selfish lot. Several of them conceded that in my surveys. It's not all their fault. Law school and law professors pretty much demand complete allegiance from students in time and energy. But none of that acquits students from being so self-absorbed as to not treat their loved ones properly. One researcher of graduate student marriages noted that students sometimes "believe[ ] that everything should be sacrificed for the good of his or her education" and that spouses often buy into and go along with this view.[258] Inevitably, "frustration and resentment build up," causing problems.[259]

A little consideration and show of appreciation and gratitude can go a long way toward taking the edge off in a relationship where one party is sacrificing for the other. A Chinese proverb says, "When eating bamboo sprouts, remember the man who planted them." For law students, we could modify the proverb in a number of ways:

• When eating a meal prepared by a partner who worked all day at a job or taking care of your child, remember the dog-tired person standing over the stove.

• When granted the luxury of studying in solitude because your partner is trying to be quiet as a mouse so as not to disturb you, remember the lonely person in the next room.

• When writing a rent check with funds earned by the person who is postponing their own development for your sake, remember the generosity of the soul who loves you so much.

As reflected in the advice comments from law students below, many students do recognize the need to show appreciation to the loved ones who sacrifice for them. But in case your student doesn't quite get it, interrupt their explanations of personal jurisdiction to read this advice to them:

• Let your loved ones know how much you appreciate their support and that you couldn't do it without them. It's going to be a hard time for them sometimes, but I think just knowing that they are appreciated will help them through it. Also, try not to complain too much— they have stresses too and I'm sure they don't want to hear about yours all of the time.

258. Scheinkman, *supra*, at 359.   **259.** *Id.*

- Remember to be a person first, and a law student second.

- Love yourself and love the person you are with. Remember to treat them as well as you want to be treated even if you're stressed, tired or overwhelmed.

If your student still doesn't comply, you may have to lay down—appropriately enough—the law, as the following significant other advised:

> From the very beginning, you should make your partner aware of qualities or behaviors you will not tolerate. Your partner will most likely be inclined to acquire several distasteful qualities (selfishness, egomania, etc.), and you should make it clear that your relationship will not last through law school should his/her personality change for the worse.

Tips for Both of You

Communicate

It's axiomatic that effective communication is essential to the health of relationships of *all* types.[260] Of course, this is one of those "I didn't need to pay $85 for a book to tell me that" pieces of advice.[261] But as obvious as the point may be, too many couples fail to communicate about what's bothering them, which inevitably leads to resentment and conflict.

Law school will give both of you plenty of opportunities to test your communication skills. We saw in Chapter 15 that law school brings with it an inevitable level of at least some conflict in most relationships. If your student is neglecting you, talk about it. If household responsibilities aren't being shared fairly, talk about it. If your student is racking up unnecessary debt, talk about it. If your student spends too

---

260. *See, e.g.,* MALCOLM R. PARKS, COMMUNICATION CORRELATES OF PERCEIVED FRIENDSHIP DEVELOPMENT 19–20 (1977) (finding that increased depth and frequency of communication positively correlated with perceived harmony in personal relationships); Jakki Mohr & Robert Spekman, *Characteristics of Partnership Success: Partnership Attributes, Communication Behavior, and Conflict Resolution Techniques,* 15 STRATEGIC MGMT. J. 135, 144 (1994) (observing that higher levels of communication quality and participation lead to more successful business partnerships).

261. What? West put a lower price on this masterpiece? Dang, I was counting on those extra royalties to reduce my kid's loan debt when she decides to go to law school.

much time complaining, talk about it. Several students commented on the importance of communication in resolving law school-related issues.

- Always be open! Before starting law school let them know that it is going to be more time consuming than anything you have ever experienced. If you are too busy to visit, go on a date, talk on the phone, or even make it home before midnight, let them know in advance. And don't just say "I'm too busy." Actually tell them what you are doing, why you have to do it, and when you can spend time together again.

- The number one piece of advice I would give is to communicate. If you keep talking to each other, you will stay relevant in each other's lives. Law school is a time of intense stress and changes that can disorient your relationship, but if you communicate with each other, you can make those changes together and find a new balance.

- Communicate! Keep the lines of communication open. It's easy to get into a funk and not talk to each other about important topics like your own relationship. Keep talking and you will find things will work out easier!

Manage Money and Debt Frugally

We've discussed how money issues, including student loan debt, are one of the biggest and most common trouble-makers in relationships. I was fortunate to escape law school with minimal debt, in large part because my law school mates and I lived at a very low standard of living. Five of us shared a ramshackle house, so rent was cheap. We didn't use the air conditioning even though it's hot as Hades in Gainesville, Florida for much of the year. We never ate out, so food was cheap. For lunch, I took a can of tuna and piece of bread to school on most days. We picked our entertainment based on cost. Our big nights out were parties in the backyard or a couple pitchers of cheap beer during happy hours. We didn't take vacations. Our cars were falling apart. We didn't buy clothes. This isn't a sob story. To the contrary, we were probably happier then than we've ever been.

It's not as easy as it used to be to escape law school without large debt because the cost of tuition has skyrocketed over the years. While public law schools remain a better value than private schools, even public law school tuition has become hefty because of state cuts in funding to higher education. Nevertheless, I am convinced that most of today's law students could shave their loan debt by *at least 20 percent* if they lived more frugally. Compare my Spartan law school lifestyle to many of today's debt-ridden law students: they live alone without roommates, drive nice cars, eat out frequently, own smart phones and pay for monthly data plans, drink $5 cups of coffee like water (which they also buy instead of turning on the tap), enjoy $15 martinis, belong to health clubs, etc.

Many of them are doing it all on borrowed money. It reminds me of a time when my daughter was a small child. We were driving and she was barraging me with one of her gazillion requests to buy her something. It might have been "Baby Uh–Oh," a doll that soiled its diaper. I remember that being a must-have item among the toddling set at the time. Whatever it was, I said in my best Ward Cleaver voice: "Honey, that costs money. We don't have money to buy everything you want." She said innocently, "Daddy, just go to that machine that gives out the money," referring to an ATM machine. With student loan money so easily available, it seems like some students view the student loan spigot the same way my kid viewed the ATM machine: as if it's free money.

Being frugal requires short-term sacrifices. You will not be able to live the way you want. Convince your student to do it anyway. The debt your student is accruing will weigh them (and you, depending on your relationship) down for many years, directly impinging on their psyche and virtually every major life decision: what kind of job to take, whether and when to get married or have children, where to live, etc.

Students can—and should—scrimp in all areas of consumption, but the easiest way to cut expenses *substantially* is through shared living. Students sometimes mention their woes to me, and they often involve finances. One student recently complained about the size of her student debt. I asked if she lived by herself or with roommates, mentioning she could save *a lot* of money by living with roommates. She said, "I don't really like living with roommates." A couple weeks later another student told me his debt fears were tearing him apart, causing him to not be able to sleep at night and making him think about dropping out of law school. "Do you live by yourself or with roommates?" I asked. "Myself. I don't like living with roommates."

Most people don't like living with roommates. I didn't. I'm an introvert. But living communally is the single most effective way to cut student debt-load. A student can't control the direct costs of education (tuition, books, fees). They can only control their own consumption expenses and housing is the largest consumption expense of them all. Of course, if you and your student live together, this doesn't really apply to you (although in Washington Beltway-speak, no option should be considered off the table—for example, my five-person communal law school household included a husband and wife).

Here's one way to get your student's attention: Take the amount they expect to borrow over three years and go online to one of the many free sites on which you can do loan amortization calculations. Plug in the total debt, approximate interest rate, and the standard student-loan repayment schedule of ten years and show your student the monthly debt payment.

A substantial amount of information about budgeting and managing student debt is readily available, both in book form and online, including specific information for grad students dealing with loan debt. A good place to start looking is the Law School Admission Council (LSAC) website, which provides a load of information and related links on financing law   school: http://www.lsac.org/jd/finance/financial-aid-repayment.asp.

Meanwhile, so you can begin thinking about other specific ways in which your student (or you and your student together) can cut deficit spending, here's a list of the "10 Biggest Money Wasters" according to a 2011 CNN.Money compilation:

- Eating out
- ATM fees
- Gourmet coffee
- Cigarettes
- Impulse buying of stuff you don't really need

- Bundled cable and phone services
- Brand-name groceries
- Lottery tickets
- Daily internet deals
- Unused gym memberships[262]

You and your student should make a point to study the details of the Education Reconciliation Act passed by Congress in 2010. It contains significant provisions easing educational debt repayment for all loans taken out in or after 2012.[263] The Act reduces monthly payment requirements and provides an earlier loan forgiveness date. Monthly loan repayment plans are based on income. Previously, student loan payments could not exceed 15 percent of income. The Act lowers that percentage to 10 percent. Just as important, the Act changes the loan forgiveness date. Before the Act, student debt would be forgiven after twenty-five years. Now, however, student debt will be forgiven after twenty years. (Hopefully, this Act will remain intact, but with budget-cutting high on the national agenda, that's not a sure bet. Already, in the 2011 compromise to raise the ceiling on the national debt, Congress tucked in a provision that graduate students will now have to pay interest on subsidized student loans that accrues while the student is in school. Previously, interest was deferred until after graduation.)

The best news is for students interested in pursuing a career in public interest law. Many students come to law school wanting to help people. They want to practice public interest law, such as working for a non-profit organization or providing *pro bono* legal services to low-income people, but their high student debt prevents them from pursuing these internally rewarding, but low-paying jobs. For graduates who go into public interest work, the Act cuts the loan forgiveness period in half, from twenty to ten years.

Additionally, sixteen states and the District of Columbia sponsor loan repayment assistance programs for law graduates who take public interest jobs, while more than 100 law schools offer their own loan repayment assistance programs

262. Blake Ellis, *10 Biggest Money Wasters*, CNNMONEY.COM, May 18, 2011, http://money.cnn.com/galleries/2011/pf/1105/gallery.money_wasters/index.html.

263. Health Care and Education Reconciliation Act, 20 U.S.C.A. § 1001 et seq. (West 2010), *available at* http://dpc.senate.gov/healthreformbill/healthbill63.pdf. The Act originally was to take effect in 2014, but President Obama moved the date back to 2012 by way of an executive order.

for such students.[264] If your student is interested in doing public interest law, make sure they investigate the availability of these types of resources.

Take Advantage of University Counseling Services if Needed

Most universities offer free, confidential mental health counseling, including couples counseling. I regularly encourage students to take advantage of it. Last semester a student was in my office with tears running down her face, saying her husband wanted a divorce because law school had made her so unavailable. The only advice I could give her was: "Call the counseling center and set up an appointment. It's hard to work these things out on your own. Here's the number. Do it!" I hope she listened.

Find Ways to Get Away From Law School Together

We've seen that students are caught in a conundrum when it comes to making decisions about how to allocate their time between law school and outside relationships. I believe people can make time for what's important to them. I always find it annoying—even though I'm sometimes guilty of the same conduct—when a friend neglects me for a long period of time then explains in mitigation, "I'm sorry I haven't called you since the Reagan Administration, but I've been really busy."

Students can find time to spend with you if they want to. They won't be able to spend as much time as they could before law school or be as flexible in choosing when to spend time together, but these decisions do not have to be all-or-nothing choices. Law students in happy relationships find ways to spend quality time together.

One of the most common strategies for couples is to reserve "date nights." Pick a day or night of the week where law school, including law school-talk, gets put in the closet, so the two of you can just focus on each other. Date nights are a longstanding, time-tested strategy for getting undivided attention from that certain someone. Forcing them at gunpoint

---

264. LEVIT & LINDER, *supra*, at 137 (discussing loan repayment assistance programs).

to "Step away from the Contracts book" will also get their undivided attention, but will risk generating even more law-talk, not to mention five years in the slammer.

Just beware of the potential pitfall that the student will back out at the last minute, a not uncommon occurrence when dealing with overwhelmed law students faced with intense daily class preparation requirements and deadlines in courses such as Legal Research and Writing. Relationship research shows that scheduling and then cancelling date nights is worse than never scheduling them in the first place because it breeds anger and resentment.

I asked significant others whether they and their students had developed any specific ways to "get away from law school" and tend to their relationships. One replied: "Can anyone ever really get away from law school? We're still working on it and are open to suggestions. Can someone please write a book about this?" Hey, that is a great idea.

Most of the partners to law students, however, reported that they and their student had come up with effective ways to get away from law school to be together. As you'll see below, these do not involve or require expensive or excitement-filled vacations or other excursions. Often the simplest pleasures of together-time are the most fulfilling. One partner wrote that simply being in the same room when her student is studying works to overcome the fact that law school can be such an "isolating experience."

I'm going to break from my practice of limiting the number of comments in response to a survey question and give you a nice meaty list. Here's why. Not only will the answers give you some good ideas, but reading them should give you comfort and confidence in the ability of people to carry on successful relationships with law students. They did that for me. More than anything else that came out of my surveys, the answers below showed me that people who love each other can and do find time to be together even in the worst of circumstances in ways that allow them to nourish their relationships.

So here are some ways in which law students and their partners have figured out how to spend quality time together removed from the whirlpool of law school:

• My husband and I have a short, obligatory quiet time every night where we sit together but engage in "alone time" activities, such as updating our iTunes, reading, watching TV, or visiting our favorite blog sites. We do not speak during this time to allow each other to decompress and give our minds a break, but we sit together so that there is still a connection between us. Once we have had our "me" time, we talk about non-school and non-work topics, such as what we saw in the news, house projects, family news, etc. If school or work is still on our minds after decompressing and we need to talk about it, we listen and talk. We are not in the financial position where we can escape the city and go somewhere fun every month, so we escape by simply putting away our books, work, etc. and focusing on us.

• John and I have tried to plan "date nights" around his busy times and my big projects at work. We have also planned time away with our families to unwind. On one occasion, we drove three hours to my parents' house and left our daughter with them. We drove to a nearby (very small) town and had an "imaginary" vacation together. We ate sushi, ice cream and slept for eight straight hours uninterrupted at a local hotel! We have been very patient with each other about the time we share. We have an understanding if one of us is too tired to be romantic. We understand if we can't focus on a dinner conversation because of something that happened during the day. We respect each other when it comes to frustrations at home, work, or school.

• Saturday is our day to really get away from law school. We sleep in, go to the microbrewery for him to buy some beer, and watch Alabama football like we always have. He lets loose on Saturdays and really buckles down on Sundays. This day allows us to reconnect and we rarely speak of school.

• We bought season passes to a local speed circuit, where we race go-carts to blow off steam.

• Every night, we try to watch reruns of "Whose Line is it Anyway?" on television. It's ridiculously funny. I think it's better to be able to watch a comedy and laugh for thirty minutes than to sit down and watch a drama after a day full of studying and writing.

• Dinner is a pretty important part of the day to us. It signifies that the day is coming to an end and there's a period of relaxation before going to sleep. I usually do most of the cooking (since my student isn't quite as adept with a knife and seasonings), but we always play some sort of logic game or timed quiz while I cook. This promotes working together to solve problems in the game, which I believe strengthens our ability to solve problems between ourselves.

• My student and I will go on weekend trips to visit family or just spend Saturday doing what we like to do, such as eat, watch football, and eat some more. We also are faithful Christians, so church and outreach are definitely one of the ways we branch out to put law school and jobs on the back burner.

• We have found creative ways to spend time together. For example, instead of paying to park downtown, I take him to school every morning and pick him up every afternoon. I work a few blocks away so it makes sense. We get that half hour each morning and afternoon to talk, debrief after a long day, or just enjoy sitting next to each other in the car. The other benefit is that since I drop him off when I have to go in for work and pick him up after I get off, he has a few hours before his first class and a few hours after his last class to get work done. Most days this means he doesn't have to do work once we get home at night.

• After school, she and I usually spend time together exercising, talking, watching TV or movies, or playing video games. We have certain television shows that we make sure to watch each week which gives us something to look forward to that does not pertain to her school or my work. Also, on the weekends we sometimes go out for dinner and a movie or visit with friends when possible. We find these activities keep things entertaining between the two of us.

• We have "no computer days" and dinner time is always sit-down-and-talk time. After finals, we always try to get away for a weekend.

• We have weekends, or sometimes just a few hours on a Saturday or Sunday, where we just become hermits—no outside friends, just us. It's a great bonding time. We use it to share hobbies we both enjoy and to talk about things other than his school and my work. It's a fun way to reconnect.

• Before she started law school we made the pact to stay true to "us," meaning that we would still try hard to do things that bring us closer together. One thing that we do is have a "game/movie night" often. This is time that we get to spend just on us. We also always try to have dinner together. I know this may not seem like a big deal, but when you know that you have that to look forward to every night it makes things easier.

• This is a work in progress. We both knew that the first year of law school was going to be very challenging. We try to set aside one day on the weekend to do something together outside of law school. We also enjoy the simple things more. This could be things like going out to breakfast or taking a walk with the dogs in the evening.

• We take a trip after every semester to recharge our marriage—even just a small camping trip when we are broke.

• Usually we try to go out to eat so we can get out of the house. If she is at the house and not doing school work, I think she feels guilty.

• While not an overabundance of ways, there are some things we like to do to get away from school. We always try to eat together at least two times a week. On the rare occasion that we finish our homework early, we might sit down and watch TV or a movie. And definitely on the weekends we spend time together either going out or going on a date! But when we have a lot of work to do or a test on a certain week, all things not school related are, unfortunately, kept to a minimum.

• We made a "rule" that he leaves law school-talk at law school. When he is home or talking to me on the phone, we talk about how our days went and go about other conversation. I work full-time so it's the same thing for me too. I leave work-talk at work and come home to relax and focus on other things.

- Getting away from law school is a necessity. We make sure to take one night each weekend to do something we both enjoy. Most times that means we will go see a movie, but any activity to clear the mind will suffice. I believe having a specified day each week to relax provides my law student motivation and something desirable to look forward to.

- We would have dates set up, but my wife would cancel them on a regular basis. So to spend time with her, I would get involved in whatever she was doing that concerned law school like: helping her practice her oral arguments, giving my opinions on cases she was reading, and acting as the judge during her arguments. I would always ask her, "How was your day?" And then actually listen to what she was telling me about law school.

- I AM the get away from law school.

- Summer following her 1L year we literally got away for a weekend at Disney World and a week in Puerto Rico. During the school year there is no time for a physical getaway and little time for a mental one. My wife's idea of relaxing is sitting on the couch curled up with a good Con Law book—she's doing it right now! We do occasionally have little date nights that include a homemade dinner and a movie after we put our son to bed, but the dinner conversation usually pertains to Rule 12(b)(6) motions, whatever that means!

- We go out of our way to make an effort to do fun things. For example, we have gone to concerts and plays here in town. Also, we have tried to associate with other young couples where we live who aren't involved in law school.

- We don't have any specific ways of getting away from law school because our child does it for us. Our son doesn't care about law school and always manages to keep our minds on other things.

What a great list! Note that several of the partners emphasized that an important component of their getaway strategy is to not just be together, but to ensure that the pesky interloper—law school—gets left behind so it doesn't develop into an ugly ménage à trios. One significant other offered particularly blunt "getting away" advice in this regard: "How about just not talking about law school? That ever come to mind?"

Easier said than done for many law students. One fun way to interrupt the flood of law-talk is to impose a "gotcha" reminder-penalty for engaging in it during occasions when you have agreed to stuff it away for a while. For example, you could agree that if your student mentions anything about law school during your reserved time together, he or she has to perform some household chore or put a dollar in a jar for your next date night or vacation or give you a foot massage or whatever else you want to come up with.

This game will help your student realize how deeply they are mired in law school. Meanwhile, *cha-ching*, you can sit back and enjoy raking in the penalty awards, of which there will be many.

* * *

You and your student have complete control over what happens to your relationship. Law school can impinge on it, but it can't ruin it or take it away unless you allow that to happen. As one student said: "Law school does not *need* to damage a relationship. Ours is better than ever!" Another student sounded an even more optimistic note:

> YOU CAN DO IT! You can have a successful relationship and a successful law school career; it just takes hard work and understanding! Law Student: think about your significant other's feelings, put yourself in their shoes, understand that they miss you and only want the best for you. Loved One: be patient, it will be worth it in the end. Be a stronghold of encouragement, support, and back rubs (those law school books are HEAVY)!

CHAPTER 18

WHAT HAPPENS AFTER GRADUATION? CAREER OPTIONS FOR NEW LAW GRADUATES

Whenever my daughter, who recently graduated from college, tells me her latest career idea, most of which involve attending expensive graduate programs, my first question is: "So, specifically, what kinds of *actual jobs* could you get with that degree?" The answer to that question ties in with several other questions that influence my level of support for her idea. What will she be doing on a day-to-day basis? Will it fit her Myers–Briggs personality preferences? Will it be something she finds interesting? Rewarding? Will it allow her to support herself and pay back her student loans? Will it permit her to strike a proper work-life balance? She rarely has answers to these questions.

I find the same to be true of law students. Most law students, certainly 1Ls, know very little about the specific career options available to them on graduation. This chapter explains those options, including some pros and cons of each. You could help your student by getting him or her to start thinking about these possibilities sooner rather than later. I've watched far too many law students stumble blindly into the legal employment world without a clue what they were looking for or getting into. A 3L research assistant wrote after reading the chapter, "I wish I would have known all of this stuff much earlier!" You need to know it too because your student's quality of work-life is going to affect you whether you're a partner, parent, or other loved one.

In fact, this might be a good chapter to read together. Law school only lasts three or four years. A career lasts a lifetime. While there is no rush for a law student to decide what kind of lawyer they want to be, it is certainly something worth thinking about. Necessarily, the discussion in this chapter deals in generalizations that are not true of all jobs in the particular category. The focus is on basic types of and venues for legal jobs, not subject matter specialties, of which there are many.

Private Practice at a Large Law Firm

The majority of lawyers work in private practice. But to simply make a distinction between "private practice" and other types of lawyer jobs fails to account for the fact that working in private practice at a large firm versus a small firm is a difference as dramatic as night and day. By "large firm," I'm talking about firms with fifty or more lawyers. Some mega-firms exist that are substantially larger. For example, Baker & McKenzie, based in Chicago with offices in thirty-nine countries, employs more than 3000 lawyers. Between very large firms and very small firms is a wide tier of medium-sized firms. As a general rule of thumb, the more lawyers in a firm, the more the firm will tend to take on the characteristics of the large firms described below.

Many graduates come to see being hired by a large law firm as the truest measure of law school success, primarily because big firms are the ones most likely to pay the fat salaries that entice many people to come to law school. Large firms usually represent corporations and concentrate on civil rather than criminal matters, although some represent corporate defendants in complex white-collar criminal cases. Areas of law commonly engaged in by large firms include antitrust law, bankruptcy law, bond law, environmental law, health law, intellectual property law, labor and employment law, mergers and acquisitions, real estate law, securities regulation, and, increasingly, international law.

Large firms have departments of both litigation lawyers and transactional lawyers. Litigators, also called "trial lawyers," handle lawsuits. Transactional lawyers handle transactions, such as bond or real estate or securities transactions. Most people, raised on television and cinema portrayals of lawyers in which the actors are always in courtrooms, believe most lawyers are trial lawyers. But in fact only about 10 percent of lawyers are trial lawyers, and even they spend most of their time in offices rather than courtrooms.

Upsides of large firms include six-figure starting salaries and excellent benefits, highly trained staff, a sense of prestige, learning from lawyers who are likely to be among the best in their fields, working on big, important cases and transactions, eating lots of fancy meals in fancy restaurants with colleagues and clients, enjoying plush office space, and having a good springboard for moving on to another job.

That last point bears emphasizing. Not everyone is cut out for or enjoys large-firm practice, but lawyers trained at large firms usually have good opportunities for moving laterally to other legal jobs. A former student recently accepted a job at a large firm, turning down a job that offered a higher overall quality of life (except for income). He explained that he had no intention of staying at the big firm, but figured it would be good training and would create other opportunities down the road. He's right, although there is a very real danger of getting caught in the "money trap" when working at a big firm; that is, developing and getting used to a standard of living that is difficult to bail out on later down the road.

Large firm practice carries definite perks, but downsides exist as well. Large firms don't pay starting associates up to $160,000 a year for altruistic reasons. They expect a lot in return: consistent excellence and lots of billable hours. Large firms often require associates to bill 2000 or more hours annually. Doesn't sound too bad. Setting aside two weeks for vacation (don't bother), this comes out to a reasonable forty hours per week. That leaves plenty of time for trailing the sailboat behind the Escalade out to the lake cabin on weekends.

The problem is that we're talking *billable* hours, not just chronological hours. It takes a whole lot more regular hours to reach the required levels of billable hours. You can't bill clients while you're eating lunch, using the restroom, writing the presentation for your managing partner's speech to the Rotary Club, un-jamming the copy machine, or talking to your partner about who is going to pick up the kids and the dry cleaning. A generally accepted ratio of billable hours to hours worked is 2:3, meaning forty billable hours per week will require sixty hours of work.

Plus, meeting the minimum isn't enough to make you look good if the associate in the office next to you is billing 200 hours a year above the minimum. Having to account for every minute of every day adds a lot of pressure to a lawyer's life. Ask a big-firm lawyer to name the single worst aspect of their job and the answer may well be "billable hours."

Other less-than-desirable aspects of large law firms can include a more formal and regimented working environment and a hierarchy that can retard the development of young associates into autonomous lawyers. Large firms handle large matters. They don't assign them to inexperienced associates to handle on their own. In big cases or transactions, it's common to have a team of several lawyers working on the same case and the pecking order is clear. The young associates usually do the un-scintillating work (research, reviewing documents, and the like) and the higher-ups do the fun stuff like arguing in court.

Another aspect of big cases is that many of them are interminable. A new associate can come into a firm and work on a case for years, without ever seeing the beginning or end of it. We used to call our cases "Vietnams" when I was in private practice because they dragged on and on with no end in sight. No joke: A former law firm colleague of mine recently told me that portions of a case at my old law firm, which I left in 1986, are still going on![265]

It is perhaps not surprising that an ABA career-satisfaction survey of 800 lawyers showed that "far and away the least satisfied lawyers were from large firms."[266] Nevertheless, the allure of big money, glitzy perks, and prestige continue to draw most of law schools' best and brightest graduates to big-firm practice. Whether a person will enjoy working at a large firm, or in any other particular legal job, depends much on personality. My older brother was a big-firm lawyer and loved it. He couldn't understand why I wanted to become a law professor, just as I couldn't under-

---

265. Before becoming a law professor, I worked for four years at a small boutique litigation firm. Even though the firm had only about a dozen lawyers, it functioned like a big firm in terms of case selection, atmosphere, compensation, and policies. Thus, size isn't always a full-proof barometer of a firm.

266. Stephanie Francis Ward, *Pulse of the Legal Profession: 800 Lawyers Reveal What They Think About Their Lives, Their Careers and the State of the Profession*, A.B.A. J., Oct. 2007, at 30, 33.

stand why he loved working at a large firm. Everyone is different.

One cautionary observation: the golden era of guaranteed partnership at large and even small firms is a thing of the past. Back in the day, assuming one did good work, he could reasonably count on transitioning from associate to full equity partner in about five years. An equity partner is one who owns part of the firm and shares in the profits, rather than simply receiving a salary and bonuses. The standard partnership track is now seven to ten years. Moreover, many, if not most, law firms (certainly most large firms) now have two or more tiers of partnership. In other words, not all partners are created equal. Non-equity partners at large firms may be little more than glorified senior associates, although they do receive good salaries.

Many events can derail an associate from a partnership track, including a spat with a boss, an inability to generate clients, not billing enough hours, poor client relationship skills, sloppy work, or even a bad economy. At large firms, only a small percentage of beginning associates are still around come partnership time. Some move on voluntarily, while others are asked to leave.

Private Practice at a Small Law Firm

Keeping in mind that we are dealing with generalizations that will not always hold true, the pros and cons of small firms compared to large firms are reversed. Small firms offer several quality of life advantages. The atmosphere is often more collegial and laid back. Many small firms, for example, let lawyers dress casually on days they won't be meeting with clients. Because most small firms handle lots of small cases, even new lawyers get assigned their own cases to manage, which is more fun than sitting in a room sifting through boxes of documents all day, a common associate assignment in big cases at big law firms.

Billable hours may still be present at small firms, depending on the type of practice, but the expectations in terms of number may be more relaxed. One reason is that large firms have huge overhead costs for their posh office space, first-class staff, platinum benefit packages, and, of course, those large associate salaries. With lower overhead, lawyers at small firms can work fewer hours with larger profit margins. Also, a lot of small matters, such as divorces or will preparations, are handled for flat fees, eliminating billable hours from the picture.

Depending on the firm, there might also be less specialization at small firms, meaning more variety in the types of cases and clients. Small firms often handle a combination of both civil and criminal work, including a lot of standard fare from everyday life: divorces, personal injury cases, DUIs and other routine criminal cases, will preparations, simple bankruptcies, home purchase transactions, etc. Handling some of these types of cases, however, can become routine, and consequently, boring.

The biggest trade-off as compared to a large firm is financial. Beginning lawyers at small firms may start at $40–50,000 a year, sometimes even less. Retirement, health, and other benefits also are likely to be less generous than at large firms, if they exist at all. But lawyers at small firms usually end up making good livings—it just may take a while.

While many small firm lawyers are generalists, a subcategory of small firms exists called "boutique firms." These are firms that specialize in particular subject areas, such as intellectual property or real estate or personal injury law. Even though the number of lawyers is small, they may handle major matters and generate high revenues. Many of the wealthiest lawyers in America are personal injury lawyers who, usually working in small firms, represent plaintiffs who suffered catastrophic injuries caused by the defendant, although the national "tort reform" movement is putting a dent in the incomes and lifestyles of plaintiffs' personal injury lawyers.[267]

Sole Practitioners

The smallest firm of all is the sole practitioner, sometimes called solo practitioner. As the name suggests, a sole practitioner is a single lawyer running his or her own law firm. Reliable recent figures aren't available, but a 2000 study by

---

267. The tort reform movement is a battle waged by medical, business, and insurance interests to restrict personal injury litigation and damages. Common tort reform laws that may adversely affect plaintiffs' personal injury lawyers are maximum caps on certain types of damages and maximum caps on attorneys' fees. States have passed literally hundreds of tort reform statutes in recent years.

the American Bar Foundation reported that 48 percent of all lawyers are sole practitioners.[268] That figure might be high today, but a recent *ABA Journal* article said, without supporting data, that "more than 30 percent of American lawyers are solos."[269] Thus, regardless of the precise figure, hundreds of thousands of lawyers work on their own.

The biggest upside of being a sole practitioner is autonomy, one of the most valued and rarest luxuries of occupational life. Happiness research shows that autonomy correlates strongly with higher life satisfaction. "If you want happiness as a lawyer, get control of your life,"[270] advise Levit and Linder in their book, *The Happy Lawyer*. They point to numerous studies of groups ranging from college students to elderly nursing home residents that "consistently show that control is closely related to happiness."[271]

The challenges for sole practitioners, however, are substantial. In addition to dealing with the considerable hassles of running any business (e.g., keeping books, paying overhead and taxes, managing employees), sole practitioners, especially new ones, have to constantly worry about where the next client will come from.

Roughly 5 percent of law graduates "hang out their shingles" (i.e., start their own firms) upon graduating and passing the bar, but it makes more sense to get some experience—and clients—before setting out on one's own.

Prosecutors and Public Defenders

Many new lawyers opt for government jobs in the prosecuting attorney's or public defender's office. Prosecutors prosecute people charged with crime, while public defenders defend them when they lack the resources to hire a private lawyer. Most of these jobs are at the state or local level. The federal government also hires prosecutors and public defenders, but these jobs are fewer in number and much more competitive to land.

---

268. Clara N. Carson, Am. Bar Found., Lawyer Statistical Report, U.S. Legal Profession in 2000 29 (2004).

269. James Podgers, *ABA Halves Dues for Solos*, A.B.A. J., Mar. 2010, at 65.

270. Levit & Linder, *supra*, at 79.

271. *Id.* at 80.

Perhaps the biggest upside of being a prosecutor or public defender is that every day is filled with action right from the get-go. Criminal cases are more interesting than most civil cases, although often in a tragic way. With criminal dockets being so full, a new prosecutor or public defender will quickly be assigned their own case load. If your student wants to get thrown into the courtroom arena early and often, these are great jobs for that.

The crowded criminal dockets are also a negative, however, as they result in prosecutors and public defenders having enormous caseloads. Heavy caseloads can be overwhelming, especially to perfectionist types who want to do their best on every case. Stress and burnout can result. (This is true in the civil arena as well. My law school roommate's first job was as a worker's compensation attorney. He had more than 300 active cases. He used to tell me, "I malpractice every day. I don't have any choice.")

As with all government lawyer jobs, prosecutors and public defenders earn lower salaries than most private practitioners. Starting salaries for state prosecutors average around $40–50,000, about the same as the starting salaries at many smaller private law firms. The difference is that salary increases that come with experience are much lower for government lawyers than in private practice. Like most public employees, prosecutors and public defenders usually receive good benefits. Life in general is much better for their federal counterparts, who receive higher salaries and have lower caseloads and more staff and other resources.

An intangible downside of working as a prosecutor or public defender is a certain hardening of the heart that occurs as a coping mechanism. This happens to all lawyers to some extent, as we've discussed, but it may be worse for prosecutors and public defenders. Most people charged with crimes are, in fact, guilty. Some of the crimes they commit are atrocious. One can't help but be affected from dealing day in and day out with thieves, drug dealers, or worse.

Non–Criminal Government Lawyers

Federal, state, and local government agencies and departments hire non-criminal lawyers by the bunches. Precise figures are lacking, but it appears that roughly 10 percent of lawyers work for federal, state, and local governments. That's more than 100,000 lawyers. Indeed, the federal government is the largest legal employer in the country. Government agencies are involved in regulating many aspects of our daily lives: consumer protection, product safety, food and drug safety, highway safety, environmental protection, national defense, Medicare and Social Security, financial industry regulation, child welfare, education, and other areas. All of those agencies need lawyers.

Government agency lawyer positions can be great jobs in terms of quality of life. Government lawyers usually work regular hours. Sometimes they have to bring work home with them, but not nearly as often as lawyers in private practice. Job security is good. I often recommend government agency work to students with young children, students who I don't think are cut out personality-wise for the high pressure of private practice, and students who are more interested in quality of life than financial rewards.

Life satisfaction can be enhanced by the fact that government agencies exist to serve the public. Whether they always function that way, of course, is subject to debate, but that is their basic function. Government lawyers are usually on what most people would consider to be the "right" side of cases. If your student is interested, for example, in environmental law, it is probably because she cares about protecting the environment. Unfortunately, most private sector jobs in environmental law involve representing corporations that produce pollution. Working for the federal Environmental Protection Agency or a similar state agency might be a dream job for such a student. The 2007 ABA lawyer satisfaction survey showed that public sector lawyers were the happiest of all lawyer groups, with 68 percent reporting satisfaction with their career.[272]

The major tradeoff is the financial aspect. Pay scales are lower for government lawyers, but the enhanced quality of life can more than make up for the lower pay, depending on one's priorities. As with prosecutors and public defenders, salaries and benefits for federal agency lawyers are substantially better than those at the state and local levels.

272. Ward, *supra*, at 34.

Legal Services and Other Nonprofit Organizations

Many students go to law school because they want to help people and the purest way of doing that as a lawyer is by working for a legal services organization (often called a "legal-aid" organization) providing free legal services to low-income people, or for some other type of non-profit organization dedicated to advancing a public cause. The primary upside of such jobs is obvious: the satisfaction that comes from truly serving the public good, a satisfaction to which few lawyers can lay claim.

Additionally, while it varies by place and position, the hours generally are reasonable and the benefits good. As a bonus, the jobs tend to attract interesting and unique people with good values, who enjoy working collaboratively instead of competitively, which can make for a more pleasant work environment.

Overall life quality is excellent, except—here's the buzz-kill—these are the lowest-paying of all lawyer jobs. The median salary for public interest lawyers in 2010 was $42,900.[273] Also, because many public interest jobs depend on temporary grant funding that can run out, they do not always provide reliable job security. Still, many students would love to take these jobs because they really do want to contribute to society in a positive way with their law degree. Unfortunately, a lot of students are precluded from even considering public interest jobs because of their high student-loan debt. As discussed in Chapter 17, however, recent federal legislation as well as loan repayment assistance programs available in some states and at many law schools, offer the potential for substantial debt relief to students who pursue public interest legal careers.

In–House Corporate Counsel

Corporations often hire lawyers to serve in positions known as "in-house counsel," which means exactly what it sounds like. When they need a lawyer, they literally have one in the building. Large corporations sometimes have entire legal staffs. In-house counsel positions are desirable because

273. *NALP Falling Salaries Report,* *supra,* at 2.

they offer the rare combination in the legal profession of good pay and benefits and a decent quality of life, including normal working hours. In-house corporate lawyers don't have to deal with billable hours or getting clients, major sources of stress on lawyers in private practice. Often, one of the principal jobs of in-house corporate counsel is to farm out difficult legal matters to outside private law firms and oversee them.

Except at large corporations with entry-level positions, however, these jobs usually are not available to new law graduates. Most lawyers hired as corporate counsel already have experience in the particular areas in which the corporation is involved. Many of them come from government agencies with which the corporations work regularly.

Judicial Law Clerks

Although the job title doesn't sound very glamorous, judicial law clerk positions are the ultimate dream job for many law graduates. I started my legal career in such a position and remember my former mother-in-law complaining that her friends didn't get it when she bragged to them that her son-in-law was a "judicial law clerk." "Is that the best he could do?" they would ask, picturing a file clerk stooped behind a counter shuffling papers.

Highly prized, a judicial clerkship is a kind of assistant-ship working with a federal or state appellate or trial judge, usually for a one- or two-year period (although some judges hire career law clerks). Federal judicial clerkships are considered significantly more prestigious and pay higher salaries than state judicial clerkships, but both are excellent opportunities. The median salary for judicial clerkships in 2010 was $51,900,[274] but that figure is skewed by the higher federal court salaries over state court salaries.

Judicial law clerks spend most of their time researching and drafting court orders and opinions. Some of those opinions end up being published in the National Reporter System, which is fun to see. Even the wealthiest, most powerful lawyers in America can't claim ghost-written authorship of a published judicial opinion (unless they also started out as judicial law clerks). Judicial law clerks get to participate in all

274. *Id.*

types of civil and criminal cases and watch and learn from many different kinds of lawyering styles. The intensive research and writing requirements of the job fast-forward the development of both of those crucial skills. And clerkships, particularly federal clerkships, make their holders highly marketable when the clerkship is over.

If your law student possesses the type of credentials required to be a legitimate candidate for a judicial clerkship (generally the top 10 percent of the class and law review membership), urge her to pursue one—and to get an early start studying and understanding the application process. If a federal clerkship is beyond reach, your student should look into state judicial clerkships, which are somewhat less competitive, yet offer several of the same benefits.

Miscellaneous

In addition to the eight basic types of lawyer jobs described above, some new lawyers join the JAG Corps (Judge Advocate General's Corps) and practice law on behalf of one of the military branches. Their jobs may involve interpreting the rules of engagement in war settings, prosecuting or defending soldiers in court martial proceedings, or more mundane regulatory and administrative law work. Former students of mine who have joined the JAG Corps uniformly report back that it is a good experience.

A few lucky, academically excellent graduates become law professors, although usually not before a few years of well-placed practice experience, a federal judicial clerkship, and/or a graduate law degree (see below). Being a law professor may be the greatest lawyer job of all. Many lawyers have figured this out, as the number of highly qualified applicants each year far exceeds the limited number of positions available by a large margin. One reason job openings are so scarce, in addition to the fact that only a couple of hundred potential employers exist nationwide, is that the only way people usually leave these jobs is through death, retirement, or being denied tenure.

Many law graduates don't practice law at all. They use their law degrees to advance careers in other areas, such as public administration, healthcare administration, business management, or politics. Some people decide they don't enjoy law and go off into an entirely different field. I'll never forget the student who showed up in my office literally the day after her law school graduation and asked if I would write a recommendation letter for her to apply to a graduate program in social work. I asked her why and she said, "I never liked law school." And, strange as it might sound, some law students pursue a law degree simply for personal enrichment, with no intention of ever using it.

More School!

Brace yourself and hide the checkbook. Some law graduates take their newly printed Juris Doctor diploma and apply to an expensive graduate law program to get an LL.M (Master of Laws) or, less often, an S.J.D. (Doctor of Juridical Science). That's right. Law has its own graduate degrees on top of the basic J.D.

U.S. law schools offer roughly 300 LL.M degree programs in a variety of specialty areas, a number that is growing. According to the *National Law Journal*, the number of LL.M. degrees awarded by ABA-approved law schools grew 65 percent between 1999 and 2009, compared to a 13 percent growth in J.D. degrees during the same period.[275]

People seeking graduate law degrees fall into four basic categories: (1) foreign lawyers looking for an entry pass into the U.S. legal profession or for a credential to be hired in an international office of a U.S. law firm; (2) lawyers who want to become knowledgeable and marketable in a specialized field of law, such as tax law; (3) students who earned their J.D. degree at a lower-ranked law school and want to "cleanse" their resumes by getting an LL.M at a more prestigious school; and (4) people who want to become law professors, many of whom also fall under category 3. (Usually, only the law professor-types seek the S.J.D.)

The return on investment for an LL.M degree is open to question. Some criticize LL.M programs as existing primarily for the purpose of generating additional revenue for law schools, referring to them disparagingly as "cash cows." The generally recognized exception is an LL.M degree in tax law.

---

275. Karen Sloan, *'Cash Cow' or Valuable Credential?*, NAT'L L.J., Sept. 20, 2010, http://www.law.com/jsp/nlj/ PubArticlePrinterFriendlyNLJ.jsp?id= 1202472170557 & slreturn=1 & hbxlogin=1.

Because tax law is so specialized and tax-LL.Ms have been around the longest, an LL.M in tax is considered a valuable credential for students who want to be tax lawyers.[276]

If your student starts talking about getting an LL.M degree, press him for details as to why he thinks he needs it. Make sure he's not doing it just to prolong his education and avoid entering the real world. He's likely to have enough debt as it is.

* * *

Perhaps the list of basic career options for a J.D.-holder is shorter than you or your student expected, but keep in mind that a wide variety of choices exists within each of the categories in terms of type of law practiced (e.g., litigation versus transactional), subject matter area (dozens of choices are available), and types of office settings, clients, and colleagues. As or after you read this chapter, feel out your student on which of the options above sound like they might be a good fit for her, making sure she considers the lifestyle and other trade-offs involved in each one.

As discussed in Chapter 12, law school has a tendency to instill in students a value system that is not necessarily compatible with who they really are or want to be. We've talked about how "more money" is what most people think will make them happy, but also about the research showing that's true only up to the point where a person can enjoy a decent standard of living. I always fall back on that fundamental piece of advice in which I believe so strongly: Tell your student to follow their heart in making a career choice. And remind them that it's okay to get it wrong at first, as long as they are willing to change their mind later down the road and get it right.

---

276. *See id.* (quoting Gregory Shumaker, a hiring partner at Jones Day, one of the nation's largest firms, as stating "the only LL.M degree that has much of an impact on our hiring decisions is a tax LL.M").

CHAPTER 19

STUMP YOUR LAW STUDENT WITH THESE "LEGAL" QUESTIONS

This book has raised more than enough serious issues for you and your student to think about, so let's have some fun before wrapping things up. One of the annoying things about law students, as we've seen reported in the loved one comments, is that many of them become know-it-alls. It's practically impossible to win an argument with a law student, especially regarding anything "legal." Until now. This chapter contains twenty fun multiple-choice questions you can use to stump your law student. Enjoy some quality "legal" bonding time by reading the questions aloud—maybe with a glass of wine or other favorite beverage on the front porch—and seeing how many your student can guess right. The questions cover everything from completely useless trivia to important moments in legal history.

1. While some people purport to "hate" lawyers, the public remains fascinated by them, as evidenced by all the attention the legal profession receives in the entertainment world. Since the 1960s, more than fifty television series about lawyers have been produced. Well over 100 "lawyer movies" have been brought to the big screen and lawyer novelists such as John Grisham sell hundreds of millions of books. What about musical entertainment? Which of the following is *not* a real song by a popular artist?

    A.   I Fought the Law (and the Law Won)

    B.   Lawyers in Love

C. Sue Me, Sue You Blues

D. My Lawyer Bit My Doctor

E. Lawyers, Guns & Money

ANSWER: D. "My Lawyer Bit My Doctor" is not a real song, although it sounds like it could be a hit. The Bobby Fuller Four made *I Fought the Law (and the Law Won)* into a top 10 hit in 1964. Sadly, Fuller was found dead in his car shortly after he tasted fame. The death was ruled a suicide/accident, although some suspected Fuller was murdered. John Mellencamp paid homage to Fuller in his song, *R.O.C.K. in the U.S.A.* ("There was Frankie Lymon, Bobby Fuller, Mitch Ryder (they were rockin').") Jackson Brown's *Lawyers in Love* reached the Top 40 in 1983, while his album of the same name made it all the way to #8 in the charts. The sardonic *Sue Me, Sue You Blues* appeared on former Beatle George Harrison's second solo album, *Living in the Material World*, released in 1973. Like many rock stars, Harrison had been embroiled in more than his fair share of litigation, including lawsuits over the breakup of the Beatles. The song contained biting lyrics such as, "Bring your lawyer, and I'll bring mine; get together and we could have a real bad time." *Lawyers, Guns & Money* was a typically over-the-top tune from the late Warren Zevon that appeared on his 1978 album, *Excitable Boy*. It includes the classic refrain line, "Send lawyers, guns, and money; the s* * * has hit the fan."

2. Speaking of entertainment, in 2003, the American Film Institute (AFI) released its list of the top fifty heroes in movie history. How many of those top fifty movie heroes were legal professionals (lawyers or lawmakers) or common citizens who used the law to achieve progressive objectives?

A. 1

B. 4

C. 8

D. 12

E. 15

ANSWER: C. The eight legally inclined top fifty movie heroes include, in the number one spot, Atticus Finch (Gregory Peck), the Southern lawyer who fought for justice in a racially charged case in the screen adaptation of Harper Lee's book, *To Kill a Mockingbird*. Mahatma Gandhi, who was trained as a lawyer, came in #21 for *Gandhi* (Ben Kingsley). Andrew Beckett (Tom Hanks), the AIDS-afflicted corporate lawyer from *Philadelphia*, made the list at #49. Jefferson Smith (Jimmy Stewart)—the protagonist in the Frank Capra classic, *Mr. Smith Goes to Washington*—reached the #11 spot. Stewart played a character appointed to fill a vacancy as a U.S. Senator, where he confronted and fought political corruption. Erin Brockovich (Julia Roberts), a down-and-out paralegal whose sleuthing led to a class action against a toxic waste-dumping corporation in the movie of the same name, checked in at #31. At #28 we have Juror #8 (Henry Fonda) from *12 Angry Men*, the lone juror who refused to vote guilty in the trial of a teenager accused of murdering his father. The final two characters were workers who became labor union activists fighting for fair, safer working conditions: Norma Rae Webster (Sally Field), from *Norma Rae*, at #15, and Karen Silkwood (Meryl Streep), from *Silkwood*, at #47.

3. You've heard more than enough about the grueling nature of law school. Wouldn't it be great if your student could just skip it and take the bar exam without having to endure those three years of expensive torment? How many states permit people to take the bar exam and become a lawyer without ever attending law school?

A. 7

B. 2

C. 16

D. 1

E. If something sounds too good to be true, it usually is: zero.

ANSWER: A. Seven states—California, Maine, New York, Vermont, Virginia, Washington, and Wyoming—permit students to train through law office study, an apprenticeship system similar to the approach to legal studies that existed before law schools became widespread. In early American history, prospective lawyers learned primarily through the English custom of "reading the law" under the tutelage of an experienced attorney. It wasn't until the 1920s that states began to require law school attendance for admission to the bar. Apprenticeships fell largely into disuse by the 1950s. In 2009, only fifty-eight of the more than 68,000 bar-exam takers nationwide trained through law office study rather than by attending law school. While no definitive explanation exists as to why more people don't take advantage of law office apprenticeship as the path to becoming a lawyer, we can speculate about some of the reasons: few attorneys are willing and able to sign on to provide the necessary mentoring; legal employers look down on job applicants without law degrees; studying law outside of a school environment takes enormous self-motivation and discipline; and the bar-passage rate for law office apprentices is much lower than for students who attend ABA-approved law schools.

4. Under the U.S. Constitution, federal judges are appointed for life. Nice job security if you can get it. The most esteemed federal judgeships, of course, are held by the nine justices of the U.S. Supreme Court. Who was the longest-serving member in the history of the Court?

A.   Oliver Wendell Holmes, Jr.

B.   William O. Douglas

C.   Antonin Scalia

D.   John Marshall

E.   Elena Kagan

ANSWER: B.   Chief Justice John Marshall might come to mind for law students who have taken Constitutional Law. His thirty-four year tenure on the Court from 1801 until his death was not only long, but holds monumental importance in American history. Marshall authored the 1803 opinion in *Marbury v. Madison*, a still-controversial decision establishing the power of the judicial branch to review and overturn acts of the President and Congress. Oliver Wendell Holmes, Jr. is another well-known, long-serving justice, having sat on Court for thirty years from 1902–1932. But the tenure of Associate Justice William O. Douglas edges out both Marshall and Holmes for the record of longest-serving justice. Douglas sat on the Court for thirty-six years, from 1939–1975. Other Supreme Court records held by Douglas include authoring the most opinions and dissents (the liberal Douglas' dissent-writing increased as the Court became more conservative during his later years on the bench) and most marriages, with four. Douglas, nicknamed "Wild Bill" for his fiery, independent streak, was a fierce champion of liberty and individual rights who authored many memorable opinions.

Kagan is a new justice, having been appointed by President Barack Obama in 2010.

5. One of the great things about a law degree is its versatility. With so many career options, what career path should your law student take? Prosecutor, public defender, public interest lawyer ... or how about President of the United States? How many U.S. presidents out of the total of forty-three (as of 2011) graduated from law school?

A. 7

B. 13

C. 18

D. 26

ANSWER: D. A whopping 60 percent of U.S. presidents—twenty-six of the forty-three—were lawyers before being elected to the highest office in the land. They include, in chronological order, John Adams, Thomas Jefferson, James Madison, James Monroe, John Quincy Adams, Andrew Jackson, Martin Van Buren, John Tyler, James K. Polk, Millard Fillmore, Franklin Pierce, James Buchanan, Abraham Lincoln, Rutherford B. Hayes, Chester A. Arthur, Grover Cleveland (who was elected on two non-consecutive occasions), Benjamin Harrison, William McKinley, William H. Taft, Woodrow Wilson, Calvin Coolidge, Franklin Delano Roosevelt, Richard Nixon, Gerald Ford, William Jefferson Clinton, and Barack Obama.

6. One of the most difficult aspects of practicing law, not covered in law school, is getting clients. Just as doctors need patients, lawyers need clients. One can surmise that all of the local criminal defense lawyers had plenty of business during the largest mass arrest in U.S. history. How many people were arrested and where did it occur?

A. 140 in Peoria, Illinois

B. 1500 in Boston, Massachusetts

C. 12,000 in Washington, D.C.

D. 17,500 in Los Angeles, California

ANSWER: C. In May 1971, more than 500,000 anti-Vietnam War protesters descended on Washington, D.C. with the intention of shutting down the federal government by blocking the streets. As of that date, 45,000 American soldiers had died in Vietnam and more than 250,000 troops were still stationed there. At least 12,000 protesters were arrested from May 3 through May 5, including Daniel Ellsberg. Ellsberg, a former Defense Department analyst, had helped compile a report on the history of U.S. involvement in Vietnam from 1945–1968 for Defense Secretary Robert McNamara. The study, which became known as the "Pentagon Papers," exposed controversial, previously hidden truths about the scope and purpose of U.S. participation in the Vietnam War. Ellsberg leaked the Pentagon Papers to the *New York Times*, which began publishing them in installments. The Nixon administration sued for an injunction, which resulted in a landmark U.S. Supreme Court case, *New York Times Co. v. United States*, 403 U.S. 713 (1971), in which the Court ruled in favor of the newspaper by a 6–3 vote, a major victory in troubled times for the First Amendment right to free speech and a free press. Publication of the Pentagon Papers helped turn the tide of public opinion against the war. It took until June 2011, forty years to the day from the original publication of the Pentagon Papers by the *New York Times*, before the U.S. government officially declassified and released the papers.

7. Many law graduates do not practice law, choosing instead to use their J.D. degree to pursue other careers, such as in business or public administration. Some, however, take more colorful paths. Which of the following famous personalities did *not* earn a law degree?

A. Jerry Springer, talk show host

B. Geraldo Rivera, talk show host

C. Howard Cosell, sportscaster

D. Fidel Castro, former communist leader of Cuba

E. All of the above earned a law degree

ANSWER: E. Everyone on the list earned a law degree. Jerry Springer earned his J.D. in 1968 from Northwestern University. Springer has enjoyed an interesting career outside of lawyering, including as mayor of Cincinnati and as host of the *Jerry Springer Show*, famous for its tasteless on-camera confrontations. Geraldo Rivera received his degree in 1969 from Brooklyn Law School and became a journalist. He is particularly famous, or infamous, for his talk show *Geraldo*, which like Springer's show, specialized in theatrical "trash TV." Howard Cosell was a brash sportscaster who first became known for covering the fights of boxer Muhammad Ali. In 1970, Cosell became one of the original sportscasters for Monday Night Football, along with "Dandy Don" Meredith and Frank Gifford. Cosell graduated from N.Y.U. School of Law where he was a member of the law review. Fidel Castro graduated with a law degree from the University of Havana in 1950 before becoming a revolutionary communist political leader.

8. One of the requirements for entering law school is a four-year bachelor's degree. Following that, law school is another three years, with the result that most new law graduates are in their mid-twenties. How old was the youngest person to graduate from a U.S. law school?

A. 21

B. 20

C. 18

D. 14

ANSWER: C.   Kathleen Holtz started her undergraduate degree at Cal State L.A. at age ten, began law school at UCLA at fifteen, graduated three years later, and successfully passed the California bar exam in 2007, known as one of the toughest bar exams in the country. After discovering that she passed the bar, Holtz did some celebrating, but was relegated to drinking water rather than alcohol due to her youth. While still in school, Holtz began working at a law firm, the firm's confidence in her abilities apparently outweighing any concerns it might have had about child labor laws.

9. Lawyers sometimes have to make tough choices about which clients they will represent, especially in criminal matters. While not everyone would want to represent an accused killer, this country has staked much on the right of every accused person to have a fair trial in which he is represented by competent counsel. Back in colonial America, in the 1760s, tensions were building between the colonists and the British, a stand-off that worsened when two regiments of British soldiers were stationed in Boston in 1768. On the night of March 5, 1770, a riot broke out over a dispute regarding whether a British officer had paid a debt to a local wigmaker. The result was the Boston Massacre, in which British soldiers fired on and killed five American colonists. Who was

the courageous American lawyer who took on the unenviable job of defending the British soldiers?

A. William Livingston
B. John Adams
C. John Jay
D. Samuel Chase
E. F. Lee Bailey

ANSWER: B. Although it was an unpopular, even dangerous, decision at the time, thirty-four-year-old John Adams, who would go on to become America's second president, agreed to represent the British soldiers. He argued successfully at trial that it was an understandable reaction for the soldiers to shoot when provoked by a chaotic, belligerent mob that was pelting them with debris. The jury acquitted all of the soldiers except two, who were convicted of manslaughter and had their thumbs branded with the letter *M*. Adams' representation of the soldiers stood as a shining beacon of America's dedication to just legal proceedings. Historically, there was no right to the assistance of counsel for those accused of serious crimes in England or its colonies, but the framers of the U.S. Constitution found this denial to be contrary to essential justice. Even before the Sixth Amendment enshrined the right to counsel in the Constitution, most states already had recognized such a right. Adams' law practice suffered because of his decision, dropping to half its previous level, but as a much older man, Adams called the case "one of the most gallant, generous, manly, and disinterested actions of my whole life, and one of the best pieces of service I ever rendered my country." A full account of the interesting Boston Massacre trial is available as part of the University of Missouri–Kansas City School of Law's "Famous Trials" project, easily located online.

10.   The number of both accredited and unaccredited law schools continues to grow. In 2011, the nation had 200 ABA-accredited law schools and a few dozen unaccredited law schools. One state, however, has bucked the trend. Which state does not have a law school?

A. Wyoming
B. Alaska
C. North Dakota
D. South Dakota

ANSWER: B. Alaska, ranked 47th among U.S. states in population, is the only state that does not have a law school. All of the state's attorneys received their law degrees elsewhere. The *Alaska Law Review* is, interestingly enough, published by Duke University, which is located in Durham, NC. Go figure. Wyoming, North Dakota, and South Dakota each have one law school. At the other extreme, California, as of this writing, has sixty-five law schools (twenty ABA-accredited law schools, eighteen state-accredited law schools, and twenty-seven unaccredited law schools).

11. Law firms typically take the names of their founding partners, and then sometimes add more names as the firm grows. Occasionally, this results in some amusing law firm names, much like the weird name conjunctions from wedding announcements comedian Jay Leno entertained audiences with on *The Tonight Show*. Which of the following is *not* the name of a real law firm?

A. Low, Ball & Lynch

B. Bickers & Bickers

C. Rush, Rush & Delay

D. Dewey, Cheatem & Howe

E. Boring & Leach

ANSWER: D. Dewey, Cheatem & Howe is a classic fictional law firm name that has made appearances in a variety of forums. The other names are real.

12. From reading this book, you are now keenly aware that many law students and lawyers are highly competitive by nature. Which of the following world records was set by lawyers?

A. Largest three-legged race

B. Most consecutive holes of golf played

C. Largest mass streaking event

D. Most people dressed as Smurfs

E. Most martinis consumed in twenty-four hours

ANSWER: A. In 2009, in Hong Kong, 160 lawyers paired up, tied their legs together, and raced 200 meters. The other records are not held by lawyers—yet. Raymond Lasater, of Lebanon, TN, played 1530 consecutive holes of golf, or 85 rounds, using luminous balls, a feat that took 62 hours, 20 minutes to complete. The world record for the largest mass streak happened at the University of Georgia in 1974 with 1543 naked participants. At a nightclub in Swansea, Wales, 2510 people dressed as Smurfs in 2009. It is unknown who has consumed the most martinis in one day and lived to tell the tale, but it's rumored that professional wrestler Andre the Giant once drank 156 beers in a single sitting.

13.   As mentioned, most full-time law students are twenty-somethings. In part-time evening-division programs, a large percentage of the students are older, often in their thirties or forties. We've already covered the youngest person ever to graduate from a U.S. law school, but how old was the oldest student to do so?

    A.   63

    B.   51

    C.   93

    D.   79

ANSWER: D.   In 2009, Alice Thomas successfully graduated from the Pacific McGeorge School of Law in California at the age of seventy-nine and began her career in a field where she can relate to her clients: elder law. Not only was she older than her classmates, she was older than all of her professors except one. Asked why she went to law school so late in life, she said, "When you quit learning something, you might as well crawl into a coffin and pull the dirt in after you."

14.   Way back in the day, around the sixteenth century, European courts used to put animals on trial. They even had counsel appointed to represent them. No joke. The practice apparently developed from the Mosaic Law that "if an ox gore a man or a woman that they die, then the ox shall be surely stoned, but the owner of the ox shall be quit." Thomas Frost documented ninety-two such trials in France in his 1897 essay, *Trials of Animals*. The critters often received the ultimate sanction: the death penalty. Which of the following legal executions of animals occurred in twentieth-century America?

    A.   Strangling of a chicken for pecking out the eyes of its owner's neighbor

B. Electrocution of a lion for escaping from the zoo and killing three people

C. Hanging of a circus elephant for killing its keeper

D. Lethal injection of a goat for biting the hand of a child at a petting zoo

E. Firing squad for a hamster who fraternized with a gerbil

ANSWER: C. An elephant known as Mary had been a circus performer for about twenty years before she killed her keeper, Walter "Red" Eldridge, in 1916 in Erwin, TN. Mary was walking along the road one day with her keeper when she tried to eat a watermelon that was on the ground. Red prodded her ear with a hook and Mary became enraged, stomping his head until he died. As a result, Mary was hanged. The execution was more of a lynching than a legitimate legal proceeding. The poor elephant didn't even receive a kangaroo court. The owner decided to hang Mary at the urging of the townspeople. Mary was not represented by counsel in the proceedings. While Mary is gone, her legend lives on. Singer-songwriter Chuck Brodsky recorded a tune called "Mary the Elephant," and playwright Caleb Lewis wrote a play about Mary entitled *Clinchfield*, which debuted in 2009.

15. All countries have their own legal codes, which are compilations of written laws, such as statutes (as opposed to judicial opinions, or "common law"). U.S. law students, for example, study portions of the United States Code, the set of federal statutes passed by Congress, in many different courses. Which of the following was the first legal code in human history, portions of which still survive today?

A. Code of Hammurabi

B. Justinian's Institutes

C. Code of Ur–Nammu

D. Ten Commandments

E. Morse Code

ANSWER: C. While the Code of Hammurabi is often cited as the first code of law, dating to about 1790 B.C., the Code of Ur–Nammu was written three hundred years earlier. It is said to have been written by King Ur–Nammu of Ur, a city in ancient Sumer, which is now part of Iraq. Portions of the Code still remain. Here are a few sample laws: "If a man has cut off another man's foot, he is to pay ten shekels." "If a man commits a robbery, he will be killed." "If someone severs the nose of another man with a copper knife, he must pay two-thirds of a mina of silver." Fun stuff! The Ten Commandments date to around 1446 B.C. Justinian's Institutes were compiled in A.D. 533 for Justinian, an Eastern Roman Emperor in what is now Turkey. The Morse Code is not a legal code, but a famous international communication code consisting of "dots and dashes."

16.   Law school attracts more than its fair share of excellent athletes. When I was in law school at the University of Florida, our law school's intramural basketball team had two former players from the Florida Gators playing on it. You should have seen the looks on the faces of opposing teams when our 6' 8" center was slamming down backward dunks. Needless to say, the team finished the season unbeaten after a string of lopsided victories. Which of the following all-time great professional sports coaches or athletes did *not* attend law school?

  A.   Phil Jackson, future Hall of Fame NBA coach

  B.   Steve Young, Hall of Fame NFL quarterback

  C.   George Mikan, Hall of Fame NBA center

  D.   Tony LaRussa, future Hall of Fame MLB manager

  E.   Vince Lombardi, Hall of Fame NFL coach

ANSWER: A.   Phil Jackson, who has won the most NBA championships as a coach, is known for his sharp intellect, but did not attend law school. Steve Young graduated from law school on his journey toward throwing a record six touchdowns and winning the 1995 Super Bowl for the San Francisco 49ers, adding to a long list of his other NFL records. One of professional basketball's first superstar "big men" in the 1950s, George Mikan began his second career as a lawyer. Tony LaRussa has a law degree from Florida State University to go along with his record as one of the winningest managers in Major League Baseball history and one of only two to win the World Series in both the American and National Leagues. Vince Lombardi, the legendary Green Bay Packers coach whose name is emblazoned on the NFL's championship trophy, attended night law school classes at

Fordham before eventually settling on coaching as his preferred occupation.

17. New law schools keep popping up all the time, a trend that leaves many insiders scratching their heads in an era where graduates of existing schools are finding it hard to find jobs. Which of the following was the first law school established in the United States?

A. Harvard Law School

B. Litchfield Law School

C. Willamette College of Law

D. William & Mary Law School

E. Yale Law School

ANSWER: B. As with many things in the law, the answer to this question is contested. Professor Nate Oman lays out the facts on the legal blog, *Concurring Opinion*: Harvard claims to be "the oldest continuously operating law school" in the United States based on its endowment of a position for a law professor, the Royal Professorship of Law Harvard College, in 1806. William & Mary's claim is similarly based on the appointment of a law professor at the university in 1779. But in terms of an actual "law school," the winner appears to be Litchfield. In 1784, Tapping Reeve founded Litchfield Law School in western Connecticut. Reeve, a former Princeton instructor who trained lawyers through the old apprenticeship method, found he had too many apprentices and established Litchfield as a formal training ground. Litchfield became a first-rate educational institution that produced some distinguished alumni, including one U.S. Vice President, three U.S. Supreme Court justices, and twenty-eight U.S. Senators. While Litchfield Law School no longer exists, "Litchfield Law School" teeshirts can still be purchased online. Hmm, was Litchfield also the first in the lucrative field of university merchandising and licensing? Yale Law School traces its origins to the early decades of the nineteenth century with the founding of New Haven Law School, which began its affiliation with Yale in the 1820s. The Willamette College of Law, in Salem, Oregon, was established in 1883.

18. The United States has the reputation as a litigious culture, a reputation made worse by highly publicized media reports of frivolous lawsuits, such as the $57 million lawsuit

322 COMPANION TEXT TO LAW SCHOOL

filed in Washington, D.C. a few years back against a drycleaner over a pair of lost pants. The good news is that courts are quite adept at recognizing frivolous suits when they see them and dismissing them without a trial. But because we value the right of access to the courts, it's difficult to prevent people from filing meritless suits in the first place. Many of the most notorious filers of frivolous lawsuits are prisoners with too much time on their hands. One such inmate is, as of this writing, a federal prisoner in Kentucky, who has filed approximately 1000 lawsuits against just about anyone and anything. We'll omit his name to avoid giving him more publicity, but who or which of the following has *not* been named as a defendant in a lawsuit filed by this litigious inmate?

A. Michael Jordan
B. Elvis Presley
C. *The Shawshank Redemption* (the movie)
D. The e coli virus
E. Thanksgiving

ANSWER: A. Among the listed answers, only the NBA's greatest superstar has escaped the prisoner's writ wrath, at least so far. Other defendants named in his lawsuits include former President George W. Bush, Martha Stewart, Lady Gaga, NFL quarterback Michael Vick, Grand Theft Auto (the videogame), Plato and Nostradamus, the planet Pluto, and the Garden of Eden. His lawsuits are invariably dismissed by the courts. To help curb the tide of inmate litigation, Congress passed the Prisoner Litigation Reform Act ("PLRA") in 1996, a partial goal of which was to make it more difficult for prisoners to abuse the court system. One provision (28 U.S.C. § 1915(g)) established a type of "three strikes and you're out" rule whereby prisoners who have had three federal suits dismissed as frivolous are precluded from filing any more suits unless they can show that they are in "imminent danger of serious physical harm."

19. Women make up nearly half of all law students, but it hasn't always been that way. For most of U.S. history, women were discriminated against in legal education and also in the legal profession. In 1873, the U.S. Supreme Court rejected, by an 8–1 vote, legal pioneer Myra Bradwell's lawsuit seeking to force the State of Illinois to allow her to

practice law. Bradwell had studied law as an apprentice and passed the Illinois bar exam, but the state refused to grant her admission. Writing for the Court, Justice Joseph Bradley said: "The natural and proper timidity and delicacy which belongs to the female sex evidently unfits it for many of the occupations of civil life." Bradwell v. State, 83 U.S. (16 Wall.) 130, 141 (1873). Not one of the Court's finer moments. Which was the first law school in the United States to admit a female student?

A. University of California–Berkeley

B. Washington University

C. Columbia University

D. George Washington University

E. Yale University

ANSWER: B. In 1869, Washington University in St. Louis, then known as St. Louis Law School, became the first law school to admit female students. Among the first female students at St. Louis Law School was Lemma Barkaloo. Barkaloo applied to Washington University, reportedly after being denied admission by Columbia Law School because of her gender. Although Barkaloo did not graduate from law school, she did go on to pass the Missouri bar exam in 1870. Unfortunately, she never had the opportunity to establish herself as a lawyer, dying from typhoid fever soon after passing the bar.

20. Representing close to half of today's collective law student body, women obviously have made great strides in legal education. Most of the progress has occurred in the past few decades. But how are women treated in the legal marketplace? What percentage of current law firm partners are women?

A. 5

B. 10

C. 20

D. 30

E. 45

ANSWER: C. Making up only 20 percent of law firm partners in the United States, women lawyers continue to lag behind men in partnership status by a wide margin. Some recent data suggest progress is being made. A 2010 study by the Project for Attorney Retention found that 34 percent of new partners in 2010 were women, up from 28 percent in 2009.

* * *

How did your student fare on the test? Here's a highly scientific scoring scale to evaluate your student's potential for success in the legal profession: 15–20 correct answers: Your student is on their way to becoming a U.S. Supreme Court Justice. 10–15 correct answers: Your student is on their way to becoming a rich partner in a large law firm. 5–10 correct answers: Your student is on their way to becoming a state court trial judge. 0–5 correct answers: Your student is on their way to becoming a member of the U.S. Congress.

POSTSCRIPT

It's another hot, humid Mid-South summer day as I write these final words. Another school year has come and gone. My Facebook news feed is filled with news that several of my current and former students are engaged or getting married. Others are taking vacations with their families or friends. Still others are celebrating anniversaries, births of children, and other family milestones.

The entries and photos make me smile, in part because I remember meeting many of their significant others, parents, friends, siblings, and children when the students brought them to Torts class back when they were 1Ls. They all made it through law school with their relationships intact. Law school ends and life goes on for all.

You've learned an awful lot about law school in this book. Not all of it has been happy news. To the contrary, some of it was gloomy. If nothing else, you now know that law school is truly a one-of-a-kind, life-changing experience that can only be appreciated by those who have lived through it. That goes for students and their loved ones alike. And while we saw that law school can add stress and conflict to relationships with law students, we also saw that it doesn't have to cause permanent harm to them. Only students and their loved ones have control over that.

I hope this book succeeded in enlightening you about the law school experience and your student's valorous journey through it, while also making you aware of the potential potholes, wrong turns, and other obstacles along the way, not only for students but for the people close to them. Most important, I hope it equipped you with sufficient information, insights, and strategies to navigate around those obstacles.

The day will arrive quicker than you think—I guarantee it[277]—when law school will be in the rear-view mirror and your student will be cruising toward the next challenge and

---

277. "Guarantee" is subject to the usual disclaimers, waivers, exculpatory clauses, limitations of remedy, and reservations of rights that I'm sure your law student will be excited to explain to you in excruciating detail.

destination in life. Casebooks, hypotheticals, the memo, law school gossip, exam stress—they'll all be only memories. You may even miss them. Okay, probably not, but anything's possible.

You've noticed my fondness for song references. Let's go ahead and sum up your law school trip in popular music. After reading this book, a reasonable prelude to your shared journey into legal education could be these lyrics from the Hoosiers: "I'm worried what the future holds, the future holds, I'm starting to worry about Ray [or Ramona; i.e., your student]."[278] In the midst of the madness, you and your student may both find yourselves pogo-ing to the Ramones' "I Wanna Be Sedated."[279] On graduation day, the refrain of a 1980 song by the New Zealand band Split Enz might resonate: "I hope I never have to see you again."[280]

But when all is said and done, a Green Day classic may best capture the mixed highs and low of the law school odyssey: "It's something unpredictable, but in the end it's right. I hope you ha[ve] the time of your life."[281]

Good luck to all of you!

278. GARRY BONNER, ALAN GORDON, ALAN SHARLAND, IRWIN SPARKES & MARTIN SKARENDAHL, WORRIED ABOUT RAY (RCA 2007). The Hoosiers aren't from Indiana; they're a London band. The similarity of "Worried about Ray" to the 1967 hit "Happy Together" by the Turtles resulted in the writers of the latter (Bonner and Gordon) receiving co-credit for the song.

279. JOEY RAMONE, I WANNA BE SEDATED (Sire 1979).

280. TIM FINN, I HOPE I NEVER (Mushroom Records 1980).

281. BILLIE JOE ARMSTRONG, GOOD RIDDANCE (TIME OF YOUR LIFE) (Reprise 1997).

APPENDIX

SAMPLE CASE

The majority of your law student's life will be made up of reading "cases"—i.e., judicial opinions penned by appellate courts—so it might be helpful for you to see what one looks like. Below is an edited version of a famous torts case called *Katko v. Briney*, which most law students read in their first semester. Most of the cases law students read are more complicated than *Katko*, but few are more interesting or generate more classroom discussion.

Katko involved a trespasser, the plaintiff Marvin Katko, who broke into an unoccupied farmhouse looking for old bottles and jars he considered to be antiques. The defendants, Edward and Bertha Briney, tired of people breaking into the farmhouse over the years, had set up a hidden shotgun trap that went off and blew away a substantial portion of Katko's leg when he opened an inside bedroom door. Katko sued and won a sizable award, including extra "punitive damages" intended to punish the Brineys for their conduct and deter similar conduct by others. The Brineys had to sell a major portion of their farm to pay the judgment. The appellate court, in the opinion below, upheld the award on the principle that life, even the life of a criminal, is more valuable than property.

Among other things, the case is useful to demonstrate the point of Chapter 5 that few things in the law are cut and dried. On the one hand, the result offends, even outrages, many people. How could a criminal break into a house and successfully sue the owners for injuries received? It seems preposterous. On the other hand, do we really want to live in a society where people can set hidden deadly traps on their property? What if Katko had been a child? When I ask my Torts students to raise their hands if they ever illegally entered a structure on someone else's property as kids, the vast majority of them do so, even the ones outraged by the result. Remember, this was an unoccupied remote farmhouse—not a home in which the Brineys lived. A tough case

327

with tough issues—just another day in the indefinite life of a law student.

Every night when your law student disappears into a room with her books, this is the kind of stuff she'll be reading. As is true of the edited versions of cases that appear in casebooks, I've inserted ellipses to indicate portions of the opinion that have been excised:

Katko v. Briney

183 N.W.2d 257 (Iowa 1971)

MOORE, CHIEF JUSTICE:

The primary issue presented here is whether an owner may protect personal property in an unoccupied boarded-up farm house against trespassers and thieves by a spring gun capable of inflicting death or serious injury.

We are not here concerned with a man's right to protect his home and members of his family. Defendants' home was several miles from the scene of the incident to which we refer infra.

Plaintiff's action is for damages resulting from serious injury caused by a shot from a 20–gauge spring shotgun set by defendants in a bedroom of an old farm house which had been uninhabited for several years. Plaintiff and his companion, Marvin McDonough, had broken and entered the house to find and steal old bottles and dated fruit jars which they considered antiques.

At defendants' request plaintiff's action was tried to a jury consisting of residents of the community where defendants' property was located. The jury returned a verdict for plaintiff and against defendants for $20,000 actual and $10,000 punitive damages.

After careful consideration of defendants' motions for judgment notwithstanding the verdict and for new trial, the experienced and capable trial judge overruled them and entered judgment on the verdict. Thus we have this appeal by defendants.

I. In this action our review of the record as made by the parties in the lower court is for the correction of errors at law. . . .

II. Most of the facts are not disputed. In 1957 defendant
Bertha L. Briney inherited her parents' farm land in Mahaska and Monroe Counties. Included was an 80-acre tract in
southwest Mahaska County where her grandparents and
parents had lived. No one occupied the house thereafter. Her
husband, Edward, attempted to care for the land. He kept no
farm machinery thereon. The outbuildings became dilapidat-
ed.

For about 10 years, 1957 to 1967, there occurred a series
of trespassing and housebreaking events with loss of some
household items, the breaking of windows and 'messing up of
the property in general.' The latest occurred June 8, 1967,
prior to the event on July 16, 1967 herein involved.

Defendants through the years boarded up the windows
and doors in an attempt to stop the intrusions. They had
posted 'no trespass' signs on the land several years before
1967. The nearest one was 35 feet from the house. On June
11, 1967 defendants set 'a shotgun trap' in the north bedroom. After Mr. Briney cleaned and oiled his 20-gauge shotgun, the power of which he was well aware, defendants took
it to the old house where they secured it to an iron bed with
the barrel pointed at the bedroom door. It was rigged with
wire from the doorknob to the gun's trigger so it would fire
when the door was opened. Briney first pointed the gun so an
intruder would be hit in the stomach but at Mrs. Briney's
suggestion it was lowered to hit the legs. He admitted he did
so 'because I was mad and tired of being tormented' but 'he
did not intend to injure anyone.' He gave no explanation of
why he used a loaded shell and set it to hit a person already
in the house. Tin was nailed over the bedroom window. The
spring gun could not be seen from the outside. No warning of
its presence was posted. . . .

Prior to July 16, 1967, plaintiff and McDonough had been
to the premises and found several old bottles and fruit jars
which they took and added to their collection of antiques. . . .
They entered the old house by removing a board from a porch
window which was without glass. While McDonough was
looking around the kitchen area plaintiff went to another
part of the house. As he started to open the north bedroom
door the shotgun went off striking him in the right leg above
the ankle bone. Much of his leg, including part of the tibia,
was blown away. Only by McDonough's assistance was plain-

tiff able to get out of the house and after crawling some distance was put in his vehicle and rushed to a doctor and then to a hospital. He remained in the hospital 40 days.

Plaintiff's doctor testified he seriously considered amputation but eventually the healing process was successful. . . .

There was undenied medical testimony plaintiff had a permanent deformity, a loss of tissue, and a shortening of the leg. . . .

III.   Plaintiff testified he knew he had no right to break and enter the house with intent to steal bottles and fruit jars therefrom. He further testified he had entered a plea of guilty to larceny in the nighttime of property of less than $20 value from a private building. He stated he had been fined $50 and costs and paroled during good behavior from a 60-day jail sentence. Other than minor traffic charges this was plaintiff's first brush with the law. . . .

IV.   The main thrust of defendants' defense in the trial court and on this appeal is that 'the law permits use of a spring gun in a dwelling or warehouse for the purpose of preventing the unlawful entry of a burglar or thief.' They repeated this contention in their exceptions to the trial court's instructions 2, 5 and 6. . . .

Instruction 6 stated: 'An owner of premises is prohibited from willfully or intentionally injuring a trespasser by means of force that either takes life or inflicts great bodily injury; and therefore a person owning a premise is prohibited from setting out 'spring guns' and like dangerous devices which will likely take life or inflict great bodily injury, for the purpose of harming trespassers. The fact that the trespasser may be acting in violation of the law does not change the rule. The only time when such conduct of setting a 'spring gun' or a like dangerous device is justified would be when the trespasser was committing a felony of violence or a felony punishable by death, or where the trespasser was endangering human life by his act' . . .

The overwhelming weight of authority, both textbook and case law, supports the trial court's statement of the applicable principles of law.

Prosser on Torts, Third Edition, pages 116–118, states:

'[T]he law has always placed a higher value upon human safety than upon mere rights in property, it is the accepted rule that there is no privilege to use any force calculated to cause death or serious bodily injury to repel the threat to land or chattels, unless there is also such a threat to the defendant's personal safety as to justify a self-defense. ... [S]pring guns and other man-killing devices are not justifiable against a mere trespasser, or even a petty thief. They are privileged only against those upon whom the landowner, if he were present in person would be free to inflict injury of the same kind.'

Restatement of Torts, section 85, page 180, states: 'The value of human life and limb, not only to the individual concerned but also to society, so outweighs the interest of a possessor of land in excluding from it those whom he is not willing to admit thereto that a possessor of land has, as is stated in s 79, no privilege to use force intended or likely to cause death or serious harm against another whom the possessor sees about to enter his premises or meddle with his chattel, unless the intrusion threatens death or serious bodily harm to the occupiers or users of the premises. ... A possessor of land cannot do indirectly and by a mechanical device that which, were he present, he could not do immediately and in person. Therefore, he cannot gain a privilege to install, for the purpose of protecting his land from intrusions harmless to the lives and limbs of the occupiers or users of it, a mechanical device whose only purpose is to inflict death or serious harm upon such as may intrude, by giving notice of his intention to inflict, by mechanical means and indirectly, harm which he could not, even after request, inflict directly were he present.' ...

In Hooker v. Miller, 37 Iowa 613, we held defendant vineyard owner liable for damages resulting from a spring gun shot although plaintiff was a trespasser and there to steal grapes. At pages 614, 615, this statement is made: 'This court has held that a mere trespass against property other than a dwelling is not a sufficient justification to authorize the use of a deadly weapon by the owner in its defense; and that if death results in such a case it will be murder, though the killing be actually necessary to prevent the trespass. ...

The facts in Allison v. Fiscus, 156 Ohio 120, 110 N.E.2d 237, 44 A.L.R.2d 369, decided in 1951, are very similar to the case at bar. There plaintiff's right to damages was recognized for injuries received when he feloniously broke a door latch and started to enter defendant's warehouse with intent to steal. As he entered a trap of two sticks of dynamite buried under the doorway by defendant owner was set off and plaintiff seriously injured. The court held the question whether a particular trap was justified as a use of reasonable and necessary force against a trespasser engaged in the commission of a felony should have been submitted to the jury. The Ohio Supreme Court recognized plaintiff's right to recover punitive or exemplary damages in addition to compensatory damages. . . .

In addition to civil liability many jurisdictions hold a land owner criminally liable for serious injuries or homicide caused by spring guns or other set devices. . . .

The legal principles stated by the trial court in instructions 2, 5 and 6 are well established and supported by the authorities cited and quoted supra. There is no merit in defendants' objections and exceptions thereto. Defendants' various motions based on the same reasons stated in exceptions to instructions were properly overruled.

V.   Plaintiff's claim and the jury's allowance of punitive damages, under the trial court's instructions relating thereto, were not at any time or in any manner challenged by defendants in the trial court as not allowable. We therefore are not presented with the problem of whether the $10,000 award should be allowed to stand.

We express no opinion as to whether punitive damages are allowable in this type of case. If defendants' attorneys wanted that issue decided it was their duty to raise it in the trial court. . . .

Study and careful consideration of defendants' contentions on appeal reveal no reversible error.

Affirmed.

(The dissenting opinion of Justice Larson is omitted.)

GLOSSARY

> Just about every law school story contains words I
> don't understand. When he's talking about law school,
> I just need to carry around a law dictionary.
>
> —Significant other to a law
> student

One of the steepest early challenges new law students face
is that the law and law school have their own vocabularies.
Because law students are obsessed with talking about their
sojourn toward the citadel of lawyer-dom, that new language
invariably spills over into the lives of the student's loved
ones. To help you follow your student's conversations and
also refresh your memory about terminology used in this
book, below is a glossary of law school terminology. To decide
which entries to include, I asked my research assistants:
"What are the words and terms, other than ones pertaining
to legal doctrines, that the loved ones of law students are
most likely to hear their students talking about in everyday
conversation?"

Definitions of legal rules are not included, not because you
won't be hearing about some of them, but because accurate
descriptions of all the legal rules law students cover would
require much more than a glossary at the back of a book. It
would require, well, a legal dictionary. We'll leave it to your
student to define those principles for you. Plenty of online
sources offer definitions of legal terms, so if you have an
insatiable burning desire to understand adverse possession or
personal jurisdiction before your student can expound on
them, just plug the words into a search engine. Immediately
afterwards, plug in "Support Groups for Loved Ones of Law
Students."

For glossary entries that are discussed in detail in the
book, a short definition is offered with a reference to the
chapter where the entry is covered. If your student hasn't
started law school yet, reading this glossary together might

be a helpful, if caffeine-necessitating, law school bonding exercise. These are all terms your student will need to know.

ABA   See American Bar Association.

Affirm   A disposition or outcome of an appellate court proceeding in which the appellate court agrees with or "affirms" the lower court's decision in the case. See also Reverse.

American Bar Association (ABA)   The national professional organization of lawyers with roughly 400,000 members (membership is voluntary). The ABA is responsible for accrediting law schools pursuant to uniform standards. When people talk about "accredited" or "unaccredited" law schools, they are referring to ABA-accreditation. The organization engages in many other activities, including promulgating the body of ethical rules governing lawyers, lobbying on behalf of the legal profession, and sponsoring continuing legal education programs.

ADR   See Alternative Dispute Resolution.

Alternative Dispute Resolution (ADR)   A broad term referring to means of resolving legal disputes that do not involve traditional trials, such as mediation and arbitration. As more and more court systems and contracts mandate that the parties to a dispute participate in mediation or arbitration, ADR courses are becoming more prominent in law schools.

Answer   The defendant's written response to a lawsuit. The answer responds to the allegations in the plaintiff's complaint and raises any defenses the defendant might have, as well as any counterclaims that might exist against the plaintiff. See also Complaint.

ALWD Manual   A book compiled by the Association of Legal Writing Directors setting forth rules on how to cite to legal authority in written documents. The *ALWD Manual* competes with the much more widely used *Bluebook*. Far more than in other disciplines, law students spend considerable time learning rules of citation style. See also Authority, Bluebook, Citation Style.

Appeal   The proceeding initiated by the loser in a lawsuit to have the case reviewed by a higher court. To bring an appeal, the party must identify a particular error or errors alleged to have occurred in the lower court proceedings. Because of the case method, law students spend most of their time studying appeals rather than trials. See also Case Method.

Appellant The party who files an appeal after receiving an adverse decision in a lower court. See also Appellee.

Appellate Brief A document that a lawyer submits to an appellate court arguing the client's position on appeal. Most first-year students write an appellate brief in the second semester of their Legal Research and Writing course, and students who participate in moot court will write additional briefs in their 2L and 3L years. Writing their appellate brief usually is a student's first attempt at drafting a persuasive court document. Contrary to the name, appellate briefs are not brief, containing 30–40 pages of detailed legal analysis.

Appellate Court A court that hears appeals of lower court decisions. There are two types of appellate courts: intermediate appellate courts sandwiched between a trial court and the supreme court, and the supreme courts themselves (one for each state and the U.S. Supreme Court for the federal system). See also Appeal.

Appellee The party responding to the appellant's appeal. While the appellant is arguing that an error was made in the lower court, the appellee is usually arguing that the lower court decision was correct and should be affirmed by the appellate court. See also Appellant.

Associate The entry-level position for a law graduate at a private law firm. Associate is the status below partner. Depending on the firm, new lawyers generally serve as associates for seven to ten years before qualifying for partnership, although a lot of events can happen along the way to derail a person's partnership track. See also Partner.

Authority A source of law that supports an assertion in a legal argument. Legal authority is divided into two basic categories: primary (principally judicial opinions and statutes) and secondary (treatises, law review articles, etc.). Courts are required to follow primary authority in making decisions. Secondary authority is not binding on courts, although it may be very persuasive. U.S. legal proceedings are firmly committed to the principle of citing authority for nearly every oral or written proposition. This is one reason students are forced to spend so much time learning the rules for citing to authority accurately. See also ALWD Manual, Bluebook, Judicial Opinion, Judicial Precedent.

Bar, The 1 Generally, a state association of lawyers. Each state has a bar to which all licensed attorneys are members. After a person takes and passes the state bar exam, they are admitted to the state's bar. **2** A term used to refer to the legal profession as a whole, as in all lawyers are members of "the bar," or portions thereof, such as the "personal injury bar" or "criminal defense bar." **3** A short-hand way to refer to the state bar examination, the test graduates must take and pass to become licensed attorneys, as in: "What are you going to do now that you've graduated from law school?" "Study for the bar, what else?" See also Bar Exam.

Bar Exam The exam students must take and pass to become licensed to practice law in a particular state. In almost all states, the bar exam has two primary components: a state portion and the Multistate Bar Examination (MBE). The state portion has state-specific questions that can be in either or both essay and multiple-choice format. The MBE portion is a six-hour exam consisting of 200 multiple-choice questions. More than half of states have recently added a third component to their bar exams known as the Multistate Performance Test (MPT). The MPT is designed to test lawyering skills, such as the ability to analyze a legal problem, rather than knowledge of substantive law. Most states also require an exam, taken separately, on ethical rules called the Multistate Professional Responsibility Exam (MPRE). State bar exams are given in February for December grads and in July for May grads, which includes most students. See also Bar Review, BarBri, Multistate Professional Responsibility Exam (MPRE).

Bar Review 1 An expensive course lasting six or seven weeks that most law school graduates participate in immediately after graduation in preparation to take the state bar examination. See also Bar Exam, BarBri. **2** At some law schools, a weekly law student social event involving the consumption of alcohol.

BarBri The leading (some have alleged monopolistic) company providing bar exam review courses and materials to law graduates. Nearly all law graduates take this expensive (more than two thousand dollars), intensive six-to-seven week course that begins shortly after graduation. See also Bar Exam, Bar Review.

Barristers' Ball The annual social event, often with formal attire required, for the student body sponsored by the Student Government Association that usually includes cocktails, dinner, and dancing. Think of it as the law school prom. See also Student Government Association.

Black Law Students Association (BLSA) Usually referred to by its acronym, pronounced "BALSA," the national organization of African-American law students that has chapters at most U.S. law schools. Similar organizations exist for Hispanic, Asian, and other law student groups. See also Student Organizations.

Black Letter Law The established rules and principles in any given subject area of law.

Black's Law Dictionary The most widely used legal dictionary. Most law students purchase an abridged paperback version (the ninth edition hardback version is 1940 pages) to look up the many unfamiliar legal terms they will encounter in their casebooks during the early weeks of law school.

Bluebook 1 The uniform guide to citations in legal writing that most law schools, law reviews, and many court systems require students and lawyers to follow. The 2010 nineteenth edition contains 511 pages of incredibly detailed rules. Should a comma be italicized in a legal citation? Only the *Bluebook* knows for sure. The *Bluebook* is described in Chapter 4. See also ALWD Manual, Authority, Citation Style. **2** Booklets of blank, lined paper with blue covers that students who handwrite their exams, rather than take them on computer as most modern law students do, are required to use in answering essay questions.

Bluebooking The process of checking and correcting legal citations to conform to the *Bluebook*. See also ALWD Manual, Bluebook, Citation Style.

Book Brief or **Book-Briefing** A technique used by law students who choose not to invest the time necessary to prepare independent case briefs to capture the essential components (e.g., facts, holding, reasoning) of a judicial opinion assigned for class reading. Book-briefing involves using the margins of the casebook and various colored highlighters to brief the case in the book rather than on a separate sheet of paper or computer file. While book-briefing is looked down on by many professors, it is a common method of class preparation for many upper-level students, and some unwise 1Ls. See also Case Brief, Casebook, Judicial Opinion.

Canned Brief   A form of commercial study aid, canned briefs are pre-packaged case briefs (summaries of judicial opinions) keyed to specific courses and/or casebooks. Some students attempt to rely on canned briefs rather than to prepare their own case briefs. Canned briefs are sometimes inaccurate and are despised by most law professors. Students who rely on canned briefs are missing the point of case-briefing, which is to learn how to dissect a judicial opinion. See also Book Brief or Book-Briefing, Case Brief, Casebook, Judicial Opinion, Study Aid.

CALI   An acronym for "Computer Assisted Legal Instruction." CALI is a non-profit consortium of law professors providing free, online practice questions called "CALI exercises" to law students covering most law school subjects. Many law students work "CALIs" throughout the semester, and especially before exams, to help master the material they are learning.

CALI Award   See Top Paper Award.

CALI Exercises   See CALI.

Callback Interview   The third phase in the application process for a job at a law firm, the first two being sending in a resume and sitting for the first interview, which is often held at the law school. Callback interviews generally are in-depth and lengthy, and can involve meeting all or many of the firm's attorneys at the law firm's offices. Receiving a callback interview is a good sign that the student is being seriously considered for the position. See also On-Campus Interview.

Case   See Judicial Opinion.

Case Law   See Judicial Opinion.

Case Brief   A short summary (less than one page) of the key aspects of a judicial opinion. Most professors expect students, especially first-year students, to prepare case briefs for each of the cases they are assigned to read. The standard components of a case brief are the: facts of the case, procedural history of the case, holding or principal rule of law from the case, and the court's reasoning. Many upper-level students and some first-year students choose book-briefing or canned briefs over real case-briefing. See also Book Brief or Book-Briefing, Canned Brief, Judicial Opinion.

Case Comment A student-written law review article approximately 10–15 pages in length analyzing a recent noteworthy judicial opinion. A case comment reviews the facts, reasoning, and result of the case, and provides analysis of the importance and soundness of the court's opinion. Law students who compete for membership on the law review will often write a case comment as part of the law review's write-on competition. Some law reviews also publish student case comments. See also Law Review, Write-on Competition.

Case Method The law school teaching methodology by which students learn the law from reading appellate judicial opinions collected and organized into casebooks by subject matter, as distinguished from reading textbooks that explain the law in an expository fashion. The case method works hand-in-hand with the Socratic method. The case method is described in Chapter 6. See also Casebook, Socratic Method.

Casebook The thick, heavy, and expensive mostly red, blue, black, or brownish-red books that your student will be lugging around and pouring over day and night. A casebook is a compilation of appellate judicial opinions in a particular subject matter designed to work with the case and Socratic methods of law school teaching. See also Case Method, Judicial Opinion, Socratic Method.

Cause of Action See Claim.

Cert or **Certiorari** See Writ of Certiorari.

Circuit Court of Appeal See U.S. Circuit Court of Appeal.

Citation See Citation Style.

Citation Style All written attributions to legal authority (e.g., judicial opinions, statutes, treatises) must adhere to a uniform citation style that is most commonly derived from the *Bluebook*, but which may also come from the competing *ALWD Manual*. Citation style is designed to inform readers how to find the source (by giving, for example, the volume, page number, and date) and also to ensure the credibility of the cited source. Most assertions in legal writing require cited authority to back them up. Depending on whether it is an academic article or a court document, citations are placed either in footnotes (academic) or included as part of the text (most court documents). Getting citation style correct is a painstaking process. Citation style generally is taught in first-year Legal Research and Writing courses. True mastery of citation style usually occurs only among students, many of whom confess to being *"Bluebook*-nerds," who serve on the law review. See also ALWD Manual, Authority, Bluebook, Law Review, Legal Research and Writing.

Civil Law Legal System A type of legal system followed in large portions of the world such as Europe and Latin America, but not in the United States. In civil law systems, the primary source of law comes from "codes," which are organized books of statutes written by legislatures. In common law systems, such as the United States, the primary source of law is case law or judicial precedent, although that is changing as common law systems shift more and more emphasis to legislation and regulatory rules. See also Common Law Legal System, Judicial Precedent, Statute.

Civ Pro See Civil Procedure.

Civil Procedure A required first-year course covering the rules governing the conduct of civil (i.e., non-criminal) lawsuits, primarily the Federal Rules of Civil Procedure. The course is commonly referred to by students as "Civ Pro." Civil Procedure is discussed in Chapter 4.

Claim Any assertion of law and facts that may entitle a party in a lawsuit to a legal remedy (such as money, property, or an injunction). Examples include claims alleging breach of contract or that the defendant's negligence caused injury to the plaintiff.

CLE See Continuing Legal Education.

Clerkship See Judicial Law Clerk and Summer Clerkship.

Client A person or entity represented by a lawyer in legal matters.

Clinic See Legal Clinic.

Common Law See Common Law Legal System.

Common Law Legal System A legal system in which the primary source of law is judge-made law; that is, law written and developed by judges in judicial opinions. The United States operates under a common law legal system, whereas most countries follow a civil law legal system, in which law comes primarily from books of statutes known as "codes."

Students spend most of their first year studying common law. In upper-level years, students take several courses focusing on statutes, but even in those courses, students usually study judicial opinions interpreting the statutes. The common law is described in Chapter 3. See also Civil Law Legal System, Judicial Opinion, Judicial Precedent, Statute.

Complaint The document that a plaintiff files with a court to commence a lawsuit, also known as a "petition" in some states. The complaint outlines the plaintiff's claims and the basic factual allegations supporting the claims. See also Answer, Claim.

Computerized Legal Research Legal research used to be conducted exclusively in thick, musty books, but most modern legal research is done using computer databases. Several of these exist, but two heavyweights dominate the market: LexisNexis and Westlaw. While there are differences between the two services, both databases contain millions of judicial opinions, statutes, law review articles, and other sources of legal authority, as well as public record and news libraries. Attorneys pay handsomely to use these subscription-based computer legal research services. Law schools pay institutional bulk rates so that students and professors can use the services without payment. New students immediately become familiar with LexisNexis and Westlaw through their on-campus training and marketing efforts. The latter will result in your student getting a lot of free pizza and trinkets bearing corporate logos (T-shirts, cups, pens, etc.).

Con Law See Constitutional Law.

Concurrence or **Concurring Opinion** See Judicial Opinion.

Constitutional Law Known to students as "Con Law," a course that focuses on judicial interpretations of the U.S. Constitution by the U.S. Supreme Court. Con Law is a required course at most schools, and a required first-year course at about one-half of law schools.

Continuing Legal Education (CLE) Educational courses usually lasting one day or part of a day that are intended to keep lawyers up-to-date on the law. Most states require lawyers to earn a minimum number of CLE hours each year to maintain their licenses, unless they go on inactive status. Many "CLEs," as they are called, are held at law schools, where students often are permitted to attend without payment.

Contracts A required first-year course that covers the law of contracts, including the elements of a valid contract, remedies for breach of contract, and defenses to contract enforcement. Contracts is described in Chapter 4.

Course Outline A summary in an outline format of the legal rules covered in a specific course. Most first-year students, certainly most of the best students, prepare their own course outlines for each course. Some students rely on course outlines prepared by and handed down from previous students, missing the primary learning value of outlines, which is the process of preparing them. Many students also purchase commercial course outlines, which are a type of study aid available in a number of brands. See also Study Aids.

CREAC A mnemonic that stands for "Conclusion, Rule, Explanation, Analysis, Conclusion" that many law schools teach as a format for legal writing and analysis in conjunction with the law office memoranda and appellate brief assignments that are part of first-year required Legal Research and Writing courses. See also Appellate Brief, IRAC, Law Office Memorandum, Legal Research and Writing.

Criminal Law A required first-year course that covers substantive criminal law, including the elements of criminal offenses and defenses, sentencing, and the policies behind the administration of the criminal justice system. Criminal Law is described in Chapter 4.

Curriculum Vitae A "c.v.," as it is known, is what most people would call a "job resume." A c.v. is longer and more complete than a typical resume, including detailed information about the person's education, employment history, publications, presentations, and other achievements. An experienced law professor's c.v., for example, may run from ten to twenty pages. Law students, on the other hand, are well-advised to not allow their resumes to exceed one page and should always refer to the document as a "resume," not as a curriculum vitae or c.v.

C.V. See Curriculum Vitae.

Damages The monetary remedy that a plaintiff seeks in a lawsuit against a defendant. The most common type of money damages are intended to compensate the plaintiff for harm caused by the defendant. Punitive damages, which are controversial and uncommon in other nations, may be added in cases where the defendant's conduct was particularly egregious for the purposes of punishing the defendant and deterring similar wrongful conduct.

Dissent or **Dissenting Opinion**   See Judicial Opinion.

E & E   See Examples and Explanations.

Elements   The components that comprise a civil claim (e.g., breach of contract) or a criminal offense (e.g., burglary), which the plaintiff or, in a criminal case, the government must prove to establish the validity of the case. For example, the elements of the tort of battery are: (1) a volitional act; (2) intended to inflict a harmful or offensive bodily contact; and (3) such a contact results. First-year students must learn and are tested on the elements of dozens of claims, crimes, and defenses. Essay questions on law school exams often require students to identify potential claims or crimes from a fact pattern and apply the elements to the facts to determine their validity. See also Claim.

Emanuel Law Outlines   A brand of commercial study aid that provides concise explanations of the law in an outline format, and which is available for most traditional law school courses. See also Study Aids.

Examples & Explanations   Called "E & Es" by students, a brand of commercial study aid that provides succinct descriptions of the law, followed by problem examples and analyses of the examples. E & Es are one of the most popular study aids, in large part because they require students to apply the same kinds of problem-solving skills as in law school classes and on exams. See also Study Aids.

Externship   Externships involve placing students with a government agency (such as a prosecuting attorney's office or public defender's office) or a court for a semester, during which time the student earns credit hours while learning under the supervision of experienced lawyers.

Fact-Finder   See Trial Court.

Flashcards   A short-hand title for the "Law in a Flash" series of law student study aids. Available for a variety of law school subjects, flashcards have questions on the front and answers on the back. See also Study Aids.

Gilbert Law Summaries Usually referred to as "Gilberts," one of the longest-running brands of commercial study aids, available for most law school courses, which succinctly explain the law in different subject areas. See also Study Aids.

Gunner A pejorative label for students who volunteer frequently in class, usually with a misguided air of opinionated arrogance and know-it-all-ness. Gunners are described in Chapter 8.

Holding The primary point of resolution of a case by a court in a judicial opinion. For many cases, the "holding of the case" will be synonymous with the "rule of the case." Students are expected to come to class knowing the holding of each case, as well as the facts and reasoning. One of the most common questions professors ask in using the Socratic method is, "What did the court hold?" Sometimes the holding of a case is clearly stated by the court, but often it will be hidden between the lines and difficult to ascertain. See also Judicial Opinion.

Hornbook Hornbooks are distinctive green, authoritative single-volume treatises on the law of a particular subject. Back in the day, hornbooks were commonly used as student study aids. Most modern students purchase less in-depth, less-expensive study aids. Hornbooks are viewed as much more authoritative than other types of study aids. For example, courts frequently cite to hornbooks in their opinions, but would not be caught dead citing to other types of law school study aids. See also Study Aids.

Hypo See Hypothetical.

Hypothetical Usually called "hypos," a popular law school teaching tool consisting of a short, usually fictitious set of facts described by a professor in class that requires students to apply the rules they are learning to solve legal problems. Depending on the professor, hypotheticals can be outlandish, entertaining, and thought-provoking. Students often discuss and ponder hypos outside of class with their fellow students and at home with their loved ones. Most law school and bar exam essay questions take the form of enlarged hypotheticals, involving more facts and actors than the short versions presented in class, but calling on students to apply the same types of problem-solving skills.

IRAC   A mnemonic that stands for "Issue, Rule, Analysis, Conclusion," IRAC is often taught to students as the standard structure for analyzing a legal problem in a written format. See also Appellate Brief, CREAC, Law Office Memorandum.

J.D.   See Juris Doctor.

Judge Benjamin Cardozo   A former U.S. Circuit Court of Appeals judge and later U.S. Supreme Court Justice known for his keen intellect and excellent writing skill who penned many famous, widely studied judicial opinions. First-year students usually study several Cardozo opinions, including, in their Torts course, one of the most famous and memorable cases in American jurisprudential history: *Palsgraf v. Long Island Railroad Co.*

Judge Hand or **Judge Hand's Formula**   See Learned Hand.

Judicial Law Clerk   An assistant to a judge who helps with legal research, order- and opinion-writing, and other matters. "Clerkships," as they are known, are prestigious, coveted positions that many top law students seek to obtain. Clerkships are available at all levels of the state and federal judicial system (both trial and appellate courts). Most clerkships last one or two years, although some judges hire permanent law clerks. Judicial clerkships are described in Chapter 18.

Judicial Opinion   The integral component of the case method of legal study, judicial opinions are the focal point of a law student's studies. When law students talk about having to read and study "cases," they're referring to written judicial opinions, almost always from an appellate court (rather than a trial court). A judicial opinion is a court's written judgment in a case. It generally contains a review of the facts, the procedural history of the lawsuit (i.e., an explanation of the previous proceedings in the case), a statement of the applicable law, the court's reasoning applying that law to the facts of the case, and the final outcome. Opinions issued by appellate courts, which are made up of several members, may contain more than one opinion if the judges disagree: the "majority opinion" (the opinion that is legally binding and which is endorsed by a majority of the judges who heard the case); a "concurring opinion" (written by a judge who agrees with the outcome of the case, but not with the reasoning of the majority); and a "dissenting opinion" (written by a judge who disagrees with the majority's reasoning and result). Judicial opinions are described in Chapter 3. See also Case Method.

Judicial Precedent Previously issued judicial opinions that are relevant to the case at hand. Under the U.S. common law legal system, judicial precedent can be binding in deciding a current case, depending on the similarity of the cases and the court which decided the previous case. For example, decisions of the U.S. Supreme Court constitute binding precedent on all other courts of the land. See also Authority, Common Law Legal System, Judicial Opinion.

Juris Doctor Also called a J.D., the professional degree a law student receives upon graduating from law school.

Justice, Supreme Court Any judge who serves on a state supreme court or the U.S. Supreme Court. The most famous justices, of course, are those nine wise men and women who sit on the U.S. Supreme Court, one chief justice and eight associate justices. Judges who serve on courts other than supreme courts are called "judges," not justices.

Kaplan A test preparation company that offers courses and materials to help students prepare for the LSAT and the Multistate Bar Exam (MBE). Most first-year law students know Kaplan for its LSAT prep courses that many of them take before applying to law school. See also Bar Review, LSAT.

Law Clerk See Judicial Law Clerk and Summer Clerkship.

Law Journal See Law Review.

Law Office Memorandum The first major legal writing assignment that most law students will complete in their required first-year Legal Research and Writing course. "The memo," as it's called, is generally a 5–15 page document written to a fictitious law firm partner explaining the law applicable to a client's or potential client's legal issue. Most schools divide the memo assignment into two parts: the "closed universe" memo and the "open universe" memo. For the former, the instructor provides students with the necessary research materials (e.g., judicial opinions, statutes), while the latter requires the students to conduct their own research. These memos play large roles in the life of a 1L and are described in Chapters 4 and 8. See also Legal Research and Writing.

Law Review A student-run publication that publishes scholarly articles written by law professors, judges, practitioners, and law students about different legal issues. Membership on the law review is one of law school's highest honors. Students usually become eligible to participate on law review through a write-on competition held in the summer after their first year. Law review is discussed in Chapter 2. See also Write-on Competition.

Learned Hand A judge with a great name who sat on the U.S. Court of Appeals for the Second Circuit, famous among law students mostly for his algebraic formula for determining when conduct is negligent under tort law, which he set forth in a case called *United States v. Carroll Towing Co.* Judge Hand's formula for negligence is described in Chapter 12.

Legal Authority See Authority.

Legal Clinic A for-credit, limited-enrollment course that allows upper-level students to represent real clients, usually low-income individuals, under the direct supervision of an experienced attorney. Some clinics are general in nature, handling a variety of different types of ordinary cases. Most clinics are specialized, however. Depending on the law school, students may find clinics in tax law, elder law, immigration law, family law, or other areas.

Legal Research and Writing The required first-year course, which travels under a variety of names depending on the particular school, in which students are taught legal research and written and oral communication skills. Legal Research and Writing courses are described in Chapter 4. See also Appellate Brief, Law Office Memorandum, Oral Argument.

Legalines A long-running brand of study aid that offers condensed case briefs and black letter legal principles keyed to the most popular casebooks in most core law school courses. See also Study Aids.

LexisNexis See Computerized Legal Research.

LexisNexis Web Courses. Online course sites set up by professors using the LexisNexis platform. See also TWEN.

Litigation   The process of bringing and carrying on a lawsuit. When a law student or lawyer says they do or want to do "litigation" as a career, they are talking about filing, defending, and otherwise engaging in lawsuits on behalf of their clients. Contrary to popular belief, most lawyers do not practice in the area of litigation. Rather, they engage in what is called "transactional law," which involves handling business transactions. See also Transactional Law.

LSAC   The acronym for the "Law School Admission Council," a non-profit organization that provides services to law schools and prospective law students pertaining to law school admissions. Your student's first dealing with legal education will be through the LSAC, which administers the LSAT and processes applications for law schools. See also LSAT.

LSAT   The acronym for the "Law School Admission Test." The LSAT is the challenging, standardized test required for law school admission. It primarily tests analytical skills, logic, and reading comprehension. A law school applicant's LSAT score plays a prominent role in determining which law schools a student can gain admission to. As a rule of thumb, the higher a law school's ranking, the higher the LSAT score required to get admitted. See also LSAC.

Majority or **Majority Opinion**.   See Judicial Opinion.

Mandatory Curve   The slang term for a grade normalization policy. Most law schools have some form of grade normalization policy requiring or recommending to professors that grades fall into specified ranges, often requiring certain percentages of each grade (e.g., 10–15 percent A- or above). The policies come in many formats, making it impossible to generalize about them. Students usually oppose grade normalization policies, thinking it forces professors to give lower grades than they otherwise would give. This can be true, but the policies can work the other way as well, forcing some professors to give higher grades than they otherwise would give. With so much depending on class rank, students actually benefit from grade normalization policies because they ensure consistent, evenhanded treatment among students in different sections and in different courses. Absent a grade normalization policy, a single outlying professor (i.e., an unusually high or low grader) can throw the class rank out of whack for an entire class.

MBE   See Bar Exam.

Memo, The See Law Office Memorandum.

Mock Trial A co-curricular activity in which student teams participate in simulated trials, often as part of a competition, either within the school or among several schools. The students act as trial lawyers, making opening statements, examining and cross-examining witnesses, admitting documentary evidence, making objections, and delivering closing arguments.

Moot Court A co-curricular activity in which student teams participate in simulated appellate court proceedings, including analyzing an appellate record, writing an appellate brief, and presenting an oral argument in front of panels of judges. Some schools have a first-year intramural moot court competition as part of their Legal Research and Writing program. Outside moot court competitions are prominent on the landscape of legal education, with many national competitions being held each year. Moot court is described in Chapter 2.

MPRE See Multistate Professional Responsibility Exam.

MPT See Bar Exam.

Multistate Bar Exam (MBE) See Bar Exam.

Multistate Performance Test (MPT) See Bar Exam.

Multistate Professional Responsibility Exam (MPRE) A two-hour, sixty-question multiple-choice exam, held separately from the regular bar exam, that is required for bar admission in forty-six states. The exam, known by its acronym, tests knowledge of the rules of professional responsibility (also called the "rules of ethics") governing lawyers. At most law schools, students take a required course in the rules of professional responsibility in their second or third year.

Note, Law Review A scholarly paper that 2L law review members research and compose on a legal topic of their choosing as part of the requirements for law review membership. A typical note runs from 30–50 pages with around 200 footnotes. The best notes are selected for publication in the law review. See also Law Review.

Nutshells A long-running series of study aid offering books in more than 130 legal subjects. As the name suggests, the books are concise summaries of the law in particular areas. See also Study Aids.

On-Campus Interview The interviews legal employers hold at law schools for prospective summer clerkships or permanent associate positions. See also Associate, Callback Interview, Summer Clerkship.

Oral Argument An oral presentation to a panel of appellate court judges, usually three in number, in which a lawyer advances the legal arguments supporting the client's case on appeal, answering questions from the judges along the way. At most schools, 1L students are required to make an oral argument in the second semester as part of their Legal Research and Writing course. The oral argument assignment is discussed in Chapter 4. See also Appeal, Appellate Court, Legal Research and Writing.

Order of the Coif A law school honor society that exists at select law schools, with membership reserved for students who graduate in the top 10 percent of their class. Order of the Coif is considered to be a high law school honor.

Orientation An introduction to law school typically held the week before classes begin. The length and content of orientations vary by school, but typical events include a session on how to read and brief cases, a panel discussion with upper-level students and/or faculty on how to succeed in law school, and social mixers. Upper-level students often serve as small group orientation leaders, and are a good source of information and tips to incoming students. You might find yourself attending a portion of orientation, as approximately one-half of law schools have special orientation sessions geared toward married students or students and their families.

P.A.D. See Phi Alpha Delta.

Partner A senior position in a law firm to which associates aspire. Law firm partnerships are discussed in Chapter 18. See also Associate.

Phi Alpha Delta (P.A.D.) One of two national legal fraternities that has chapters at most law schools (the other is Phi Delta Phi). While both law fraternities promote themselves as professional and social organizations, P.A.D.'s activities tend to be more socially oriented. Membership is not exclusive: if you pay the membership fee, you're in. See also Phi Delta Phi.

Phi Delta Phi   One of two national legal fraternities that has chapters at most law schools. At some schools, Phi Delta Phi has a more academic focus than P.A.D., the other major national law school fraternity. Some chapters require a minimum GPA to join. See also Phi Alpha Delta.

Pro Bono   Meaning "for the public good" in Latin, *pro bono* work is legal services performed free of charge to people who cannot afford to hire a lawyer. Lawyers are expected to render some *pro bono* work as part of their professional obligation or to contribute money to legal services agencies that provide such services. Many law schools have *pro bono* service requirements for students, providing that students must devote a certain number of hours to a qualifying cause or organization as a condition to graduating.

Precedent   See Judicial Precedent.

Property   A required first-year course that covers the law governing the ownership and transfer of interests in real and personal property. Real property is land and things attached to land. Personal property is portable goods such as this book. Property is discussed in Chapter 4.

Public Interest Law   An umbrella term describing legal work geared toward advancing social justice and/or public welfare. Public interest law can involve working at a government agency, a non-profit organization, or representing clients on a *pro bono* basis. Public interest law can be seen as the flipside of the for-profit, private sector work that most lawyers do, although all lawyers are expected to support *pro bono* work as part of their professional obligation. See also Pro Bono.

Regulation   A legally binding rule promulgated by a federal or state administrative agency, such as the Environmental Protection Agency or the Food and Drug Administration. Regulations are to be distinguished from statutes, which are passed by Congress or state legislatures. See also Statute.

Reporter   A book containing a chronological collection of appellate judicial opinions from a particular court or jurisdiction. For example, the United States Reports collects all opinions of the U.S. Supreme Court from 1759 through the present in several hundred volumes. Each of the individual volumes in the set is called a "reporter." Law school libraries contain complete sets of all the relevant reporters, which consume miles of shelf space. In the past, law firm libraries also contained extensive sets of reporters, and many still do, although the availability of computerized legal research has made it easier to cut library maintenance costs and save space in law libraries of all types. New law students usually learn to find judicial opinions in the bound reporters in their Legal Research and Writing course before learning and being allowed to resort to computerized legal research. See also Computerized Legal Research.

Restatements of the Law A series of influential legal treatises, well-known to law students, that are written and published by the American Law Institute, an organization of prominent legal scholars, including lawyers, judges, and law professors. "Restatements," as they are called, set forth the black letter rules of law in clear terms. Restatements are not binding authority on courts—which means a court does not have to follow them in making a decision—but they are nevertheless very persuasive, especially in certain areas of law such as Torts and Contracts. See also Authority, Black Letter Law.

Reverse A disposition or outcome of an appellate court proceeding in which the court overturns or "reverses" the decision of the lower court, often sending the case back to the lower court for further proceedings, such as a new trial. See also Affirm.

SBA See Student Government Association.

SCOTUS An acronym for the Supreme Court of the United States.

SGA See Student Government Association.

Shepardize Shepard's is a trademark-protected service for checking the subsequent history of a judicial opinion to see if it has been reversed, distinguished, followed, or rejected by other courts. Today, "Shepardize" is often used as a generic verb for checking the subsequent history of cases, whether using Shepard's or a competing product. As you might imagine, a lawyer citing to a case that has been reversed or otherwise overturned is a large no-no. All 1Ls are taught the importance of checking the subsequent history of cases before citing them as legal authority.

Socratic Method The predominant law school teaching style, particularly in the first year, wherein professors cold-call on students to engage in a dialogue about a judicial opinion assigned for class reading. The Socratic method goes hand in hand with the case method of law school teaching, in which students learn the law from reading and analyzing judicial opinions collected in casebooks, rather than from reading expository text explaining the law. The Socratic and case methods are described in Chapter 6. See also Case Method, Casebook.

Statute   A law passed by Congress or a state legislature and signed into law by, respectively, the U.S. president or the governor of the state. Statutory law should be distinguished from case law, which is the body of judge-made law that emanates from judicial opinions. Law students spend most of their first year studying case law, but take several courses in their upper-level years that focus on statutory law. See also Judicial Opinion, Judicial Precedent, Regulation.

Student Government Association (SGA)   Called the Student Bar Association or SBA at some schools, the elected body of student representatives at a law school. All law schools have a SGA. The officers, elected by students, usually include a president, vice-president, treasurer, secretary, and representatives for each class (i.e., 1L, 2L, and 3L) and often each section within a class. Depending on the school, the SGA may focus on meaningful activities such as organizing community service events or may focus mostly on organizing social events. Most SGAs do some of both. See also Student Organization.

Student Organization   A term referring to any law school student-run organization, of which there are many. These include national organizations such as the Black Law Students Association and the Federalist Society, which have chapters at most law schools, as well as many home-grown organizations unique to a particular school. Common types of student organizations appeal to particular political persuasions, social causes (such as animal rights), and legal interests (such as sports law or environmental law). Many schools also have student organizations aimed at married students or students with children. Student organizations allow students to explore legal causes or subjects that are of special interest to them and to meet and network with like-minded people.

Study Aids   Any of the many series of books intended to explain the law to students clearly and succinctly. Study aids are available for most law school courses, and most law students buy at least some study aids to help them understand the material and prepare for exams. Many students buy study aids for every course. Dozens of competing types and formats of study aids are available. A few of the more prominent series are listed in this Glossary. See also Emanuel Law Outlines, Examples & Explanations, Flashcards, Gilbert Law Summaries, Legalines, Nutshells.

Summer Associate   See Summer Clerkship.

Summer Clerkship   A term for a summer job at a law firm, also referred to as a summer associate position, which is to be distinguished from a "judicial clerkship." Most first-year students begin vying for summer clerkships in their second semester. During summer clerkships, students primarily perform legal research, but they might also be invited to attend depositions, trials, and client interviews. Many summer clerkships lead to offers of permanent associate jobs at the firm. Summer clerkships at prestigious firms pay well and can be good resume boosters.

Supreme Court of the United States (SCOTUS)   The highest court in the United States, made up of nine justices nominated by the president and confirmed by the U.S. Senate. Decisions of the U.S. Supreme Court are the "law of the land," binding under the constitution on all other courts and—under the principle of judicial review established by the Court in *Marbury v. Madison*—also on the executive and legislative branches of government. First-year students study Supreme Court judicial opinions primarily in Civil Procedure and Constitutional Law, a first-year course at roughly one-half of law schools.

Torts   A required first-year course studying the law of liability for civil wrongs other than breaches of contract. Most of the course involves claims arising from personal injury. Torts is described in Chapter 4.

Top Paper Award   The generic term for the award given to the student who receives the highest grade in a given course, usually as determined by the final exam. At most law schools, top paper awards are called "CALI Awards" because they are sponsored by the CALI (Computer-Assisted Legal Instruction) organization. In the old days, top paper awards were called "Book Awards," because the recipient received a book as a prize and some older professors still use that term, sometimes as a verb, as in: "Sarah is an excellent student. In fact, she booked my course." Receiving the top paper award in a course is a coveted honor and good resume booster. See also CALI.

Transactional Law A broad term describing legal practice that does not involve litigation (i.e., handling lawsuits). Transactional law includes negotiating, structuring, drafting documents for, and handling business deals of all types. Most lawyers engage in some form of transactional law practice. See also Litigation.

Trial Court The court at the bottom of the hierarchical judicial system, either state or federal, where lawsuits originate and where pretrial and trial proceedings take place (as distinguished from appellate courts, where appeals take place). See also Appellate Court.

TWEN An acronym for "The West Education Network," TWEN is a widely used online tool that allows law professors to set up "course sites" for their individual courses that can contain course materials, discussion boards, calendars, quizzes, relevant web links, and other features. Students should register for their professors' TWEN sites as soon as possible on arrival to law school. Many professors rely on TWEN as the primary portal of communication with students outside of class.

UCC See Uniform Commercial Code

Uniform Commercial Code (UCC) Usually just called the "UCC," a compilation of statutes that regulates a variety of commercial transactions, including sales, banking, and collateralized transactions. Drafted as model legislation by the National Conference of Commissioners on Uniform State Laws, all states have adopted the UCC in whole or in part as part of their state statutes. First-year students study portions of Article 2 (Sales) of the UCC in their Contracts course.

U. S. Circuit Court of Appeal One of thirteen regional appellate courts within the federal court system that hear appeals from the U.S. District Courts (the trial courts in the federal system). U.S. Circuit Courts of Appeal are the most powerful tribunals in the land below the U.S. Supreme Court. See also Appellate Court, Trial Court.

U.S. District Court A trial court within the federal judicial system.

U.S. News & World Report Rankings   The annual law school rankings by the national news magazine. Each year, the magazine ranks all ABA-accredited law schools. While the magazine's ranking methodology has been severely criticized, the rankings are widely referenced by law students, law faculty, and law school administrations.

Westlaw   See Computerized Legal Research.

Writ of Certiorari   The process by which the U.S. Supreme Court decides to review most of the cases it hears. The vast majority of the cases accepted for review by the U.S. Supreme Court are heard because the Court discretionarily chooses to hear them, rather than because the parties have a "right" of appeal to the Court. The Writ of Certiorari is the means by which the Court exercises that discretion. Perhaps because both law students and lawyers struggle to spell and pronounce the term correctly, "certiorari" is usually shortened to "cert," as in "cert petition" and "denial of cert." The process is initiated by a party to a qualifying case filing a petition for a writ of certiorari with the Court. If the Court grants "cert review" and agrees to hear the case, it is an indication that the case involves issues of national significance and/or is causing confusion and disagreement among the lower courts. Out of nearly 10,000 cert petitions filed with the Court each year, the Court grants cert (that is, agrees to review) only about 100 cases.

Write-on Competition   The competition that students participate in during the summer after their first year in an effort to gain an invitation to participate on the law review. The competition usually involves writing a case comment (summary and analysis of a recent case) and a test of the student's mastery of *Bluebook* citation style. Law review is discussed in Chapter 2. See also Bluebook, Case Comment, Citation Style, Law Review.

Writing Sample   A sample of a student's legal writing that is often required as part of a legal job application. First-year students often polish up their Legal Research and Writing law office memorandum or appellate brief to use as a writing sample when applying for their first summer job. See also Appellate Brief, Law Office Memorandum, Summer Clerkship.

ACKNOWLEDGMENTS

I couldn't have written this book without a lot of help from a lot of people. One of the great blessings of being a law professor is being able to work with outstanding students hired as faculty research assistants. For this project, I benefitted tremendously from these research assistants at the University of Memphis Cecil C. Humphreys School of Law: Jessica Farmer, Russell Hayes, Sally Joyner, Jane Marie Lewis, Jonathan Lindsey, Natalie Malone, Eric McEnerney, Sarah Spitzer, and Meredith Blake Stewart. Several law professors gave input, including Professors David W. Case, Bill Childs, Donna S. Harkness, Barbara Kritchevsky, Steve Mulroy, Janet Richards, Eugene Shapiro, and Jodi Wilson. Particular thanks are owed to Professors Nancy Levit and Mary Pat Treuthart for generously reading and commenting on a draft of the manuscript. Other help came courtesy of Phil Handwerk of the Law School Admission Council, Lindsay Paige Watkins of the Law School Survey of Student Engagement, Susan Cartier Liebel of Solo Practice University, and Sue Ann McClellan, Assistant Dean for Admissions at the University of Memphis law school.

Special gratitude is owed to all of the current and former law students and their partners whose comments fill so many of these pages. Quite simply, there would be no *Companion Text* without the insights from these students and companions in response to my surveys and other questions. They include, in addition to a few random lawyer friends: students and their partners from the California Western School of Law and Seattle University College of Law; former students of mine at the University of Arkansas at Little Rock Bowen School of Law and Florida International University College of Law; and my current and former students, along with their partners, at the University of Memphis. I'm particularly grateful to Section 11 of the 2010 entering law school class at the University of Memphis for their patience and willingness to respond to my many requests for help and information.

Student, lawyer, and loved one contributors include, in addition to most of my research assistants: Marvin E. Adams, Rebecca Alcover, Keith Atkinson, Sarah Atkinson, Stephanie Marie Bada, Salwa Bahhur, Brook Barnes, Stephen Barnes, Susan Barnes, Rebecca Blair Beaty, Samantha Bennett, Jonathan Bettis, Julie Bigsby, David Billetdeaux, Jessie Wallace Birchfield, Emily Blaiss, Nathan Bobo, Roger Bolick, Martin Boury, Tessa Boury, Kim Bowers, Jamaal Boykin, Melissa Dorn Bratton, Kimberly Greathouse Brown, Lori L. Burrows, Cullen Byrne, Neely Campbell, Warren P. Campbell, Aaron James Chaplin, Melanie Chung–Tims, Andrew Collup, David Cooley, Scott Cooper, Janelle Crandall, Edwin Cruz, Naomi Cruz, Tiffany Davidson, Tamara Davis, Elisabeth Dawson, Peter Dawson, Jason Dayley, Jacob Dennis, James Marshall Digmon, Elizabeth Dove, Andy Droke, Jamie Droke, Casey DuBose, Tina Duvall, Charles Richard Edwards, Jamie Ewing, Charles Ferrante, Meaghan E. Fitzgerald, J. Flanders, Mandy Floyd, Marcus Floyd, Gaspar Forteza, Bennett Foster, Andrew Ryan Francisco, William Christopher Frulla, James Fyke, Libba W. Fyke, Michael Gibbons, Caroline Giovannetti, Whitney Goode, DeLeith Duke Gossett, Kamron Graham, Jenna Griffin, Seth Andrew Guess, Ryan Hagenbrok, Jennifer Hames, Scott Hampel, Amanda Harmon, Adraine N. Harris, Angela Harris, Cheyne Harris, Christian Harris, Christopher Hart, April Hayes, Jerry Hayes, Andrew Hays, Karen Leigh Henson, Johnathon Clyde Hershman, Christy Hickman–Baker, Rebecca Keaton Hinds, Anna Hinnenkamp–Faulk, Jacob Hinton, Jordan Hinton, Laura Hollar, Andrew Holt, Devon Horak, Chad Horner, Michael Roy Houbre, Zach Hoyt, Jennifer Hull, Justin Irick, Amy Dunn Johnson, Matthew Johnson, Ross Johnson, Kelly Jordan, Christy De Zayas Jurado, Joseph Michael Kendrick, Katie Kiihnl, Armen Kiramijyan, Kathy Williams Kostopoulos, Ashley Landman–Smith, Judy Lansky, Erica Lindsey, Jesse Lords, Meredith Alston Lucas, Suzanne Ritter Lumpkin, Kevin Magennis, Rob Malin, Brandon Malone, Kate Mara, Breanne Martin, Torr Martin, Shannon Mashburn, Jonathan Meredith, Danielle McCollum, Hannah McDonald, Julie Zellner McDonald, Shane McKinnie, Cherie McKnight, Eric Micai, Jill Micai, Landon Mills, Eric Montierth, Lindsay Montierth, Jonathan Mosley, Starr Mosley, Leighann Ness, Bill O'Connor, Julie O'Connor, James P. Olson, Mary Olszewska, Krystle Ouellette, Brooke–Augusta Owen, Tyler Parks, Melissa Patten,

Darrell Phillips, Rachel Phillips, Tammy Phillips, Robert Todd Pinckley, Lynne Trulock Ravellette, Ryan Reaves, Allison Leigh Renfro, Kimberly Rice, Bryan Riley, Atina Rizk, Pam Roberts, Jane Portis Roeder, Ashley Jordan Russell, Ash Sammour, Adrian Santos, Anna Rudman Santos, Ginger Stuart Schafer, Laura Schencker, Eric Setterlund, Robyn Silva, Jeremy Smith, Sheldon Smith, Cliff Sward, Ken David Swindle, Henry Talbot, Lisa Goeden Taylor, Adam Blake Thomas, Monica Timmerman, Brett Toney, Mary Trachian–Bradley, Ashlinn Turnbow, Josh Turnbow, Mary Wagner, Jonathan Warren, Gina Helms White, Chad Wilgenbusch, Vallie Peake Wilkerson, Benjamin Bradley Wilkins, Elizabeth Ann Smith Wilson, and Danna Woods Young.

Forgive me if I left anyone out and thanks again to all. Quite a few comment contributors not listed above requested anonymity, but I want to give them a shout-out as well. (By the way, all of the comments are anonymous in the sense that there is no way to match them with individuals.)

Finally, thanks to all of the great folks at Thomson West, the publisher, for their help and support throughout this project.

A few portions of this book were borrowed from my previous writings, including *1L of a Ride*, my humor columns in the *American Bar Association Journal*, and my parody of legal education, *The Law School Trip*.

ABOUT THE AUTHOR

Andrew J. McClurg is a nationally and internationally recognized law professor, primarily in the area of tort law. He holds the Herbert Herff Chair of Excellence in Law at the University of Memphis Cecil C. Humphreys School of Law. From 2002–2006, he was a member of the founding faculty at the Florida International University College of Law. Previously, he was the Nadine H. Baum Distinguished Professor of Law at the University of Arkansas at Little Rock, and also has taught at Wake Forest University, the University of Colorado, and Golden Gate University. McClurg is the recipient of numerous law school and university awards for his teaching and scholarly publications.

The "Companion Text" to Law School is a follow-up to his law school prep book, *1L of a Ride: A Well–Traveled Professor's Roadmap to Success in the First Year of Law School* (West 2009), which is assigned as required or recommended reading at law schools throughout the country. McClurg is also the editor of an innovative series of comparative law texts published by the Carolina Academic Press.

In addition to his several books, McClurg has published numerous scholarly law review and other articles, which have been quoted and cited by hundreds of legal scholars and many courts. He has been interviewed on National Public Radio and quoted as a legal expert by *Time, U.S. News and World Report*, the *New York Times*, the *Wall Street Journal*, and dozens of other media sources.

For four years, McClurg was the monthly humor columnist for the *American Bar Association Journal*, the official publication of the American legal profession, and is the editor of lawhaha.com, an academically oriented legal humor blog.

Prior to joining academia, McClurg served as a law clerk to a federal district court judge and worked four years as a trial lawyer. He graduated Order of the Coif from the University of Florida College of Law where he was a member of the law review.

He welcomes all reader comments, relevant anecdotes, or insights about this book.

Index

INDEX

INDEX

Law students—Cont'd
Conversation topics of—Cont'd
Complaints, in general, 104–05, 209
Courses, 103–04
Generally, 84–109
Law, The, 98–102
Professors, 88–89
Coping with lower than expected grades by, 138–41
Cynicism and skepticism as traits in, 175–80, 227
Debt-load, 154–55, 246–51, 284–88
Demographics of, 15–16
Depression in. *See* Psychological distress in students.
Desire to have loved ones understand
Classes are intense and require preparation, 214–15
Competitiveness of students, 218–19
Exams are stressful, 215–16
Importance of grades and class rank, 216–18
Law school is all-consuming and intense, 211–13
Time is limited, 211
Workload is enormous, 219–21
Dreams about law school by, 84–85, 277
Emotional detachment in, 102, 184–87, 268
Friendships/bonding with fellow students, 5, 85, 90–92, 132, 144, 146, 192–94, 237–39
Gossip among, 89, 92–93, 96–98, 219, 277
Legalistic view of life among, 162–67
List of stress factors for, 135–58
Love-hate relationship with law school, 209
Number of, 15, 17
Obsession with discussing law school, 3–4, 84–109, 270–72, 278–79, 293
Obsessive-compulsiveness as a trait of, 123–26, 151, 162, 223, 232
Over-awareness of risks among, 163–67
Part-time or night students. *See* Part-time students.
Personality changes in caused by law school. *See* Personalities of law students.
Psychological distress in. *See* Psychological distress in students.
Quality of, 207, 239
Relationships with. *See* Loved ones; Relationships.

Law students—Cont'd
Stresses in. *See* Psychological distress in students; Stress.
Substance abuse among. *See* Substance abuse.
Tendency to become argumentative as a trait of, 161, 170–75, 224
Tendency to over-analyze as a trait of, 167–70, 179
Things never to say to, 9, 110–20
Uncertainty as a cause of frustration in, 58–63, 135–37, 140
Uncertainty of career choices by, 116–17, 295
Workload. *See* Workload.
Law Student Survey of Student Engagement (LSSSE), 134, 154, 190
Law, The
As a conversation topic, 98–102
Civil law. *See* Common law, As distinguished from civil law.
Common law. *See* Common law.
Private compared to public, 34
Uncertainty of, 58–63
United States legal system as compared to other countries, 34–35
See also Curriculum (and individual first-year course listings).
Law office memorandum. *See* Legal Research and Writing.
Lawyers
As a noble profession, 1–2, 118–20
As superior thinkers, 64–65, 70–71
"Doctor" as a title for, 12
Explanation of disdain for, 119
Job satisfaction among, 275, 298, 303
Jokes about, 118–20
Perceptions of, 118–20
Rates of depression among, 126
Substance abuse by. *See* Substance abuse.
Types of jobs available to, 295–308
Legal education. *See* Law school.
Legal Research and Writing, first-year course in, 25, 41–42, 277, 289
Appellate brief in, 37, 53, 103, 145
As a focal point of student complaining, 48–51, 87, 103–04, 245, 274
Book versus computer research in, 48–49
Citation style in. *See* Citation style.
Differences from other first-year courses, 47–48
Explanation of, 47–53
Feedback in, 50–51, 103–04, 129, 140
Fewer credit hours for as compared to other courses, 48

367

†